RIGHT CONDUCT

Theories and Applications

RIGHT CONDUCT
Theories and Applications

MICHAEL D. BAYLES

Westminster Institute for Ethics and Human Values
Westminster College
London, Canada

AND

KENNETH HENLEY

Florida International University
Miami, Florida

RANDOM HOUSE

NEW YORK

First Edition

9 8 7 6 5 4 3 2 1

Copyright © 1983 by Random House, Inc.

LIBRARY OF CONGRESS CATALOGING IN PUBLICATION DATA

Main entry under title:

Right conduct.

   Bibliography: p.
   1. Ethics—Addresses, essays, lectures.   I. Bayles,
Michael D.   II. Henley, Kenneth.
BJ1012.R49   1982   170   82–13198
ISBN 0–394–32609–1

Manufactured in the United States of America

Cover design by Stacie Rogoff
Cover art: Culver Pictures

Preface

Many issues of social ethics confront contemporary society. In response to this, over the last decade or so, many philosophers have returned to an examination of ethical problems. Enrollments in ethics courses have increased, and various courses on specialized topics—bioethics, business ethics, professional ethics—have developed. Yet the majority of students still take only one general course in ethics. This book has been designed to acquaint introductory students with ethical theory as well as to present to them various approaches to interesting topics of practical concern.

Our primary principle in editing this book has been to emphasize the relationship of theory to practice. This principle has significantly influenced the structure of the text. First, we have focused exclusively on theories of conduct and have omitted material dealing primarily with metaethics, such as the meaning of the word "good" or such questions as "Why be moral?" Second, the applications have been chosen to illustrate different theoretical approaches to debatable issues. Some topics, such as war, have been omitted because they do not readily exhibit the variety of theoretical approaches. Others, such as racism, have been omitted because no philosopher today seriously argues for racism.

Part I sets out six basic ethical theories: natural law, natural rights, Kantianism, contractarianism, and utilitarianism, both act and rule. Classical and contemporary sources are used to illustrate both historical origins and modern formulations of theories. This part should be studied before the student goes on to Part II, which deals with applications.

In Part II, the selections have been chosen to illustrate the different theoretical approaches presented in Part I; each of the three selections in a chapter illustrates a theory from a chapter in Part I. Although many authors of the selections do not fully subscribe to the views they have been chosen to illustrate, their selections exhibit an argument form of a particular type of theory. The chapters have been ordered to consider problems of life and death, sexual morality and the relations between the sexes, and more general issues of economics and the future. However, an instructor can use them in any order he or she wishes. Each chapter stands independently.

This text arose from our dissatisfaction with the materials that we have each used in approximately ten years of teaching ethics. Despite the fact that natural law and natural-rights arguments figure prominently in discussions of contemporary issues, it has been difficult to obtain class materials representing them. We have also found that many students need considerable assistance in understanding selections and are often unable to take satisfactory notes in class. They need concise expositions that they can examine repeatedly. Consequently, we have provided rather extensive introductions to each chapter setting out the major problems and views. In these introductions, we have striven to be objective and impartial, not favoring one theory over another. We have also tried to choose materials of differing levels of difficulty. Our experience indicates that students have most difficulty with abstract considerations of theory, and the chapters on applications should help increase understanding of theories by providing an opportunity for a more detailed consideration of particular aspects of them. As a basis for testing views and classroom discussion, we have provided a brief actual case at the beginning of each chapter on applications.

In preparing this text, we have received the advice of many reviewers, both at the preliminary outline stage and after the penultimate draft. Although it was impossible to accommodate all their suggestions, because some were conflicting and space was limited, the book is undoubtedly better for their help.

Finally, we wish to thank Michael Rumball and Bernard Bouchard for their assistance in finding suitable selections and preparing bibliographies; Lois Weston and Patricia Roe for efficiently typing parts of the manuscript; and Nancy Margolis for helping to improve the style of some of the introductions.

Contents

RIGHT CONDUCT

Theories and Applications

General Introduction: The Importance and Possibility of Ethics

A normative ethical theory is a principle (or a set of principles) that can be used to decide what morally ought to be done, along with the supporting reasons for such a principle. Principles are general guidelines for right conduct. The principles in ethical theories are very general, so that they will apply to every situation one encounters. The principle to treat others as you would have them treat you (the Golden Rule) is a good example of the general sort found in ethical theories. From it one can work out more specific principles or rules for truth telling, killing, and so on. The injunction "Do not lie" is also general, but there are many ethical problems it does not cover, such as those concerning killing.

One must understand the reasoning supporting a principle in order to apply that principle intelligently to practical moral problems. For example, a person who does not understand the point of the Golden Rule might think it means that he should give everyone a computer game for Christmas if that is what he wants himself. As there are competing theories of right conduct, the reasoning for each theory tries to show why its principles are correct. Such reasoning, however, will probably fail to convince everyone. Ethical theories are at least as controversial as are practical moral problems.

The Study of Ethics Why then should one study theories of right conduct? Since there is controversy over theory, why not confront moral problems directly without separate treatment of theory? Some people go so far as to say that theories only serve to rationalize moral views that really stem from other sources (such as childhood training or religious beliefs).

Indeed, theories can be used to justify beliefs already held—and perhaps, this is to some extent inevitable. Almost all theories try to justify some central ethical beliefs, such as the wrongness of torturing people for pleasure. But there is a difference between mere rationalization, with the goal of rigidly keeping all one's beliefs, and justification of central beliefs, with the goal of making one's beliefs consistent and rational. Consistency will almost always require changes in some less central particular belief. For example, if one believes that women should be treated as equal to men, one may have to abandon a belief that it is permissible to exclude

1

girls from Little League baseball teams. But even if many beliefs remain untouched, a given ethical theory should not necessarily be considered mere rationalization. After all, many of the moral beliefs commonly taught to children are rationally justifiable. And it would make little sense to suggest that most very central moral beliefs are *mistaken*. What would it be like to discover that intentional cruelty, murder, rape, lying, and stealing are all morally acceptable? Any theory that would lead to such conclusions is incorrect, simply because these conclusions are unacceptable. It might make sense to suggest that all our talk about morality is a sham, but that is a different matter; if morality is an illusion, then no moral beliefs can be either mistaken or correct.

This text does not consider various philosophical claims that would call into question the central moral beliefs held within our society. For instance, there are philosophers who defend *egoism*, the view that one ought always to promote one's own interests, as the only rational basis for deciding what to do. This view clearly undercuts most moral thought, because a consideration of the interests and well-being of others is built into such basic moral concepts as individual rights, the general welfare, and obligation. Some egoists consider their view to be a normative ethical theory, in competition with other ethical theories. But it is tidier to think of egoism as a theory that is normative but not in the same category as other theories; egoism is an attack upon the rationality of most moral thought, not a particular theory of moral thought. The egoist really offers a theory of what counts as rational conduct, a theory in which it is irrational to consider the interests of others (except as these interests have some effect on one's own interests).

There is also a practical reason for excluding egoism in this text. Whatever the theoretical strengths and weaknesses of egoism, it is of no use in settling moral, social, and legal disputes between people. When people disagree about what ought to be done, it will not help to appeal to the principle that each person ought to promote his or her own interests; those interests often conflict, otherwise there would have been no practical problem to begin with. This practical uselessness of egoism is perhaps connected to the theoretical distinction between egoism and normative theories of *moral* conduct. Principles of right conduct are centrally concerned with guiding human action where there is conflict between the competing interests and values of different persons. They necessarily aim at considering the interests and values of many people. Egoism condemns this aim as irrational.

So one should expect that most of one's central moral beliefs will survive examination of the theories in this text. The changes and additions that theory can make to a person's moral beliefs come mainly in the area of difficult or new cases. One of the chief benefits of studying ethical theory is that one learns to think clearly and systematically when confronted with cases about which one's moral beliefs may be shaky or even unformed. Ethical theory will uncover the principles implicit in most of one's central moral beliefs and so enable one to think clearly and consistently. And because they are general, theoretical principles can be applied to new problems (for instance, those created by changing social conditions or advances in technology).

Another important benefit of ethical theory is an increased ability to understand and respect the viewpoints of others. Once one comes to see the principles and concepts that underlie other views, moral disagreement is less likely to lead to accusations of bad intentions. The abortion controversy is a good illustration of the need for understanding the theoretical basis of moral disagreement. Each side accuses the other of bad faith but does not bother to investigate the differing theory of right conduct that would make sense of the opposing view. The study of ethical theory makes it possible to see how a reasonable and well-intentioned person can hold a moral view different from one's own.

But the most important benefit of studying ethics is the increased ability to reason about moral questions. Without appeal to principles, a moral judgment about a particular problem will seem unreasoned. In fact, most people do appeal to general principles when judging particular cases. For example, people often ask, "But what if everyone did that?" Such an appeal is the beginning of theory; but the philosophical study of the principles of right conduct uncovers general principles more systematically and with greater carefulness. Rather than being satisfied with giving a general principle as the reason for a particular moral judgment, the theorist goes further and seeks to give reasons for accepting the general principle itself. There is a continuity between practical moral thought in ordinary life and ethical theory as a philosophical inquiry. The only ways to avoid ethical theory altogether are to abstain from making moral judgments or to view moral judgments as mere expressions of personal preferences.

Subjectivism   Many people, in fact, do hold to the views of *subjectivism*, thinking that moral judgments are simply expressions of personal preferences: that morality is a "matter of opinion." By this phrase they mean to deny that there is any objective way of determining what is morally correct. This may seem perfectly logical, but one must be careful. It is important to distinguish between two different views:

1. Moral judgments merely express the preferences of the speaker.
2. Moral judgments are never known to be true.

If the first view is correct, then the second is false, for a person can certainly know his or her own preferences. But good reasons exist for rejecting the view that moral judgments merely express personal preferences.

Two people with different preferences do not disagree about anything. If Jane likes cabbage, but Bob does not, then Jane can say, "I like cabbage," and Bob can say, "I do not like cabbage." Both of them will be saying something true, since the pronoun "I" stands for a different person in each sentence.

This is not the case with moral judgments. If Jane says, "A pregnant woman has a moral right to an abortion," and Bob says, "A pregnant woman does not have a moral right to an abortion," they cannot both be correct. Jane and Bob *disagree* concerning a moral question. Furthermore, they cannot simply "agree to disagree." What people think about this moral question (and many others) influences their position on legislation and such social policy as government funding for abortions. There may be some moral questions without social consequences (there is dispute about this), but even such seemingly personal issues as sexual morality raise in some minds questions of family structure and the social surroundings affecting society at large. More important, a moral judgment, unlike a mere personal preference, has implications for the conduct of others. Though Jane can eat cabbage and Bob leave it on his plate, on abortion each makes a claim about what everyone has (or has not) a right to do. Bob will not criticize Jane for eating cabbage, but he will criticize Jane for having an abortion. It makes no sense to ask someone for reasons justifying a dislike of cabbage; it does make sense to ask for reasons when a moral judgment is made. Moral principles aim to resolve disputes about how everyone ought to act; mere personal preferences do not address such matters. Therefore, moral judgments cannot be mere expressions of personal preferences.

Skepticism   But what about the claim of *skepticism* that moral judgments can never be known to be true? In this view, although Jane and Bob are making contradictory claims about something distinct from personal preferences (namely, a moral right to have an abortion), nevertheless, there can be no knowledge concerning this topic. Furthermore, no other moral question is on any firmer footing, for there simply is no such thing as *knowing* that an action is right or wrong.

Much depends upon what is built into the word "know" in this skeptical view. A specific area of philosophy (epistemology, or the theory of knowledge) deals with the difficult question of what justifies a claim to know something. Some theorists have very demanding standards for admitting that someone *really* knows something—so demanding that there is doubt concerning even the most obvious knowledge claims about ordinary experience (such as the knowledge claim that you are now reading this book). Other theorists have argued that knowledge is reasoned true belief and that this standard is met often by claims to knowledge in ordinary life. Such arguments are of great philosophical interest; but it is of greater practical interest (and still of philosophical interest) to explore the reasoning found in moral thinking.

And so it will be assumed in this text that most central moral beliefs are known to be correct (for instance, that gratuitous intentional cruelty is wrong). The competing ethical theories considered here do not disagree about most central moral judgments, although each theory offers a different justification of these central judgments, which can make a difference in difficult and new problems. But it matters little whether *knowledge* is claimed concerning these very central judgments. One can ignore the issue of knowledge altogether, and simply say that it is unreasonable to question most central judgments when discussing practical moral questions. When Bob and Jane disagree about abortion, they are apt to agree on general and basic principles that may be assumed to play some role in every reasonable person's moral thought. The disagreement will involve such things as the importance or weight attached to various principles; the application of general principles to difficult or borderline cases; and the exact meaning of central terms, such as "person" or "human being." General skepticism about moral knowledge has no role in practical disputes because it removes the basis for discussion and guidance. It does not even allow one to conclude that one ought to be tolerant of the views of others, for that also is a moral claim one could not know to be correct.

However, in both applied ethics and normative ethical theory there is room for doubt about whether one knows what ought to be done in a particular controversial problematic case like abortion. One of the benefits of ethical theory is an increased understanding of difficult cases, where correct answers are hard to come by. Serious study of both theories and facts might lead to skepticism about any claim to know the truth on a particular difficult issue. In a difficult or new area of application, there may be a breakdown in the moral reasoning that ordinarily leads to clear solutions. But since practical problems *must* be solved—human lives cannot stand still in the face of moral dilemmas—a resolution of these problems must be found. Moral thought here parallels legal thought; a decision must be made, even if there is still room for doubt about what the law or morality requires. It is in such problematic cases that ethical theory is of the greatest practical use, even if in the end it would be claiming too much to say that one *knows* what ought to be done.

Relativism   Two additional views sometimes block people from serious study of ethical theory and applied ethics: social relativism and theological relativism. Both of these views are forms of *ethical relativism,* the view that the truth or falsehood of moral judgments is relative to some authority. One other form of ethical relativism has already been discussed, the view that moral judgments are expressions of personal preferences. As already explained, this personal relativism is a mistaken view of what moral judgments are about. Other forms of relativism are mistaken in the same respect.

Social relativism places society in the role of absolute moral authority. In this view, moral judgments are relative to the society in which they are made. The judgment that abortion is wrong will be true if made in a society in which that is the prevalent belief, and the judgment that abortion is permissible will be true in a society which shares that belief. For the social relativist, the sentence, "It is wrong to hold human beings in slavery," is neither true nor false until some assumption is made concerning the society in which the judgment is made.

But the society about which a moral judgment is made is not always the society within which the judgment is made. For instance, people now commonly make moral claims about actions and social institutions found in Nazi Germany or in the United States before the Civil War (or before the civil rights movement of the 1960s). How is a social relativist going to analyze such cross-society judgments? Either the truth of the judgment depends upon the society within which it is made, or the truth depends upon the society about which the judgment is made, or the cross-society judgment is neither true nor false (because it does not make sense). None of these alternatives will allow for a genuine disagreement between societies about moral questions. For genuine disagreement, it must be possible for members of one society to think that a prevalent moral belief of another society is confused or incorrect. According to social relativism, the prevalent moral beliefs of any society are necessarily true. And yet it is common for people to criticize the prevalent moral beliefs of other (or earlier) societies.

When abolitionists criticized slavery as immoral in the early nineteenth century, they were not denying that in slave-owning societies the prevalent belief was that slavery was justified morally. Just as personal relativism fails to allow for the meaningfulness of moral evaluation between persons, so social relativism fails to allow for the meaningfulness of moral evaluation between societies.

Furthermore, the fact of moral disagreement *within* societies cannot be squared with the social-relativist view of moral judgments. In civilized societies, some people will always criticize prevalent moral beliefs. The ability to use moral concepts to attack majority beliefs shows that society is not an absolute moral authority. If moral judgments meant what social relativists say they do, then social critics could not significantly express their disagreement with the majority. Because their views are in the minority, they must be incorrect. But this is not so. Not only can critics make significant minority moral judgments, they also can reason with the majority using a shared structure of moral argument.

It is important to distinguish between social relativism and the commonsense view that people are influenced by the moral beliefs prevalent in their society. Social influence on moral beliefs is as inevitable as it is on other kinds of belief. But there is no reason to lose confidence in most central moral beliefs merely because they are part of human culture, passed from generation to generation by the processes of socialization and education. In order for critics to reason with their opponents, moral criticism of prevalent practices must depend upon some shared core of moral values and principles. Even slaveholders shared with abolitionists the most basic concepts of justice and compassion, though there was serious disagreement about the application of these concepts. Reasoned disagreement about particular issues is only possible when there is a background of agreement on basic concepts. If human beings were to encounter alien rational beings who found *all* human moral conceptions unintelligible, then moral discourse (including moral disagreement) between the two species would be impossible. It is a philosophically interesting question whether this bit of science fiction is a genuine possibility. But moral concepts in human societies are not so diverse as to make meaningful discourse between different societies impossible in *every* respect (though there may be some cases in which concepts differ enough to close off some kinds of cross-society discourse). Not only do critics within societies sometimes manage to modify prevalent moral beliefs on particular issues, but sometimes societies influence other societies. And with contemporary technology, the boundaries between societies are increasingly blurring; social relativism is coming to be of less practical than theoretical interest.

Theological relativism places God in the role of absolute moral authority. In this view, moral judgments are true if they express God's preferences. If it is assumed that only one God exists and that this being does not change, then theological relativism escapes one major difficulty of personal and social relativism—at least in theory. Personal and social relativism fail to account for objective truth in discourse between persons and societies simply because there are many persons with differing preferences, and many societies with differing moral beliefs. But for the theological relativist, there is an objective truth at issue in moral discourse between persons and societies, and this truth is discovered by learning the will of God.

However, this theoretical strength disappears if the theological relativist adopts the view that God's will is *arbitrary*, that it is based upon no reasons, or based upon reasons that no human being can understand. If human beings cannot discover the will of God through reasoning, the question of what God wills must be determined by revelation. But if it is so determined there is no way to decide rationally whether a purported divine revelation is indeed an expression of God's will. So even though there is one unchanging God, there will be many different views of what that God wills and no way to judge between them. The objectivity found at the level of theory disappears then in practice, leaving the same breakdown in moral reasoning as that found in personal and social relativism. It can be of no use to appeal to the arbitrary will of God when disagreement exists concerning both what the divine will is and whether there is a God at all. Moral reasoning must be able to cross boundaries between religions and between sects within religions and to cross the boundary between theists and nontheists.

A theological relativist, nevertheless, may argue that God wills that human beings do what is morally right and that God has given human beings freedom to act and with that freedom the use of rational thought to distinguish between right and wrong. According to this approach, a person should use the God-given ability to reason in order to determine whether an action is right—and thus whether God wills that action. Here God's will is not arbitrary, for it is based upon reasons that human beings can understand. Purported revelations from God (such as the Bible or Koran) might serve as the starting place for rational reflection concerning right conduct, but whether a particular command is in fact an expression of God's will must be decided using human reasoning.

This second approach to discovering God's will allows the theist to discuss moral problems with those in other religious traditions and even with nontheists. It may seem confusing to call this view a form of theological relativism, since in normative ethics there is no need to speak of God; but there are people who do speak of God while holding this view, and they may wish to claim that they do what is right in order to obey God. As they understand it, right conduct is backed by divine authority, although it can be determined independently using human reasoning.

Moral Concepts   Several concepts are central to moral thought and are used by all ethical theories. The concept of *value* ("the good" and "the bad") plays a role in much moral thought. Competing ethical theories often have differing views of what is *intrinsically good*, that is, what is good in itself. Intrinsic goods are contrasted with *instrumental goods,* which are valued only because they are instrumental in bringing about other goods. For instance, happiness is often considered an intrinsic good; and everyone considers a visit to the dentist instrumentally good rather than intrinsically good. Some theories set up a plurality of intrinsic goods (for instance, human life, friendship, knowledge). Other theories insist that there is only one kind of intrinsic good (for instance, pleasure). The difference between a plurality of goods and only one intrinsic good is important. In thinking about a moral problem, one might want to compare the amount of intrinsic good produced by alternative actions. If several different values are at stake, comparing goods is like adding apples and rivers. Only a theory with *one* intrinsic value can treat the comparison as a matter of simple arithmetic.

Theories of right conduct are theories of what one morally ought to do. It is possible to make subtle distinctions between a moral obligation and a moral duty, but here no distinction will be made. The contrary of doing what one ought to do is to do something morally wrong. Both the concept of obligation and that of moral wrong can be defined by the concept of the morally permitted. Most human actions are neither obligatory nor wrong, since both doing the actions and not doing them is permissible. A moral *wrong* is that which is not permitted; a moral *obligation* is something that it is not permitted to leave undone. Not all moral thinking concerns obligation; for instance, moral thinking that concentrates on questions of character and the virtues often proceeds without explicit use of the concept of obligation. One might consider it morally praiseworthy to risk one's own life in order to save someone else, but this need not be considered obligatory.

Another fundamental concept is the concept of a *right*, understood in the sense of such phrases as "human rights" and "civil rights." A right is a valid claim or entitlement that a person can make to restrict the conduct of others in their dealings with him or her. If there are no other conflicting moral considerations, it is obligatory to respect an individual's rights. However, moral problems often involve conflicts between individuals, each of whom has a right that deserves some respect. One important purpose of ethical theories is to help resolve such conflicts of rights, as well as conflicts of rights with other moral considerations.

Some people distinguish between *negative* and *positive* rights. Most commonly recognized rights are negative, requiring only that others not interfere with the right holder's life, conduct, or property. Thus the "right to life" is usually understood as the right not to be killed, rather than the right to be provided with the means to continue to live. If there is a positive right to life, then much more direct help to the needy is morally obligatory than is ordinarily supposed (see the selection by James Sterba in Chapter 11). The extent of positive rights is one of the most controversial questions in ethical theory.

Ethical Theories   Each ethical theory includes an account of value, obligation, and rights. However, these concepts are not of equal importance for each theory. Some theories derive obligations and rights from values; other theories establish rights and obligations independent of values. Most of these latter theories take rights as fundamental.

Theories that base obligations and rights on values are called *teleological* (from *telos,* meaning "goal," or "end"). The values are the end, and conduct is evaluated in terms of these ends. The simplest form of teleological theory is the evaluation of conduct as a means to an end. Theories of this sort, such as utilitarianism (see Chapter 3), are *consequentialist.* That is, they evaluate conduct as right or wrong depending solely upon the value of the consequences of the conduct. However, not all teleological theories are consequentialist. In evaluating conduct as right or wrong, some consider intentions and motives as well as consequences. And teleological theories that recognize many basic values will not be consequentialist, since comparing the value of the consequences of alternative actions is not always possible. Natural-law theory (see Chapter 1) is an example of a teleological theory that is not consequentialist.

Those theories that do not base all obligations and rights upon values are called *deontological* theories. Deontological comes from the Greek word *deon,* "that which is binding." The concept of obligation or duty is thus central for deontologists, but not all deontological theories take duty as primary. For example, natural-rights theory (see Chapter 1) takes rights as fundamental and establishes obligations or duties on the basis of rights. Other theories, such as Kant's (see Chapter 2), do not establish all duties on the basis of rights. The contractarian theory (see Chapter 2) is also a deontological theory.

These classifications are useful only insofar as they help indicate the general structure of the theory. One must then consider the principles and the reasons supporting them. Part I provides a detailed examination of the theories. Part II considers the application of the theories to particular moral problems. In examining the applications one should keep in mind that different people using the same theory can come to different conclusions, because they differ as to interpretation of the facts or because the theories give reasons to support different resolutions of problems. Thus, in examining the applications of theories, one should also consider what light the application sheds on the theory and how it might be applied to yet other problems.

part I

THEORIES

chapter 1

Natural Law and Natural Rights

INTRODUCTION

Two Kinds of Law: Prescriptive and Descriptive People live together in societies. Within each society there are social rules that regulate
conduct. Informal customs and formal laws are used to fit individuals into
the life of the social group. Children learn these rules as they grow up.
Violations are punished either informally or through such formal institutions as courts. These customs and laws are *prescriptive*, prescribing or
commanding how people ought to act.

There is quite a different concept of law used both in everyday life and
in science. Scientific laws are *descriptive*, describing what does in fact happen under certain conditions. The laws of gravity are examples of descriptive laws. And in everyday life, people use less precise "laws" to explain
what happens to them. (For instance, "People who haven't had enough
sleep are irritable.") Descriptive laws do not say what ought to happen.

Prescriptive and descriptive laws seem very different. Yet it is possible
to attempt to connect them. The term *natural law* is used in ethics to
mean a set of prescriptive rules of conduct rather than the causal, scientific
laws that describe natural processes. Why then is the word "natural" used?
These prescriptive laws are called natural because they are not prescribed
within some particular society for the regulation of its own social life.
"Natural" is thus contrasted to "conventional." Unlike the prescriptive
laws of particular societies, the natural law is considered binding upon all
human beings simply because they are human beings. And natural rights
are also attributed to people regardless of the particular society to which
they belong. In the arguments for the theory of natural law and the theory
of natural rights, there is an attempt to show that the facts of human nature determine the basic prescriptive laws that all human beings ought to
follow. The facts of human nature are described in descriptive laws, so in
these theories prescriptive laws of conduct are derived from descriptive
laws of human nature.

Nature and Convention The theory of natural law and the theory of
natural rights both provide an account of right conduct that is *naturalist:*

13

the rightness of an action is determined by reference to nature rather than to convention, custom, or preferences. The nature determining right conduct is human nature, which is the same for all human beings regardless of social conventions. Cultural differences are merely imposed upon an underlying set of characteristics that constitute humanity. These unchanging characteristics can be distinguished from what is culturally relative by methods of rational inquiry. Although reason is considered the distinguishing mark of humanity, there are other natural characteristics of human beings that are essential in accounting for the distinction between right and wrong in human conduct. Reason is the governing element in human nature, but in its control of right conduct, reason must take into account other elements of complex human nature, such as sexuality and the emotions.

NATURAL LAW

Greek, Roman, and Christian Origins   The ancient Greek philosopher Aristotle (384 B.C.–322 B.C.) gave an account of the nature of human beings that has continued to influence the theory of natural law ever since. The central concept is that each kind of thing has a goal or purpose (in Greek, *telos*). According to this teleological viewpoint, it is the goal of each thing to be or act in accordance with the distinctive characteristics of its kind. The whole history of natural law in ethics stresses that actions are directed toward goals. In the *Nichomachean Ethics,* Aristotle identifies rationality as the distinctive characteristic of human nature, and thus rational activity as the proper (because natural) mode of living for human beings:

> Living is something shared by man even with plants, whereas we are after something specific. Therefore, we must rule out nutritive living, life as growth. Next comes perception; but this too is shared—in this case by horses, cows, and all animals. We are left with a life concerned with action, belonging to the rational part of man.[1]

And yet Aristotle also accepts the reality of human emotional and bodily needs. Rationality is not the only genuinely human characteristic. Right conduct aims at a truly human happiness, a happiness found in activity that expresses our distinctive rationality. But to this active life of reason must be added sufficient external goods (friends, health, family, money, and so on) to meet our equally human emotional and bodily needs.

After Aristotle, the school of philosophers called the Stoics continued to develop a natural-law theory of ethics. The Stoic school began in ancient Athens in about 300 B.C. and achieved great popularity several hundred years later during the late period of the Roman Republic and during the Roman Empire. The Stoic principle of right conduct was that one ought to follow nature rather than convention or custom. This principle, however, did not mean that human beings should pursue every whim or act on every desire. On the contrary, since the Stoics shared Aristotle's view that rationality is distinctive to human nature, following nature meant following reason.

The main difference between the Stoics and Aristotle concerned the value of external goods, for the Stoics denied Aristotle's view that a life cannot be called happy without such external goods as friends, health, family, and sufficient wealth. The Stoic view derived from a more extreme emphasis upon rationality and a disvaluing of human emotions. Thus, the Stoics offered a less biological form of naturalism, placing human beings in a radically different category from other natural things.

The Stoics stressed the distinction between the varying conventions, customs, and laws of particular societies and the unchanging rule of reason in conduct. This distinction was fleshed out in the Stoic ideal of the cosmopolitan, the citizen of the world, who is guided by nature and reason. The cosmopolitan recognizes all human beings as fellow citizens. During the empire, Roman jurists, who needed to work out a system of law dealing with persons who did not share the same customs and national laws, used the Stoic conception of the natural law binding all human beings together in a rational commonwealth. The Stoics and Roman jurists claimed that persons of differing cultures can be obligated to respect each other only if there is a natural law deriving from rationality itself.

This Roman conception of a rational law binding those of differing cultures appealed to the Christian world as well. The Christian conception of the equality of all found kinship in the Stoic ideal of the citizenship of all humanity. Christian philosophers were also attracted to Stoicism because of its insistence on humanity's special dignity and freedom. Saint Thomas Aquinas (1224–1274) gave the theory of natural law its classic expression, bringing together its Aristotelian, Stoic, and Christian elements.

Basic Human Goods   The natural abilities and inclinations of human beings are the basis of natural-law theory, for they determine what is good. The fundamental principle of right conduct is that good is to be done and promoted and evil is to be avoided. Of course, this principle is an empty and unhelpful truism without the specification of what is good and what is evil. This specification is found in the natural inclinations and abilities of all human beings. What is understood as constituting a good human life varies from society to society and even from person to person, but that variation lies within a set of limits determined by human nature. Human flourishing occurs in a life in which the inclinations basic to human nature are rationally pursued (with some success) and humanly important abilities are put to active use. What thwarts this flourishing is an evil. The constitutive elements of human flourishing are the universal human goods.

The universal human goods are: life itself, health, procreation and rearing of the young, knowledge, and relationships with other human beings in society and in friendship. Within each of these basic goods lie more specific goods, such as the good of a particular friendship. Cultural differences often mask the underlying identity of the universal human goods that exist in all human societies. A comparison with the diversity of human languages may help. Despite the huge differences found among human languages, it can be argued that there are universal characteristics —a universal grammar—deeply buried under the surface variations.[2] Even if there is no such universal grammar, the concept of one makes sense. The concept of universal human goods makes the same kind of sense, and it need not be discarded merely because of the context of cultural diversity within which these goods are pursued (for instance, the fact that family structure varies from society to society).

Teleological but Not Consequentialist   A theory is *teleological* if it considers right conduct to be determined by the goal or purpose (Greek, *telos*) of the conduct. As already explained in the section dealing with the historical origins of natural law, a teleological view of both human nature and human conduct is central to the theory of natural law. The fundamental principle of natural law is clearly teleological: good is to be done and promoted and evil to be avoided.

However, the basic human goods are considered *incommensurable*, that is, they cannot be measured using a common unit, and so they cannot be traded off one for another. For example, the good of friendship cannot be compared on a common scale with the good of knowledge. And since according to natural law, each individual human life is seen as uniquely valuable, one human life cannot be weighed against another. This incommensurability of basic values is extremely important in natural law. If one basic good could be traded off in order to promote another, the teleological structure of natural law would lead to consequentialism. *Consequentialism* is the view that right conduct is that conduct which has the best consequences, all things considered. Consequentialist theories are all teleological, for they consider right conduct to be directed toward the goal of maximizing value. But not all teleological theories are consequentialist, since if values are incommensurable, the concept of the "best consequences" is senseless. To evaluate alternative sets of consequences, one needs a unit of comparison; but if there are many basic values, then no such unit can exist. It is not possible to "maximize value" if incommensurable values are in question.

Absolute Prohibitions   Since natural law is not consequentialist, it is possible for there to be moral prohibitions which are absolute, that is, which forbid some kinds of action *whatever the consequences*. "Do not kill the innocent" is a precept based upon respect for the unique value of each human life, and it forbids killing the innocent no matter what the consequences. Each life is incommensurably valuable, so one life may not be taken in order to save another. The precept against killing the innocent is grounded teleologically, since it is derived from the fundamental principle to avoid evil, along with the distinctive natural-law view of the incommensurable value of each human life.

Intention as the Key to Moral Evaluation   In evaluating conduct, the theory of natural law considers the intention or aim of various courses of conduct. The role of intention in moral evaluation prevents natural law from judging an action solely by its consequences, as does the incommensurability of the basic human goods. The intention is determined by what the person performing the conduct wills, either as a means to a further end or as an end in itself. Thus, all intentional killing of innocent human beings is prohibited, even if the death of the innocent person is willed only as a means to some further good (for instance, saving the lives of five other innocent people). Morally speaking, an action is identified in terms of the intention of the person acting. An external view of an action, therefore, will often fail to distinguish between cases that are morally quite different.

Double Effect   The fact that moral differences can exist between externally similar actions has led to the principle of *double effect*: under certain circumstances one may rightly perform an action that has, besides the effect desired either as a means or an end, a second effect that could not rightly be willed as a means or an end. This principle helps distinguish heroic self-sacrifice from suicide. A soldier jumping on a grenade to save his comrades does not will his own death either as a means or an end, although he foresees that he may die. (If the grenade does not explode, the soldier's intentions have not been thwarted for he intended to protect others rather than to kill himself, nor did he intend his own death as a means of protecting others.)

Justice and the Social Nature of Human Beings   The theory of natural law views human beings as by nature social. This view, held by Aristotle, the Stoics, and St. Thomas Aquinas, holds that natural human sociality underlies the requirements of justice and equity. Thus, the laws of states are valid only if they are instituted by the public authority for the common good. State laws may require conduct in addition to that required by natural law, but a requirement by the public authority that citizens violate natural law is not a valid law.

And so there is a *jurisprudential* theory of natural law, which concerns itself with the validity of the laws of states. This theory developed out of the legal thought of the Stoics and Roman jurists, who saw a universal core of natural law within the laws of all civilized nations. The jurisprudential theory of natural law received new attention after World War II, for it offered a way to conceptualize the extreme case of the Nazi revisions of the German legal system.[3] A natural-law theorist would judge many Nazi revisions of the law as invalid—mere orders backed by force, rather than laws deserving at least some respect. The case of the Nazis is interesting not only from the perspective of jurisprudence. Those who understand justice as determined solely by convention or agreement must confront the implication that *morally speaking* the Nazis acted within the requirements of justice. This implication will lead most people to abandon such social relativism.

Deriving Values from Facts   The main philosophical difficulty with the theory of natural law is that it seems to derive value judgments from nonevaluative, merely factual claims about the nature of human beings. Deriving claims about what ought to be done from claims about what is the case has been called the *naturalistic fallacy*.[4] Why should people act in accordance with their nature, even if there were agreement about what nature is? Could it not equally be said that human beings ought to strive to *overcome* human nature? Furthermore, there seem to be many elements in human nature other than those designated by natural-law theorists as the basis of right conduct. For instance, there is good reason to believe that human beings have some innate aggressive tendencies, and yet few would have us follow nature in this respect.

Two interrelated questions present themselves here: (1) How can one logically derive value judgments from any factual claims at all? and (2) How can one consistently choose only some aspects of human nature as the basis of value? The response of the natural-law theorists is the same on both issues. They believe it is possible to derive values from facts and to distinguish some aspects of humanity as the basis of value, because the question of right conduct arises only for a being who is capable of rational choice.

Human beings have many aspects; but not all aspects of humanity have an equal place in rational deliberations concerning right conduct. Some natural inclinations must be resisted in order to make a life in which people's deepest needs (the universal human goods) are met. For instance, aggression must be curbed in favor of friendship and the preservation of life in society—not because sociality is natural to humanity and aggression not natural, but because the natural place of aggression in human life must be subordinate to sociality. Value judgments are grounded in what is valuable for human beings given what they are; this is a complex matter involving relationships of subordination among the many natural aspects of human beings. It is natural to avoid pain, but it is against reason (and so against human nature) to avoid pain at the expense of health (for instance, by not going to the dentist). All voluntary actions aim at some perceived good, and it is the job of reason to weigh the importance of competing goods in the light of an understanding of the incommensurable universal human goods necessary for a good human life.

It is the teleological structure of voluntary action that provides the bridge between fact and value. If all voluntary action aims at some perceived good, then voluntary action *ought* to promote the actual good and avoid the actual evil. The shift from what is in fact the case to what ought to be the case is accomplished by reason. After all, it would be irrational not to will what is actually good rather than what is a mere apparent or limited good. Most people do consider irrational those who knowingly avoid pain at the expense of health, for they rationally judge health as the more basic good. The same judgment usually is made of the person whose aggressiveness deprives him of the deep human satisfaction of friendship.

Still, the derivation of values from facts is not an exercise in pure logic. It is not a logical contradiction to embrace a life of aggression at the expense of friendship. Using the word "irrational" to criticize someone for choosing less than a fully human life is to incorporate into that term standards that go beyond mere consistency into the realm of value judgments.

Even if *some* value judgments may be justified by appeal to the actual good of human beings, a full and detailed natural-law theory of right conduct could not be given such a foundation. There are relatively few uncontroversial cases of the distinction between apparent or limited good and actual good. The case of not going to the dentist in order to avoid pain is clear-cut but rare. And such uncontroversial matters are not likely to play a crucial role in genuine moral problems. As Bernard Williams has argued, an understanding of human nature serves to "delimit the possible content of what could be regarded as a morality," but a full account of right conduct cannot be derived directly from an understanding of human nature.[5]

Human Nature and God   There are some who object to natural-law theory on quite different grounds. Existentialists, some Marxists, and some other contemporary philosophers reject the view that there is such a thing as "human nature" in the relevant sense. Human beings, they claim, continually make and remake their nature as they live in society; humanity is malleable and moldable, and people should not limit their actions in either personal or political life by any doctrine of an unchanging human nature. The natural-law idea that the function of human beings is rational activity is rejected, for human beings, they assert, cannot be said to have a function or purpose. To speak of such a function is to conceive of human beings as if they were artifacts or tools, like chairs and hammers. And so the existentialist Jean-Paul Sartre writes: "If God does not exist, there is at least one being in whom existence precedes essence, a being who exists before he can be defined by any concept. . . . Thus, there is no human nature, since there is no God to conceive it. . . . Man is nothing else but what he makes himself."[6] Thus each human being is responsible for deciding, through his or her plans and actions, what "human nature" will be.

However, the conception of human nature found in natural-law theory does not necessarily require a fundamental belief in a Creator who made human beings to serve a function, as a manufacturer makes a hammer to serve a function. Natural-law theory began in Aristotle without a background belief in a Creator. Although the development of Christian natural law presupposed a Creator, the conception of humanity as having an essential nature can perhaps be given an entirely naturalistic, scientific interpretation. The guiding idea of natural law is that there are central abilities and inclinations that set limits to what will count as human flourishing. This might be true whether or not a Creator exists.

NATURAL RIGHTS

Break with an Earlier View   The modern theory of natural rights arose in the seventeenth century and made a definite break with the

natural-law tradition out of which it grew. Natural-law theorists had insisted that human beings are social by nature. The defenders of natural
rights denied this natural sociality, insisting that the liberty of the individual is the primary moral characteristic of humanity. This individual liberty
is understood as natural, since it is independent of the laws and customs of
particular societies. The laws of states derive their legitimacy from the
agreement or consent of free individuals. The political and social philosophy of natural rights thus requires some version of a freely entered social
contract in order to justify any authority over individuals.

Primacy of Individual Rights *Individual rights* are primary within
this theory: each person has a natural right to life, liberty, and justly acquired property. The theory of natural rights is not teleological. Rather,
natural-rights theory is *deontological*—that is, it does not derive rights and
obligations from the promotion of value. Right conduct is conduct that respects the boundaries of each person's rights, regardless of whether
through that conduct good is promoted and evil avoided. Each person has
the right to live as he or she chooses (as long as an equal right is left to
others), so there are no duties to self within natural-rights theory. This dif-
ferentiates it in an important way from the theory of natural law, which
places great moral stress upon an individual's duty to lead a fully human
life.

Natural-rights theory is essentially negative in its view of morality: *not*
violating the rights of others is all that is required. And those rights are for
the most part negative rights; for instance, the natural right to life is not the
right to be provided the means to live but only the right not to be killed.
Apart from special relationships (such as parenthood), there is no duty to
help others, only a duty not to harm others. Helping others is perhaps admirable, but it is not strictly obligatory.

Minimal Government This ethical minimalism—requiring the least
possible of people—is matched by a minimalist account of the legitimate
functions of government. Government exists to protect the prior natural
rights of individuals and cannot legitimately coerce individuals to aid one
another. Both ethical and governmental minimalism derive from the fundamental natural-rights principle that right conduct respects the rights of
others, construing those rights as rights to noninterference. An absolute
value is placed upon individual freedom, regardless of the uses to which
that freedom is put. And it would be incorrect to say that the natural-
rights theorist seeks to produce the most freedom, for the rights of one individual may not be violated in order to produce more respect for the
rights of others. According to the tenets of natural-rights theory, there is
not even a teleology of freedom.

Self-Interested Rationality Natural-rights theorists paint a picture of
humanity as self-interested and rational. Self-interest is often understood
as primarily an interest in self-preservation and secondarily as an interest in
the pursuit of happiness, or the satisfaction of desire. It is humanity's rationality and self-interest, rather than any other distinct aspects of human

nature, which explain the pursuit of knowledge and even the choice of life in society, for these are viewed as rationally necessary means to promote self-interest.

Influence on the Constitution and Popular Morality   The natural-rights theorists influenced the founders of the United States. Consequently, there is an emphasis upon individual liberty and the limitation of governmental authority in the Constitution of the United States, especially in the first ten amendments, or the Bill of Rights. In the Declaration of Independence, Thomas Jefferson expressed both the individualist conception of rights and the more traditional background of natural law that was thought to justify this conception of liberty: "We hold these truths to be self-evident, that all men are created equal; that they are endowed by their Creator with certain inalienable rights; that among these, are life, liberty, and the pursuit of happiness. That, to secure these rights, governments are instituted among men, deriving their just powers from the consent of the governed."

The natural right to liberty sets limits to all legitimate interference with the individual (whether governmental or social). A modern corollary to this is the *right to privacy*, which has become central to contemporary natural-rights theory. This idea of the "right to be left alone" has evolved within United States constitutional law (for instance, the constitutional right to terminate pregnancy as determined in *Roe* v. *Wade* is based upon it), but it is also appealed to informally in much current moral debate. It is common to hear controversial conduct defended on the grounds that as long as no one else is harmed, the conduct is the "business" only of those engaged in it. This view that self-regarding conduct (directly affecting only those consenting to it) ought to be free from not only government interference but even from the interference of moral disapproval by society is the equivalent in popular moral thought of the more technical legal concept of the right of privacy.[7]

Readings   The selection from Saint Thomas Aquinas sets out the fundamental principle of right conduct and then specifies the good and the evil by reference to the basic natural inclinations of human beings. Aquinas then argues that the natural law encompasses all virtuous actions —that the natural law is unchanging.

Germain Grisez and Russell Shaw give a contemporary version of the theory of natural law. The principle of right conduct is that one must remain open to all fundamental human goods (or purposes). Grisez and Shaw then explain eight "modes of responsibility" which follow from that principle: commitment to a harmonious set of values, impartiality, benevolence, detachment, fidelity, efficiency, duties deriving from social roles, and the absolute prohibition of directly acting against one of the fundamental human goods. In a passage not printed below, the fundamental human goods are given as: life, play, aesthetic experience, speculative knowledge, integrity, authenticity, friendship, and religion.

The selections from John Locke set out the natural-rights conception of human beings as equal in liberty in the state of nature, with natural rights to life, liberty, and property. Locke explains how property is acquired in a state of nature (by mixing one's labor with the object) and also discusses how the introduction of money allows the just acquisition of wealth beyond what can be used and thus allows for economic inequality without violation of natural rights. He then explains the origin of government as a means of protecting life and property and the limitations on governmental authority due to the natural rights of individuals, from whose consent government derives all legitimacy.

The selection from Robert Nozick offers his account of the "entitlement theory" of justice in property. This theory traces justice in property to a series of events conferring title rather than to any supposed just pattern of distribution. According to Nozick, everyone has a moral right to dispose of property as he or she chooses.

Notes

[1] Aristotle, *Nichomachean Ethics*, book 1, chap. 7, in *The Philosophy of Aristotle*, trans. A. E. Wardman, ed. R. Bambrough (New York: New American Library, 1963), p. 293.

[2] See especially Noam Chomsky, *Language and Mind* (New York: Harcourt, Brace & World, 1968), pp. 69–85.

[3] See Lon Fuller, "Positivism and Fidelity to Law—A Reply to Professor Hart," *Harvard Law Review* 71 (1958): 630–72.

[4] The phrase derives from George E. Moore, *Principia Ethica* (Cambridge: Cambridge University Press, 1903). For a clear discussion of the naturalistic fallacy, see William Frankena, "The Naturalistic Fallacy," *Mind*, 48 (1939): 464–77.

[5] Bernard Williams, *Morality: An Introduction to Ethics* (New York: Harper & Row, 1972), p. 66. In discussing Aristotle's emphasis on rationality as the "distinguishing mark of man," Williams offers a valuable defense of the place of the emotions in human life. This point is also relevant to Kant's ethics, with its Stoic emphasis on rationality beyond that found in Aristotle.

[6] Jean-Paul Sartre, "Existentialism," in *Existentialism and Human Emotions*, trans. B. Frechtman (New York: Philosophical Library, 1957), p. 15.

[7] The utilitarian John Stuart Mill wrote a classic defense of the principle that self-regarding conduct ought to be free from interference by society, either through law or the informal coercion of moral opinion; he claimed, however, that his argument appealed only to utility and not to any doctrine of natural rights. Nevertheless, Mill's *On Liberty* belongs within the tradition of John Locke and individual rights.

Bibliography on Natural Law and Natural Rights

Natural Law

Aquinas, St. Thomas. *Basic Writings of Saint Thomas Aquinas*. 2 vols. Edited by Anton C. Pegis. New York: Random House, 1945. The "Treatise on Law" from the *Summa Theologica* is found in the second volume.

Copleston, Frederick C. *Aquinas*. Baltimore, Md.: Penguin Books, 1955. Chapter 5.

Donagan, Alan. *The Theory of Morality*. Chicago, Ill.: University of Chicago Press, 1977.

(For the Stoic, Christian, and Jewish understanding of morality, see pages 1–9; for a discussion of Aquinas and Kant on the fundamental moral principle, see pages 57–66.)

Finnis, John. *Natural Law and Natural Rights*. New York: Oxford University Press, 1979.

Grisez, Germain G. "The First Principle of Practical Reason: A Commentary on the *Summa Theologica*, 1–2, Question 94, Article 2," *Natural Law Forum* (now *The American Journal of Jurisprudence*) 10 (1965): 168–201.

"Natural Law." *The Encyclopedia of Philosophy*. New York: Macmillan, 1967. Vol. 5, pp. 450–454.

O'Connor, D. J. *Aquinas and Natural Law*. London: Macmillan, 1968.

Simon, Yves R. *The Tradition of Natural Law: A Philosopher's Reflections*. New York: Fordham University Press, 1965.

Natural Rights

Hart, Herbert L. A. "Are There Any Natural Rights?" *Philosophical Review* 64 (1955): 175–91.

Hayek, Frederick A. *The Constitution of Liberty*. Chicago, Ill.: University of Chicago Press, 1960.

_____. *Law, Legislation, and Liberty*. Vol. 1. *Rules and Order*. Chicago, Ill.: University of Chicago Press, 1973.

Locke, John. *The Second Treatise of Government*. Several editions.

Nozick, Robert. *Anarchy, State, and Utopia*. New York: Basic Books, 1974.

Paul, Jeffrey, ed. *Reading Nozick*. Totowa, N.J.: Rowman and Littlefield, 1981.

Schochet, Gordon, ed. *Life, Liberty, and Property: Essays on Locke's Political Ideas*, Belmont, Calif.: Wadsworth, 1971.

SAINT THOMAS AQUINAS
ON NATURAL LAW

Second Article

WHETHER THE NATURAL LAW CONTAINS SEVERAL PRECEPTS. OR ONLY ONE?

We proceed thus to the Second Article:—

Objection 1. It would seem that the natural law contains, not several precepts, but only one. For law is a kind of precept, as was stated above. If therefore there were many precepts of the natural law, it would follow that there are also many natural laws.

Obj. 2. Further, the natural law is consequent upon human nature. But human nature, as a whole, is one, though, as to its parts, it is manifold. Therefore, either there is but one precept of the law of nature because of the unity of nature as a whole, or there are many by reason of the number of parts of human nature. The result would be that even things relating to the inclination of the concupiscible power would belong to the natural law.

From St. Thomas Aquinas, *Summa Theologica*, I–II, Question 94, articles 2–5, in *Basic Writings of Saint Thomas Aquinas*, ed. Anton C. Pegis (New York: Random House, 1945), vol. 2, pp. 773–780. By permission of the A. C. Pegis Estate.

Obj. 3. Further, law is something pertaining to reason, as was stated above. Now reason is but one in man. Therefore there is only one precept of the natural law.

On the contrary, The precepts of the natural law in man stand in relation to operable matters as first principles do to matters of demonstration. But there are several first indemonstrable principles. Therefore there are also several precepts of the natural law.

I answer that, As was stated above, the precepts of the natural law are to the practical reason what the first principles of demonstrations are to the speculative reason, because both are self-evident principles. Now a thing is said to be self-evident in two ways: first, in itself; secondly, in relation to us. Any proposition is said to be self-evident in itself, if its predicate is contained in the notion of the subject; even though it may happen that to one who does not know the definition of the subject, such a proposition is not self-evident. For instance, this proposition, *Man is a rational being,* is, in its very nature, self-evident, since he who says *man,* says *a rational being;* and yet to one who does not know what a man *is,* this proposition is not self-evident. Hence it is that, as Boethius says, certain axioms or propositions are universally self-evident to all; and such are the propositions whose terms are known to all, as, *Every whole is greater that its part,* and, *Things equal to one and the same are equal to one another.* But some propositions are self-evident only to the wise, who understand the meaning of the terms of such propositions. Thus to one who understands that an angel is not a body, it is self-evident that an angel is not circumscriptively in a place. But this is not evident to the unlearned, for they cannot grasp it.

Now a certain order is to be found in those things that are apprehended by men. For that which first falls under apprehension is *being,* the understanding of which is included in all things whatsoever a man apprehends. Therefore the first indemonstrable principle is that *the same thing cannot be affirmed and denied at the same time,* which is based on the notion of *being* and *not-being:* and on this principle all others are based, as is stated in *Metaph.* iv. Now as *being* is the first thing that falls under the apprehension absolutely, so *good* is the first thing that falls under the apprehension of the practical reason, which is directed to action (since every agent acts for an end, which has the nature of good). Consequently, the first principle in the practical reason is one founded on the nature of good, viz., that *good is that which all things seek after.* Hence this is the first precept of law, that *good is to be done and promoted, and evil is to be avoided.* All other precepts of the natural law are based upon this; so that all the things which the practical reason naturally apprehends as man's good belong to the precepts of the natural law under the form of things to be done or avoided.

Since, however, good has the nature of an end, and evil, the nature of the contrary, hence it is that all those things to which man has a natural inclination are naturally apprehended by reason as being good, and consequently as objects of pursuit, and their contraries as evil, and objects of avoidance. Therefore, the order of the precepts of the natural law is according to the order of natural inclinations. For there is in man, first of all, an inclination to good in accordance with the nature which he has in common with all substances, inasmuch, namely, as every substance seeks the preservation of its own being, according to its nature; and by reason of this inclination, whatever is a means of preserving human life, and of warding off its obstacles, belongs to the natural law. Secondly, there is in man an inclination to things that pertain to him more specially, according to that nature which he has in common with other animals; and in virtue of this inclination, those things are said to belong to the natural law *which nature has taught to all animals,* such as sexual intercourse, the education of offspring and so forth. Thirdly, there is in man an inclination to good according to the nature of his reason, which nature is proper to him. Thus man has a natural inclination to know the truth about God, and to live in society; and in this respect, whatever pertains to this inclination belongs to the natural law: *e.g.,* to shun ignorance, to avoid offending those among whom one has to live, and other such things regarding the above inclination.

Reply Obj. 1. All these precepts of the law of nature have the character of one natural law, inasmuch as they flow from one first precept.

Reply Obj. 2. All the inclinations of any parts whatsoever of human nature, *e.g.,* of the concupiscible and irascible parts, in so far as they are ruled by reason, belong to the natural law, and are reduced to one first precept, as was stated above. And thus the precepts of the natural law are many in themselves, but they are based on one common foundation.

Reply Obj. 3. Although reason is one in itself, yet it directs all things regarding man: so that whatever can be ruled by reason is contained under the law of reason.

Third Article

WHETHER ALL THE ACTS OF THE VIRTUES ARE PRESCRIBED BY THE NATURAL LAW?

We proceed thus to the Third Article:—

Objection 1. It would seem that not all the acts of the virtues are prescribed by the natural law. For, as was stated above, it is of the nature of law that it be ordained to the common good. But some acts of the virtues are ordained to the private good of the individual, as is evident especially in regard to acts of temperance. Therefore, not all the acts of the virtues are the subject of natural law.

Obj. 2. Further, every sin is opposed to some virtuous act. If therefore all the acts of the virtues are prescribed by the natural law, it seems to follow that all sins are against nature: whereas this applies to certain special sins.

Obj. 3. Further, those things which are according to nature are com-

mon to all. But the acts of the virtues are not common to all, since a thing
is virtuous in one, and vicious in another. Therefore, not all the acts of the
virtues are prescribed by the natural law.

On the contrary, Damascene says that *virtues are natural*. Therefore
virtuous acts also are subject to the natural law.

I answer that, We may speak of virtuous acts in two ways: first, in so
far as they are virtuous; secondly, as such and such acts considered in their
proper species. If, then, we are speaking of the acts of the virtues in so far
as they are virtuous, thus all virtuous acts belong to the natural law. For it
has been stated that to the natural law belongs everything to which a man
is inclined according to his nature. Now each thing is inclined naturally to
an operation that is suitable to it according to its form: *e.g.*, fire is inclined
to give heat. Therefore, since the rational soul is the proper form of man,
there is in every man a natural inclination to act according to reason; and
this is to act according to virtue. Consequently, considered thus, all the
acts of the virtues are prescribed by the natural law, since each one's reason
naturally dictates to him to act virtuously. But if we speak of virtuous acts,
considered in themselves, *i.e.*, in their proper species, thus not all virtuous
acts are prescribed by the natural law. For many things are done virtuously, to which nature does not primarily incline, but which, through the
inquiry of reason, have been found by men to be conducive to well-living.

Reply Obj. 1. Temperance is about the natural concupiscences of food,
drink and sexual matters, which are indeed ordained to the common good
of nature, just as other matters of law are ordained to the moral common
good.

Reply Obj. 2. By human nature we may mean either that which is
proper to man, and in this sense all sins, as being against reason, are also
against nature, as Damascene states; or we may mean that nature which is
common to man and other animals, and in this sense, certain special sins
are said to be against nature: *e.g.*, contrary to sexual intercourse, which is
natural to all animals, is unisexual lust, which has received the special
name of the unnatural crime.

Reply Obj. 3. This argument considers acts in themselves. For it is owing to the various conditions of men that certain acts are virtuous for some,
as being proportioned and becoming to them, while they are vicious for
others, as not being proportioned to them.

Fourth Article

WHETHER THE NATURAL LAW IS THE SAME IN ALL MEN?

We proceed thus to the Fourth Article:—

Objection 1. It would seem that the natural law is not the same in all.
For it is stated in the *Decretals* that *the natural law is that which is contained in the Law and the Gospel.* But this is not common to all men, because, as it is written (*Rom.* x. 16), *all do not obey the gospel.* Therefore
the natural law is not the same in all men.

Obj. 2. Further, *Things which are according to the law are said to be just,* as is stated in *Ethics* v. But it is stated in the same book that nothing is so just for all as not to be subject to change in regard to some men. Therefore even the natural law is not the same in all men.

Obj. 3. Further, as was stated above, to the natural law belongs everything to which a man is inclined according to his nature. Now different men are naturally inclined to different things—some to the desire of pleasures, others to the desire of honors, and other men to other things. Therefore, there is not one natural law for all.

On the contrary, Isidore says: *The natural law is common to all nations.*

I answer that, As we have stated above, to the natural law belong those things to which a man is inclined naturally; and among these it is proper to man to be inclined to act according to reason. Now it belongs to the reason to proceed from what is common to what is proper, as is stated in *Physics* i. The speculative reason, however, is differently situated, in this matter, from the practical reason. For, since the speculative reason is concerned chiefly with necessary things, which cannot be otherwise than they are, its proper conclusions, like the universal principles, contain the truth without fail. The practical reason, on the other hand, is concerned with contingent matters, which is the domain of human actions: and, consequently, although there is necessity in the common principles, the more we descend towards the particular, the more frequently we encounter defects. Accordingly, then, in speculative matters truth is the same in all men, both as to principles and as to conclusions; although the truth is not known to all as regards the conclusions, but only as regards the principles which are called *common notions*. But in matters of action, truth or practical rectitude is not the same for all as to what is particular, but only as to the common principles; and where there is the same rectitude in relation to particulars, it is not equally known to all.

It is therefore evident that, as regards the common principles whether of speculative or of practical reason, truth or rectitude is the same for all, and is equally known by all. But as to the proper conclusions of the speculative reason, the truth is the same for all, but it is not equally known to all. Thus, it is true for all that the three angles of a triangle are together equal to two right angles, although it is not known to all. But as to the proper conclusions of the practical reason, neither is the truth or rectitude the same for all, nor, where it is the same, is it equally known by all. Thus, it is right and true for all to act according to reason, and from this principle it follows, as a proper conclusion, that goods entrusted to another should be restored to their owner. Now this is true for the majority of cases. But it may happen in a particular case that it would be injurious, and therefore unreasonable, to restore goods held in trust; for instance, if they are claimed for the purpose of fighting against one's country. And this principle will be found to fail the more, according as we descend further towards the particular, *e.g.*, if one were to say that goods held in trust should be restored with such and such a guarantee, or in such and such a way; because the greater the number of conditions added, the greater the number of ways in which the principle may fail, so that it be not right to restore or not to restore.

Consequently, we must say that the natural law, as to the first common principles, is the same for all, both as to rectitude and as to knowledge. But as to certain more particular aspects, which are conclusions, as it were, of those common principles, it is the same for all in the majority of cases, both as to rectitude and as to knowledge; and yet in some few cases it may fail, both as to rectitude, by reason of certain obstacles (just as natures subject to generation and corruption fail in some few cases because of some obstacle), and as to knowledge, since in some the reason is perverted by passion, or evil habit, or an evil disposition of nature. Thus at one time theft, although it is expressly contrary to the natural law, was not considered wrong among the Germans, as Julius Caesar relates.

Reply Obj. 1. The meaning of the sentence quoted is not that whatever is contained in the Law and the Gospel belongs to the natural law, since they contain many things that are above nature; but that whatever belongs to the natural law is fully contained in them. Therefore Gratian, after saying that *the natural law is what is contained in the Law and the Gospel,* adds at once, by way of example, *by which everyone is commanded to do to others as he would be done by.*

Reply Obj. 2. The saying of the Philosopher is to be understood of things that are naturally just, not as common principles, but as conclusions drawn from them, having rectitude in the majority of cases, but failing in a few.

Reply Obj. 3. Just as in man reason rules and commands the other powers, so all the natural inclinations belonging to the other powers must needs be directed according to reason. Therefore it is universally right for all men that all their inclinations should be directed according to reason.

Fifth Article

WHETHER THE NATURAL LAW CAN BE CHANGED?

We proceed thus to the Fifth Article:—

Objection 1. It would seem that the natural law can be changed. For on *Ecclus.* xvii. 9 (*He gave them instructions, and the law of life*) the *Gloss* says: *He wished the law of the letter to be written, in order to correct the law of nature.* But that which is corrected is changed. Therefore the natural law can be changed.

Obj. 2. Further, the slaying of the innocent, adultery and theft are against the natural law. But we find these things changed by God: as when God commanded Abraham to slay his innocent son (*Gen.* xxii. 2); and when He ordered the Jews to borrow and purloin the vessels of the Egyptians (*Exod.* xii. 35); and when He commanded Osee to take to himself *a wife of fornications* (*Osee* i. 2). Therefore the natural law can be changed.

Obj. 3. Further, Isidore says that *the possession of all things in common, and universal freedom, are matters of natural law.* But these things are seen to be changed by human laws. Therefore it seems that the natural law is subject to change.

On the contrary, It is said in the *Decretals: The natural law dates from the creation of the rational creature. It does not vary according to time, but remains unchangeable.*

I answer that, A change in the natural law may be understood in two ways. First, by way of addition. In this sense, nothing hinders the natural law from being changed, since many things for the benefit of human life have been added over and above the natural law, both by the divine law and by human laws.

Secondly, a change in the natural law may be understood by way of subtraction, so that what previously was according to the natural law, ceases to be so. In this sense, the natural law is altogether unchangeable in its first principles. But in its secondary principles, which, as we have said, are certain detailed proximate conclusions drawn from the first principles, the natural law is not changed so that what it prescribes be not right in most cases. But it may be changed in some particular cases of rare occurrence, through some special causes hindering the observance of such precepts, as was stated above.

Reply Obj. 1. The written law is said to be given for the correction of the natural law, either because it supplies what was wanting to the natural law, or because the natural law was so perverted in the hearts of some men, as to certain matters, that they esteemed those things good which are naturally evil; which perversion stood in need of correction.

Reply Obj. 2. All men alike, both guilty and innocent, die the death of nature; which death of nature is inflicted by the power of God because of original sin, according to *I Kings* ii. 6: *The Lord killeth and maketh alive.* Consequently, by the command of God, death can be inflicted on any man, guilty or innocent, without any injustice whatever.—In like manner, adultery is intercourse with another's wife; who is allotted to him by the law emanating from God. Consequently intercourse with any woman, by the command of God, is neither adultery nor fornication.—The same applies to theft, which is the taking of another's property. For whatever is taken by the command of God, to Whom all things belong, is not taken against the will of its owner, whereas it is in this that theft consists.—Nor is it only in human things that whatever is commanded by God is right; but also in natural things, whatever is done by God is, in some way, natural, as was stated in the First Part.

Reply Obj. 3. A thing is said to belong to the natural law in two ways. First, because nature inclines thereto: *e.g.,* that one should not do harm to another. Secondly, because nature did not bring with it the contrary. Thus, we might say that for man to be naked is of the natural law, because nature did not give him clothes, but art invented them. In this sense, *the possession of all things in common and universal freedom* are said to be of the natural law, because, namely, the distinction of possessions and slavery were not brought in by nature, but devised by human reason for the benefit of human life. Accordingly, the law of nature was not changed in this respect, except by addition. . . .

GERMAIN GRISEZ AND RUSSELL SHAW
A NATURAL LAW THEORY

CHOICE—EXCLUSIVISTIC AND INCLUSIVISTIC

. . . One way of choosing can be called "exclusive" or, better perhaps, "exclusivistic." It may be objected that all choice is exclusivistic, since in choosing one thing an individual naturally excludes the things not chosen.

While this is certainly the case, it ignores the fact that there are two radically different attitudes which one can bring to choosing. In making a choice among alternatives one can do so in such a way—and with such an attitude—that those things which are not chosen are also not positively rejected, or one's attitude can be such that the alternatives not chosen *are* rejected. The second way of choosing—with an attitude that positively rejects the alternatives not chosen—is exclusivistic choice. . . .

But it is also possible to choose with an inclusive—or, better, an inclusivistic—attitude. This means simply that while choosing one alternative out of two or more, one continues to respect the values present in the alternatives that were not chosen. A person who chooses in this way in effect acknowledges his own limitations—no one can be or do everything—but he does not shift the blame, as it were, onto the options-not-chosen by denying their value. . . .

We ought always to choose inclusivistically. For consistent inclusivism in choice is in fact the criterion of moral goodness we have been seeking, whereas moral evil consists in choosing exclusivistically. Indeed, it can be said that no one chooses precisely to do *what is morally wrong*; one rather makes choices *in a way* that is morally wrong—in an exclusivistic manner.

This is so because, upon reflection, it becomes apparent that inclusivistic choice corresponds to . . . the meaning of the moral "ought"—the fullest possible realization of ourselves as free. When we choose inclusivistically we remain open to further self-realization even in directions we have not chosen. Even though we have chosen X—instead of Y or Z—we continue to acknowledge the good that is in Y and Z and, in doing so, we remain open to the possibility of realizing that good, given different circumstances. We have not closed off growth in any area of life (which is to say, growth in ourselves).

From Germain Grisez and Russell Shaw, *Beyond The New Morality: The Responsibilities of Freedom* (Notre Dame, Ind.: University of Notre Dame Press, 1974), pp. 88, 90–91, 108–14, 118–21, 128–33. Copyright 1974, University of Notre Dame Press, Notre Dame, Indiana 46556.

By contrast, because it involves an attitude which denies the value of that which is not chosen, exclusivistic choice not only prevents self-realization in these directions here and now but tends to block it permanently by creating a mind-set which denies the goodness that is there. . . .

MODES OF RESPONSIBILITY

. . . If one's attitude toward all the fundamental human purposes were open and inclusivistic (the basic criterion of moral goodness), he would not live for passing satisfactions or for specific future objectives. He would instead commit himself to the realization of basic purposes with which he could identify to such an extent that the free actions by which he realized them would in fact constitute him as the person he was. Furthermore, he would make a number of such commitments—large, third-level actions like marrying or engaging in a profession. And, further still, he would strive to make his commitments consistent with one another, so that they formed a harmonious framework for his life. This, then, is the first mode of responsibility: consistent commitment to a harmonious set of purposes or values.

Negatively, this mode of responsibility rules out a certain kind of premoral spontaneity, in which a man in effect puts himself at the service of a desire or inclination which is not harmonized with the rest of his fundamental life-purposes. Many people do in fact spend a great part of their lives in the service of such goals—pleasure, wealth, status, and so forth—which do not represent rational commitments but instead originated as mere wants or cravings. Such unreflective, slavish activity has nothing to do with a free, self-determined life.

At the same time there is a place for spontaneity within morality. For the individual who has integrated his commitments into a consistent pattern, spontaneous action within this pattern becomes almost second nature. But spontaneity in this case will be in line with one's commitments rather than something that precedes commitment. From the perspective of this mode of responsibility, immorality consists in using one's mature powers in the service of infantile goals, while morality means organizing one's life around basic commitments and acting within the pattern one has created by this organization.

A second mode of responsibility is that if one has an open and inclusivistic attitude toward all the fundamental human purposes, he will at all times take into account all of the goods, and will, furthermore, do so not merely as they apply to himself but as they apply to all other men. He will not regard himself as a special case, demanding concessions and special treatment he is unwilling to grant to others. He will regularly ask himself questions such as "How would I like it if somebody did this to me?" and "What would happen if everybody acted as I wish to act?"

It is no secret that this moral rule is violated frequently in ordinary experience. Violations are especially common on the part of people who have undergone a change in their state of life and no longer remember how things looked "on the other side." How many parents, one wonders, inflict injustices on their children which they, as children suffering the same injustices at the hands of *their* parents, vowed never to be guilty of in adult life?

A third mode of responsibility, also involving relationships with others, might be described simply as openness: willingness to help others, desire to see them develop and perfect themselves by realizing to the fullest the goods of which they are capable. A person with this attitude is not defensive or selfish about protecting his own position of excellence or superiority in relation to others.

A striking example is provided by the good teacher who genuinely rejoices in seeing his students progress in their particular discipline or skill, even if the students come in time to outshine the teacher. A man with this attitude will also accept and take satisfaction in the ways in which other people are different from him; he will not demand that everyone mirror his tastes and enthusiasms.

Morality, from the viewpoint of this mode of responsibility, is often expressed in willingness to accept responsibility for the needs of another even where there is no structured relationship with the other which compels one to do so. Conversely, immorality is apparent in the actions of persons who feel no responsibility for others with whom they come into contact in unstructured relationships (e.g., the driver who does not stop or send help back to a stranded motorist). To insist on having a clear-cut duty before doing what is necessary to help someone else reflects an immoral attitude.

DETACHMENT AND FIDELITY

"Detachment" is the word which characterizes a fourth mode of responsibility. Its contrary is manifested by people who are so oriented toward one purpose that its frustration or loss is a shattering experience which drains their lives of meaning. Someone with a morally good attitude, an openness to all human goods, will not be so totally destroyed by the loss of any one good, no matter how genuinely painful the loss may be. . . .

A person with a religious turn of mind may object at this point that what has just been said cannot apply to loving God above all else—something to which every man ought to be totally dedicated, and dedicated above everything else. This is true, so long as one keeps in mind that God is not an aspect of the human personality, that God transcends all human goods, and that, properly understood, love of God implies love of all human goods; implies, in other words, precisely the morally good attitude we have been attempting to describe. However, it *is* possible to overidentify with and overcommit oneself to the human good of religion, in which case the aberration in question is what is called "religious fanaticism."

The fifth mode of responsibility complements detachment. While prepared to accept the loss of particular satisfactions and achievements without regarding this as a final loss of his personhood, a man should nevertheless remain committed to his ideals. He should, in other words, practice fidelity. A person with such an attitude will persist in seeking to realize realistically realizable purposes; by contrast, a person with an immoral attitude will tend to give up rather easily upon encountering problems and obstacles.

Fidelity or stability in commitment to purposes is not the same thing as mere constancy, much less rigidity. It implies continuing effort to explore new ways of better serving the purposes to which one is committed. Furthermore, it involves refusal to narrow down a human good to those particular expressions of it with which one happens to be familiar. A creative and open approach to living is not only consistent with but essential to genuine fidelity. . . .

Detachment on the one hand and fidelity on the other balance each other in the life of an individual. They enable a man to strike a mean between the immoral extremes of fanaticism and noninvolvement. They also rule out an attitude of unwillingness to attempt difficult things and thereby risk failure.

Morality does not require one to take needless risks or to be unrealistic about circumstances, including one's own abilities, and the consequent chances of failing in an undertaking. But a person with a morally good attitude will be inclined to push beyond what he and others have already accomplished and to take reasonable chances in the process, aware that many good and important things in life will never be done except by people who are willing to run the risk of failing in the attempt to do them.

PURSUIT OF LIMITED OBJECTIVES

Under the sixth mode of responsibility one will seek specific ends which contribute to realization of the broader, deeper purposes to which he has dedicated his life. The pursuit of specific objectives which can be attained by definite, limited means should always be included within the framework of our basic self-constitution.

This may seem a surprising thing to say in view of the many occasions on which we have up to now criticized the pursuit of limited objectives. The point of this criticism, however, has been that it is wrong to limit one's morality, and one's life, merely to this. But, provided life is grounded upon and built around commitment to a consistent set of purposes, it is not only good sense but one's responsibility to, as it were, put flesh on the bones of these commitments by pursuing limited ends which further their realization. . . .

Where, morally speaking, efficiency is possible, it is a virtue, although it is no virtue if it means achieving a limited objective at the expense of violating some basic good. Waste and inefficiency, by contrast, are signs of vice, although it is no vice to be judged "inefficient" in the pursuit of an objective when "efficiency" would require the violation of fundamental human goods.

Thus a nation might be judged inefficient in defending itself against aggression, even to the point of allowing itself to be overrun and conquered. But there would be nothing immoral about such inefficiency—it would in fact reflect an entirely moral attitude—if the efficiency in question came down in cold fact to repelling the aggression by merciless bombing of the potential invader's civilian population.

The modes of responsibility, as the last example suggested, apply not only to individuals but also to communities in their common action. In other words, they hold not only for men singly but for men collectively. Each mode of responsibility has a social as well as an individual dimension. . . .

COMMUNITIES AND DUTIES

Each of us has a variety of social roles arising from membership in various communities, and each of these social roles carries with it a variety of duties. To see why these duties normally are real *moral* responsibilities (why, that is, they concern good and evil and why they involve our self-determination) it is necessary to bear in mind what constitutes a genuine community.

A crowd of people brought together by accident or force—by something extrinsic to the members of the group—is not a community. . . . A community is characterized by shared commitment on the part of its members to the realization of some fundamental human purpose or purposes and by structures and activity appropriate to bringing this about.

In many respects a family is a model community. Its members are joined by ties of blood and mutual dependence, to be sure, but also by a joint commitment to common purposes of a very basic and intimate sort. Where such a commitment is lacking, a particular family may exist as a socioeconomic unit—as a kind of convenient arrangement—but it is not a genuine "community" as the word is understood and used here.

Definite structures and activity are required for the realization of the purposes which constitute a community. Institutions are necessary to articulate the purposes to which the community members are committed. All this in turn gives rise to various roles—what one might call "job descriptions"—for the different community members. Within the family, for instance, "father" refers to one role, "mother" to another, "eldest son" to a third, and so on.

The fulfillment of these roles will require that the persons filling them act in certain ways. These required ways of acting are duties, and a duty may be defined as something one has a responsibility for doing or not doing by virtue of one's role in a particular community. Just as we all have many social roles, so we have many duties: as a student, as a citizen, as a family member, as an employer or employee, and so on.

A community cannot function efficiently if its members do not live up to their roles and fulfill their duties. But true as this is, it is not this which makes duties genuine moral responsibilities. The aspect of moral responsibility enters in, rather, because of the fact that the members of a community are engaged in a joint . . . action seeking the realization of a fundamental human purpose or purposes.

A community member who does not fulfill his role and live up to his duties is in effect seeking to enjoy participation in the common good for which the community is organized without putting into it what is required of him if the community is to continue to realize the good for which it exists. He is trying to get something for nothing, to enjoy a free ride, at the expense of the other community members. Moreover, he is undermining the community at its roots by refusing to do his part to realize its purposes. If enough members behave in this way, the result, sooner or later, will be the collapse of the community and the end of the possibility that *this* community will realize its constituting purposes. . . .

Having said this, however, it is necessary to add two important qualifications. First, our duties as community members are real moral responsibilities only if the community itself is a genuine one. Second, when duties conflict with one another—as they sometimes do—our moral responsibility is limited to fulfilling only one of the conflicting duties, but deciding which one is not at all easy. . . .

A pure community in which there are no elements of injustice and exploitation is a very rare thing. Indeed, it is doubtful whether such a phenomenon ever does exist in our imperfect world. Certainly, the large-scale societies of which we are all members are not pure communities. They have aspects of genuine community, but they have less attractive aspects as well. And our duties as members of such a society are true moral responsibilities only when they arise from the community aspect of the society rather than from its unjust and exploitative aspects.

Nations, including the United States, are such societies, partly community and partly a highly complex structure to facilitate self-interest and exploitation. To say this is not to engage in breast-beating or viewing with alarm; it is simply to state the evident fact of the matter. . . .

ETHICAL ABSOLUTES

Are there ethical absolutes? Are there principles which should never be violated and therefore things which should never be done, regardless of circumstances and consequences?

Most people, almost instinctively, would answer Yes, and would then go on to cite some action which they feel should never be performed: purposely to torture a small child, for instance. Yet for many ethical theorists in our times the answer is No. For them there are no ethical absolutes and therefore no actions which can flatly be ruled out as being beyond the pale of acceptable human behavior. . . .

Our eighth mode of responsibility states unequivocally that there are such actions. It may be put quite simply: it is never right to act directly against one of the fundamental human goods. But while it is easy enough to state this principle, it is more difficult to show what it means. The question is far removed from idle speculation, however. Indeed, it is one of the most burning ethical issues of our times, an issue of far-reaching practical ramifications for individual and social life.

DUTIES AND RESPONSIBILITIES

In our discussion of duties we saw that many of our moral responsibilities arise from duties (which in turn arise from our structured social relationships with other people). Such responsibilities have true moral force, but they are not absolute. This is evident in the fact that they can and sometimes do conflict with one another. A man's responsibilities arising from his duties as a husband may sometimes come into conflict with his responsibilities as an employee. Both sets of duties are real, but in a particular situation an individual may not be able to respond to both.

In such a case a person must fulfill one set of duties and neglect the other. Provided he is being honest about the facts and his response to the facts, he can do so with a clear conscience, in the knowledge that these duties, while real, are not absolute responsibilities and, where circumstances require, can be neglected in favor of other, equally pressing duties.

However, there are other responsibilities which do not arise from duties and which are not conditional but absolute. They are founded instead on the implications of the ideal of openness to all the goods constitutive of the human person. Openness to the human goods is the basis of a right moral attitude.

In acting directly against any one of them we make that against which we act a means to an ulterior end. But the goods that go to make up personhood are themselves the ends of human action, and as such they should not be treated as if they were mere means to other ends. Because each of these goods is, as we have seen, the supreme good in its own way, no one of them can be subordinated to another as a means to an end. Thus the minimum requirement for a morally correct attitude (and action) is simultaneous respect for all the basic goods: respect which means in practice refusing to violate any fundamental good in order to achieve another.

The seven modes of responsibility we have examined previously are positive: they tell us what to do. But this eighth mode is negative. It tells us what we ought *not* to do. It is not correct to suppose that all morality is summed up in prohibitions ("thou shalt not"), even though it is sometimes caricatured that way. But it is also a mistake to overlook the extremely strong binding force of this negative mode of responsibility: one should never act directly against any of the fundamental human goods.

It is essential to remember that these goods are what human life and human action are all about. The goods are not abstractions existing "out there" beyond us and other people. Rather, as we experience them, the goods are aspects of human persons, ourselves or others, aspects which either already exist in actuality or have the potential of being realized. Thus, to act directly against one of the fundamental goods is to violate an actual or possible aspect of the personhood of a real person or persons: to violate "life," for example, means violating somebody's life. This amounts to using a human person as a means to an end.

ARE THERE INALIENABLE RIGHTS?

Critics of the view that there are ethical absolutes sometimes refer to them disparagingly as "legalistic absolutes." Rhetoric aside, the implication is that this position exalts law (legalism) at the expense of the person. Yet the defense of ethical absolutes, properly understood, does not mean assigning primacy to bloodless law over flesh-and-blood persons. On the contrary, it constitutes a defense of the person and his inalienable rights.

If there are no absolute responsibilities, there are no inalienable rights. If it were true that any action, no matter what, is permitted in certain circumstances, then no good intrinsic to the person would be safe from invasion and suppression provided the justifying circumstances existed. In such a case it would always be possible to conceive of circumstances in which the person could be sacrificed to the attainment of ulterior ends.

Instead of being the norm and source from which other things receive their value, the human person would become simply one more item or commodity with a relative value, inviolable only up to the point at which it became expedient to violate him in order to achieve some objective. It would then make no sense at all to speak of the "infinite value" of the human person. Far from being infinite, the value of a person would be quite specific and quantifiable, something to be weighed calculatingly in the balance against other values.

Often it is assumed that this sort of weighing of human goods (and human persons) is possible. This assumption enters in, tacitly in many instances, as a result of confusion between the fundamental goods constitutive of the person, which are always open-ended and never fully defined (because one can never say that one of these goods has been totally realized and exhausted by oneself or others), and a specific objective which is never completely identical with the person.

Typically, an individual with such an attitude will think along the following lines: Two lives are better than one; therefore if two innocent lives can be saved by sacrificing one innocent life, it is entirely right and proper to sacrifice the one life in order to save the two.

An example dramatizes this attitude. In wartime a military commander is confronted with a group of prisoners who possess important information about the enemy's plans. He needs the information in order to prevent loss of life among his own men, but the prisoners will not tell him what he wants to know. In order to compel the prisoners to talk, he has one of them executed as an example to the others and thereby frightens the survivors into divulging the desired information. Thus, by taking one life he has saved other lives, and according to the principle that two lives are better than one (or twenty better than two, or two thousand better than twenty, and so on) his action is not only expedient but morally right.

One arrives at a very different judgment, however, if human life is regarded not as a concrete, specific, essentially quantifiable object but as a good in which each person participates but which none exhausts or sums up in himself. In such a view of reality it is simply not possible to make the sort of calculation which weighs lives against each other (my life is more valuable than John's life, John's life is more valuable than Ed's and Tom's combined, etc.) and thus determines whose life shall be respected and whose sacrificed. The value of life, each human life, is incalculable, not in any merely poetic sense but simply because it is something not susceptible to calculation, measurement, weighing, and balancing.

Traditionally this point has been expressed by the statement that the end does not justify the means. This is simply a way of saying that the direct violation of any good intrinsic to the person cannot be justified by the good result which such a violation will bring about. What is extrinsic to human persons may be used for the good of persons, but what is intrinsic to persons has a kind of sacredness and may not be violated.

JOHN LOCKE
NATURAL RIGHTS AND CIVIL SOCIETY

OF THE STATE OF NATURE

4. To understand political power aright, and derive it from its original, we must consider what estate all men are naturally in, and that is, a state of perfect freedom to order their actions, and dispose of their possessions and persons as they think fit, within the bounds of the law of Nature, without asking leave or depending upon the will of any other man.

A state also of equality, wherein all the power and jurisdiction is reciprocal, no one having more than another, there being nothing more evident than that creatures of the same species and rank, promiscuously born to all the same advantages of Nature, and the use of the same faculties, should also be equal one amongst another, without subordination or subjection, unless the lord and master of them all should, by any manifest declaration of his will, set one above another, and confer on him, by an evident and clear appointment, an undoubted right to dominion and sovereignty. . . .

6. But though this be a state of liberty, yet it is not a state of licence;

From John Locke, *Two Treatises of Government* (1690).

though man in that state have an uncontrollable liberty to dispose of his person or possessions, yet he has not liberty to destroy himself, or so much as any creature in his possession, but where some nobler use than its bare preservation calls for it. The state of Nature has a law of Nature to govern it, which obliges every one, and reason, which is that law, teaches all mankind who will but consult it, that being all equal and independent, no one ought to harm another in his life, health, liberty or possessions; for men being all the workmanship of one omnipotent and infinitely wise Maker; all the servants of one sovereign Master, sent into the world by His order and about His business; they are His property, whose workmanship they are made to last during His, not one another's pleasure. And, being furnished with like faculties, sharing all in one community of Nature, there cannot be supposed any such subordination among us that may authorise us to destroy one another, as if we were made for one another's uses, as the inferior ranks of creatures are for ours. Every one as he is bound to preserve himself, and not to quit his station willfully, so by the like reason, when his own preservation comes not in competition, ought he as much as he can to preserve the rest of mankind, and not unless it be to do justice on an offender, take away or impair the life, or what tends to the preservation of the life, the liberty, health, limb, or goods of another.

7. And that all men may be restrained from invading others' rights, and from doing hurt to one another, and the law of Nature be observed, which willeth the peace and preservation of all mankind, the execution of the law of Nature is in that state put into every man's hands, whereby every one has a right to punish the transgressors of that law to such a degree as may hinder its violation. For the law of Nature would, as all other laws that concern men in this world, be in vain if there were nobody that in the state of Nature had a power to execute that law, and thereby preserve the innocent and restrain offenders; and if any one in the state of Nature may punish another for any evil he has done, every one may do so. For in that state of perfect equality, where naturally there is no superiority or jurisdiction of one over another, what any may do in prosecution of that law, every one must needs have a right to do. . . .

14. It is often asked as a mighty objection, where are, or ever were, there any men in such a state of Nature? To which it may suffice as an answer at present, that since all princes and rulers of "independent" governments all through the world are in a state of Nature, it is plain the world never was, nor never will be, without numbers of men in that state. I have named all governors of "independent" communities, whether they are, or are not, in league with others; for it is not every compact that puts an end to the state of Nature between men, but only this one of agreeing together mutually to enter into one community, and make one body politic; other promises and compacts men may make one with another, and yet still be in the state of Nature. The promises and bargains for truck, etc., between the two men in Soldania, in or between a Swiss and an Indian, in the woods of America, are binding to them, though they are perfectly in a

state of Nature in reference to one another for truth, and keeping of faith belongs to men as men, and not as members of society. . . .

OF PROPERTY

27. Though the earth and all inferior creatures be common to all men, yet every man has a "property" in his own "person." This nobody has any right to but himself. The "labour" of his body and the "work" of his hands, we may say, are properly his. Whatsoever, then, he removes out of the state that Nature hath provided and left it in, he hath mixed his labour with it, and joined to it something that is his own, and thereby makes it his property. It being by him removed from the common state Nature placed it in, it hath by this labour something annexed to it that excludes the common right of other men. For this "labour" being the unquestionable property of the labourer, no man but he can have a right to what that is once joined to, at least where there is enough, and as good left in common for others.

28. He that is nourished by the acorns he picked up under an oak, or the apples he gathered from the trees in the wood, has certainly appropriated them to himself. Nobody can deny but the nourishment is his. I ask, then, when did they begin to be his? when digested? or when he ate? or when he boiled? or when he brought them home? or when he picked them up? And it is plain, if the first gathering made them not his, nothing else could. That labour put a distinction between them and common. That added something to them more than Nature, the common mother of all, had done, and so they became his private right. And will any one say he had no right to those acorns or apples he thus appropriated because he had not the consent of all mankind to make them his? Was it a robbery thus to assume to himself what belonged to all in common? If such a consent as that was necessary, man had starved, notwithstanding the plenty God had given him. We see in commons, which remain so by compact, that it is the taking any part of what is common, and removing it out of the state Nature leaves it in, which begins the property, without which the common is of no use. And the taking of this or that part does not depend on the express consent of all the commoners. Thus, the grass my horse has bit, the turfs my servant has cut, and the ore I have digged in any place, where I have a right to them in common with others, become my property without the assignation or consent of anybody. The labour that was mine, removing them out of that common state they were in, hath fixed my property in them. . . .

31. It will, perhaps, be objected to this, that if gathering the acorns or other fruits of the earth, etc., makes a right to them, then any one may engross as much as he will. To which I answer, Not so. The same law of Nature that does by this means give us property, does also bound that property too. "God has given us all things richly." Is the voice of reason confirmed by inspiration? But how far has He given it us—"to enjoy"? As

much as any one can make use of to any advantage of life before it spoils, so much he may by his labour fix a property in. Whatever is beyond this is more than his share, and belongs to others. Nothing was made by God for man to spoil or destroy. And thus considering the plenty of natural provisions there was a long time in the world, and the few spenders, and to how small a part of that provision the industry of one man could extend itself and engross it to the prejudice of others, especially keeping within the bounds set by reason of what might serve for his use, there could be then little room for quarrels or contentions about property so established. . . .

46. The greatest part of things really useful to the life of man, and such as the necessity of subsisting made the first commoners of the world look after—as it doth the Americans now—are generally things of short duration, such as—if they are not consumed by use—will decay and perish of themselves. Gold, silver, and diamonds are things that fancy or agreement hath put the value on, more than real use and the necessary support of life. Now of those good things which Nature hath provided in common, every one hath a right (as hath been said) to as much as he could use, and had a property in all he could effect with his labour; all that his industry could extend to, to alter from the state Nature had put it in, was his. He that gathered a hundred bushels of acorns or apples had thereby a property in them; they were his goods as soon as gathered. He was only to look that he used them before they spoiled, else he took more than his share, and robbed others. And, indeed, it was a foolish thing, as well as dishonest, to hoard up more than he could make use of. If he gave away a part to anybody else, so that it perished not uselessly in his possession, these he also made use of. And if he also bartered away plums that would have rotted in a week, for nuts that would last good for his eating a whole year, he did no injury; he wasted not the common stock; destroyed no part of the portion of goods that belonged to others, so long as nothing perished uselessly in his hands. Again, if he would give his nuts for a piece of metal, pleased with its colour, or exchange his sheep for shells, or wool for a sparkling pebble or a diamond, and keep those by him all his life, he invaded not the right of others; he might heap up as much of these durable things as he pleased; the exceeding of the bounds of his just property not lying in the largeness of his possession, but the perishing of anything uselessly in it.

47. And thus came in the use of money; some lasting thing that men might keep without spoiling, and that, by mutual consent, men would take in exchange for the truly useful but perishable supports of life.

48. And as different degrees of industry were apt to give men possessions in different proportions, so this invention of money gave them the opportunity to continue and enlarge them. . . .

50. But since gold and silver, being little useful to the life of man, in proportion to food, raiment, and carriage, has its value only from the consent of men—whereof labour yet makes in great part the measure—it is plain that the consent of men have agreed to a disproportionate and un-

equal possession of the earth—I mean out of the bounds of society and compact; for in governments the laws regulate it; they having, by consent, found out and agreed in a way how a man may, rightfully and without injury, possess more than he himself can make use of by receiving gold and silver, which may continue long in a man's possession without decaying for the overplus, and agreeing those metals should have a value. . . .

OF POLITICAL OR CIVIL SOCIETY

87. Man being born, as has been proved, with a title to perfect freedom and an uncontrolled enjoyment of all the rights and privileges of the law of Nature, equally with any other man, or number of men in the world, hath by nature a power not only to preserve his property—that is, his life, liberty, and estate, against the injuries and attempts of other men, but to judge of and punish the breaches of that law in others, as he is persuaded the offence deserves, even with death itself, in crimes where the heinousness of the fact, in his opinion, requires it. But because no political society can be, nor subsist, without having in itself the power to preserve the property, and in order thereunto punish the offences of all those of that society, there, and there only, is political society where every one of the members hath quitted this natural power, resigned it up into the hands of the community in all cases that exclude him not from appealing for protection to the law established by it. And thus all private judgment of every particular member being excluded, the community comes to be umpire, and by understanding indifferent rules and men authorised by the community for their execution, decides all the differences that may happen between any members of that society concerning any matter of right, and punishes those offences which any member hath committed against the society with such penalties as the law has established; whereby it is easy to discern who are, and are not, in political society together. Those who are united into one body, and have a common established law and judicature to appeal to, with authority to decide controversies between them and punish offenders, are in civil society one with another; but those who have no such common appeal, I mean on earth, are still in the state of Nature, each being where there is no other, judge for himself and executioner; which is, as I have before showed it, the perfect state of Nature. . . .

95. MEN being, as has been said, by nature all free, equal, and independent, no one can be put out of this estate and subjected to the political power of another without his own consent, which is done by agreeing with other men, to join and unite into a community for their comfortable, safe, and peaceable living, one amongst another, in a secure enjoyment of their properties, and a greater security against any that are not of it. This any number of men may do, because it injures not the freedom of the rest; they are left, as they were, in the liberty of the state of Nature. When any number of men have so consented to make one community or government, they are thereby presently incorporated, and make one body politic, wherein the majority have a right to act and conclude the rest.

96. For, when any number of men have, by the consent of every individual, made a community, they have thereby made that community one body, with a power to act as one body, which is only by the will and determination of the majority. For that which acts any community, being only the consent of the individuals of it, and it being one body, must move one way, it is necessary the body should move that way whither the greater force carries it, which is the consent of the majority, or else it is impossible it should act or continue one body, one community, which the consent of every individual that united into it agreed that it should; and so every one is bound by that consent to be concluded by the majority. And therefore we see that in assemblies empowered to act by positive laws where no number is set by that positive law which empowers them, the act of the majority passes for the act of the whole, and of course determines as having, by the law of Nature and reason, the power of the whole. . . .

99. Whosoever, therefore, out of a state of Nature unite into a community, must be understood to give up all the power necessary to the ends for which they unite into society to the majority of the community, unless they expressly agreed in any number greater than the majority. And this is done by barely agreeing to unite into one political society, which is all the compact that is, or needs be, between the individuals that enter into or make up a commonwealth. And thus, that which begins and actually constitutes any political society is nothing but the consent of any number of freemen capable of majority, to unite and incorporate into such a society. And this is that, and that only, which did or could give beginning to any lawful government in the world. . . .

OF THE EXTENT OF THE LEGISLATIVE POWER

135. Though the legislative, whether placed in one or more, whether it be always in being or only by intervals, though it be the supreme power in every commonwealth, yet, first, it is not, nor can possibly be, absolutely arbitrary over the lives and fortunes of the people. For it being but the joint power of every member of the society given up to that person or assembly which is legislator, it can be no more than those persons had in a state of Nature before they entered into society, and gave it up to the community. For nobody can transfer to another more power than he has in himself, and nobody has an absolute arbitrary power over himself, or over any other, to destroy his own life, or take away the life or property of another. A man, as has been proved, cannot subject himself to the arbitrary power of another; and having, in the state of Nature, no arbitrary power over the life, liberty, or possession of another, but only so much as the law of Nature gave him for the preservation of himself and the rest of mankind, this is all he doth, or can give up to the commonwealth, and by it to the legislative power, so that the legislative can have no more than this. Their power in the utmost bounds of it is limited to the public good of the society. It is a power that hath no other end but preservation, and therefore can never have a right to destroy, enslave, or designedly to impoverish

the subjects; the obligations of the law of Nature cease not in society, but only in many cases are drawn closer, and have, by human laws, known penalties annexed to them to enforce their observation. Thus the law of Nature stands as an eternal rule to all men, legislators as well as others. The rules that they make for other men's actions must, as well as their own and other men's actions, be conformable to the law of Nature—*i.e.,* to the will of God, of which that is a declaration, and the fundamental law of Nature being the preservation of mankind, no human sanction can be good or valid against it.

136. Secondly, the legislative or supreme authority cannot assume to itself a power to rule by extemporary arbitrary decrees, but is bound to dispense justice and decide the rights of the subject by promulgated standing laws, and known authorised judges. For the law of Nature being unwritten, and so nowhere to be found but in the minds of men, they who, through passion or interest, shall miscite or misapply it, cannot so easily be convinced of their mistake where there is no established judge; and so it serves not as it aught, to determine the rights and fence the properties of those that live under it, especially where every one is judge, interpreter, and executioner of it too, and that in his own case; and he that has right on his side, having ordinarily but his own single strength, hath not force enough to defend himself from injuries or punish delinquents. To avoid these inconveniencies which disorder men's properties in the state of Nature, men unite into societies that they may have the united strength of the whole society to secure and defend their properties, and may have standing rules to bound it by which every one may know what is his. To this end it is that men give up all their natural power to the society they enter into, and the community put the legislative power into such hands as they think fit, with this trust, that they shall be governed by declared laws, or else their peace, quiet, and property will still be at the same uncertainty as it was in the state of Nature. . . .

138. Thirdly, the supreme power cannot take from any man any part of his property without his own consent. For the preservation of property being the end of government, and that for which men enter into society, it necessarily supposes and requires that the people should have property, without which they must be supposed to lose that by entering into society which was the end for which they entered into it; too gross an absurdity for any man to own. Men, therefore, in society having property, they have such a right to the goods, which by the law of the community are theirs, that nobody hath a right to take them, or any part of them, from them without their own consent; without this they have no property at all. For I have truly no property in that which another can by right take from me when he pleases against my consent. Hence it is a mistake to think that the supreme or legislative power of any commonwealth can do what it will, and dispose of the estates of the subject arbitrarily, or take any part of them at pleasure. This is not much to be feared in governments where the legislative consists wholly or in part in assemblies which are variable,

whose members upon the dissolution of the assembly are subjects under the common laws of their country, equally with the rest. But in governments where the legislative is in one lasting assembly, always in being, or in one man as in absolute monarchies, there is danger still, that they will think themselves to have a distinct interest from the rest of the community, and so will be apt to increase their own riches and power by taking what they think fit from the people. For a man's property is not at all secure, though there be good and equitable laws to set the bounds of it between him and his fellow-subjects, if he who commands those subjects have power to take from any private man what part he pleases of his property, and use and dispose of it as he thinks good.

ROBERT NOZICK

DISTRIBUTIVE JUSTICE

THE ENTITLEMENT THEORY

The subject of justice in holdings consists of three major topics. The first is the *original acquisition of holdings,* the appropriation of unheld things. This includes the issues of how unheld things may come to be held, the process, or processes, by which unheld things may come to be held, the things that may come to be held by these processes, the extent of what comes to be held by a particular process, and so on. We shall refer to the complicated truth about this topic, which we shall not formulate here, as the principle of justice in acquisition. The second topic concerns the *transfer of holdings* from one person to another. By what processes may a person transfer holdings to another? How may a person acquire a holding from another who holds it? Under this topic come general descriptions of voluntary exchange, and gift and (on the other hand) fraud, as well as reference to particular conventional details fixed upon in a given society. The complicated truth about this subject (with placeholders for conventional details) we shall call the principle of justice in transfer. (And we shall suppose it also includes principles governing how a person may divest himself of a holding, passing it into an unheld state.)

If the world were wholly just, the following inductive definition would exhaustively cover the subject of justice in holdings,

    1.   A person who acquires a holding in accordance with the principle of justice in acquisition is entitled to that holding.

    2.   A person who acquires a holding in accordance with the principle of justice in transfer, from someone else entitled to the holding, is entitled to the holding.

From Robert Nozick, *Anarchy, State, and Utopia* (New York: Basic Books, 1974), pp. 150–60. Reprinted by permission.

3. No one is entitled to a holding except by (repeated) applications of 1 and 2.

The complete principle of distributive justice would say simply that a distribution is just if everyone is entitled to the holdings they possess under the distribution.

A distribution is just if it arises from another just distribution by legitimate means. The legitimate means of moving from one distribution to another are specified by the principle of justice in transfer. The legitimate first "moves" are specified by the principle of justice in acquisition.[1] Whatever arises from a just situation by just steps is itself just. The means of change specified by the principle of justice in transfer preserve justice. As correct rules of inference are truth-preserving, and any conclusion deduced via repeated application of such rules from only true premises is itself true, so the means of transition from one situation to another specified by the principle of justice in transfer are justice-preserving, and any situation actually arising from repeated transitions in accordance with the principle from a just situation is itself just. The parallel between justice-preserving transformations and truth-preserving transformations illuminates where it fails as well as where it holds. That a conclusion could have been deduced by truth-preserving means from premises that are true suffices to show its truth. That from a just situation a situation *could* have arisen via justice-preserving means does *not* suffice to show its justice. The fact that a thief's victims voluntarily *could* have presented him with gifts does not entitle the thief to his ill-gotten gains. Justice in holdings is historical; it depends upon what actually has happened. We shall return to this point later.

Not all actual situations are generated in accordance with the two principles of justice in holdings: the principle of justice in acquisition and the principle of justice in transfer. Some people steal from others, or defraud them, or enslave them, seizing their product and preventing them from living as they choose, or forcibly exclude others from competing in exchanges. None of these are permissible modes of transition from one situation to another. And some persons acquire holdings by means not sanctioned by the principle of justice in acquisition. The existence of past injustice (previous violations of the first two principles of justice in holdings) raise the third major topic under justice in holdings: the rectification of injustice in holdings. If past injustice has shaped present holdings in various ways, some identifiable and some not, what now, if anything, ought to be done to rectify these injustices? What obligations do the performers of injustice have toward those whose position is worse than it would have been had the injustice not been done? Or, than it would have been had compensation been paid promptly? How, if at all, do things change if the beneficiaries and those made worse off are not the direct parties in the act of injustice, but, for example, their descendants? Is an injustice done to someone whose holding was itself based upon an unrectified injustice? How far back must one go in wiping clean the historical slate of injustices? What may victims of injustice permissibly do in order to rectify the injustices being done to them, including the many injustices done by persons acting through their government? I do not know of a thorough or theoretically sophisticated treatment of such issues.[2] Idealizing greatly, let us suppose theoretical investigation will produce a principle of rectification. This principle uses historical information about previous situations and injustices done in them (as defined by the first two principles of justice and rights against interference), and information about the actual course of events that flowed from these injustices, until the present, and it yields a description (or descriptions) of holdings in the society. The principle of rectification presumably will make use of its best estimate of subjunctive information about what would have occurred (or a probability distribution over what might have occurred, using the expected value) if the injustice had not taken place. If the actual description of holdings turns out not to be one of the descriptions yielded by the principle, then one of the descriptions yielded must be realized.

The general outlines of the theory of justice in holdings are that the holdings of a person are just if he is entitled to them by the principles of justice in acquisition and transfer, or by the principle of rectification of injustice (as specified by the first two principles). If each person's holdings are just, then the total set (distribution) of holdings is just. To turn these general outlines into a specific theory we would have to specify the details of each of the three principles of justice in holdings: the principle of acquisition of holdings, the principle of transfer of holdings, and the principle of rectification of violations of the first two principles. I shall not attempt that task here. . . .

HISTORICAL PRINCIPLES AND END-RESULT PRINCIPLES

The general outlines of the entitlement theory illuminate the nature and defects of other conceptions of distributive justice. The entitlement theory of justice in distribution is *historical;* whether a distribution is just depends upon how it came about. In contrast, *current time-slice principles* of justice hold that the justice of a distribution is determined by how things are distributed (who has what) as judged by some *structural* principle(s) of just distribution. A utilitarian who judges between any two distributions by seeing which has the greater sum of utility and, if the sums tie, applies some fixed equality criterion to choose the more equal distribution, would hold a current time-slice principle of justice. As would someone who had a fixed schedule of trade-offs between the sum of happiness and equality. According to a current time-slice principle, all that needs to be looked at, in judging the justice of a distribution, is who ends up with what; in comparing any two distributions one need look only at the matrix presenting the distributions. No further information need be fed into a principle of justice. It is a consequence of such principles of justice that any two structurally identical distributions are equally just. (Two distributions are structurally identical if they present the same profile, but perhaps have different persons occupying the particular slots. My having ten and your having five, and my having five and your having ten are structurally identical distributions.) Welfare economics is the theory of current time-slice principles of justice. The subject is conceived as operating on matrices representing only current information about distribution. This, as well as some of the usual conditions (for example, the choice of distribution is invariant under relabeling of columns), guarantees that welfare economics will be a current time-slice theory, with all of its inadequacies.

Most persons do not accept current time-slice principles as constituting the whole story about distributive shares. They think it relevant in assessing the justice of a situation to consider not only the distribution it embodies, but also how that distribution came about. If some persons are in prison for murder or war crimes, we do not say that to assess the justice of the distribution in the society we must look only at what this person has, and that person has, and that person has, . . . at the current time. We think it relevant to ask whether someone did something so that he *deserved* to be punished, deserved to have a lower share. Most will agree to the relevance of further information with regard to punishments and penalties. Consider also desired things. One traditional socialist view is that workers are entitled to the product and full fruits of their labor; they have earned it; a distribution is unjust if it does not give the workers what they are entitled to. Such entitlements are based upon some past history. No socialist holding this view would find it comforting to be told that because the actual distribution A happens to coincide structurally with the one he desires D, A therefore is no less just than D; it differs only in that the ''parasitic'' owners of capital receive under A what the workers are entitled to under D; and the workers receive under A what the owners are entitled to under D; namely very little. This socialist rightly, in my view, holds onto the notions of earning, producing, entitlement, desert, and so forth, and he rejects current time-slice principles that look only to the structure of the resulting set of holdings. (The set of holdings resulting from what? Isn't it implausible that how holdings are produced and come to exist has no effect at all on who should hold what?) His mistake lies in his view of what entitlements arise out of what sorts of productive processes.

We construe the position we discuss too narrowly by speaking of *current* time-slice principles. Nothing is changed if structural principles operate upon a time sequence of current time-slice profiles and, for example, give someone more now to counterbalance the less he has had earlier. A utilitarian or an egalitarian or any mixture of the two over time will inherit the difficulties of his more myopic comrades. He is not helped by the fact that *some* of the information others consider relevant in assessing a distribution is reflected, unrecoverably, in past matrices. Henceforth, we shall refer to such unhistorical principles of distributive justice, including the current time-slice principles, as *end-result principles* or *end-state principles*.

In contrast to end-result principles of justice, *historical principles* of justice hold that past circumstances or actions of people can create differential entitlements or differential deserts to things. An injustice can be worked by moving from one distribution to another structurally identical one, for the second, in profile the same, may violate people's entitlements or deserts; it may not fit the actual history.

PATTERNING

The entitlement principles of justice in holdings that we have sketched are historical principles of justice. To better understand their precise character, we shall distinguish them from another subclass of the historical principles. Consider, as an example, the principle of distribution according to moral merit. This principle requires that total distributive shares vary directly with moral merit; no person should have a greater share than anyone whose moral merit is greater. (If moral merit could be not merely ordered but measured on an interval or ratio scale, stronger principles could be formulated.) Or consider the principle that results by substituting "usefulness to society" for "moral merit" in the previous principle. Or instead of "distribute according to moral merit," or "distribute according to usefulness to society," we might consider "distribute according to the weighted sum of moral merit, usefulness to society, and need," with the weights of the different dimensions equal. Let us call a principle of distribution *patterned* if it specifies that a distribution is to vary along with some natural dimension, weighted sum of natural dimensions, or lexicographic ordering of natural dimensions. And let us say a distribution is patterned if it accords with some patterned principle. (I speak of natural dimensions, admittedly without a general criterion for them, because for any set of holdings some artificial dimensions can be gimmicked up to vary along with the distribution of the set.) The principle of distribution in accordance with moral merit is a patterned historical principle, which specifies a patterned distribution. "Distribute according to I.Q." is a patterned principle that looks to information not contained in distributional matrices. It is not historical, however, in that it does not look to any past actions creating differential entitlements to evaluate a distribution; it requires only distributional matrices whose columns are labeled by I.Q. scores. The distribution in a society, however, may be composed of such simple patterned distributions, without itself being simply patterned. Different sectors may operate different patterns, or some combination of patterns may operate in different proportions across a society. A distribution composed in this manner, from a small number of patterned distributions, we also shall term "patterned." And we extend the use of "pattern" to include the overall designs put forth by combinations of end-state principles.

Almost every suggested principle of distributive justice is patterned: to each according to his moral merit, or needs, or marginal product, or how hard he tries, or the weighted sum of the foregoing, and so on. The principle of entitlement we have sketched is *not* patterned. There is no one natural dimension or weighted sum or combination of a small number of natural dimensions that yields the distributions generated in accordance with the principle of entitlement. The set of holdings that results when some persons receive their marginal products, others win at gambling, others receive a share of their mate's income, others receive gifts from foundations, others receive interest on loans, other receive gifts from admirers, others receive returns on investment, others make for themselves much of what they have, others find things, and so on, will not be patterned. Heavy strands of patterns will run through it; significant portions of the variance in holdings will be accounted for by pattern-variables. If most people most of the time choose to transfer some of their entitlements to others only in exchange for something from them, then a large part of what many people hold will vary with what they held that others wanted. More details are provided by the theory of marginal productivity. But gifts to relatives, charitable donations, bequests to children, and the like, are not best conceived, in the first instance, in this manner. Ignoring the strands of pattern, let us suppose for the moment that a distribution actually arrived at by the operation of the principle of entitlement is random with respect to any pattern. Though the resulting set of holdings will be unpatterned, it will not be incomprehensible, for it can be seen as arising from the operation of a small number of principles. These principles specify how an initial distribution may arise (the principle of acquisition of holdings) and how distributions may be transformed into others (the principle of transfer of holdings). The process whereby the set of holdings is generated will be intelligible, though the set of holdings itself that results from this process will be unpatterned.

The writings of F. A. Hayek focus less than is usually done upon what patterning distributive justice requires. Hayek argues that we cannot know enough about each person's situation to distribute to each according to his moral merit (but would justice demand we do so if we did have this knowledge?); and he goes on to say, ''our objection is against all attempts to impress upon society a deliberately chosen pattern of distribution, whether it be an order of equality or of inequality.''[3] However, Hayek concludes that in a free society there will be distribution in accordance with value rather than moral merit; that is, in accordance with the perceived value of a person's actions and services to others. Despite his rejection of a patterned conception of distributive justice, Hayek himself suggests a pattern he thinks justifiable: distribution in accordance with the perceived benefits given to others, leaving room for the complaint that a free society does not realize exactly this pattern. Stating this patterned strand of a free capitalist society more precisely, we get ''To each according to how much he benefits others who have the resources for benefiting those who benefit them.'' This will seem arbitrary unless some acceptable initial set of holdings is specified, or unless it is held that the operation of the system over time washes out any significant effects from the initial set of holdings. As an example of the latter, if almost anyone would have bought a car from

Henry Ford, the supposition that it was an arbitrary matter who held the money then (and so bought) would not place Henry Ford's earnings under a cloud. In any event, *his* coming to hold it is not arbitrary. Distribution according to benefits to others *is* a major patterned strand in a free capitalist society, as Hayek correctly points out, but it is only a strand and does not constitute the whole pattern of a system of entitlements (namely, inheritance, gifts for arbitrary reasons, charity, and so on) or a standard that one should insist a society fit. Will people tolerate for long a system yielding distributions that they believe are unpatterned? No doubt people will not long accept a distribution they believe is *unjust*. People want their society to be and to look just. But must the look of justice reside in a resulting pattern rather than in the underlying generating principles? We are in no position to conclude that the inhabitants of a society embodying an entitlement conception of justice in holdings will find it unacceptable. Still, it must be granted that were people's reasons for transferring some of their holdings to others always irrational or arbitrary, we would find this disturbing. (Suppose people always determined what holdings they would transfer, and to whom, by using a random device.) We feel more comfortable upholding the justice of an entitlement system if most of the transfers under it are done for reasons. This does not mean necessarily that all deserve what holdings they receive. It means only that there is a purpose or point to someone's transferring a holding to one person rather than to another; that usually we can see what the transferrer thinks he's gaining, what cause he thinks he's serving, what goals he thinks he's helping to achieve, and so forth. Since in a capitalist society people often transfer holdings to others in accordance with how much they perceive these others benefiting them, the fabric constituted by the individual transactions and transfers is largely reasonable and intelligible. (Gifts to loved ones, bequests to children, charity to the needy also are nonarbitrary components of the fabric.) In stressing the large strand of distribution in accordance with benefit to others, Hayek shows the point of many transfers, and so shows that the system of transfer of entitlements is not just spinning its gears aimlessly. The system of entitlements is defensible when constituted by the individual aims of individual transactions. No overarching aim is needed, no distributional pattern is required.

To think that the task of a theory of distributive justice is to fill in the blank in "to each according to his _____" is to be predisposed to search for a pattern; and the separate treatment of "from each according to his _____" treats production and distribution as two separate and independent issues. On an entitlement view these are *not* two separate questions. Whoever makes something, having bought or contracted for all other held resources used in the process (transferring some of his holdings for these cooperating factors), is entitled to it. The situation is *not* one of something's getting made, and there being an open question of who is to get it. Things come into the world already attached to people having entitlements over them. From the point of view of the historical entitlement conception of justice in holdings, those who start afresh to complete "to each according to his _____" treat objects as if they appeared from nowhere, out of nothing. A complete theory of justice might cover this limit case as well; perhaps here is a use for the usual conceptions of distributive justice.

So entrenched are maxims of the usual form that perhaps we should present the entitlement conception as a competitor. Ignoring acquisition and rectification, we might say:

> From each according to what he chooses to do, to each according to what he makes for himself (perhaps with the contracted aid of others) and what others choose to do for him and choose to give him of what they've been given previously (under this maxim) and haven't yet expended or transferred.

This, the discerning reader will have noticed, has its defects as a slogan. So as a summary and great simplification (and not as a maxim with any independent meaning) we have:

> *From each as they choose, to each as they are chosen.*

Notes

[1] Applications of the principle of justice in acquisition may also occur as part of the move from one distribution to another. You may find an unheld thing now and appropriate it. Acquisitions also are to be understood as included when, to simplify, I speak only of transitions by transfers.

[2] See, however, the useful book by Boris Bittker, *The Case for Black Reparations* (New York: Random House, 1973).

[3] F. A. Hayek, *The Constitution of Liberty* (Chicago: University of Chicago Press, 1960), p. 87.

chapter *2*

Kant and Contractarianism

INTRODUCTION

KANT

Rationality as the Key to Morality   The natural-law account of right conduct emphasized rationality as the distinguishing characteristic of humanity. But other distinct features were also considered morally relevant. For instance, the social nature of human beings was understood as the natural basis of the requirements of justice. The seventeenth-century natural-rights theorists, however, emphasized a more individualist and self-interested rationality as the key to right conduct. Immanuel Kant (1724–1804) shared with the modern natural-rights theorists this narrowing of the basis of right conduct to rationality alone, but he differed from them in an insistence that self-interest, too, must be excluded as a component of the rationality which determines right conduct.

In Kant the emphasis upon disinterested rationality frees ethical theory as its most abstract level from any connection with human beings as a specific biological species. Right conduct has the same basis for all rational beings, whether human, extraterrestrial, or even angelic. It is in applying the fundamental principle of right conduct to cases that one must take into account the specifics of human nature. At this level of application to cases, Kant often argues just as the natural-law theorists did. This traditional part of Kant has had little influence, but Kant's more innovative attempt to free basic ethical theory from any relation to specific human nature has been tremendously influential.

The Rational Self as the Source of Morality   Kant's basic ethical theory is characterized by an emphasis upon rationality as the source of moral law. Kant traces the basic forms of scientific thought back to the operation of the mind of the knower rather than to an external reality independent of the knower. To interpret the world in terms of cause and effect was thus a necessity grounded in the rational faculties of the interpreter. Kant could then trace moral judgments back to that same rationality of the interpreter: on the one hand, one must interpret the world causally in order to

53

know and to understand it, while on the other hand, in order to act at all, one must interpret one's own actions as freely chosen. Kant finds the key to morality in this necessary presupposition of freedom by every rational being who acts. There are two ways of looking at human conduct, each determined by its context. Within the context of scientific inquiry, human conduct is a part of the natural order of causal laws; within the context of practical reasoning (deciding what one will do), human conduct is under self-imposed "laws of freedom," which are derived from the rational will (also called "practical reason" by Kant).

Autonomy *Autonomy* (from the Greek words *autos*, meaning "self," and *nomos*, meaning "law") is the self-legislative characteristic of rational agents, by virtue of which they are free. For Kant, autonomy (and so freedom) is not the same thing as mere subjective and arbitrary personal decision. The *nomic* ("lawlike") aspect of autonomy is central in Kant's account of both free action and right conduct. Autonomy requires that the merely personal and arbitrary be subordinated to the requirements of reason, which are the same for all rational beings. It is by virtue of this impersonality and regularity that free agents bring a moral order to their actions comparable to the causal order in the realm of nature.

Many followers of Kant, however, emphasize not the nomic aspect of autonomy but its other aspect, the *self*, which is seen as governing the actions of free rational agents rather than anything external. But this view of autonomy is really no more than *self-determination*—that is, the ability and right of rational agents to make choices in their own lives. Such contemporary proponents of autonomy are using Kantian language to express what is essentially an individualistic, natural-rights viewpoint. There is nothing individualistic about Kant's conception of autonomy, for the order that each individual rationally imposes on conduct is understood by him as unvarying from person to person.

For Kant freedom from external determination is no more important than is freedom from internal determination by any aspect of the self other than reason. Kant did not count as autonomous actions those resulting from the agent's own desires if they are uncontrolled by reason. According to Kant, not only can an agent lack autonomy by submitting himself blindly to external authority, he can lack autonomy by becoming a slave to his own passions. This attitude is indicative of a great Stoic influence on Kant.

Hypothetical Versus Categorical Imperatives What is the order that reason imposes on conduct? Kant distinguishes between two kinds of rational control over conduct. The first kind is the rationality of choosing the best available means to achieve one's goals. The rational conclusion that given a certain goal or end one *ought* to adopt certain means is called a *hypothetical imperative* by Kant. The imperative, or command, to adopt the means holds good only on the hypothesis that one has the goal. To Kant happiness is the only goal that all people *must* have. General rules, which he calls "counsels of prudence," ordinarily tend to promote happiness, but the means to happiness are indeterminate. Most goals, however, Kant understands as *contingent*, that is, some people have the goal and some do not. Hypothetical imperatives called "rules of skill" outline determinate means to contingent ends.

Suppose, for instance, that an obese person goes to a physician and, after ruling out other causes of obesity, the physician prescribes that the patient ought to eat less if he wants to lose weight. The patient wants to lose weight and acts rationally by following the imperative. The patient will then lose weight. Suppose also that the patient thinks that losing weight will substantially contribute to his happiness. But after losing weight there may, in fact, be no gain in happiness, even though it was reasonable to think that there would be. In Kant's view, happiness is a goal for which we inevitably strive, but the recipe for success cannot be surely given even by well-informed, rational deliberation.

There are thus no universal and certain hypothetical imperatives, for either the goals are contingent or the means are uncertain. Nevertheless, Kant thought that there are imperatives prescribed by reason universally and with certainty. These imperatives bring order to conduct in an entirely different way than do hypothetical imperatives. It is through this second kind of rational control over conduct, these *categorical imperatives*, that the agent becomes aware of his freedom from his own desires and passions. An imperative prescribes conduct categorically if the prescription holds good without any hypothesis about the goals or ends of the agent. Not even happiness may be presupposed as a goal by a categorical imperative.

What does reason command categorically? Many philosophers would answer, "Nothing." The eighteenth-century British philosopher David Hume insisted that "reason is, and ought only to be the slave of the passions, and can never pretend to any other office than to serve and obey them."[1] In other words, Hume was denying that there can be categorical imperatives. But Kant thought that the rationality of each person imposes on his conduct a requirement independent of the particular desires, passions, and feelings that he happens to have. These inclinations are the basis of hypothetical imperatives, having happiness as their final goal. But apart from these contingent inclinations, reason demands categorically (without any "if" clause, whether explicit or implicit) that each person bring order to his conduct through obedience to universal principles.

Universality is the formal characteristic of law—whether laws of cause and effect, laws of states, or moral law. Form is here contrasted with content. In this understanding, the laws of Newtonian physics and the laws against murder have entirely different contents or topics, but both are universal in form, covering all occurrences of a certain kind. Universality—the form of law—is all that remains for reason to command once the content provided by the inclinations is left out of consideration. Following from this, the *categorical imperative* is the command of reason that conduct ought to follow universal moral principles.

Kant considers the conscious following of universal moral principles as the only unconditional good. All other good things are conditioned upon the desires and needs that lead to their pursuit. If human beings had no need and no desire for food or sexual pleasure, neither of these would be good for human beings. Their goodness is thus conditional. But a will to obey universal moral principles is good without any such condition of need or desire. "Nothing in the world—indeed nothing even beyond the world —can possibly be conceived which could be called good without qualification except a *good will.*"[2] This is the opening sentence of the first section of Kant's *Foundations of the Metaphysics of Morals.* Only rational agents are capable of acting out of respect for universal principles, and it is this respect for the moral law that is good without condition. The moral worth of such a good will does not depend upon the results or consequences of the action performed, but rather upon the intention of the agent to act out of respect for universal moral principles.

The Categorical Imperative   Kant provides five different formulations of the categorical imperative.[3] The first formula simply expresses the form of law: "Act only according to that maxim by which you can at the same time will that it should become a universal law."[4] The maxim of an action is the subjective principle upon which the agent proposes to act, and it expresses the intention of the agent. Thus the first formulation of the categorical imperative commands that the subjective, personal intention of the agent be such that it could be willed by the agent not only as his own intention in this particular case but also as the intention of all rational agents in similar circumstances. The subjective maxim must be *universalizable.* So, for instance, before a person decides to cheat a friend in order to make money, he should ask himself whether he can will that everyone adopt this intention in similar circumstances.

The second formulation of the categorical imperative uses the concept of a causal law of nature as an aid to imagining what it would be like for a kind of conduct to become universal: "Act as though the maxim of your action were by your will to become a universal law of nature."[5] This formulation emphasizes the analogy between causal laws, which bring order to the natural world, and the laws of freedom, which bring order to the actions of free agents. Imagine that the agent's intentions will determine not only how the agent will act but also how everyone will *necessarily* act. It will then become clear whether the intention can be universalized.

The third formulation is especially interesting, for it introduces the idea of *respect for persons,* that is, the intention to treat rational, free agents (including oneself) as valuable in themselves, rather than merely as means to the satisfaction of desires or inclinations. In this third formulation, Kant uses "humanity" to mean the distinguishing feature of humanity—rationality—rather than the whole of human nature: "Act so that you treat humanity, whether in your own person or in that of another, always as an end and never as a means only."[6] Thus, it is wrong to manipulate someone as if he were a mere tool rather than a rational agent and valuable as a person independent of his usefulness. How can one show a lack of respect for one's own humanity or rational personhood? If a person views himself as having value only to the extent that his inclinations are satisfied—if he lets the pursuit of pleasure become the overriding end of his life—then he has failed to respect his own value as a rational agent whose ultimate worth is found in the goodness of his will.

The fourth and fifth formulations return to the language of law rather than that of respect for persons found in the third. The fourth formulation emphasizes the autonomy of the rational agent, who is his own legislator: "Act only so that the will through its maxims could regard itself at the same time as universally lawgiving."[7] The fifth formulation emphasizes the identity of the rationality of all persons by imagining them all joined in a *realm of ends*, a legislative assembly of all "ends in themselves," or persons. This final formulation states: "Every rational being must act as if he, by his maxims, were at all times a legislative member in the universal realm of ends."[8]

Perfect and Imperfect Duties The categorical imperative functions in two different ways as a rational control over conduct: it forbids or requires certain quite specific kinds of action, and it requires the adoption of certain general goals, leaving it up to the individual to decide what actions to perform in furthering those goals. In the first case, the duties are *perfect*, that is, they are perfectly determined and clear, leaving no room for personal variation. It is, for instance, a perfect duty not to cheat in order to make money. In the second case, the duties are *imperfect*, that is, they are only general guidelines that leave room for personal choice over particular actions. It is an imperfect duty to help others, for though it is a universal principle that everyone ought to pursue the goal of helping others, how, when, and whom to help cannot be specified except by the individual agent. H. J. Paton has explained the distinction using the third formulation of respect for persons: "We transgress perfect duties by treating any person merely as a means. We transgress imperfect duties by failing to treat a person as an end, even though we do not actively treat him merely as a means."[9] And this applies to one's treatment of oneself as well as of others. For instance, one has a perfect duty not to kill oneself (according to Kant) and an imperfect duty to develop one's talents and abilities.

A maxim that proposes a violation of perfect duty cannot be universalized, for the state of affairs in which it would be universally adopted cannot be consistently described. The maxim "I will deceive in order to obtain a loan" could not be followed universally, for once such deception came to be common, no one would trust anyone enough to make a loan. The immoral agent wants to make a special exception for himself, while unable to will that the same conduct be generally adopted. The immoral agent is a kind of parasite upon the general practice of right conduct. But it is irrational to think that what is permissible for one person is not permissible for all.

A maxim that proposes a violation of imperfect duty cannot be universalized, for although its universal adoption can be consistently described, the agent cannot will such universal adoption without a conflict. Thus, it is impossible to will that no one should help others, for the agent would be depriving himself of possible aid. For Kant, finite rational beings necessarily have their own happiness as a goal. To universalize the maxim not to help others, an agent would have to abandon the goal of his own happiness, for there are possible circumstances in which he would need the help of others. Consideration of the likelihood of ever needing the help of others is irrelevant. The argument depends upon the structure of rationality in beings with needs and desires, rather than upon the calculations of self-interest of the particular person who is deliberating.

Difficulties with the Theory   One major difficulty with Kant's theory is that it provides no standard for deciding *what* maxim the agent must test for universality. The intention of the agent can be described correctly in many different ways and at many different levels of generality or specificity. For instance, "I will tell a lie in order to protect an innocent human life" is a universalizable maxim. It would not be self-defeating if everyone lied in order to save innocent human lives, for such lies would be rare and trust would still be general. But for Kant the maxim of *all* lying was a highly general description of intention, such as "I will tell a lie in order to achieve my ends." This maxim cannot be universalized, so Kant considered all lying wrong.

There is a comparable problem with the formula of respect for persons. If someone lies to a would-be murderer, does he treat the other as a mere means and thereby fail to respect him as a person? Understood as simply lying in order to get one's own way, it would be natural to speak of manipulation in this case. But if one describes the action as lying in order to prevent another from murdering, it is more natural to understand the deception as a way of showing respect for both the personhood of the intended victim and that of the would-be murderer.[10] Neither the test of universalization nor the test of respect for persons can provide a clear reason for choosing a highly general description of intention.

Perhaps Kant's theory of right conduct loses its intended rigor because of this multiplicity of possible maxims to describe the agent's intentions. But Kant was more concerned with the integrity of the agent as a conscious, rational being than with fine distinctions in difficult cases—although he does argue many such cases with a certainty that fails to convince. The ideas of universalizability and of respect for persons as ends in themselves work better as an account of goodness of will, for who can doubt the blameworthiness of a conscious intent to make an exception in one's own favor, or to treat a person as a mere tool?

Kant thinks that a full account of right conduct can be generated from these ideas when they are accompanied by an understanding of human life. Although this may not be possible, his ideas are still instructive. Why should there not remain difficult, even irresolvable cases even if the fundamental principle of right conduct is understood? Most immoral conduct results not from ignorance of the right in difficult cases but from selfishness, confusion, and self-deception. Kant combats these sources of immorality with his insistence on clarity of intention and motive and through the ideas of universality and impartiality.

The Dignity of Persons   Impartiality and clarity of intention and motive seem uncontroversial elements in an account of right conduct. What makes Kant distinct? Kant places a special emphasis on the absolute value of persons as ends in themselves, and this is very controversial. In the natural-law tradition, each human life is incommensurably valuable, and this value attaches to the life as a whole rather than solely to the rationality of the person. For Kant, persons have a special dignity deriving solely from their rationality and the freedom which that rationality brings. Thus Kant is not a consequentialist; he recognizes the existence of incommensurable values as does the natural-law theorist. The value of persons as rational, free agents is not merely incommensurable, but it is so great that the dignity of persons is the only unconditional value. Kant differs from the natural-law tradition by his radical separation of the rational self from other aspects of the self. It is thus possible for a Kantian to say that a living human being no longer has the distinctive dignity of a person if, for instance, he has suffered severe and irreparable brain damage. However, in arguing cases, Kant himself tends to support traditional natural-law positions that do not separate the value of rationality and the value of human life.

Structure of the Theory   Kant is not a teleologist; he does not base right conduct on the promotion of value. There are, however, teleological components within Kant's theory. The imperfect duties, for instance, require that one promote certain values (the perfection of the self and the happiness of others). But the pursuit of these obligatory ends is itself limited by the perfect duties, so that even here conduct is not evaluated solely in terms of the promotion of a good end. Thus Kant's theory is deontological, for right conduct is not derived from the promotion of good ends. The basic structure of his theory is similar to that of the theory of natural rights. But while natural-rights theory places absolute value on the liberty of the individual, Kant places absolute value on the freedom that rationality makes possible. Kant thus can make sense of the idea of duties to self; natural-rights theory has no conceptual room for anything but duties to others. And underneath the basic deontological structure, Kant includes imperfect duties both to self and others; these imperfect duties are positive, requiring the promotion of good ends beyond anything found in such contemporary natural-rights theorists as Nozick.

CONTRACTARIANISM

The Connection with Kant   Many recent philosophers have been influenced by the Kantian idea of universal moral principles requiring respect for persons as ends in themselves. The contemporary American philosopher John Rawls, for instance, has developed an account of justice that has roots in Locke, Rousseau, and Kant. The guiding idea behind this account is the social contract in a form similar to that underlying the fifth formulation of Kant's categorical imperative: "Every rational being must act as if he, by his maxims, were at all times a legislative member in the universal realm of ends." In this formula Kant uses the conception of the social contract found in Jean-Jacques Rousseau (1712–1778), although he interprets it in his own distinctive way.[11] Kant's understanding of the social contract is entirely conceptual. It does not involve any question of the historical origin of societies in positing an initial contract; nor, in its recognition of social obligations, is there any question of actual contractual undertakings by individuals. So Kant's formulation includes the all-important phrase "as if." The "universal realm of ends" consists of an imaginary community of all rational beings ("ends in themselves"), who are establishing rules of right conduct that will bind each and all.

The Original Position and the Veil of Ignorance   John Rawls has made this Kantian version of contract more determinate by describing the equivalent of the realm of ends in terms of an *original position*, the state of nature found in Locke and Rousseau. Within the original position, the parties to the social contract deliberate about the rules of right conduct that will be strictly followed once they enter society. The imaginative assumption of strict compliance is equivalent to the Kantian requirement that the rules be universal. In his important book *A Theory of Justice*, Rawls indicates that a contractarian account can be given of almost all principles of right conduct, although he works out in detail only the specific principles determining the justice of the basic structure of society.

The original position is a hypothetical, imaginary situation meant to embody basic constraints on arguments for moral principles. These constraints are Kantian for the most part. They are equality; impartiality; not taking advantage of accidental features of one's particular situation; and the assumption of the generality, universality, and publicity of the principles that are to be justified. Impartiality and equality are insured imaginatively by the *veil of ignorance* that hides from the persons in the original position all particular facts about themselves. Each person is ignorant of his own place in society (social and economic), ignorant of his own particular talents and abilities, indeed ignorant of everything that can distinguish one person from another in the particular society into which he will enter. But each person in the original position does know the general principles of social theory and human psychology. In order to justify more specific principles, the contractors will know general facts about their particular society (such as the level of technology), but for the justification of the basic principles of justice these facts, too, will be hidden behind the veil of ignorance.

Self-Interest and Primary Goods   Another important feature of the original position is the assumption that each person is motivated by self-interest, giving no consideration to the interests of others. This assumption imparts an un-Kantian flavor to Rawls, but given the veil of ignorance there is no real self-interest at work, even in the original position. Behind the veil of ignorance one cannot distinguish between one's own interests and the interests of others. The motivational assumption of self-interest is an imaginative way of capturing Kant's insight that the structure of rationality for finite beings (with needs and desires) includes the necessary goal of happiness.

And so Rawls justifies principles of right conduct by imagining an original position of equality in which rational persons, ignorant of all particular information about themselves but informed about general facts, decide upon the principles that will be publicly acknowledged and strictly followed in the society they will form. In deciding these principles, each person seeks to further his own interests. Rawls specifies the interests to be furthered: rights and liberties, powers and opportunities, income and wealth, and self-respect. Rawls chooses these *primary goods* on the ground that "these goods normally have a use whatever a person's rational plan of life."[12]

Rawls considers self-respect the most important of the primary goods. This accords with his view that the original position captures the Kantian idea of respect for persons as ends in themselves. The veil of ignorance makes it impossible to promote one's own self-respect without promoting everyone's self-respect, and so promoting self-respect is the same as promoting respect for persons.

The Two Principles of Justice Rawls argues in great detail that rational contractors in the original position of equality would agree upon two principles of justice for the basic structure of society. The first principle states that "each person is to have an equal right to the most extensive total system of equal basic liberties compatible with a similar system of liberty for all." According to the second principle, "social and economic inequalities are to be arranged so that they are both: (a) to the greatest benefit of the least advantaged. . . , and (b) attached to offices and positions open to all under conditions of fair equality of opportunity."[13]

These two principles are ranked in order of priority, so that the first principle has complete priority over the second: equal basic liberties cannot be sacrificed as a means to secure social and economic goals.[14] (Further details of the two principles are omitted here.)

In a complete contractarian account of right conduct, the veil of ignorance would be gradually lifted, allowing more and more facts to be known by the contractors. Contractors must know all general facts morally relevant to deciding between alternative principles, however specific the topic of those principles. The only facts that can never enter into a contractarian solution of a moral problem are facts that allow contractors to identify their own particular interests as individuals or members of a class, for this knowledge would destroy the original position as an imaginative model of Kantian impartiality.

Readings The selection from Kant's *Foundations of the Metaphysics* *of Morals* gives an extensive analysis of rational principles of conduct, both hypothetical and categorical. The foundational principle of right conduct, the categorical imperative, is then formulated in several versions and applied to examples.

The selection from Onora Nell explains the way in which Kant's categorical imperative can be used to decide whether one has a perfect (non-discretionary) duty by applying the test of contradiction in conception. She emphasizes that intention is embedded within the context of assumptions about the way the world is, and she draws a distinction between highly specific descriptions of an action and the actual intention of the agent. Both of these points are essential in applying the categorical imperative.

The selection by John Rawls is from the introductory sections of *A Theory of Justice*. In it, he outlines the general idea of contractarianism and the original position. He also briefly explains the two principles of justice.

Notes

[1] David Hume, *A Treatise of Human Nature*, ed. L. A. Selby-Bigge (Oxford: Clarendon Press, 1888), p. 415.

[2] Immanuel Kant, *Foundations of the Metaphysics of Morals*, trans. Lewis White Beck (Indianapolis, Ind.: Bobbs-Merrill, 1959), p. 9.

[3] Kant himself numbered these formulations so that there are only three, counting the second as a version of the first and the fifth as a version of the fourth.

[4] Kant, *Foundations*, p. 39.

[5] Ibid.

[6] Ibid., p. 47.

[7] Ibid., p. 52.

[8] Ibid., p. 57.

[9] H. J. Paton, *The Categorical Imperative* (New York: Harper & Row, 1967), p. 172.

[10] For Kant's rigorist rejection of all lying, see "Concerning the Common Saying: This May Be True in Theory but Does Not Apply in Practice," in *The Philosophy of Kant*, trans. Carl J. Friedrich (New York: Modern Library, 1949).

[11] For Rousseau's influence on Kant, see Ernst Cassirer, *Rousseau, Kant, and Goethe* (New York: Harper & Row, 1963).

[12] John Rawls, *A Theory of Justice* (Cambridge, Mass.: Harvard University Press, 1971), p. 62.

[13] Ibid., p. 302.

[14] Ibid., p. 63.

Bibliography on Kant and Contractarianism

Aune, Bruce. *Kant's Theory of Morals*. Princeton, N. J.: Princeton University Press, 1979.

Barry, Brian. *The Liberal Theory of Justice: A Critical Examination of the Principal Doctrines in* A Theory of Justice *by John Rawls*. Oxford: Clarendon Press, 1973.

Blocker, H. Gene, ed. *John Rawls' Theory of Social Justice*. Cambridge: Cambridge University Press, 1979.

Daniels, Norman, ed. *Reading Rawls*. New York: Basic Books, 1975.

Donagan, Alan. *The Theory of Morality*. Chicago, Ill.: University of Chicago Press, 1977.

Gregor, Mary J. *Laws of Freedom: A Study of Kant's Method of Applying the Categorical Imperative in the* Metaphysik der Sitten. Oxford: Basil Blackwell, 1963.

Kant, Immanuel. *Foundations of the Metaphysics of Morals: With Critical Essays*. Translated by Lewis White Beck. Edited by Robert Paul Wolff. Indianapolis, Ind.: Bobbs-Merrill, 1959.

_____. *The Doctrine of Virtue*. Translated by Mary J. Gregor. Philadelphia, Pa.: University of Pennsylvania Press, 1964.

_____. *The Metaphysical Elements of Justice*. Translated by John Ladd. Indianapolis, Ind.: Bobbs-Merrill, 1965.

Murphy, Jeffrie G. *Kant: The Philosophy of Right*. London: Macmillan, 1970.

Nell, Onora. *Acting on Principle: An Essay on Kantian Ethics*. New York: Columbia University Press, 1975.

Paton, H. J. *The Categorical Imperative*. New York: Harper & Row, 1967.

Rawls, John. *A Theory of Justice*. Cambridge, Mass.: Harvard University Press, 1971.

Richards, David A. J. *A Theory of Reasons for Action*. Oxford: Clarendon Press, 1971.

Wolff, Robert Paul. *Understanding Rawls*. Princeton, N.J.: Princeton University Press, 1977.

IMMANUEL KANT

THE CATEGORICAL IMPERATIVE

All imperatives command either hypothetically or categorically. The former present the practical necessity of a possible action as a means to achieving something else which one desires (or which one may possibly desire). The categorical imperative would be one which presented an action as of itself objectively necessary, without regard to any other end.

Since every practical law presents a possible action as good and thus as necessary for a subject practically determinable by reason, all imperatives are formulas of the determination of action which is necessary by the principle of a will which is in any way good. If the action is good only as a means to something else, the imperative is hypothetical; but if it is thought of as good in itself, and hence as necessary in a will which of itself conforms to reason as the principle of this will, the imperative is categorical.

The imperative thus says what action possible to me would be good, and it presents the practical rule in relation to a will which does not forthwith perform an action simply because it is good, in part because the subject does not always know that the action is good and in part (when he does know it) because his maxims can still be opposed to the objective principles of practical reason.

The hypothetical imperative, therefore, says only that the action is good to some purpose, possible or actual. In the [415] former case it is a

From Immanuel Kant: *Foundations of the Metaphysics of Morals*, translated by Lewis White Beck, pp. 31–49, © 1959 by the Bobbs-Merrill Co., Inc., reprinted by permission of the publisher. (Bracketed numbers indicate the pages of the Prussian Akademie edition.)

problematical, in the latter an assertorical, practical principle. The categorical imperative, which declares the action to be of itself objectively necessary without making any reference to a purpose, i.e., without having any other end, holds as an apodictical (practical) principle.

We can think of that which is possible through the mere powers of some rational being as a possible purpose of any will. As a consequence, the principles of action, in so far as they are thought of as necessary to attain a possible purpose which can be achieved by them, are in reality infinitely numerous. All sciences have some practical part which consists of problems of some end which is possible for us and of imperatives as to how it can be reached. These can therefore generally be called imperatives of skill. Whether the end is reasonable and good is not in question at all, for the question is only of what must be done in order to attain it. The precepts to be followed by a physician in order to cure his patient and by a poisoner in order to bring about certain death are of equal value in so far as each does that which will perfectly accomplish his purpose. Since in early youth we do not know what ends may occur to us in the course of life, parents seek to let their children learn a great many things and provide for skill in the use of means to all sorts of arbitrary ends among which they cannot determine whether any one of them may later become an actual purpose of their pupil, though it is possible that he may some day have it as his actual purpose. And this anxiety is so great that they commonly neglect to form and correct their judgment on the worth of things which they may make their ends.

There is one end, however, which we may presuppose as actual in all rational beings so far as imperatives apply to them, i.e., so far as they are dependent beings; there is one purpose not only which they *can* have but which we can presuppose that they all *do* have by a necessity of nature. This purpose is happiness. The hypothetical imperative which represents the practical necessity of action as means to the promotion of happiness is an assertorical imperative. We may not expound it as merely necessary to an uncertain and a merely possible purpose, but as necessary to a purpose which we can a priori and with assurance assume for everyone [416] because it belongs to his essence. Skill in the choice of means to one's own highest welfare can be called prudence[1] in the narrowest sense. Thus the imperative which refers to the choice of means to one's own happiness, i.e., the precept of prudence, is still only hypothetical; the action is not absolutely commanded but commanded only as a means to another end.

Finally, there is one imperative which directly commands a certain conduct without making its condition some purpose to be reached by it. This imperative is categorical. It concerns not the material of the action and its intended result but the form and the principle from which it results. What is essentially good in it consists in the intention, the result being what it may. This imperative may be called the imperative of morality.

Volition according to these three principles is plainly distinguished by dissimilarity in the constraint to which they subject the will. In order to clarify this dissimilarity, I believe that they are most suitably named if one says that they are either rules of skill, counsels of prudence, or commands (laws) of morality, respectively. For law alone implies the concept of an unconditional and objective and hence universally valid necessity, and commands are laws which must be obeyed, even against inclination. Counsels do indeed involve necessity, but a necessity that can hold only under a subjectively contingent condition, i.e., whether this or that man counts this or that as part of his happiness; but the categorical imperative, on the other hand, is restricted by no condition. As absolutely, though practically, necessary it can be called a command in the strict sense. We could also call the first imperative technical (belonging to art), the second pragmatic[2] (belonging to well [417] fare), and the third moral (belonging to free conduct as such, i.e., to morals).

The question now arises: how are all these imperatives possible? This question does not require an answer as to how the action which the imperative commands can be performed but merely as to how the constraint of the will, which the imperative expresses in the problem, can be conceived. How an imperative of skill is possible requires no particular discussion. Whoever wills the end, so far as reason has decisive influence on his action, wills also the indispensably necessary means to it that lie in his power. This proposition, in what concerns the will, is analytical; for, in willing an object as my effect, my causality as an acting cause, i.e., the use of the means, is already thought, and the imperative derives the concept of necessary actions to this end from the concept of willing this end. Synthetical propositions undoubtedly are necessary in determining the means to a proposed end, but they do not concern the ground, the act of the will, but only the way to make the object real. Mathematics teaches, by synthetical propositions only, that in order to bisect a line according to an infallible principle I must make two intersecting arcs from each of its extremities; but if I know the proposed result can be obtained only by such an action, then it is an analytical proposition that, if I fully will the effect, I must also will the action necessary to produce it. For it is one and the same thing to conceive of something as an effect which is in a certain way possible through me and to conceive of myself as acting in this way.

If it were only easy to give a definite concept of happiness, the imperatives of prudence would completely correspond to those of skill and would be likewise analytical. For it could be said in this case as well as in the former that whoever [418] wills the end wills also (necessarily according to reason) the only means to it which are in his power. But it is a misfortune that the concept of happiness is so indefinite that, although each person wishes to attain it, he can never definitely and self-consistently state what it is he really wishes and wills. The reason for this is that all elements which belong to the concept of happiness are empirical, i.e., they must be taken from experience, while for the idea of happiness an absolute whole, a maximum, of well-being is needed in my present and in every future condition. Now it is impossible even for a most clear-sighted and most capable but finite being to form here a definite concept of that which he really wills. If he wills riches, how much anxiety, envy, and intrigue might he not thereby draw upon his shoulders! If he wills much knowledge and vision, perhaps it might become only an eye that much sharper to show him as more dreadful the evils which are now hidden from him and which are yet unavoidable, or to burden his desires—which already sufficiently engage him—with even more needs! If he wills a long life, who guarantees that it will not be long misery? If he wills at least health, how often has not the discomfort of the body restrained him from excesses into which perfect health would have led him? In short, he is not capable, on any principle and with complete certainty, of ascertaining what would make him truly happy; omniscience would be needed for this. He cannot, therefore, act according to definite principles so as to be happy, but only according to empirical counsels, e.g., those of diet, economy, courtesy, restraint, etc., which are shown by experience best to promote welfare on the average. Hence the imperatives of prudence cannot, in the strict sense, command, i.e., present actions objectively as practically necessary; thus they are to be taken as counsels (*consilia*) rather than as commands (*praecepta*) of reason, and the task of determining infallibly and universally what action will promote the happiness of a rational being is completely unsolvable. There can be no imperative which would, in the strict sense, command us to do what makes for happiness, because happiness is an ideal not of reason but of imagination, depending only on empirical grounds which one would expect in vain to determine an [419] action through which the totality of consequences—which is in fact infinite—could be achieved. Assuming that the means to happiness could be infallibly stated, this imperative of prudence would be an analytical proposition, for it differs from the imperative of skill only in that its end is given, while in the latter case it is merely possible. Since both, however, only command the means to that which one presupposes, the imperative which commands the willing of the means to him who wills the end is in both cases analytical. There is, consequently, no difficulty in seeing the possibility of such an imperative.

To see how the imperative of morality is possible is, then, without doubt the only question needing an answer. It is not hypothetical, and thus the objectively conceived necessity cannot be supported by any presupposition, as was the case with the hypothetical imperatives. But it must not be overlooked that it cannot be shown by any example (i.e., it cannot be empirically shown) whether or not there is such an imperative; it is rather to be suspected that all imperatives which appear to be categorical may yet be hypothetical, but in a hidden way. For instance, when it is said, "Thou shalt not make a false promise," we assume that the necessity of this avoidance is not a mere counsel for the sake of escaping some other evil, so that it would read, "Thou shalt not make a false promise so that, if it comes to light, thou ruinest thy credit"; we assume rather that an action of this kind must be regarded as of itself bad and that the imperative of the prohibition is categorical. But we cannot show with certainty by any example that the will is here determined by the law alone without any other incentives, even though this appears to be the case. For it is always possible that secret fear of disgrace, and perhaps also obscure apprehension of other dangers, may have had an influence on the will. Who can prove by experience the non-existence of a cause when experience shows us only that we do not perceive the cause? But in such a case the so-called moral imperative, which as such appears to be categorical and unconditional, would be actually only a pragmatic precept which makes us attentive to our own advantage and teaches us to consider it.

Thus we shall have to investigate purely a priori the possibility of a categorical imperative, for we do not have the [420] advantage that experience would give us the reality of this imperative, so that the [demonstration of its] possibility would be necessary only for its explanation and not for its establishment. In the meantime, this much may at least be seen: the categorical imperative alone can be taken as a practical *law*, while all the others may be called principles of the will but not laws. This is because what is necessary merely for the attainment of an arbitrary purpose can be regarded as itself contingent, and we get rid of the precept once we give up the purpose, whereas the unconditional command leaves the will no freedom to choose the opposite. Thus it alone implies the necessity which we require of a law.

Secondly, in the case of the categorical imperative or law of morality, the cause of difficulty in discerning its possibility is very weighty. This imperative is an a priori synthetical practical proposition,[3] and, since to discern the possibility of propositions of this sort is so difficult in theoretical knowledge, it may well be gathered that it will be no less difficult in the practical.

In attacking this problem, we will first inquire whether the mere concept of a categorical imperative does not also furnish the formula containing the proposition which alone can be a categorical imperative. For even when we know the formula of the imperative, to learn how such an absolute law is possible will require difficult and special labors which we shall postpone to the last section.

If I think of a hypothetical imperative as such, I do not know what it will contain until the condition is stated [under which it is an imperative]. But if I think of a categorical imperative, I know immediately what it contains. For since the imperative contains besides the law only the necessity [421] that the maxim[4] should accord with this law, while the law contains no condition to which it is restricted, there is nothing remaining in it except the universality of law as such to which the maxim of the action should conform; and in effect this conformity alone is represented as necessary by the imperative.

There is, therefore, only one categorical imperative. It is: Act only according to that maxim by which you can at the same time will that it should become a universal law.

Now if all imperatives of duty can be derived from this one imperative as a principle, we can at least show what we understand by the concept of duty and what it means, even though it remain undecided whether that which is called duty is an empty concept or not.

The universality of law according to which effects are produced constitutes what is properly called nature in the most general sense (as to form), i.e., the existence of things so far as it is determined by universal laws. [By analogy], then, the universal imperative of duty can be expressed as follows: Act as though the maxim of your action were by your will to become a universal law of nature.

We shall now enumerate some duties, adopting the usual division of them into duties to ourselves and to others and into perfect and imperfect duties.[5]

1. A man who is reduced to despair by a series of evils feels a weariness with life but is still in possession of his reason [422] sufficiently to ask whether it would not be contrary to his duty to himself to take his own life. Now he asks whether the maxim of his action could become a universal law of nature. His maxim, however, is: For love of myself, I make it my principle to shorten my life when by a longer duration it threatens more evil than satisfaction. But it is questionable whether this principle of self-love could become a universal law of nature. One immediately sees a contradiction in a system of nature whose law would be to destroy life by the feeling whose special office is to impel the improvement of life. In this case it would not exist as nature; hence that maxim cannot obtain as a law of nature, and thus it wholly contradicts the supreme principle of all duty.

2. Another man finds himself forced by need to borrow money. He well knows that he will not be able to repay it, but he also sees that nothing will be loaned him if he does not firmly promise to repay it at a certain time. He desires to make such a promise, but he has enough conscience to ask himself whether it is not improper and opposed to duty to relieve his distress in such a way. Now, assuming he does decide to do so, the maxim of his action would be as follows: When I believe myself to be in need of money, I will borrow money and promise to repay it, although I know I shall never do so. Now this principle of self-love or of his own benefit may very well be compatible with his whole future welfare, but the question is whether it is right. He changes the pretension of self-love into a universal law and then puts the question: How would it be if my maxim became a universal law? He immediately sees that it could never hold as a universal law of nature and be consistent with itself; rather it must necessarily contradict itself. For the universality of a law which says that anyone who believes himself to be in need could promise what he pleased with the intention of not fulfilling it would make the promise itself and the end to be accomplished by it impossible; no one would believe what was promised to him but would only laugh at any such assertion as vain pretense.

3. A third finds in himself a talent which could, by means of some cultivation, make him in many respects a useful [423] man. But he finds

himself in comfortable circumstances and prefers indulgence in pleasure to troubling himself with broadening and improving his fortunate natural gifts. Now, however, let him ask whether his maxim of neglecting his gifts, besides agreeing with his propensity to idle amusement, agrees also with what is called duty. He sees that a system of nature could indeed exist in accordance with such a law, even though man (like the inhabitants of the South Sea Islands) should let his talents rust and resolve to devote his life merely to idleness, indulgence, and propagation—in a word, to pleasure. But he cannot possibly will that this should become a universal law of nature or that it should be implanted in us by a natural instinct. For, as a rational being, he necessarily wills that all his faculties should be developed, inasmuch as they are given to him for all sorts of possible purposes.

4. A fourth man, for whom things are going well, sees that others (whom he could help) have to struggle with great hardships, and he asks, "What concern of mine is it? Let each one be as happy as heaven wills, or as he can make himself; I will not take anything from him or even envy him; but to his welfare or to his assistance in time of need I have no desire to contribute." If such a way of thinking were a universal law of nature, certainly the human race could exist, and without doubt even better than in a state where everyone talks of sympathy and good will, or even exerts himself occasionally to practice them while, on the other hand, he cheats when he can and betrays or otherwise violates the rights of man. Now although it is possible that a universal law of nature according to that maxim could exist, it is nevertheless impossible to will that such a principle should hold everywhere as a law of nature. For a will which resolved this would conflict with itself, since instances can often arise in which he would need the love and sympathy of others, and in which he would have robbed himself, by such a law of nature springing from his own will, of all hope of the aid he desires.

The foregoing are a few of the many actual duties, or at least of duties we hold to be actual, whose derivation from the one stated principle is clear. We must be able to will that [424] a maxim of our action become a universal law; this is the canon of the moral estimation of our action generally. Some actions are of such a nature that their maxim cannot even be *thought* as a universal law of nature without contradiction, far from it being possible that one could will that it should be such. In others this internal impossibility is not found, though it is still impossible to *will* that their maxim should be raised to the universality of a law of nature, because such a will would contradict itself. We easily see that the former maxim conflicts with the stricter or narrower (imprescriptible) duty, the latter with broader (meritorious) duty. Thus all duties, so far as the kind of obligation (not the object of their action) is concerned, have been completely exhibited by these examples in their dependence on the one principle.

When we observe ourselves in any transgression of a duty, we find that we do not actually will that our maxim should become a universal law. That is impossible for us; rather, the contrary of this maxim should remain as a law generally, and we only take the liberty of making an exception to it for ourselves or for the sake of our inclination, and for this one occasion. Consequently, if we weighed everything from one and the same standpoint, namely, reason, we would come upon a contradiction in our own will, viz., that a certain principle is objectively necessary as a universal law and yet subjectively does not hold universally by rather admits exceptions. However, since we regard our action at one time from the point of view of a will wholly conformable to reason and then from that of a will affected by inclinations, there is actually no contradiction, but rather an opposition of inclination to the precept of reason (*antagonismus*). In this the universality of the principle (*universalitas*) is changed into mere generality (*generalitas*), whereby the practical principle of reason meets the maxim halfway. Although this cannot be justified in our own impartial judgment, it does show that we actually acknowledge the validity of the categorical imperative and allow ourselves (with all respect to it) only a few exceptions which seem to us to be unimportant and forced upon us.

We have thus at least established that if duty is a concept [425] which is to have significance and actual legislation for our actions, it can be expressed only in categorical imperatives and not at all in hypothetical ones. For every application of it we have also clearly exhibited the content of the categorical imperative which must contain the principle of all duty (if there is such). This is itself very much. But we are not yet advanced far enough to prove a priori that that kind of imperative really exists, that there is a practical law which of itself commands absolutely and without any incentives, and that obedience to this law is duty.

With a view to attaining this, it is extremely important to remember that we must not let ourselves think that the reality of this principle can be derived from the particular constitution of human nature. For duty is practical unconditional necessity of action; it must, therefore, hold for all rational beings (to which alone an imperative can apply), and only for that reason can it be a law for all human wills. Whatever is derived from the particular natural situation of man as such, or from certain feelings and propensities, or even from a particular tendency of the human reason which might not hold necessarily for the will of every rational being (if such a tendency is possible), can give a maxim valid for us but not a law; that is, it can give a subjective principle by which we might act only if we have the propensity and inclination, but not an objective principle by which we would be directed to act even if all our propensity, inclination, and natural tendency were opposed to it. This is so far the case that the sublimity and intrinsic worth of the command is the better shown in a duty the fewer subjective causes there are for it and the more there are against it; the latter do not weaken the constraint of the law or diminish its validity. . . .

The question then is: Is it a necessary law for all rational beings that they should always judge their actions by such maxims as they themselves could will to serve as universal laws? If it is such a law, it must be connected (wholly a priori) with the concept of the will of a rational being as such. But in order to discover this connection we must, however reluctantly, take a step into metaphysics, although into a region of it different from speculative philosophy, i.e., into metaphysics of morals. In a practical philosophy it is not a question of assuming grounds for what happens but of assuming laws of what ought to happen even though it may never happen —that is to say, objective, practical laws. Hence in practical philosophy we need not inquire into the reasons why [427] something pleases or displeases, how the pleasure of mere feeling differs from taste, and whether this is distinct from a general satisfaction of reason. Nor need we ask on what the feeling of pleasure or displeasure rests, how desires and inclinations arise, and how, finally, maxims arise from desires and inclination under the co-operation of reason. For all these matters belong to an empirical psychology, which would be the second part of physics if we consider it as philosophy of nature so far as it rests on empirical laws. But here it is a question of objectively practical laws and thus of the relation of a will to itself so far as it determines itself only by reason; for everything which has a relation to the empirical automatically falls away, because if reason of itself alone determines conduct it must necessarily do so a priori. The possibility of reason thus determining conduct must now be investigated

The will is thought of as a faculty of determining itself to action in accordance with the conception of certain laws. Such a faculty can be found only in rational beings. That which serves the will as the objective ground of its self-determination is an end, and, if it is given by reason alone, it must hold alike for all rational beings. On the other hand, that which contains the ground of the possibility of the action, whose result is an end, is called the means. The subjective ground of desire is the incentive, while the objective ground of volition is the motive. Thus arises the distinction between subjective ends, which rest on incentives, and objective ends, which depend on motives valid for every rational being. Practical principles are formal when they disregard all subjective ends; they are material when they have subjective ends, and thus certain incentives, as their basis. The ends which a rational being arbitrarily proposes to himself as consequences of his action are material ends and are without exception only relative, for only their relation to a particularly constituted faculty of desire in the subject gives them their worth. And this worth cannot, therefore, afford any universal principles for all rational beings or valid and necessary principles for every volition. That is, they cannot give rise to any practical laws. [428] All these relative ends, therefore, are grounds for hypothetical imperatives only.

But suppose that there were something the existence of which in itself had absolute worth, something which, as an end in itself, could be a ground of definite laws. In it and only in it could lie the ground of a possible categorical imperative, i.e., of a practical law.

Now, I say, man and, in general, every rational being exists as an end in himself and not merely as a means to be arbitrarily used by this or that will. In all his actions, whether they are directed to himself or to other rational beings, he must always be regarded at the same time as an end. All objects of inclinations have only a conditional worth, for if the inclinations and the needs founded on them did not exist, their object would be without worth. The inclinations themselves as the sources of needs, however, are so lacking in absolute worth that the universal wish of every rational being must be indeed to free himself completely from them. Therefore, the worth of any objects to be obtained by our actions is at all times conditional. Beings whose existence does not depend on our will but on nature, if they are not rational beings, have only a relative worth as means and are therefore called "things"; on the other hand, rational beings are designated "persons" because their nature indicates that they are ends in themselves, i.e., things which may not be used merely as means. Such a being is thus an object of respect and, so far, restricts all [arbitrary] choice. Such beings are not merely subjective ends whose existence as a result of our action has a worth for us, but are objective ends, i.e., beings whose existence in itself is an end. Such an end is one for which no other end can be substituted, to which these beings should serve merely as means. For, without them, nothing of absolute worth could be found, and if all worth is conditional and thus contingent, no supreme practical principle for reason could be found anywhere.

Thus if there is to be a supreme practical principle and a categorical imperative for the human will, it must be one that forms an objective principle of the will from the conception of that which is necessarily an end for everyone because it is an end in itself. Hence this objective principle can serve [429] as a universal practical law. The ground of this principle is: rational nature exists as an end in itself. Man necessarily thinks of his own existence in this way; thus far it is a subjective principle of human actions. Also every other rational being thinks of his existence by means of the same rational ground which holds also for myself;[6] thus it is at the same time an objective principle from which, as supreme practical ground, it must be possible to derive all laws of the will. The practical imperative, therefore, is the following: Act so that you treat humanity, whether in your own person or in that of another, always as an end and never as a means only. Let us now see whether this can be achieved.

To return to our previous examples:

First, according to the concept of necessary duty to one's self, he who contemplates suicide will ask himself whether his action can be consistent with the idea of humanity as an end in itself. If, in order to escape from burdensome circumstances, he destroys himself, he uses a person merely as a means to maintain a tolerable condition up to the end of life. Man, however, is not a thing, and thus not something to be used merely as a means; he must always be regarded in all his actions as an end in himself. Therefore, I cannot dispose of man in my own person so as to mutilate, corrupt, or kill him. (It belongs to ethics proper to define more accurately this basic principle so as to avoid all misunderstanding, e.g., as to the amputation of limbs in order to preserve myself, or to exposing my life to danger in order to save it; I must, therefore, omit them here.)

Second, as concerns necessary or obligatory duties to others, he who intends a deceitful promise to others sees immediately that he intends to use another man merely as a means, without the latter containing the end in himself at the same time. For he whom I want to use for my own purposes by means of such a promise cannot possibly assent to my mode of acting [430] against him and cannot contain the end of this action in himself. This conflict against the principle of other men is even clearer if we cite examples of attacks on their freedom and property. For then it is clear that he who transgresses the rights of men intends to make use of the persons of others merely as a means, without considering that, as rational beings, they must always be esteemed at the same time as ends, i.e., only as beings who must be able to contain in themselves the end of the very same action.[7]

Third, with regard to contingent (meritorious) duty to one's self, it is not sufficient that the action not conflict with humanity in our person as an end in itself; it must also harmonize with it. Now in humanity there are capacities for greater perfection which belong to the end of nature with respect to humanity in our own person; to neglect these might perhaps be consistent with the preservation of humanity as an end in itself but not with the furtherance of that end.

Fourth, with regard to meritorious duty to others, the natural end which all men have is their own happiness. Humanity might indeed exist if no one contributed to the happiness of others, provided he did not intentionally detract from it; but this harmony with humanity as an end in itself is only negative rather than positive if everyone does not also endeavor, so far as he can, to further the ends of others. For the ends of any person, who is an end in himself, must as far as possible also be my end, if that conception of an end in itself is to have its full effect on me. . . .

Notes

[1] The word "prudence" may be taken in two senses, and it may bear the name of prudence with reference to things of the world and private prudence. The former sense means the skill of a man in having an influence on others so as to use them for his own purposes. The latter is the ability to unite all these purposes to his own lasting advantage. The worth of the first is finally reduced to the latter, and of one who is prudent in the former sense but not in the latter we might better say that he is clever and cunning yet, on the whole, imprudent.

[2] It seems to me that the proper meaning of the word "pragmatic" could be most accurately defined in this way. For sanctions which properly flow not from the law of states as necessary statutes but from provision for the general welfare are called pragmatic. A history is pragmatically composed when it teaches prudence, i.e., instructs the world how it could provide for its interest better than, or at least as well as, has been done in the past.

[3] I connect a priori, and hence necessarily, the action with the will without supposing as a condition that there is any inclination [to the action] (though I do so only objectively, i.e., under the idea of a reason which would have complete power over all subjective motives).

This is, therefore, a practical proposition which does not analytically derive the willing of an action from some other volition already presupposed (for we do not have such a perfect will); it rather connects it directly with the concept of the will of a rational being as something which is not contained within it.

⁴ A maxim is the subjective principle of acting and must be distinguished from the objective principle, i.e., the practical law. The former contains the practical rule which reason determines according to the conditions of the subject (often its ignorance or inclinations) and is thus the principle according to which the subject acts. The law, on the other hand, is the objective principle valid for every rational being, and the principle by which it ought to act, i.e., an imperative.

⁵ It must be noted here that I reserve the division of duties for a future *Metaphysics of Morals* and that the division here stands as only an arbitrary one (chosen in order to arrange my examples). For the rest, by a perfect duty I here understand a duty which permits no exception in the interest of inclination; thus I have not merely outer but also inner perfect duties. This runs contrary to the usage adopted in the schools, but I am not disposed to defend it here because it is all one to my purpose whether this is conceded or not.

⁶ Here I present this proposition as a postulate, but in the last section grounds for it will be found.

⁷ Let it not be thought that the banal *"quod tibi non vis fieri, etc.,"* could here serve as guide or principle, for it is only derived from the principle and is restricted by various limitations. It cannot be a universal law, because it contains the ground neither of duties to one's self nor of the benevolent duties to others (for many a man would gladly consent that others should not benefit him, provided only that he might be excused from showing benevolence to them). Nor does it contain the ground of obligatory duties to another, for the criminal would argue on this ground against the judge who sentences him. And so on.

ONORA NELL
APPLYING THE CATEGORICAL IMPERATIVE

The Formula of Universal Law states in the first place a criterion for coherent intentions, and only via this a test for maxims of duty. This explains why Kant includes the qualification "simultaneously" or "at the same time as" in the formula. Intentions are datable. Unless two intentions are held at the same time, there is no possibility of their being inconsistent. If the presence or absence of a contradiction between intentions is to discriminate maxims of duty from other maxims, then one must assume that the intentions can be ascribed to the same agent at the same time.

One might, however, wonder whether there can ever be any contradiction between intending to do some act and the intention that everyone similarly situated do the same act. If we consider the two intentions schematically it would seem impossible. For they would be, respectively:

(3¹) I will – – – – if . . . .

(6) Everyone will – – – – if . . . .

From Onora Nell, *Acting on Principle: An Essay on Kantian Ethics* (New York: Columbia University Press, 1975), pp. 70-74. Reprinted by permission.

Rather it seems that (3¹) is an instantiation of (6), and that no contradiction would ever be possible. But to draw this conclusion is to take too limited a view of what it is to have an intention. If I intend to, say, rob a bank, I intend also some sufficient set of conditions to realize my ends and the normal, predictable results of the success of my intended action. For instance, I intend the continued existence of the bank I plan to rob, that I be neither discovered nor interrupted during the theft, and that I shall use or enjoy the fruits of the theft. These are not separate intentions which a person who intends to rob a bank may or may not have; they are part and parcel of normal intentions to rob banks. Similarly if I intend *qua* universal legislator that everyone should rob some bank, then I must also intend some conditions sufficient for them to do so and the normal and predictable results of their succeeding in doing so. But I cannot intend that everybody be not interrupted or discovered in their theft from a bank and be able to use or enjoy the fruits of their theft. I must intend the normal and predictable results of the success of any course of action which I intend, and the normal result of everyone's stealing from banks is that banks will take ever greater precautions to impede and discover thieves and to prevent them using or enjoying their loot. Failing successful prevention, banks, as we know them, would close down.

I cannot intend a system of nature in which everybody does what I do. So if my maxim is to rob a bank I cannot universalize it. In my capacity as universal legislator, I would intend that all theft from banks and, hence, my theft from a bank and the use and enjoyment of its results become increasingly difficult and eventually impossible; yet in my private capacity I intend that my theft from a bank be feasible and successful. If an agent does act on the maxim of robbing a bank, or on any other maxim whose universalization would require him to have self-contradictory intentions, then the outcome will be ". . . . no contradiction, but rather an opposition to the precept of reason (antagonismus), whereby the universality of the principle (universalitas) is turned to mere generality (generalitas)."¹

In such cases we intend that we should be an exception to the universal law, and that the law be not really universal. In the example given, we intend both that banks continue to exist in their present form, as part of the necessary conditions for the robberies we intend, and that banks do not continue to exist in their present form, as part of the normal and predictable results of the robberies we intend. Rational beings cannot intend a society of bank robbers.

The derivation of a contradiction from the intentions of an agent trying to universalize his maxim of bank robbing depends upon the generality of that maxim. But each bank robbery can be described and may be intended much more specifically. Suppose a person with red hair named Ignatz MacGillycuddy . . . intends to rob a bank exactly northeast of his house at 5 P.M. on a Thursday. He discovers that he can without contradiction intend a system of nature in which any red-headed person named Ignatz MacGillycuddy who has a bank exactly northeast of his house robs that bank at 5 P.M. on a Thursday, and that his own robbery take place in such a system of nature. Is this robbery then not forbidden? . . .

. . . A person cannot simply *claim* a highly specific maxim, as in the Ignatz MacGillycuddy example. He must, in fact, intend his act to be contingent on those restrictions and not merely pursued by these means if he is to hold his maxim is specific and so universalizable. He must demonstrate (perhaps only to his own satisfaction) that he would drop his project of bank robbing if his hair turned gray or 5 P.M. passed or the bank turned out to be north-northeast of his house and so on. On the whole, I believe, agents who are honest will not claim to have highly specific maxims. They know that when they claim that they will rob a bank of a specified sort in a specified way, etc., their project is not really contingent upon these specifications. As always, Kant places great reliance on agents being honest and careful in stating what it is that they intend to do. In general, the contradiction in conception test is extremely sensitive to the details of agents' maxims. Some of the consequences of this sensitivity will be discussed in chapters 6 and 7. . . .

This interpretation of the contradiction in conception test proposes a far from mechanical method for determining whether acting on a maxim is compatible with duty. But the method is still relatively clear and definite. It asks whether we can simultaneously intend to do x (assuming that we must intend some set of conditions sufficient for the successful carrying out of our intentions and the normal and predictable results of successful execution) and intend everyone else to do x (assuming again that we must intend some conditions sufficient for the successful execution of their intentions and the normal and predictable results of such execution). No appeal is made in this interpretation of the test to particular desires or inclinations or to particular empirical situations. Naturally an agent who is working out what his intentions commit him to must take certain empirical facts into account. But a limit is placed on the sort of empirical material which may be adduced in testing a maxim by the relevance of the empirical material to the coherence of the agent's intentions. There are still good reasons for calling the contradictions which may be derived from applications of this test "inner impossibilities." They mark an incoherence *within* the intentions of a particular agent.

Only given a certain background of empirical facts can an agent's intentions to do an act be determinate. For only given these can he work out whether there is some feasible means for executing his intention and what the normal and predictable results of successful execution of the intention would be. But just which sorts of facts may or must an agent assume to see what exactly his intentions commit him to?

If this cannot be stated carefully we shall be back with a problem like that of providing a relevant description of an act. Is it, for instance, permissible for an agent testing the maxim of embezzlement to assume as an empirical fact that he will not be apprehended? Or is this not part of the normal and predictable results of successful embezzling? The answer in such cases is that he may do so only if he assumes also that, if everyone else embezzles, they will not be apprehended. The only sense in which Kant does rely upon the notion of a system of nature in the statement of the contradiction in conception test is that he requires that we ask "Whether if the action you propose should take place by a law of nature of which you yourself were a part you could regard it as possible through your will."[2] Appeal cannot be made to empirical facts such as that not everyone will do likewise or that this act will (or will not) serve as a bad example. For the hypothesis against which a maxim is tested is precisely that others do the same, whether or not because of the example given.

But this is not a sufficient restriction on the sorts of empirical circumstance which a man may assume in determining what his intentions commit him to. He must assume, not only that he belongs to the same system of nature as others, but, if he is seeing whether his maxim is a maxim of human duty, he must assume that he belongs to that system of nature to which men belong. He cannot, for instance, assume that a duplicate of stolen property is somehow miraculously presented to the owner, who is therefore not deprived while the thief enjoys the original. If we did live in such a system of nature, precautions against theft would presumably never be taken and the maxim of thieving could consistently be universalized. But this is no reason for rejecting the interpretation of the test. One would not expect the moral status of theft to be the same in such a system of nature as it is in our own.

Tests of the capacity of maxims to guide any human moral choices must assume those natural laws in whose context all human society operates—that men are mortal and learn from experience; that material goods are not infinitely abundant and are desired, and additional specific laws of this sort. No doubt it is not entirely clear which generalizations about the human condition are laws of nature, but this is a question which judgment is not powerless to solve. The fact that agents testing the rightness and moral worth of acts done or proposed have to make judgments of this sort does, however, show once again how far from mechanical this test is. To apply it fairly, agents must assess their intentions and the probable results of their success with complete honesty. This fact may account for the enormous stress which Kant places on duties such as integrity and conscientiousness. . . .

Notes

[1] Immanuel Kant, *G.* (*Foundations*), Akademie edition, p. 424.
[2] *K. P. V.* (*Critique of Practical Reason*), Akademie edition, p. 69.

JOHN RAWLS
A CONTRACTARIAN THEORY OF JUSTICE

THE MAIN IDEA OF THE THEORY OF JUSTICE

My aim is to present a conception of justice which generalizes and carries to a higher level of abstraction the familiar theory of the social contract as found, say, in Locke, Rousseau, and Kant.[1] In order to do this we are not to think of the original contract as one to enter a particular society or to set up a particular form of government. Rather, the guiding idea is that the principles of justice for the basic structure of society are the object of the original agreement. They are the principles that free and rational persons concerned to further their own interests would accept in an initial position of equality as defining the fundamental terms of their association. These principles are to regulate all further agreements; they specify the kinds of social cooperation that can be entered into and the forms of government that can be established. This way of regarding the principles of justice I shall call justice as fairness.

Thus we are to imagine that those who engage in social cooperation choose together, in one joint act, the principles which are to assign basic rights and duties and to determine the division of social benefits. Men are to decide in advance how they are to regulate their claims against one another and what is to be the foundation charter of their society. Just as each person must decide by rational reflection what constitutes his good, that is, the system of ends which it is rational for him to pursue, so a group of persons must decide once and for all what is to count among them as just and unjust. The choice which rational men would make in this hypothetical situation of equal liberty, assuming for the present that this choice problem has a solution, determines the principles of justice.

In justice as fairness the original position of equality corresponds to the state of nature in the traditional theory of the social contract. This original position is not, of course, thought of as an actual historical state of affairs, much less as a primitive condition of culture. It is understood as a purely hypothetical situation characterized so as to lead to a certain conception of justice.[2] Among the essential features of this situation is that no one knows his place in society, his class position or social status, nor does any one know his fortune in the distribution of natural assets and abilities, his intelligence, strength, and the like. I shall even assume that the parties do not know their conceptions of the good or their special psychological propensities. The principles of justice are chosen behind a veil of ignorance. This ensures that no one is advantaged or disadvantaged in the choice of principles by the outcome of natural chance or the contingency of social circumstances. Since all are similarly situated and no one is able to design principles to favor his particular condition, the principles of justice are the result of a fair agreement or bargain. For given the circumstances of the original position, the symmetry of everyone's relations to each other, this initial situation is fair between individuals as moral persons, that is, as rational beings with their own ends and capable, I shall assume, of a sense of justice. The original position is, one might say, the appropriate initial status quo, and thus the fundamental agreements reached in it are fair. This explains the propriety of the name "justice as fairness": it conveys the idea that the principles of justice are agreed to in an initial situation that is fair. The name does not mean that the concepts of justice and fairness are the same, any more than the phrase "poetry as metaphor" means that the concepts of poetry and metaphor are the same.

Justice as fairness begins, as I have said, with one of the most general of all choices which persons might make together, namely, with the choice of the first principles of a conception of justice which is to regulate all subsequent criticism and reform of institutions. Then, having chosen a conception of justice, we can suppose that they are to choose a constitution and a legislature to enact laws, and so on, all in accordance with the principles of justice initially agreed upon. Our social situation is just if it is such that by this sequence of hypothetical agreements we would have con tracted into the general system of rules which defines it. Moreover, assuming that the original position does determine a set of principles (that is, that a particular conception of justice would be chosen), it will then be true that whenever social institutions satisfy these principles those engaged in them can say to one another that they are cooperating on terms to which they would agree if they were free and equal persons whose relations with respect to one another were fair. They could all view their arrangements as meeting the stipulations which they would acknowledge in an initial situation that embodies widely accepted and reasonable constraints on the choice of principles. The general recognition of this fact would provide the basis for a public acceptance of the corresponding principles of justice. No society can, of course, be a scheme of cooperation which men enter voluntarily in a literal sense; each person finds himself placed at birth in some particular position in some particular society, and the nature of this position materially affects his life prospects. Yet a society satisfying the principles of justice as fairness comes as close as a society can to being a voluntary scheme, for its meets the principles which free and equal persons would assent to under circumstances that are fair. In this sense its members are autonomous and the obligations they recognize self-imposed.

One feature of justice as fairness is to think of the parties in the initial situation as rational and mutually disinterested. This does not mean that the parties are egoists, that is, individuals with only certain kinds of interests, say in wealth, prestige, and domination. But they are conceived as not taking an interest in one another's interests. They are to presume that even their spiritual aims may be opposed, in the way that the aims of those of different religions may be opposed. Moreover, the concept of rationality must be interpreted as far as possible in the narrow sense, standard in economic theory, of taking the most effective means to given ends. I shall modify this concept to some extent . . , but one must try to avoid introducing into it any controversial ethical elements. The initial situation must be characterized by stipulations that are widely accepted.

In working out the conception of justice as fairness one main task clearly is to determine which principles of justice would be chosen in the original position. To do this we must describe this situation in some detail and formulate with care the problem of choice which it presents. These matters I shall take up in the immediately succeeding chapters. It may be observed, however, that once the principles of justice are thought of as arising from an original agreement in a situation of equality, it is an open question whether the principle of utility would be acknowledged. Offhand it hardly seems likely that persons who view themselves as equals, entitled to press their claims upon one another, would agree to a principle which may require lesser life prospects for some simply for the sake of a greater sum of advantages enjoyed by others. Since each desires to protect his interests, his capacity to advance his conception of the good, no one has a reason to acquiesce in an enduring loss for himself in order to bring about a greater net balance of satisfaction. In the absence of strong and lasting benevolent impulses, a rational man would not accept a basic structure merely because it maximized the algebraic sum of advantages irrespective of its permanent effects on his own basic rights and interests. Thus it seems that the principle of utility is incompatible with the conception of social cooperation among equals for mutual advantage. It appears to be inconsistent with the idea of reciprocity implicit in the notion of a well-ordered society. Or, at any rate, so I shall argue.

I shall maintain instead that the persons in the initial situation would choose two rather different principles: the first requires equality in the assignment of basic rights and duties, while the second holds that social and economic inequalities, for example inequalities of wealth and authority, are just only if they result in compensating benefits for everyone, and in particular for the least advantaged members of society. These principles rule out justifying institutions on the grounds that the hardships of some are offset by a greater good in the aggregate. It may be expedient but it is not just that some should have less in order that others may prosper. But there is no injustice in the greater benefits earned by a few provided that the situation of persons not so fortunate is thereby improved. The intuitive idea is that since everyone's well-being depends upon a scheme of cooperation without which no one could have a satisfactory life, the division of advantages should be such as to draw forth the willing cooperation of everyone taking part in it, including those less well situated. Yet this can be expected only if reasonable terms are proposed. The two principles mentioned seem to be a fair agreement on the basis of which those better endowed, or more fortunate in their social position, neither of which we can be said to deserve, could expect the willing cooperation of others when some workable scheme is a necessary condition of the welfare of all.[3] Once we decide to look for a conception of justice that nullifies the accidents of natural endowment and the contingencies of social circumstances as counters in quest for political and economic advantage, we are led to these principles. They express the result of leaving aside those aspects of the social world that seem arbitrary from a moral point of view. . . .

A final remark. Justice as fairness is not a complete contract theory. For it is clear that the contractarian idea can be extended to the choice of more or less an entire ethical system, that is, to a system including principles for all the virtues and not only for justice. Now for the most part I shall consider only principles of justice and others closely related to them; I make no attempt to discuss the virtues in a systematic way. Obviously if justice as fairness succeeds reasonably well, a next step would be to study the more general view suggested by the name "rightness as fairness." But even this wider theory fails to embrace all moral relationships, since it would seem to include only our relations with other persons and to leave out of account how we are to conduct ourselves toward animals and the rest of nature. I do not contend that the contract notion offers a way to approach these questions which are certainly of the first importance; and I shall have to put them aside. We must recognize the limited scope of justice as fairness and of the general type of view that it exemplifies. How far its conclusions must be revised once these other matters are understood cannot be decided in advance. . . .

TWO PRINCIPLES OF JUSTICE

I shall now state in a provisional form the two principles of justice that I believe would be chosen in the original position. In this section I wish to make only the most general comments, and therefore the first formulation of these principles is tentative. As we go on I shall run through several formulations and approximate step by step the final statement to be given much later. I believe that doing this allows the exposition to proceed in a natural way.

The first statement of the two principles reads as follows.

> First: each person is to have an equal right to the most extensive basic liberty compatible with a similar liberty for others.
>
> Second: social and economic inequalities are to be arranged so that they are both (a) reasonably expected to be to everyone's advantage, and (b) attached to positions and offices open to all. . . .

By way of general comment, these principles primarily apply, as I have said, to the basic structure of society. They are to govern the assignment of rights and duties and to regulate the distribution of social and economic advantages. As their formulation suggests, these principles presuppose that the social structure can be divided into two more or less distinct parts, the first principle applying to the one, the second to the other. They distinguish between those aspects of the social system that define and secure the equal liberties of citizenship and those that specify and establish social and economic inequalities. The basic liberties of citizens are, roughly speaking, political liberty (the right to vote and to be eligible for public office) together with freedom of speech and assembly; liberty of conscience and freedom of thought; freedom of the person along with the right to hold (personal) property; and freedom from arbitrary arrest and seizure as defined by the concept of the rule of law. These liberties are all required to be equal by the first principle, since citizens of a just society are to have the same basic rights.

The second principle applies, in the first approximation, to the distribution of income and wealth and to the design of organizations that make use of differences in authority and responsibility, or chains of command. While the distribution of wealth and income need not be equal, it must be to everyone's advantage, and at the same time, positions of authority and offices of command must be accessible to all. One applies the second principle by holding positions open, and then, subject to this constraint, arranges social and economic inequalities so that everyone benefits.

These principles are to be arranged in a serial order with the first principle prior to the second. This ordering means that a departure from the institutions of equal liberty required by the first principle cannot be justified by, or compensated for, by greater social and economic advantages. The distribution of wealth and income, and the hierarchies of authority, must be consistent with both the liberties of equal citizenship and equality of opportunity.

It is clear that these principles are rather specific in their content, and their acceptance rests on certain assumptions that I must eventually try to explain and justify. A theory of justice depends upon a theory of society in ways that will become evident as we proceed. For the present, it should be observed that the two principles (and this holds for all formulations) are a special case of a more general conception of justice that can be expressed as follows.

> All social values—liberty and opportunity, income and wealth, and the bases of self-respect—are to be distributed equally unless an unequal distribution of any, or all, of these values is to everyone's advantage.

Injustice, then, is simply inequalities that are not to the benefit of all. Of course, this conception is extremely vague and requires interpretation.

As a first step, suppose that the basic structure of society distributes certain primary goods, that is, things that every rational man is presumed to want. These goods normally have a use whatever a person's rational plan of life. For simplicity, assume that the chief primary goods at the disposition of society are rights and liberties, powers and opportunities, income and wealth. (Later on in Part Three the primary good of self-respect has a central place.) These are the social primary goods. Other primary goods such as health and vigor, intelligence and imagination, are natural goods; although their possession is influenced by the basic structure, they are not so directly under its control. Imagine, then, a hypothetical initial arrangement in which all the social primary goods are equally distributed: everyone has similar rights and duties, and income and wealth are evenly shared. This state of affairs provides a benchmark for judging improvements. If certain inequalities of wealth and organizational powers would make everyone better off than in this hypothetical starting situation, then they accord with the general conception.

Now it is possible, at least theoretically, that by giving up some of their fundamental liberties men are sufficiently compensated by the resulting social and economic gains. The general conception of justice imposes no restrictions on what sort of inequalities are permissible; it only requires that everyone's position be improved. We need not suppose anything so drastic as consenting to a condition of slavery. Imagine instead that men forego certain political rights when the economic returns are significant and their capacity to influence the course of policy by the exercise of these rights would be marginal in any case. It is this kind of exchange which the two principles as stated rule out; being arranged in serial order they do not permit exchanges between basic liberties and economic and social gains. The serial ordering of principles expresses an underlying preference among primary social goods. When this preference is rational so likewise is the choice of these principles in this order.

In developing justice as fairness I shall, for the most part, leave aside the general conception of justice and examine instead the special case of the two principles in serial order. The advantage of this procedure is that from the first the matter of priorities is recognized and an effort made to find principles to deal with it. One is led to attend throughout to the conditions under which the acknowledgment of the absolute weight of liberty with respect to social and economic advantages, as defined by the lexical order of the two principles, would be reasonable. Offhand, this ranking appears extreme and too special a case to be of much interest; but there is more justification for it than would appear at first sight. Or at any rate, so I shall maintain. . . . Furthermore, the distinction between fundamental rights and liberties and economic and social benefits marks a difference among primary social goods that one should try to exploit. It suggests an important division in the social system. Of course, the distinctions drawn and the ordering proposed are bound to be at best only approximations. There are surely circumstances in which they fail. But it is essential to depict clearly the main lines of a reasonable conception of justice; and under many conditions anyway, the two principles in serial order may serve well enough. When necessary we can fall back on the more general conception.

The fact that the two principles apply to institutions has certain consequences. Several points illustrate this. First of all, the rights and liberties referred to by these principles are those which are defined by the public rules of the basic structure. Whether men are free is determined by the rights and duties established by the major institutions of society. Liberty is a certain pattern of social forms. The first principle simply requires that certain sorts of rules, those defining basic liberties, apply to everyone equally and that they allow the most extensive liberty compatible with a like liberty for all. The only reason for circumscribing the rights defining liberty and making men's freedom less extensive than it might otherwise be is that these equal rights as institutionally defined would interfere with one another.

Another thing to bear in mind is that when principles mention persons, or require that everyone gain from an inequality, the reference is to representative persons holding the various social positions, or offices, or whatever, established by the basic structure. Thus in applying the second principle I assume that it is possible to assign an expectation of well-being to representative individuals holding these positions. This expectation indicates their life prospects as viewed from their social station. In general, the expectations of representative persons depend upon the distribution of rights and duties throughout the basic structure. When this changes, expectations change. I assume, then, that expectations are connected: by raising the prospects of the representative man in one position we presumably increase or decrease the prospects of representative men in other positions. Since it applies to institutional forms, the second principle (or rather the first part of it) refers to the expectations of representative individuals. As I shall discuss below, neither principle applies to distributions of particular goods to particular individuals who may be identified by their proper names. The situation where someone is considering how to allocate certain commodities to needy persons who are known to him is not within the scope of the principles. They are meant to regulate basic institutional arrangements. We must not assume that there is much similarity from the standpoint of justice between an administrative allotment of goods to specific persons and the appropriate design of society. Our common sense intuitions for the former may be a poor guide to the latter.

Now the second principle insists that each person benefit from permissible inequalities in the basic structure. This means that it must be reasonable for each relevant representative man defined by this structure, when he views it as a going concern, to prefer his prospects with the inequality to his prospects without it. One is not allowed to justify differences in income or organizational powers on the ground that the disadvantages of those in one position are outweighed by the greater advantages of those in another. Much less can infringements of liberty be counterbalanced in this way. Applied to the basic structure, the principle of utility would have us maximize the sum of expectations of representative men (weighted by the number of persons they represent, on the classical view); and this would permit us to compensate for the losses of some by the gains of others. Instead, the two principles require that everyone benefit from economic and social inequalities. It is obvious, however, that there are indefinitely many ways in which all may be advantaged when the initial arrangement of equality is taken as a benchmark. How then are we to choose among these possibilities? The principles must be specified so that they yield a determinate conclusion. I now turn to this problem.

Notes

[1] As the text suggests, I shall regard Locke's *Second Treatise of Government,* Rousseau's *The Social Contract,* and Kant's ethical works beginning with *The Foundations of the Metaphysics of Morals* as definitive of the contract tradition. For all of its greatness, Hobbes's *Leviathan* raises special problems. A general historical survey is provided by J. W. Gough, *The Social Contract,* 2nd ed. (Oxford, The Clarendon Press, 1957), and Otto Gierke, *Natural Law and the Theory of Society,* trans. with an introduction by Ernest Barker (Cambridge, The University Press, 1934). A presentation of the contract view as primarily an ethical theory is to be found in G. R. Grice, *The Grounds of Moral Judgment* (Cambridge, The University Press, 1967).

[2] Kant is clear that the original agreement is hypothetical. See *The Metaphysics of Morals,* pt. I (*Rechtslehre*), especially §§47, 52; and pt. II of the essay "Concerning the Common Saying: This May Be True in Theory but It Does Not Apply in Practice," in *Kant's Political Writings,* ed. Hans Reiss and trans. by H. B. Nisbet (Cambridge, The University Press, 1970), pp. 73–87. See Georges Vlachos, *La Pensée politique de Kant* (Paris, Presses Universitaires de France, 1962), pp. 326–335; and J. G. Murphy, *Kant: The Philosophy of Right* (London, Macmillan, 1970), pp. 109–112, 133–136, for a further discussion.

[3] For the formulation of this intuitive idea I am indebted to Allan Gibbard.

chapter *3*

*U*tilitarianism

INTRODUCTION

At approximately the same time Kant was developing his theory of ethics, the English philosopher Jeremy Bentham (1748–1832) was formulating his theory of utilitarianism. Although philosophers before Bentham, especially David Hume, had developed theories with utilitarian aspects, he was the first to provide a systematic formulation of the view much as it is discussed today. Bentham's primary statement of utilitarianism is presented in his book *The Principles of Morals and Legislation* first published in 1789. As the book's title indicates, the theory has a political as well as a personal orientation.

Although working out its details is often difficult, part of utilitarianism's attraction is the simplicity of its central idea. According to the utilitarian, the rightness and wrongness of conduct depends solely on its consequences; thus it is a consequentialist theory. The criterion of ethical conduct is to produce as great a balance of good over bad as possible. Happiness is the only intrinsic good, and unhappiness the only intrinsic bad. Each person's happiness is as important as is anyone else's. Conduct is right or wrong depending upon whether it produces as much *net utility* (the balance of happiness over unhappiness) as anything else that could be done.

Bentham and his close friend James Mill sought to educate a successor to lead the ethical and political movement that they started in the early nineteenth century. They developed a very strict educational plan for James Mill's oldest son, John Stuart. From about the age of three, John was trained to be the intellectual leader of the utilitarian movement. Bentham and the elder Mill were quite successful, and John Stuart Mill (1806–1873) became the leading philosopher in Great Britain, making significant contributions to logic, metaphysics, ethics, political philosophy, and economics.

The impact of utilitarian ideas in the nineteenth century was great. Utilitarianism significantly influenced the British penal and electoral reforms of that century. But though these were important achievements, the reforms did not improve the lot of the average person as much as Bentham and the Mills had hoped they would.

At the beginning of the twentieth century, George E. Moore severely attacked utilitarianism by rejecting the view of Bentham and Mill that the sole end of ethics is happiness or pleasure.[1] Moore, however, still held that the rightness and wrongness of conduct depends on its consequences. During the 1930s even that aspect of utilitarian theory was severely criticized by W. David Ross.[2] In many ways, however, utilitarian ideas were still alive and significantly affected society through their incorporation into legal and economic thought.

Since the 1950s philosophers have had a renewed interest in utilitarian theory. One reason for this increased interest is the distinction, never made explicit by Bentham or Mill, between two types of utilitarianism. One version of the theory—*act utilitarianism*—directly determines the rightness and wrongness of conduct by considering the utility of particular acts. The other version—*rule utilitarianism*—indirectly determines the rightness and wrongness of conduct by judging acts by their conformity to rules and judging rules by their utility.

Act Utilitarianism The following is a formulation of a representative act-utilitarian principle:

> An act is permissible if, and only if, its net utility is at least as great as that of any alternative act the agent could perform in the situation.

The crucial concept involved is that of net utility, usually simply termed utility. The net utility of an act is the sum of its good (positive) and bad (negative) consequences. Bentham and Mill considered pleasure (happiness) to be the only intrinsic good and pain (unhappiness) the only intrinsic evil. Other theorists, such as Moore, expand this understanding, believing that things other than pleasure and pain are also intrinsically good and bad. Most contemporary utilitarians consider the satisfaction of interests or preferences to be that which is intrinsically good and their frustration to be that which is intrinsically bad. The following discussion refers to happiness and unhappiness as intrinsically good and bad, leaving open whether they are to be equated with pleasure and pain, satisfaction and frustration, or something else.

Determining the net utility of an act requires three steps. First, one sums all the happiness that will be caused by the act. Second, one sums all the unhappiness that will be caused by the act. Third, one in effect subtracts the unhappiness from the happiness. This result is the net utility, which is negative if the act will produce more unhappiness than happiness and positive if the consequences are vice versa.

This concept of utility requires that one can mathematically compare the happiness and unhappiness of different people, or, as it is said, make mathematical comparisons of interpersonal utility. To sum up the happiness an act, say, Fred's eating ice cream or Sharon's earning a bachelor's degree, produces, one must be able to assign standard units of happiness to it. One must also be able to assign the same standard units to unhappiness. There are two problems involved. First, it might not always be possible to assign definite units to the pleasure a person gets through the performance of a particular action. For example, it might not be possible to figure out exactly how many units of happiness Fred gets from eating ice cream, as compared to playing tennis. Second, even if one could do that for each person, there is no way to be certain that the units assigned for Fred are the same as those assigned for Sharon. A number of philosophers and economists have struggled to develop a system of making mathematical comparisons, but as yet no one has provided a generally accepted method for so doing.

To determine which act or acts are morally permissible in a situation, one must go through the following three steps. (1) One must determine all the alternative acts that could be performed. People learning to reason in a utilitarian manner often forget to consider all the available alternatives. For example, suppose one is trying to decide whether to study or to go to a movie. There are not just two alternatives available. One could also, perhaps, study for a while and then go to the movie when one is tired, take a shorter break by watching a half-hour television show, go for a walk, or commit suicide. Some of these actions, such as committing suicide, are not plausibly going to produce as much utility as others and can practically be ignored. (2) As described previously, one must determine the net utility of each of the alternative acts. (3) One determines which acts have at least as much net utility as any of the others. Any of these acts will be morally permissible. If one act has more net utility than any other, then it is obligatory and no other act is permissible. In some situations, it will be discovered that none of the acts has a positive net utility. The act-utilitarian principle does not imply that they are all wrong; it simply implies that the one(s) with the least balance of unhappiness over happiness is (are) permissible. In short, if all acts will on balance cause net unhappiness, or disutility, then act utilitarianism implies that one should do what will cause the least net unhappiness.

A few points should be noted about act-utilitarian theory. It differs from Kantian theory in that only the consequences of actions are considered relevant to determining their rightness, whereas Kant and others believe that something other than the utility of consequences is morally relevant. Also, although it shares some characteristics with egoism, it differs from egoism by considering the happiness and unhappiness of everyone equally. An egoist is concerned only with the consequences for himself, but a utilitarian does not consider the consequences for himself to be of any more importance than are the consequences for others. Nor does the act-utilitarian principle state that one should aim for "the greatest happiness of the greatest number," a conception that does not make sense in some situations. Suppose one act will affect five people and produce a net utility of ten units and the only alternative act will affect ten persons and produce a net utility of five units. The second act will produce happiness for more people, but the first one will produce more happiness overall.

Seeking the greatest happiness for the greatest number does not tell one what to do in this situation. Such a formulation tries to maximize two independent variables—happiness and number of people—at the same time, something that is not always possible.

Three widely influential criticisms of act utilitarianism should be considered here. The first criticism pertains to promise keeping. According to act utilitarianism, one has an obligation to keep a promise if and only if no other act has as much utility as keeping it does. (If another act has the same net utility, then keeping the promise is permissible but not obligatory.) Suppose one has borrowed money from a friend and promised to repay it. After a couple of weeks one earns enough money to repay the friend, but funds are being collected for famine relief in a particularly desperate country. Assume that, everything considered, giving the money to famine relief would have more net utility than would repaying the friend. According to act utilitarianism, it is not permissible to repay the friend; instead, one has an obligation to give it to famine relief (assuming no other alternative has as much net utility as that act does). But, the critics claim, one is obligated to repay one's friend. Therefore, act utilitarianism is not a correct principle.

Short of abandoning or modifying the theory, the act utilitarian can give two different replies to this type of criticism. He or she can claim that when one examines the situation in detail, repaying one's friend does have greater net utility, for one must consider the extra disappointment breaking one's promise will cause the friend, the bad example it will set, and the bad effect it will have on one's character. Usually repaying one's friend will have more net utility. In some cases, however, even if all these factors are taken into account, giving to famine relief might have greater utility. If so, act utilitarianism implies that one is obligated to break the promise. At this point, the utilitarian can simply reply that it is mistaken to think that it would be wrong to break the promise.

The critics claim that the promise-keeping example shows that something other than consequences is relevant to determining the rightness of conduct. One should keep one's promise because one promised. The promise was something made in the past and is not a matter of the future consequences of promise keeping. The obligation to keep promises, they claim, is a "backward-looking" obligation, and act utilitarianism cannot account for such considerations because it is solely "forward looking." Other commonsense obligations, such as gratitude, are also backward looking.

The second criticism of act utilitarianism pertains to justice. Suppose the finance minister of a country is trying to decide between two economic policies. Policy A will produce tremendous economic growth, but most of the benefits will accrue to the upper 30 percent of the population. Policy B will produce much less economic growth, but the benefits will be more widely and evenly distributed. Further suppose that policy A will produce more net utility than policy B. Assuming that no other policy has as much net utility as A, according to act utilitarianism, the finance minister has an obligation to choose policy A; it would be wrong to choose policy B. According to the critics, since one is not obligated to make the rich richer, act utilitarianism must be incorrect.

An act utilitarian can try to argue on the facts that policy B will have more net utility than policy A. In general, dollar for dollar, economic benefits to the poor produce more happiness than economic benefits to the rich, because they provide goods more essential for happiness. Nonetheless, if policy A would produce many more goods for the wealthy 30 percent of the population than would policy B, it will still have more net utility. Alternately, the act utilitarian can simply accept the implications and defend the moral correctness of policy A. Of course, one can also abandon or try to revise the theory.

The underlying difficulty brought out by this example is that act utilitarianism does not consider the distribution of utility, only its amount. It thus, according to critics, ignores the important consideration of equality of distribution. Although utilitarians count the happiness of each person equally, a greater amount of happiness for one person outweighs a lesser amount of unhappiness for another, no matter how happy the first person already is or how unhappy the second person already is.

The third criticism of act utilitarianism pertains to cooperative conduct and, in particular, to what are called *maximizing conditions*.[3] These are situations in which most people need to act the same way to obtain great utility, but most utility will be achieved if a few people do not act that way. Say, for instance, that due to the energy shortage, the government has asked everyone to lower their thermostat to sixty-five degrees. Now June, a cold-blooded act utilitarian, reasons as follows. If everyone lowers the thermostat to sixty-five, more energy will be saved than needs to be. As I am very cold-blooded, chilly temperatures cause me more unhappiness than they do other people. If I keep my thermostat at seventy-two degrees, I will not encourage others to do so because I live alone and no one will know. Consequently, it is permissible for me to leave my thermostat at seventy-two degrees, because it will give me happiness and will not cause anyone else unhappiness. The critics have two objections to this form of act-utilitarian reasoning. First, it is unfair for June to leave her thermostat at seventy-two degrees when everyone else must turn theirs down. Second, suppose that everyone reasoned as June does. Then everyone would leave the thermostat at seventy-two degrees; no energy would be saved; and an economic or energy disaster (no heat at all) would occur.

Utilitarians can argue that their theory does not imply it is permissible for everyone to leave the thermostat at seventy-two degrees. Only cold-blooded persons can do so. Alternately, they can accept the implications and say that it is permissible for everyone to do so, unless the government adopts a policy (such as fines or higher energy prices) making it more attractive for persons to turn down their thermostats. The critics, however, claim that the example shows that utilitarianism ignores considerations of fairness.

Rule Utilitarianism The following is a formulation of a general rule-utilitarian principle:

> An act is permissible if, and only if, it is not prohibited by a rule to which conformance would have at least as much net utility as conformance to any other rule applicable to the situation.

By this principle, often called *primitive rule utilitarianism,* an act is not evaluated as right or wrong by directly considering its utility but by considering whether it is prohibited by a rule. An act prohibited by a relevant rule is wrong. The chief difficulty with this theory, many critics claim, is that it produces the same results as act utilitarianism. For example, consider promise keeping. Conforming to a rule that it is always wrong to break promises would not have as much utility as conforming to one that allowed exceptions. When would it be most useful to allow exceptions? Whenever more utility would result from breaking a promise than in keeping it. Thus, it would seem the most useful rule would be, "It is wrong to break promises except when doing so has as much utility as does keeping them." Although some philosophers argue that primitive rule utilitarianism does not always give the same results as act utilitarianism, it would be likely to have the same results as does act utilitarianism, if applied in the objectionable cases considered in the preceding section.

However, if one considers the utility of accepting rules, otherwise known as *acceptance utility,* rather than of conforming to them, one does not get the same results as with act utilitarianism. In practicing acceptance utility, one does not assume that people will always conform to the rules; one can allow for people not always doing what, in a reflective moment, they would think is right.

A major problem with primitive rule utilitarianism is that it evaluates the utility of one rule at a time, although different rules might conflict in any given situation. Also, while it is always possible to work out a rule for a particular situation, one may end up with so many rules that it would be difficult to remember them all. Consequently, it is usually better to consider the utility of different sets of rules, or moral codes. A useful code would be composed of rather simple rules, including a rule or two explaining what to do in the event of rule conflict. Nonetheless, in most cases one will have to consider differences between codes, each having different rules applicable to the kind of situation one is confronted with.

A rule-utilitarian principle making allowances for these considerations can be formulated as follows:

> An act is permissible if, and only if, it is not prohibited by a set of rules the acceptance of which would have at least as much net utility as the acceptance of any other set.

Actually, the steps in rule-utilitarian reasoning are quite similar to those in act-utilitarian reasoning. (1) One must determine the relevant codes. As noted above, one need not consider every code, only those having particular rules applicable to the type of situation confronted (keeping promises, showing gratitude, distributing goods, and so on). Usually then, one can simply consider alternative rules applicable to the type of situation. As with act utilitarianism, a common failing is a lack of imagination in considering alternative rules. For example, with regard to promise keeping, the choice is not simply between the two rules "Never break promises" or "Never break promises unless more net utility will result from doing so." One should consider relevant rules with other exceptive clauses, such as "Never break promises unless they were coerced, or if breaking them can save a life." (2) One must determine the net utility of the acceptance of each of the various relevant rules, or sets of rules. (3) One picks a rule, or set of rules, the acceptance of which has at least as much net utility as the acceptance of any other. (4) One must ask whether this rule, or set of rules, prohibits the act in question. If so, it is wrong; if not, it is permissible.

Perhaps the strongest argument for rule utilitarianism is that while it retains the concern for the utility of conduct, it avoids some of the objectionable implications of act utilitarianism. Consider the example of breaking a promise to repay a loan in order to give the money to famine relief. A rule that "It is wrong to break promises unless doing so will produce more net utility" would probably not have as much net acceptance utility as another rule. If people were permitted to break promises whenever they happened to think more net utility would result, because of bias or improper calculations of utility they would break promises much of the time. Consequently, rules with more precise exceptions are better. Nor is it likely that a rule which permitted breaking promises to repay loans in order to give to famine relief would have as much acceptance utility as a rule that did not. Famines occur rather frequently. In many cases, people who loaned money could not rely on getting their money back. Consequently, they might be less inclined to loan money, and few people would be able to borrow. Moreover, a code with high acceptance utility would probably include other rules specifically providing for famine relief, so there would be no need to include such an exception in a rule about promise keeping. Consequently, the rule utilitarian would likely imply that it would be wrong to break the promise made in the example.

Now consider the example of leaving the thermostat at seventy-two degrees. Suppose the rule stated that it is wrong not to lower one's thermostat to sixty-five degrees unless one is cold-blooded. The acceptance utility of such a rule is apt to be much less than that of a rule without that exceptive condition. As stated, the rule leaves too much leeway for people to make exceptions in their own favor. Quite likely, so many people would decide that they were cold-blooded and, therefore, free to keep the heat up that most of the utility of lowering thermostats would be lost. This is not to say that a rule with as high an acceptance utility as any other would not contain some exceptions. Exceptions, for instance, might be admitted for people who are very sick, or for the elderly.

Rule utilitarianism does not, however, diverge from act utilitarianism in the example of justice and economic policy. The choice between policies is in effect a choice between two rules. By hypothesis, policy A, in which most benefits go to the rich, has the higher utility. The resentment of the poor resulting from its primarily benefiting the rich might decrease its utility, but if most of the people accepted the high-growth policy, then resentment would be minimized. People do not resent policies they approve of. Thus, rule utilitarianism, like act utilitarianism, is concerned only with the amount of utility, *not* with its distribution.

Two criticisms of rule utilitarianism should be mentioned. The first is the act utilitarians' charge that rule utilitarians are guilty of *superstitious rule worship*. Their argument is simple. Like us, they say, rule utilitarians claim to be interested in promoting happiness, yet their theory prescribes different acts from ours. Our theory prescribes the acts that produce as much utility as possible; rule utilitarianism does not. In short, rule utilitarians do not permit breaking rules even when they admit there may be more utility in breaking than in following them. Why then do they follow the rules? Because of superstitious rule worship.

The second criticism usually comes from nonutilitarians.[4] Rule utilitarianism holds that one should follow those rules which would have as much utility as possible *if* they were accepted. But suppose the rules are not in fact accepted. Rule utilitarianism would still imply that one should follow the rules, whether acceptance is hypothetical or real. Sometimes this will lead a person to make a useless sacrifice. Consider again the energy shortage. Suppose the legislature has failed to act, but as high a net utility as possible would result if everyone accepted the rule to lower thermostats to sixty-five degrees, unless they were seriously ill or over seventy years of age. The vast majority of people do not accept the rule, therefore, do not lower their thermostats, and energy shortages occur. Meanwhile, the rule utilitarian has turned his thermostat down to sixty-five degrees. Why? Because it is required by the rule that *would* have as much utility as possible *if* it were accepted. The result is that the rule utilitarian makes a useless sacrifice. He is chilly when others are warm, and when the energy runs out, his heat will be shut off just like everyone else's. This is a ridiculous consequence, of course. Moreover, the useless sacrifices need not be made by rule utilitarians; their actions can lead to sacrifices by others. For example, suppose the government does not have a social security system, but a rule utilitarian concludes that such a system would be best. Consequently, instead of caring for his parents when they are old as everyone else in the society does, he simply makes an "extra" contribution to the government in the amount he calculated he would have to pay under a social security system. His parents receive nothing; they have made a useless sacrifice.

When faced with these objections, rule utilitarians can claim that in fact their theory does not have the objectionable implications. Alternately, they can accept the implications and suggest that our beliefs should be reformed. As a last resort, they can abandon or modify their theory.

Readings The selection from John Stuart Mill provides his statement of utilitarianism and his argument for it. Mill believes that he can justify acceptance of utilitarianism if he can show that happiness and only happiness is intrinsically good. His argument, however, is frequently said to contain a number of logical fallacies. A distinguishing aspect of his theory is the suggestion that some kinds of pleasure are preferable to others. The more preferable ones he calls higher and believes to be chiefly intellectual. In this respect, he differs markedly from Bentham who considered all pleasures to be on a par.

The selection by J. J. C. Smart is a contemporary statement and defense of act utilitarianism (which he calls "extreme utilitarianism"). Smart replies to some of the criticisms of act utilitarianism given above. He also criticizes rule utilitarianism ("restricted utilitarianism") as superstitious rule worship.

The last selection by R. B. Brandt is a statement of rule utilitarianism. He explains the notion of accepting a rule and explains why it is best to consider sets of rules. He also indicates the types of rules he thinks would be justified. In his recent important book, *A Theory of the Good and the Right*,[5] Brandt has given a much more detailed defense of a modified form of his theory.

Notes

[1] *Principia Ethica* (Cambridge: Cambridge University Press, 1903).

[2] W. David Ross, *The Right and the Good* (Oxford: Clarendon Press, 1930) and *Foundations of Ethics* (Oxford: Clarendon Press, 1939).

[3] David Lyons, *Forms and Limits of Utilitarianism* (Oxford: Clarendon Press, 1965), pp. 128–31.

[4] See B. J. Diggs, "A comment on 'Some Merits of One Form of Rule-Utilitarianism,'" in *Readings in Contemporary Ethical Theory*, ed. Kenneth Pahel and Marvin Schiller (Englewood Cliffs, N.J.: Prentice-Hall, 1970), pp. 307–17.

[5] (Oxford: Clarendon Press, 1979).

Bibliography on Utilitarianism

Bayles, Michael D., ed. *Contemporary Utilitarianism.* Garden City, N.Y.: Doubleday, Anchor Books, 1968; reprint, Gloucester, Mass.: Peter Smith, 1978.

Bentham, Jeremy. *An Introduction to the Principles of Morals and Legislation.* 1789. Several editions.

Brandt, Richard B. *A Theory of the Good and the Right.* Oxford: Clarendon Press, 1979.

Feldman, Fred. *Introductory Ethics.* Englewood Cliffs, N.J.: Prentice-Hall, 1978. Chapters 2–5.

Lyons, David. *Forms and Limits of Utilitarianism.* Oxford: Clarendon Press, 1965.

Mill, John Stuart. *Utilitarianism with Critical Essays.* Edited by Samuel Gorovitz. Indianapolis, Ind.: Bobbs-Merrill, 1971.

Narveson, Jan. *Morality and Utility.* Baltimore, Md.: Johns Hopkins Press, 1967.

Sartorius, Rolf E. *Individual Conduct and Social Norms: A Utilitarian Account of Social Union and the Rule of Law.* Encino, Calif.: Dickenson Publishing, 1975. Especially Chapter 2.

Sidgwick, Henry. *The Methods of Ethics.* 7th ed. London: Macmillan, 1907. Book IV.

Singer, Marcus George. *Generalization in Ethics.* New York: Knopf, 1961. Especially Chapter 7.

Smart, J. J. C., and Williams, Bernard. *Utilitarianism: For and Against.* Cambridge: Cambridge University Press, 1973.

"Symposium on Utilitarianism." *Noûs* 10 (1976): 101–244.

JOHN STUART MILL
UTILITARIANISM

CHAPTER II   WHAT UTILITARIANISM IS

. . . The creed which accepts as the foundation of morals, Utility, or the Greatest Happiness Principle, holds that actions are right in proportion as they tend to promote happiness, wrong as they tend to produce the reverse of happiness. By happiness is intended pleasure, and the absence of pain; by unhappiness, pain, and the privation of pleasure. To give a clear view of the moral standard set up by the theory, much more requires to be said; in particular, what things it includes in the ideas of pain and pleasure; and to what extent this is left an open question. But these supplementary explanations do not affect the theory of life on which this theory of morality is grounded—namely, that pleasure, and freedom from pain, are the only things desirable as ends; and that all desirable things (which are as numerous in the utilitarian as in any other scheme) are desirable either for the pleasure inherent in themselves, or as means to the promotion of pleasure and the prevention of pain.

Now, such a theory of life excites in many minds, and among them in some of the most estimable in feeling and purpose, inveterate dislike. To suppose that life has (as they express it) no higher end than pleasure—no better and nobler object of desire and pursuit—they designate as utterly mean and grovelling; as a doctrine worthy only of swine, to whom the followers of Epicurus were, at a very early period, contemptuously likened; and modern holders of the doctrine are occasionally made the subject of equally polite comparisons by its German, French, and English assailants.

When thus attacked, the Epicureans have always answered, that it is not they, but their accusers, who represent human nature in a degrading light; since the accusation supposes human beings to be capable of no pleasures except those of which swine are capable. If this supposition were true, the charge could not be gainsaid, but would then be no longer an imputation; for if the sources of pleasure were precisely the same to human beings and to swine, the rule of life which is good enough for the one would be good enough for the other. The comparison of the Epicurean life to that of beasts is felt as degrading, precisely because a beast's pleasures

From John Stuart Mill, *Utilitarianism* (1861).

do not satisfy a human being's conception of happiness. Human beings have faculties more elevated than the animal appetites, and when once made conscious of them, do not regard anything as happiness which does not include their gratification. I do not, indeed, consider the Epicureans to have been by any means faultless in drawing out their scheme of consequences from the utilitarian principle. To do this in any sufficient manner, many Stoic, as well as Christian elements require to be included. But there is no known Epicurean theory of life which does not assign to the pleasures of the intellect, of the feelings and imagination, and of the moral sentiments, a much higher value as pleasures than to those of mere sensation. It must be admitted, however, that utilitarian writers in general have placed the superiority of mental over bodily pleasures chiefly in the greater permanency, safety, uncostliness, etc., of the former—that is, in their circumstantial advantages rather than in their intrinsic nature. And on all these points utilitarians have fully proved their case; but they might have taken the other, and, as it may be called, higher ground, with entire consistency. It is quite compatible with the principle of utility to recognise the fact, that some *kinds* of pleasure are more desirable and more valuable than others. It would be absurd that while, in estimating all other things, quality is considered as well as quantity, the estimation of pleasures should be supposed to depend on quantity alone.

If I am asked, what I mean by difference of quality in pleasures, or what makes one pleasure more valuable than another, merely as a pleasure, except its being greater in amount, there is but one possible answer. Of two pleasures, if there be one to which all or almost all who have experience of both give a decided preference, irrespective of any feeling of moral obligation to prefer it, that is the more desirable pleasure. If one of the two is, by those who are competently acquainted with both, placed so far above the other that they prefer it, even though knowing it to be attended with a greater amount of discontent, and would not resign it for any quantity of the other pleasure which their nature is capable of, we are justified in ascribing to the preferred enjoyment a superiority in quality, so far out-weighing quantity as to render it, in comparison, of small account.

Now it is an unquestionable fact that those who are equally acquainted with, and equally capable of appreciating and enjoying, both, do give a most marked preference to the manner of existence which employs their higher faculties. Few human creatures would consent to be changed into any of the lower animals, for a promise of the fullest allowance of a beast's pleasures; no intelligent human being would consent to be a fool, no instructed person would be an ignoramus, no person of feeling and conscience would be selfish and base, even though they should be persuaded that the fool, the dunce, or the rascal is better satisfied with his lot than they are with theirs. They would not resign what they possess more than he for the most complete satisfaction of all the desires which they have in common with him. If they ever fancy they would, it is only in cases of unhappiness so extreme, that to escape from it they would exchange their lot for almost any other, however undesirable in their own eyes. A being of higher faculties requires more to make him happy, is capable probably of more acute suffering, and certainly accessible to it at more points, than one of an inferior type; but in spite of these liabilities, he can never really wish to sink into what he feels to be a lower grade of existence. We may give what explanation we please of this unwillingness; we may attribute it to pride, a name which is given indiscriminately to some of the most and to some of the least estimable feelings of which mankind are capable: we may refer it to the love of liberty and personal independence, an appeal to which was with the Stoics one of the most effective means for the inculcation of it; to the love of power, or to the love of excitement, both of which do really enter into and contribute to it: but its most appropriate appellation is a sense of dignity, which all human beings possess in one form or another, and in some, though by no means in exact, proportion to their higher faculties, and which is so essential a part of the happiness of those in whom it is strong, that nothing which conflicts with it could be, otherwise than momentarily, an object of desire to them. Whoever supposes that this preference takes place at a sacrifice of happiness—that the superior being, in anything like equal circumstances, is not happier than the inferior—confounds the two very different ideas, of happiness, and content. It is indisputable that the being whose capacities of enjoyment are low, has the greatest chance of having them fully satisfied; and a highly endowed being will always feel that any happiness which he can look for, as the world is constituted, is imperfect. But he can learn to bear its imperfections, if they are at all bearable; and they will not make him envy the being who is indeed unconscious of the imperfections, but only because he feels not at all the good which those imperfections qualify. It is better to be a human being dissatisfied than a pig satisfied; better to be Socrates dissatisfied than a fool satisfied. And if the fool, or the pig, are of a different opinion, it is because they only know their own side of the question. The other party to the comparison knows both sides.

It may be objected, that many who are capable of the higher pleasures, occasionally, under the influence of temptation, postpone them to the lower. But this is quite compatible with a full appreciation of the intrinsic superiority of the higher. Men often, from infirmity of character, make their election for the nearer good, though they know it to be the less valuable; and this no less when the choice is between two bodily pleasures, than when it is between bodily and mental. They pursue sensual indulgences to the injury of health, though perfectly aware that health is the greater good. It may be further objected, that many who begin with youthful enthusiasm for everything noble, as they advance in years sink into indolence and selfishness. But I do not believe that those who undergo this very common change, voluntarily choose the lower description of pleasures in preference to the higher. I believe that before they devote themselves exclusively to the one, they have already become incapable of the other. Capacity for the nobler feelings is in most natures a very tender plant, easily killed, not only by hostile influences, but by mere want of sustenance; and in the majority of young persons it speedily dies away if the occupations to which their position in life has devoted them, and the society into which it has thrown them, are not favourable to keeping that higher capacity in exercise. Men lose their high aspirations as they lose their intellectual tastes, because they have not time or opportunity for indulging them; and they addict themselves to inferior pleasures, not because they deliberately prefer them, but because they are either the only ones to which they have access, or the only ones which they are any longer capable of enjoying. It may be questioned whether any one who has remained equally susceptible to both classes of pleasures, ever knowingly and calmly preferred the lower; though many, in all ages, have broken down in an ineffectual attempt to combine both.

From this verdict of the only competent judges, I apprehend there can be no appeal. On a question which is the best worth having of two pleasures, or which of two modes of existence is the most grateful to the feelings, apart from its moral attributes and from its consequences, the judgment of those who are qualified by knowledge of both, or, if they differ, that of the majority among them, must be admitted as final. And there needs be the less hesitation to accept this judgment respecting the quality of pleasures, since there is no other tribunal to be referred to even on the question of quantity. What means are there of determining which is the acutest of two pains, or the intensest of two pleasurable sensations, except the general suffrage of those who are familiar with both? Neither pains nor pleasures are homogeneous, and pain is always heterogeneous with pleasure. What is there to decide whether a particular pleasure is worth purchasing at the cost of a particular pain, except the feelings and judgment of the experienced? When, therefore, those feelings and judgment declare the pleasures derived from the higher faculties to be preferable *in kind,* apart from the question of intensity, to those of which the animal nature, disjoined from the higher faculties, is susceptible, they are entitled on this subject to the same regard.

I have dwelt on this point, as being a necessary part of a perfectly just conception of Utility or Happiness, considered as the directive rule of human conduct. But it is by no means an indispensable condition to the acceptance of the utilitarian standard; for that standard is not the agent's own greatest happiness, but the greatest amount of happiness altogether; and if it may possibly be doubted whether a noble character is always the happier for its nobleness, there can be no doubt that it makes other people happier, and that the world in general is immensely a gainer by it. Utilitarianism, therefore, could only attain its end by the general cultivation of nobleness of character, even if each individual were only benefited by the nobleness of others, and his own, so far as happiness is concerned, were a sheer deduction from the benefit. But the bare enunciation of such an absurdity as this last, renders refutation superfluous.

According to the Greatest Happiness Principle, as above explained, the ultimate end, with reference to and for the sake of which all other things are desirable (whether we are considering our own good or that of other people), is an existence exempt as far as possible from pain, and as rich as possible in enjoyments, both in point of quantity and quality; the test of quality, and the rule for measuring it against quantity, being the preference felt by those who in their opportunities of experience, to which must be added their habits of self-consciousness and self-observation, are best furnished with the means of comparison. This, being, according to the utilitarian opinion, the end of human action, is necessarily also the standard of morality; which may accordingly be defined, the rules and precepts for human conduct, by the observance of which an existence such as has been described might be, to the greatest extent possible, secured to all mankind; and not to them only, but, so far as the nature of things admits, to the whole sentient creation. . . .

The objectors to utilitarianism cannot always be charged with representing it in a discreditable light. On the contrary, those among them who entertain anything like a just idea of its disinterested character, sometimes find fault with its standard as being too high for humanity. They say it is exacting too much to require that people shall always act from the inducement of promoting the general interests of society. But this is to mistake the very meaning of a standard of morals, and confound the rule of action with the motive of it. It is the business of ethics to tell us what are our duties, or by what test we may know them; but no system of ethics requires that the sole motive of all we do shall be a feeling of duty; on the contrary, ninety-nine hundredths of all our actions are done from other motives, and rightly so done, if the rule of duty does not condemn them. It is the more unjust to utilitarianism that this particular misapprehension should be made a ground of objection to it, inasmuch as utilitarian moralists have gone beyond almost all others in affirming that the motive has nothing to do with the morality of the action, though much with the worth of the agent. He who saves a fellow-creature from drowning does what is morally right, whether his motive be duty, or the hope of being paid for his trouble; he who betrays the friend that trusts him, is guilty of a crime, even if his object be to serve another friend to whom he is under greater obligation. But to speak only of actions done from the motive of duty, and in direct obedience to principle: it is a misapprehension of the utilitarian mode of thought, to conceive it as implying that people should fix their minds upon so wide a generality as the world, or society at large. The great majority of good actions are intended not for the benefit of the world, but for that of individuals, of which the good of the world is made up; and the thoughts of the most virtuous man need not on these occasions travel beyond the particular persons concerned, except so far as is necessary to assure himself that in benefiting them he is not violating the rights, that is, the legitimate and authorised expectations, of any one else. The multiplication of happiness is, according to the utilitarian ethics, the object of virtue: the occasions on which any person (except one in a thousand) has it in his power to do this on an extended scale, in other words to be a public benefactor, are but exceptional; and on these occasions alone is he called on to consider public utility; in every other case, private utility, the interest or happiness of some few persons, is all he has to attend to. Those alone the influence of whose actions extends to society in general, need concern themselves habitually about so large an object. In the case of abstinences indeed—of things which people forbear to do from moral considerations, though the consequences in the particular case might be beneficial—it would be unworthy of an intelligent agent not to be consciously aware that the action is of a class which, if practised generally, would be generally injurious, and that this is the ground of the obligation to abstain from it. The amount of regard for the public interest implied in this recognition, is no greater than is demanded by every system of morals, for they all enjoin to abstain from whatever is manifestly pernicious to society. . . .

CHAPTER IV   OF WHAT SORT OF PROOF THE PRINCIPLE OF UTILITY IS SUSCEPTIBLE

It has already been remarked, that questions of ultimate ends do not admit of proof, in the ordinary acceptation of the term. To be incapable of proof by reasoning is common to all first principles; to the first premises of our knowledge, as well as to those of our conduct. But the former, being matters of fact, may be the subject of a direct appeal to the faculties which judge of fact—namely, our senses, and our internal consciousness. Can an appeal be made to the same faculties on questions of practical ends? Or by what other faculty is cognisance taken of them?

Questions about ends are, in other words, questions what things are desirable. The utilitarian doctrine is, that happiness is desirable, and the only thing desirable, as an end; all other things being only desirable as means to that end. What ought to be required of this doctrine—what conditions is it requisite that the doctrine should fulfil—to make good its claim to be believed?

The only proof capable of being given that an object is visible, is that people actually see it. The only proof that a sound is audible, is that people hear it: and so of the other sources of our experience. In like manner, I apprehend, the sole evidence it is possible to produce that anything is desirable, is that people do actually desire it. If the end which the utilitarian doctrine proposes to itself were not, in theory and in practice, acknowledged to be an end, nothing could ever convince any person that it was so. No reason can be given why the general happiness is desirable, except that each person, so far as he believes it to be attainable, desires his own happiness. This, however, being a fact, we have not only all the proof which the case admits of, but all which it is possible to require, that happiness is a good: that each person's happiness is a good to that person, and the general happiness, therefore, a good to the aggregate of all persons. Happiness has made out its title as *one* of the ends of conduct, and consequently one of the criteria of morality.

But it has not, by this alone, proved itself to be the sole criterion. To do that, it would seem, by the same rule, necessary to show, not only that people desire happiness, but that they never desire anything else. . . .

We have now, then, an answer to the question, of what sort of proof the principle of utility is susceptible. If the opinion which I have now stated is psychologically true—if human nature is so constituted as to desire nothing which is not either a part of happiness or a means of happiness, we can have no other proof, and we require no other, that these are the only things desirable. If so, happiness is the sole end of human action, and the promotion of it the test by which to judge of all human conduct; from whence it necessarily follows that it must be the criterion of morality, since a part is included in the whole.

And now to decide whether this is really so; whether mankind do desire nothing for itself but that which is a pleasure to them, or of which the absence is a pain; we have evidently arrived at a question of fact and experience, dependent, like all similar questions, upon evidence. It can only be determined by practised self-consciousness and self-observation, assisted by observation of others. I believe that these sources of evidence, impartially consulted, will declare that desiring a thing and finding it pleasant, aversion to it and thinking of it as painful, are phenomena entirely inseparable, or rather two parts of the same phenomenon; in strictness of language, two different modes of naming the same psychological fact: that to think of an object as desirable (unless for the sake of its consequences), and to think of it as pleasant, are one and the same thing; and that to desire anything, except in proportion as the idea of it is pleasant, is a physical and metaphysical impossibility.

J. J. C. SMART
EXTREME AND RESTRICTED UTILITARIANISM[1]

I

Utilitarianism is the doctrine that the rightness of actions is to be judged by their consequences. What do we mean by 'actions' here? Do we mean particular actions or do we mean classes of actions? According to which way we interpret the word 'actions' we get two different theories, both of which merit the appellation 'utilitarian'.

(1) If by 'actions' we mean particular individual actions we get the sort of doctrine held by Bentham, Sidgwick, and Moore. According to this doctrine we test individual actions by their consequences, and general rules, like 'keep promises', are mere rules of thumb which we use only to avoid

From J. J. C. Smart, *The Philosophical Quarterly*, 6 (1956): 344–54, with revisions. Reprinted by permission of the author and *The Philosophical Quarterly*. Since publication of this article, Professor Smart has preferred to follow Brandt's terminology of "act" and "rule utilitarianism" instead of "extreme" and "restricted utilitarianism."

the necessity of estimating the probable consequences of our actions at every step. The rightness or wrongness of keeping a promise on a particular occasion depends only on the goodness or badness of the consequences of keeping or of breaking the promise on that particular occasion. Of course part of the consequences of breaking the promise, and a part to which we will normally ascribe decisive importance, will be the weakening of faith in the institution of promising. However, if the goodness of the consequences of breaking the rule is *in toto* greater than the goodness of the consequences of keeping it, then we must break the rule, irrespective of whether the goodness of the consequences of *everybody's* obeying the rule is or is not greater than the consequences of *everybody's* breaking it. To put it shortly, rules do not matter, save *per accidens* as rules of thumb and as *de facto* social institutions with which the utilitarian has to reckon when estimating consequences. I shall call this doctrine 'extreme utilitarianism'.

(2) A more modest form of utilitarianism has recently become fashionable. . . . Part of its charm is that it appears to resolve the dispute in moral philosophy between intuitionists and utilitarians in a way which is very neat. The[se] . . . philosophers hold, or seem to hold, that moral rules are more than rules of thumb. In general the rightness of an action is *not* to be tested by evaluating its consequences but only by considering whether or not it falls under a certain rule. Whether the rule is to be considered an acceptable moral rule, is, however, to be decided by considering the consequences of adopting the rule. Broadly, then, actions are to be tested by rules and rules by consequences. The only cases in which we must test an individual action directly by its consequences are (*a*) when the action comes under two different rules, one of which enjoins it and one of which forbids it, and (*b*) when there is no rule whatever that governs the given case. I shall call this doctrine 'restricted utilitarianism'. . . .

The issue between extreme and restricted utilitarianism can be illustrated by considering the remark 'But suppose everyone did the same'. (Cf. A. K. Stout's article in *The Australasian Journal of Philosophy*, Vol. 32, pp. 1–29.) Stout distinguishes two forms of the universalisation principle, the causal form and the hypothetical form. To say that you ought not to do an action A because it would have bad results if everyone (or many people) did action A may be merely to point out that while the action A would otherwise be the optimific one, nevertheless when you take into account that doing A will probably cause other people to do A too, you can see that A is not, on a broad view, really optimific. If this causal influence could be avoided (as may happen in the case of a secret desert island promise) then we would disregard the universalisation principle. This is the causal form of the principle. A person who accepted the universalisation principle in its hypothetical form would be one who was concerned only with what would happen *if* everyone did the action A: he would be totally unconcerned with the question of whether in fact everyone would do the action A. That is, he might say that it would be wrong not to vote because it would have bad results if everyone took this attitude, and he would be totally unmoved by arguments purporting to show that my refusing to vote has no effect whatever on other people's propensity to vote. Making use of Stout's distinction, we can say that an extreme utilitarian would apply the universalisation principle in the causal form, while a restricted utilitarian would apply it in the hypothetical form.

How are we to decide the issue between extreme and restricted utilitarianism? I wish to repudiate at the outset that milk and water approach which describes itself sometimes as 'investigating what is implicit in the common moral consciousness' and sometimes as 'investigating how people ordinarily talk about morality'. We have only to read the newspaper correspondence about capital punishment or about what should be done with Formosa to realise that the common moral consciousness is in part made up of superstitious elements, of morally bad elements, and of logically confused elements. I address myself to good hearted and benevolent people and so I hope that if we rid ourselves of the logical confusion the superstitious and morally bad elements will largely fall away. For even among good hearted and benevolent people it is possible to find superstitious and morally bad reasons for moral beliefs. These superstitious and morally bad reasons hide behind the protective screen of logical confusion. With people who are not logically confused but who are openly superstitious or morally bad I can of course do nothing. That is, our ultimate pro attitudes may be different. Nevertheless I propose to rely on *my own* moral consciousness and to appeal to *your* moral consciousness and to forget about what people ordinarily say. 'The obligation to obey a rule', says Nowell-Smith (*Ethics*, p. 239), 'does not, *in the opinion of ordinary men*', (my italics), 'rest on the beneficial consequences of obeying it in a particular case'. What does this prove? Surely it is more than likely that ordinary men are confused here. Philosophers should be able to examine the question more rationally.

II

For an extreme utilitarian moral rules are rules of thumb. In practice the extreme utilitarian will mostly guide his conduct by appealing to the rules ('do not lie', 'do not break promises', etc.) of common sense morality. This is not because there is anything sacrosanct in the rules themselves but because he can argue that probably he will most often act in an extreme utilitarian way if he does not think as a utilitarian. For one thing, actions have frequently to be done in a hurry. Imagine a man seeing a person drowning. He jumps in and rescues him. There is no time to reason the matter out, but usually this will be the course of action which an extreme utilitarian would recommend if he did reason the matter out. If, however, the man drowning had been drowning in a river near Berchtesgaden in 1938, and if he had had the well known black forelock and moustache of Adolf Hitler, an extreme utilitarian would, if he had time, work out the probability of the man's being the villainous dictator, and if the probability were high enough he would, on extreme utilitarian grounds, leave him to drown. The rescuer, however, has not time. He trusts to his instincts and dives in and rescues the man. And this trusting to instincts and to moral rules can be justified on extreme utilitarian grounds. Furthermore, an extreme utilitarian who knew that the drowning man was Hitler would nevertheless praise the rescuer, not condemn him. For by praising the man he is strengthening a courageous and benevolent disposition of mind, and in general this disposition has great positive utility. (Next time, perhaps it will be Winston Churchill that the man saves!) We must never forget that an extreme utilitarian may praise actions which he knows to be wrong. Saving Hitler was wrong, but it was a member of a class of actions which are generally right, and the motive to do actions of this class is in general an optimific one. In considering questions of praise and blame it is not the expediency of the praised or blamed action that is at issue, but the expediency of the praise. It can be expedient to praise an inexpedient action and inexpedient to praise an expedient one.

Lack of time is not the only reason why an extreme utilitarian may, on extreme utilitarian principles, trust to rules of common sense morality. He knows that in particular cases where his own interests are involved his calculations are likely to be biased in his own favour. Suppose that he is unhappily married and is deciding whether to get divorced. He will in all probability greatly exaggerate his own unhappiness (and possibly his wife's) and greatly underestimate the harm done to his children by the break up of the family. He will probably also underestimate the likely harm done by the weakening of the general faith in marriage vows. So probably he will come to the correct extreme utilitarian conclusion if he does not in this instance think as an extreme utilitarian but trusts to common sense morality.

There are many more and subtle points that could be made in connection with the relation between extreme utilitarianism and the morality of common sense. All those that I have just made and many more will be found in Book IV Chapters 3–5 of Sidgwick's *Methods of Ethics*. I think that this book is the best book ever written on ethics, and that these chapters are the best chapters of the book. As they occur so near the end of a very long book they are unduly neglected. I refer the reader, then, to Sidgwick for the classical exposition of the relation between (extreme) utilitarianism and the morality of common sense. One further point raised by Sidgwick in this connection is whether an (extreme) utilitarian ought on (extreme) utilitarian principles to propagate (extreme) utilitarianism among the public. As most people are not very philosophical and not good at empirical calculations, it is probable that they will most often act in an extreme utilitarian way if they do not try to think as extreme utilitarians. We have seen how easy it would be to misapply the extreme utilitarian criterion in the case of divorce. Sidgwick seems to think it quite probable that an extreme utilitarian should not propagate his doctrine too widely. However, the great danger to humanity comes nowadays on the plane of public morality—not private morality. There is a greater danger to humanity from the hydrogen bomb than from an increase of the divorce rate, regrettable though that might be, and there seems no doubt that extreme utilitarianism makes for good sense in international relations. . . . I myself have no hesitation in saying that on extreme utilitarian principles we ought to propagate extreme utilitarianism as widely as possible. But Sidgwick had respectable reasons for suspecting the opposite.

The extreme utilitarian, then, regards moral rules as rules of thumb and as sociological facts that have to be taken into account when deciding what to do, just as facts of any other sort have to be taken into account. But in themselves they do not justify any action.

III

The restricted utilitarian regards moral rules as more than rules of thumb for short-circuiting calculations of consequences. Generally, he argues, consequences are not relevant at all when we are deciding what to do in a particular case. In general, they are relevant only to deciding what rules are good reasons for acting in a certain way in particular cases. This doctrine is possibly a good account of how the modern unreflective twentieth century Englishman often thinks about morality, but surely it is monstrous as an account of how it is most rational to think about morality. Suppose that there is a rule R and that in 99% of cases the best possible results are obtained by acting in accordance with R. Then clearly R is a useful rule of thumb; if we have not time or are not impartial enough to assess the consequences of an action it is an extremely good bet that the thing to do is to act in accordance with R. But is it not monstrous to suppose that if we *have* worked out the consequences and if we have perfect faith in the impartiality of our calculations, and if we *know* that in this instance to break R will have better results than to keep it, we should nevertheless obey the rule? Is it not to erect R into a sort of idol if we keep it when breaking it will prevent, say, some avoidable misery? Is not this a form of superstitious rule-worship (easily explicable psychologically) and not the rational thought of a philosopher? . . .

Let us consider a much discussed sort of case in which the extreme utilitarian might go against the conventional moral rule. I have promised to a friend, dying on a desert island from which I am subsequently rescued, that I will see that his fortune (over which I have control) is given to a jockey club. However, when I am rescued I decide that it would be better to give the money to a hospital, which can do more good with it. It may be argued that I am wrong to give the money to the hospital. But why? (*a*) The hospital can do more good with the money than the jockey club can. (*b*) The present case is unlike most cases of promising in that no one except me knows about the promise. In breaking the promise I am doing so with complete secrecy and am doing nothing to weaken the general faith in promises. That is, a factor, which would normally keep the extreme utilitarian from promise breaking even in otherwise unoptimific cases, does not at present operate. (*c*) There is no doubt a slight weakening in my own character as an habitual promise keeper, and moreover psychological tensions will be set up in me every time I am asked what the man made me promise him to do. For clearly I shall have to say that he made me promise to give the money to the hospital, and, since I am an habitual truth teller, this will go very much against the grain with me. Indeed I am pretty sure that in practice I myself would keep the promise. But we are not discussing what my moral habits would probably make me do; we are discussing what I ought to do. Moreover, we must not forget that even if it would be most rational of me to give the money to the hospital it would also be most rational of you to punish or condemn me if you did, most improbably, find out the truth (e.g., by finding a note washed ashore in a bottle). Furthermore, I would agree that though it was most rational of me to give the money to the hospital it would be most rational of you to condemn me for it. We revert again to Sidgwick's distinction between the utility of the action and the utility of the praise of it.

Many such issues are discussed by A. K. Stout in the article to which I have already referred. I do not wish to go over the same ground again, especially as I think that Stout's arguments support my own point of view. It will be useful, however, to consider one other example that he gives. Suppose that during hot weather there is an edict that no water must be used for watering gardens. I have a garden and I reason that most people are sure to obey the edict, and that as the amount of water that I use will be by itself negligible no harm will be done if I use the water secretly. So I do use the water, thus producing some lovely flowers which give happiness to various people. Still, you may say, though the action was perhaps optimific, it was unfair and wrong.

There are several matters to consider. Certainly my action should be condemned. We revert once more to Sidgwick's distinction. A right action may be rationally condemned. Furthermore, this sort of offence is normally found out. If I have a wonderful garden when everybody else's is dry and brown there is only one explanation. So if I water my garden I am weakening my respect for law and order, and as this leads to bad results an extreme utilitarian would agree that I was wrong to water the garden. Suppose now that the case is altered and that I can keep the thing secret: there is a secluded part of the garden where I grow flowers which I give away anonymously to a home for old ladies. Are you still so sure that I did the wrong thing by watering my garden? However, this is still a weaker case than that of the hospital and the jockey club. There will be tensions set up within myself: my secret knowledge that I have broken the rule will make it hard for me to exhort others to keep the rule. These psychological ill effects in myself may be not inconsiderable: directly and indirectly they may lead to harm which is at least of the same order as the happiness that the old ladies get from the flowers. You can see that on an extreme utilitarian view there are two sides to the question.

So far I have been considering the duty of an extreme utilitarian in a predominantly non-utilitarian society. The case is altered if we consider the extreme utilitarian who lives in a society every member, or most members, of which can be expected to reason as he does. Should he water his flowers now? (Granting, what is doubtful, that in the case already considered he would have been right to water his flowers.) Clearly not. A simple argument, employing the game-theoretical concept of a mixed strategy, suggests that each extreme utilitarian should give himself a very small probability (say by tossing dice) of watering his garden. Suppose that there are m potential garden waterers and that $f(n)$ is the damage done by exactly n people watering their gardens. Now if each of them gives himself a probability p of watering his garden it is easy to calculate, in terms of p, the probabilities $p_1, p_2, \ldots p_m$ of 1, 2, $\ldots$ m persons respectively watering their gardens. Let a be the benefit to each gardener of watering his garden. Then if V is the total probable benefit to the community of gardeners we have

$$V = p_1 \left(a - f(1) \right) + p_2 \left(2a - f(2) \right) + \ldots p_m \left(ma - f(m) \right)$$

Assuming that numerical values can be given to a and to values of the function $f(n)$ we calculate the value of p for which $\dfrac{dV}{dp} = 0$. This gives the value of p which maximises the total probable benefit. In practical cases of course numerical values of $f(n)$ and a cannot be determined, but a good approximation can usually be got by taking p as equal to zero. However the mathematical analysis is of theoretical interest for the discussion of utilitarianism. Too many writers mistakenly suppose that the only two relevant alternatives are that no one does something and that everyone does it.

I now pass on to a type of case which may be thought to be the trump card of restricted utilitarianism. Consider the rule of the road. It may be said that since all that matters is that everyone should do the same it is indifferent which rule we have, 'go on the left hand side' or 'go on the right hand side'. Hence the only *reason* for going on the left hand side in British countries is that this is the rule. Here the rule does seem to be a reason, in itself, for acting in a certain way. I wish to argue against this. The rule in itself is not a reason for our actions. We would be perfectly justified in going on the right hand side if (*a*) we knew that the rule was to go on the left hand side, and (*b*) we were in a country peopled by super-anarchists who always on principle did the opposite of what they were told. This shows that the rule does not give us a reason for acting so much as an indication of the probable actions of others, which helps us to find out what would be our own most rational course of action. If we are in a country not peopled by anarchists, but by non-anarchist extreme utilitarians, we expect, other things being equal, that they will keep rules laid down for them. Knowledge of the rule enables us to predict their behavior and to harmonise our own actions with theirs. The rule 'keep to the left hand side', then, is not a logical *reason* for action but an anthropological *datum* for planning actions.

I conclude that in every case if there is a rule R the keeping of which is in general optimific, but such that in a special sort of circumstance the optimific behaviour is to break R, then in these circumstances we should break R. Of course we must consider all the less obvious effects of breaking R, such as reducing people's faith in the moral order, before coming to the conclusion that to break R is right: in fact we shall rarely come to such a conclusion. Moral rules, on the extreme utilitarian view, are rules of thumb only, but they are not bad rules of thumb. But if we *do* come to the conclusion that we should break the rule and if we have weighed in the balance our own fallibility and liability to personal bias, what good reason remains for keeping the rule? I can understand 'it is optimific' as a reason for action, but why should 'it is a member of a class of actions which are usually optimific' or 'it is a member of a class of actions which as a class are more optimific than any alternative general class' be a good reason? You might as well say that a person ought to be picked to play for Australia just because all his brothers have been, or that the Australian team should be composed entirely of the Harvey family because this would be better than composing it entirely of any other family. The extreme utilitarian does not appeal to artificial feelings, but only to our feelings of benevolence, and what better feelings can there be to appeal to? Admittedly we can have a pro-attitude to anything, even to rules, but such artificially begotten pro-attitudes smack of superstition. Let us get down to realities, human happiness and misery, and make these the objects of our pro-attitudes and anti-attitudes.

Notes

[1] Based on a paper read to the Victorian Branch of the Australasian Association of Psychology and Philosophy, October, 1955.

R. B. BRANDT

SOME MERITS OF ONE FORM OF RULE-UTILITARIANISM

. . . [I]t may be helpful to offer some "supporting remarks" which will explain some reasons why some philosophers are favorably disposed toward a utilitarian type of normative theory.

(a) The utilitarian principle provides a clear and definite procedure for determining which acts are right or wrong (praiseworthy or blameworthy),

Reprinted from *University of Colorado Studies, Series in Philosophy*, No. 3, January 1967, pp. 41–43, 48–55. Copyright © 1967 Colorado Associated University Press.

by observation and the methods of science alone and without the use of any supplementary intuitions (assuming that empirical procedures can determine when something maximizes utility), for all cases, including the complex ones about which intuitions are apt to be mute, such as whether kleptomanic behavior is blameworthy or whether it is right to break a confidence in certain circumstances. The utilitarian presumably frames his thesis so as to conform with enlightened intuitions which are clear, but his thesis, being general, has implications for all cases, including those about which his intuitions are not clear. The utilitarian principle is like a general scientific theory, which checks with observations at many points, but can also be used as a guide to beliefs on matters inaccessible to observation (like the behavior of matter at absolute zero temperature).

Utilitarianism is not the only normative theory with this desirable property; egoism is another, and, with some qualifications, so is Kant's theory.

(b) Any reasonably plausible normative theory will give a large place to consequences for welfare in the moral assessment of actions, for this consideration enters continuously and substantially into ordinary moral thinking. Theories which ostensibly make no appeal of this sort either admit utilitarian considerations by the back door, or have counterintuitive consequences. Therefore the ideal of simplicity leads us to hope for the possibility of a pure utilitarian theory. Moreover, utilitarianism avoids the necessity of weighing disparate things such as justice and utility.

(c) If a proposed course of action does not raise moral questions, it is generally regarded as rational, and its agent well-advised to perform it, if and only if it will maximize expectable utility for the agent. In a similar vein, it can be argued that society's "choice" of an institution of morality is rational and well-advised, if and only if having it will maximize expectable social utility—raise the expectable level of the average "utility curve" of the population. If morality is a system of traditional and arbitrary constraints on behavior, it cannot be viewed as a rational institution. But it can be, if the system of morality is utilitarian. In that case the institution of morality can be recommended to a person of broad human sympathies, as an institution which maximizes the expectation of general welfare; and to a selfish person, as an institution which, in the absence of particular evidence about his own case, may be expected to maximize his own expectation of welfare (his own welfare being viewed as a random sample from the population). To put it in other words, a utilitarian morality can be "vindicated" by appeal either to the humanity or to the selfishness of human beings.

To say this is not to deny that non-utilitarian moral principles may be capable of vindication in a rather similar way. For instance, to depict morality as an institution which fosters human equality is to recommend it by appeal to something which is perhaps as deep in man as his sympathy or humanity.

4. The type of utilitarianism on which I wish to focus is a form of rule-utilitarianism, as contrasted with act-utilitarianism. According to the latter

type of theory (espoused by Sidgwick and Moore), an act is objectively right if no other act the agent could perform would produce better consequences. (On this view, an act is blameworthy if and only if it is right to perform the act of blaming or condemning it; the principles of blameworthiness are a special case of the principle of objectively right actions.) Act-utilitarianism is hence a rather atomistic theory: the rightness of a single act is fixed by its effects on the world. Rule-utilitarianism, in contrast, is the view that the rightness of an act is fixed, not by its relative utility, but by the utility of having a relevant moral rule, or of most or all members of a certain class of acts being performed.

The implications of act-utilitarianism are seriously counterintuitive, and I shall ignore it except to consider whether some ostensibly different theories really are different.

5. Rule-utilitarianism may be divided into two main groups, according as the rightness of a particular act is made a function of ideal rules in some sense, or of the actual and recognized rules of a society. The variety of theory I shall explain more fully is of the former type. . . .

For convenience I shall refer to the theory as the "ideal moral code" theory. The essence of it is as follows. Let us first say that a moral code is "ideal" if its currency in a particular society would produce at least as much good per person (the total divided by the number of persons) as the currency of any other moral code. (Two different codes might meet this condition, but, in order to avoid complicated formulations, the following discussion will ignore this possibility.) Given this stipulation for the meaning of "ideal," the Ideal Moral Code theory consists in the assertion of the following thesis: *An act is right if and only if it would not be prohibited by the moral code ideal for the society; and an agent is morally blameworthy (praiseworthy) for an act if, and to the degree that, the moral code ideal in that society would condemn (praise) him for it.* It is a virtue of this theory that it is a theory both about objective rightness and about moral blameworthiness (praiseworthiness) of actions, but the assertion about blameworthiness will be virtually ignored in what follows.

8. In order to have a clear proposal before us, however, the foregoing summary statement must be filled out in three ways: (1) by explaining what it is for a moral code to have currency; (2) by making clear what is the difference between the rules of a society's moral code and the rules of its institutions; and (3) by describing how the relative utility of a moral code is to be estimated.

First, then, the notion of a moral code having currency in a society.

For a moral code to have currency in a society, two things must be true. First, a high proportion of the adults in the society must subscribe to the moral principles, or have the moral opinions, constitutive of the code. Exactly how high the proportion should be, we can hardly decide on the basis of the ordinary meaning of "the moral code"; but probably it would not be wrong to require at least ninety percent agreement. Thus, if at least 90 percent of the adults subscribe to principle A and 90 percent to principle *B*, etc., we may say that a code consisting of *A* and *B* (etc.) has currency in the society, provided the second condition is met. Second, we want to say that certain principles *A, B,* etc. belong to the moral code of a society only if they are recognized as such. That is, it must be that a large proportion of the adults of the society would respond correctly if asked, with respect to *A* and *B,* whether most members of the society subscribed to them. (It need not be required that adults base their judgments on such good evidence as recollection of moral discussions; it is enough if for some reason the correct opinion about what is accepted is widespread.) It is of course possible for certain principles to constitute a moral code with currency in a society even if some persons in the society have no moral opinions at all, or if there is disagreement, e.g., if everyone in the society disagrees with every other person with respect to at least one principle.

The more difficult question is what it is for an individual to subscribe to a moral principle or to have a moral opinion. What is it, then, for someone to think sincerely that any action of the kind *F* is wrong? (1) He is to some extent motivated to avoid actions which he thinks are *F*, and often, if asked why he does not perform such an action when it appears to be to his advantage, offers, as one of his reasons, that it is *F*. In addition, the person's motivation to avoid *F*-actions does not derive entirely from his belief that *F*-actions on his part are likely to be harmful to him or to persons to whom he is somehow attached. (2) If he thinks he has just performed an *F*-action, he feels guilty or remorseful or uncomfortable about it, unless he thinks he has some excuse—unless, for instance, he knows that at the time of action he did not think his action would be an *F*-action. "Guilt" (etc.) is not to be understood as implying some special origin such as interiorization of parental prohibitions, or as being a vestige of anxiety about punishment. It is left open that it might be an unlearned emotional response to the thought of being the cause of the suffering of another person. Any feeling which must be viewed simply as anxiety about anticipated consequences, for one's self or person to whom one is attached, is not, however, to count as a "guilt" feeling. (3) If he believes that someone has performed an *F*-action, he will tend to admire him less as a person, unless he thinks that the individual has a good excuse. He thinks that action of this sort, without excuse, reflects on character—this being spelled out, in part, by reference to traits like honesty, respect for the rights of others, and so on. (4) He thinks that these attitudes of his are correct or well justified, in some sense, but with one restriction: it is not enough if he thinks that what justifies them is simply the fact that they are shared by all or most members of his society. This restriction corresponds with our distinction between a moral conviction and something else. For instance, we are inclined to think no moral attitude is involved if an Englishman disapproves of something but says that his disapproval is justified by the fact that it is shared by "well-bred Englishmen." In such cases we are inclined to say that the individual subscribes only to a custom, or to a rule of etiquette or manners. On the other hand, if the individual thinks that what justifies his attitude unfavorable to *F*-actions is that *F*-actions are contrary to the will of God (and the individual's attitude is not merely a prudential one), or inconsistent with the welfare of mankind, or contrary to human nature, we are disposed to say the attitude is a moral attitude and the opinion expressed a moral one. And the same if he thinks his attitude justified, but can give no reason. There are perhaps other restrictions we should make on acceptable justifications (perhaps to distinguish a moral code from a code of honor), and other types of justification we should wish to list as clearly acceptable (perhaps an appeal to human equality).

9. It is important to distinguish between the moral code of a society and its institutions, or the rules of its institutions. It is especially important for the Ideal Moral Code theory, for this theory involves the conception of a moral code ideal for a society in the context of its institutions, so that it is necessary to distinguish the moral code which a society does or might have from its institutions and their rules. The distinction is also one we actually do make in our thinking, although it is blurred in some cases. (For instance, is "Honor thy father and thy mother" a moral rule, or a rule of the family institution, in our society?)

An institution is a set of positions or statuses, with which certain privileges and jobs are associated. (We can speak of these as "rights" and "duties" if we are careful to explain that we do not mean moral rights and duties.) That is, there are certain, usually nameable, positions which consist in the fact that anyone who is assigned to the position is expected to do certain things, and at the same time is expected to have certain things done for him. The individuals occupying these positions are a group of cooperating agents in a system which as a whole is thought to have the aim of serving certain ends. (E.g., a university is thought to serve the ends of education, research, etc.) The rules of the system concern jobs that must be done in order that the goals of the institution be achieved; they allocate the necessary jobs to different positions. Take, for instance, a university. There are various positions in it: the presidency, the professorial ranks, the registrars, librarians, etc. It is understood that one who occupies a certain post has certain duties, say teaching a specified number of classes or spending time working on research in the case of the instructing staff. Obviously the university cannot achieve its ends unless certain persons do the teaching, some tend to the administration, some do certain jobs in the library, and so on. . . .

If an "institution" is defined in this way, it is clear that the moral code of a society cannot itself be construed as an institution, nor its rules as rules of an institution. The moral code is society-wide, so if we were to identify its rules as institutional rules, we should presumably have to say that everyone belongs to this institution. But what is the "purpose" of society as a whole? Are there any distinctions of status, with rights and duties attached, which we could identify as the "positions" in the moral system? Can we say that moral rules consist in the assignment of jobs in such a way that the aims of the institution may be achieved? It is true that there is a certain analogy: society as a whole might be said to be aiming at the good life for all, and the moral rules of the society might be viewed as the rules with which all must conform in order to achieve this end. But the analogy is feeble. Society as a whole is obviously not an organization like a university, an educational system, the church, General Motors, etc.; there is no specific goal in the achievement of which each position has a designated role to play. Our answer to the above questions must be in the negative: morality is not an institution in the explained sense; nor are moral rules institutional expectations or rules.

The moral code of a society may, of course, have implications that bear on institutional rules. For one thing, the moral code may imply that an institutional system is morally wrong and ought to be changed. Moreover, the moral code may imply that a person has also a moral duty to do something which is his institutional job. For instance, it may be a moral rule that a person ought to do whatever he has undertaken to do, or that he ought not to accept the benefits of a position without performing its duties. Take for instance the rules, "A professor should meet his classes" or "Wives ought to make the beds." Since the professor has undertaken to do what pertains to his office, and the same for a wife, and since these tasks are known to pertain to the respective offices, the moral rule that a person is morally bound (with certain qualifications) to do what he has undertaken to do implies, in context, that the professor is morally bound to meet his classes and the wife to make the beds, other things being equal (viz., there being no contrary moral obligations in the situation). But these implications are not themselves part of the moral code. No one would say that a parent had neglected to teach his child the moral code of the society if he had neglected to teach him that professors must meet classes, and that wives must make the beds. A person becomes obligated to do these things only by participating in an institution, by taking on the status of professor or wife. Parents do not teach children to have guilt feelings about missing classes, or making beds. The moral code consists only of more general rules, defining what is to be done in certain types of situations in which practically everyone will find himself. ("Do what you have promised!")

Admittedly some rules can be both moral and institutional: "Take care of your father in his old age" might be both an institutional rule of the family organization and also a part of the moral code of a society. (In this situation, one can still raise the question whether this moral rule is optimific in a society with that institutional rule; the answer could be negative.) . . .

10. It has been proposed above that an action is right if and only if it would not be prohibited by the moral code ideal for the society in which it occurs, where a moral code is taken to be "ideal" if and only if its currency would produce at least as much good per person as the currency of any other moral code.[1] We must now give more attention to the conception of an ideal moral code, and how it may be decided when a given moral code

will produce as much good per person as any other. We may, however, reasonably bypass the familiar problems of judgments of comparative utilities, especially when different persons are involved, since these problems are faced by all moral theories that have any plausibility. We shall simply assume that rough judgments of this sort are made and can be justified.

(a) We should first notice that, as "currency" has been explained above, a moral code could not be current in a society if it were too complex to be learned or applied. We may therefore confine our consideration to codes simple enough to be absorbed by human beings, roughly in the way in which people learn actual moral codes.

(b) We have already distinguished the concept of an institution and its rules from the concept of a moral rule, or a rule of the moral code. (We have, however, pointed out that in some cases a moral rule may prescribe the same thing that is also an institutional expectation. But this is not a necessary situation, and a moral code could condemn an institutional expectation.) Therefore, in deciding how much good the currency of a specific moral system would do, we consider the institutional setting as it is, as part of the situation. We are asking which moral code would produce the most good in the long run in this setting. One good to be reckoned, of course, might be that the currency of a given moral code would tend to change the institutional system.

(c) In deciding which moral code will produce the most per person good, we must take into account the probability that certain types of situation will arise in the society. For instance, we must take for granted that people will make promises and subsequently want to break them, that people will sometimes assault other persons in order to achieve their own ends, that people will be in distress and need the assistance of others, and so on. We may not suppose that, because an ideal moral code might have certain features, it need not have other features because they will not be required; for instance, we may not suppose, on the ground that an ideal moral system would forbid everyone to purchase a gun, that such a moral system needs no provisions about the possession and use of guns—just as our present moral and legal codes have provisions about self-defense, which would be unnecessary if everyone obeyed the provision never to assault anyone.

It is true that the currency of a moral code with certain provisions might bring about a reduction in certain types of situation, e.g., the number of assaults or cases of dishonesty. And the reduction might be substantial, if the moral code were current which prohibited these offenses very strongly. (We must remember that an ideal moral code might differ from the actual one not only in what it prohibits or enjoins, but also in how strongly it prohibits or enjoins.) But it is consistent to suppose that a moral code prohibits a certain form of behavior very severely, and yet that the behavior will occur, since the "currency" of a moral code requires only 90 percent subscription to it, and a "strong" subscription, on the average, permits a great range from person to person. In any case there must be doubt whether the best moral code will prohibit many things very severely, since there are serious human costs in severe prohibitions: the burden of guilt feelings, the traumas caused by the severe criticism by others which is a part of having a strong injunction in a code, the risks of any training process which would succeed in interiorizing a severe prohibition, and so on.

(d) It would be a great oversimplification if, in assessing the comparative utility of various codes, we confined ourselves merely to counting the benefits of people doing (refraining from doing) certain things, as a result of subscribing to a certain code. To consider only this would be as absurd as estimating the utility of some feature of a legal system by attending only to the utility of people behaving in the way the law aims to make them behave—and overlooking the fact that the law only reduces and does not eliminate misbehavior, as well as the disutility of punishment to the convicted, and the cost of the administration of criminal law. In the case of morals, we must weigh the benefit of the improvement in behavior as a result of the restriction built into conscience, against the cost of the restriction—the burden of guilt feelings, the effects of the training process, etc. There is a further necessary refinement. In both law and morals we must adjust our estimates of utility by taking into account the envisaged system of excuses. That *mens rea* is required as a condition of guilt in the case of most legal offenses is most important; and it is highly important for the utility of a moral system whether accident, intent, and motives are taken into account in deciding a person's liability to moral criticism. A description of a moral code is incomplete until we have specified the severity of condemnation (by conscience or the criticism of others) to be attached to various actions, along with the excuses to be allowed as exculpating or mitigating.

Notes

[1] Some utilitarians have suggested that the right act is determined by the total net intrinsic good produced. This view can have embarrassing consequences for problems of population control. The view here advocated is that the right act is determined by the per person, average, net intrinsic good produced.

part II

APPLICATIONS

*A*bortion

INTRODUCTION

Is it morally permissible to obtain an abortion? Is abortion ever a violation of the moral rights of the fetus? Should abortion be legally prohibited? Is the choice of obtaining an abortion ever the expression of a morally blameworthy trait of character (for instance, selfishness)? These are only some of the many distinct normative questions concerning abortion. An argument advanced in answer to one question may also have implications for the answer to another, but these implications are seldom as obvious as might at first appear. This chapter will concentrate on the first two questions and the relationship between them. But the third question deserves some attention initially, if only to clarify the boundaries of the dispute.

The Legal Question   The current public debate concerning abortion is largely the result of recent changes in the law. In *Roe* v. *Wade* the Supreme Court of the United States ruled that the right of privacy includes a right to terminate pregnancy; this right, however, is not absolute; after the first three months of pregnancy, states may regulate abortion to safeguard the health of the pregnant woman and to maintain medical standards, and, during the final three months of pregnancy, states may protect fetal life, though not at the expense of the life or health of the mother.[1] Legal abortions are obtainable in many other nations. In Canada, for example, abortions are legal to preserve the physical or mental health of the pregnant woman. The argument that there is a constitutionally protected right to terminate pregnancy is found only in the United States. Legal, safe abortions are now commonplace. In the United States, several constitutional amendments have been proposed in order either to allow the states to prohibit abortion by statute, or, more directly, to give constitutional protection to the rights of human fetuses. Many are now asking whether there should be a return to prohibition of abortion in the criminal law.

Many of those seeking criminalization of abortion base their demand for the illegality of abortion on the claim that abortion is morally wrong. In its strongest form, the view states that, morally, abortion is the killing

119

of the innocent and thus the moral equivalent of murder. Weaker versions claim only that abortion violates the moral rights of the fetus and that the criminal law should give legal protection to those moral rights. Assuming for the moment that under some conditions abortion is a violation of the moral rights of the fetus, does it follow that abortion should be illegal under those conditions?

Even the natural-law theorists restrict the legitimate scope of law to a class of wrongs less extensive than the whole class of moral wrongs. Saint Thomas Aquinas, for instance, holds that "human laws do not forbid all vices . . . but only the more grievous vices . . . , and chiefly those that are injurious to others, without the prohibition of which human society could not be maintained."[2] But, argue some of the proponents of criminalization, abortion is the killing of an innocent human being (or, at least, a serious violation of the moral rights of the fetus), and this is a clear-cut case of the *kind* of wrong that should also be illegal. The law exists, it is argued, to protect individuals against infringements of their basic rights. Baruch Brody, for instance, has argued that it is not consistent to hold that abortion is the moral equivalent of murder while opposing recriminalization.[3]

If abortion is understood as a serious violation of the moral rights of the fetus, then it may be said to be a crime with a "victim," as opposed to such victimless crimes as homosexual acts between consenting adults. When victimless moral wrongs are at issue, there is a strong argument that the moral views of some should not be forced upon all through the coercion of the law. But whether the fetus can properly be considered a victim is debatable and is an important part of the moral dispute. It is this peculiarity that makes the legal question about abortion so difficult to extricate from the moral questions surrounding it.

The Supreme Court attempted to extricate itself from the moral controversy by denying that the judiciary could resolve the issue of when human life begins if physicians, theologians, and philosophers were unable to reach a consensus. The Court then turned to legal precedent, arguing that the law has never recognized the unborn as persons in the whole sense. Daniel Callahan has argued that the Court first announced its unwillingness to intervene where there was no consensus, and then, in fact, decided the matter by denying fetuses full legal personhood.[4]

But perhaps there is some sense in the Supreme Court's apparent inconsistency. It can be argued that, however unclearly, the Court did keep separate the questions of the moral status and the legal status of the unborn. The Court may be interpreted as claiming that the judiciary may not set aside the precedents of the law in order to take sides in a moral or theological dispute. Although *Roe* v. *Wade* broke new legal ground, it did not deviate from settled law in holding that the unborn are not legal persons in the whole sense. Indeed, statutes prohibiting abortion would not have existed if the unborn had been protected, as full legal persons, by the laws against homicide. The novelty of *Roe* v. *Wade* is its extension of the right of privacy to the choice to obtain an abortion, an extension that could not have been made if the law recognized the unborn as full legal persons.

A comparable argument could be made that since there is moral disagreement about the status of the unborn, there should not be a constitutional amendment making the unborn full legal persons. It can be claimed that in a pluralistic, democratic society, the Constitution itself must not become partisan concerning disputed moral and religious issues. But this argument has less force than the Court's, since it is one function of amendments to the Constitution to change basic law. Even such changes, however, can be judged by standards of consistency with the most fundamental principles embedded in the Constitution.

And so it may be possible to hold simultaneously that abortion is a serious violation of the moral rights of the fetus and yet not seek recriminalization of abortion within a pluralistic, democratic society. However, the contrary view has not been clearly refuted. It remains possible to argue with Brody that pluralism is no argument for allowing the moral equivalent of murder.

Is abortion the killing of an innocent human being? Is it a violation of the moral rights of the fetus? These questions could be definitively answered *only* if the fundamental dispute between competing ethical theories were resolved—something that has yet to be done.

Natural Law According to natural-law theory, it is always wrong to kill the innocent intentionally. Each human life is incommensurably valuable, and so it is always wrong to act on the intention to kill an innocent human being, either as a means to a further end or as an end in itself.

But is a fetus an innocent human being in the relevant sense? It is clear that in the natural-law view the unborn are included in the moral category of human beings from the moment of conception. To be human in the morally relevant sense is to be a member of a natural kind differentiated by rationality from other natural kinds. From conception, the new organism is an individual member of such a rational species. (Although no other rational species is known, if a rational species other than *Homo sapiens* were discovered, the same view would be taken of them.) The fetus has not yet developed his rationality, but the newborn infant has also not developed his rationality. Nevertheless, from the perspective of natural law both fetus and newborn infant are human beings in the moral sense.

Are the unborn *innocent* in the relevant sense? This is a much more difficult question to answer within the theory of natural law. Certainly most fetuses are innocent, in all senses, but it can be argued that if the woman's life is endangered by continuing the pregnancy, the fetus is not materially innocent. In self-defense, it is permissible to kill not only an aggressor (who is formally culpable) but also someone formally innocent (for instance, an insane person) whose actions *in fact* constitute a mortal threat. If the fetus whose continued growth threatens the life of the mother is morally like such a nonresponsible insane person, then abortions to protect the life of the pregnant woman can be justified even within the terms of natural-law theory.

If this comparison is rejected (as in current official Roman Catholic teaching), then direct abortion will be considered wrong even in order to save the life of the pregnant woman. Only "indirect" abortions will be justifiable—for instance, the removal of a cancerous uterus. In such cases the doctrine of double effect is used to argue that the action causes the death of the innocent fetus only as an unintended side effect. The intention is to save the woman's life by removing her cancerous uterus; it is incidental that there is a fetus there, and the operation would have had to be performed even if the woman had not been pregnant.

Natural-law theory thus prohibits all direct abortion, or, if the fetus is considered materially not innocent when endangering the woman's life, all direct abortion except to save the pregnant woman's life. Within natural-law theory an argument may be made that a fetus conceived as a result of rape is not materially innocent; but since the woman's life is not endangered, the appeal to the rightfulness of self-defense will be more strained than it would be in the case of an actual danger to life.

Natural Rights   It is more difficult to apply the theory of natural rights to abortion. The fundamental natural-rights principle is that one ought to respect the individual rights of others. Since natural law appeals to the precept that each human life is an incommensurable good that may not be destroyed, there is no need for natural-law theorists to settle the question of whether the fetus has rights (though rights are usually ascribed to the fetus from conception, nothing depends upon this ascription).[5] But natural-rights theorists cannot avoid this question.

Much of the debate in the United States about the morality of abortion has centered on the question of whether the fetus has rights (and at what stage of development it has those rights), for the natural-rights approach is central to both legal and moral thought in the United States. If the fetus is not a moral person in the whole sense, just as it is not a legal person in the whole sense, then the pregnant woman's right to obtain an abortion will be vindicated from the viewpoint of natural rights. Even though natural-rights theory *may* recognize some rights of nonpersons (for instance, the right of animals not to be treated cruelly), the individual rights of persons are *always* morally crucial. The woman's right to live her life as she chooses can be limited only by conflicting rights of other persons with the same claim to liberty. If the fetus (at whatever stage) has no such claim or right, then the woman has every right to choose not to carry the fetus full-term.

An even stronger argument for the woman's right to choose has been made by Judith Jarvis Thomson.[6] She has argued that even if the fetus is a person with a right to life, the woman may still, in some circumstances, have the right to choose not to carry it full-term. Thomson compares carrying a fetus to cases of rendering aid (as in the Parable of the Good Samaritan). Within the morality of respect for individual rights, no one has a duty to provide others with aid at any major risk, or even inconvenience, to himself. The right to life is not the right to be provided with what is needed in order to live. The only duties one has to provide for others at serious expense to oneself are duties that result from deliberate assumptions of responsibility; for instance, choosing to rear a child creates such a duty. And so in cases of rape, the woman has no duty to provide the fetus with the use of her womb, even if the fetus is a person with a right to life, for the woman has clearly assumed no such responsibility. And Thomson argues that the woman has no special responsibility for the fetus if she has taken *reasonable* precautions against conception and yet becomes pregnant. Thomson's argument is rooted within the ethical minimalism of the natural-rights tradition. When coupled with her view that the fetus is *not* a person, at least in the early stages of development (and so may be aborted even if the woman is responsible for becoming pregnant), Thomson's natural-rights argument constitutes a forceful defense of the woman's moral right to choose whether to terminate pregnancy.

Kant Is the fetus a person? This question is important both to natural-rights theory and to a Kantian approach. In Kant's view, there are no direct moral duties to nonpersons. (Our duty not to treat animals cruelly is indirect, for it is justified by the tendency of cruelty to animals to lead to mistreatment of persons.) According both to natural-rights theory and to Kant, freedom and rationality are criteria of personhood. The question then is whether the *potential* for rationality is sufficient for personhood, since neither the fetus nor the infant is actively rational. It would be morally incomprehensible to hold an infant (or a fetus) responsible for anything at all. Does this show that from a Kantian viewpoint, the infant and the fetus are not moral persons?

Kant himself would not have drawn this conclusion, for in applying his theory to cases he usually follows traditional views. Within the compass of Christian morality, infanticide is viewed as murder. And so Kant would not consider active rationality essential to personhood. If the infant can be a person without active rationality, then so can the fetus. It is possible then to be a Kantian and to oppose abortion as a failure to respect the humanity of the fetus as an end in itself.[7]

However, a neo-Kantian approach *can* insist on the criterion of active rationality (or some other stringent criterion) and, therefore, judge the fetus a nonperson. The argument is that the respect owed to persons derives from their status as autonomous, rational beings with goals and values of their own. But a fetus cannot be an object of such respect, for it has no autonomy and no goals. Such stringent criteria for personhood will clearly imply that infants also are nonpersons.

Could a natural-rights theorist or a neo-Kantian consider viability, the ability of the fetus to survive outside of the mother's womb, the point at which the fetus becomes a person? From the Kantian point of view, viability is morally irrelevant, for rational faculties of the fetus remain merely potential before and after viability. From the natural-rights viewpoint, however, viability may be seen as morally significant, since at the point of viability the new human being can be protected without requiring the woman to give up her own right to live as she chooses. However, this would argue not against the woman's right to terminate but rather for the protection of the viable fetus if pregnancy is terminated.

Contractarianism The contractarian answer to the moral question of abortion might seem to depend upon whether fetuses are viewed as parties to the contract by which principles of right conduct are determined. Since the contractors are viewed as engaging in rational deliberation, fetuses (and infants) are probably not contractors. However, John Rawls specifies the contractors as "heads of families . . . having a desire to further the welfare of their nearest descendants."[8] Although the parties must themselves be actively rational, they will take into account the welfare of future persons. The neo-Kantian stringency of the criterion of active rationality is thus qualified, but in a way that makes difficult the application of the theory to the abortion issue. The welfare of descendants could be promoted, arguably, by a principle that permitted pregnant women to choose abortion if the quality of life of the child would be minimal (for instance, in the case of birth defects and, perhaps, that of *unwanted* children). When one adds to this concern for the welfare of future persons the self-interest of the contractors (who do not know whether they are men or women), a contractarian approach to abortion will seem very similar to a rule-utilitarian approach.

Rule Utilitarianism The rule utilitarian seeks to adopt a general rule the acceptance of which will have at least as much net utility as the acceptance of any other rule. (See Chapter 3 for alternative formulations of rule utilitarianism.) Net utility is the balance of happiness over unhappiness resulting as the consequence of accepting the rule. Applied to abortion, this form of rule utilitarianism leads to a permissive view. An early abortion surely causes no unhappiness to the fetus and satisfies the desire of the pregnant woman to free herself of the pregnancy. A moral rule permitting women to choose early abortion seems unproblematic from this viewpoint. Even if there are occasionally desires that are frustrated (for instance, an aspiring father's desire for a child), it is a reasonable general rule that the most intense interests at issue are those of the pregnant woman herself. The future child's own happiness is threatened by any moral rule that requires a woman to continue a pregnancy against her own better judgment. Occasionally, a fetus may be aborted that would have produced more happiness (either in its own life or by benefiting others) than the sum of unhappiness that would have resulted from continuing the pregnancy against the woman's wishes. But generally, better consequences will result from allowing the woman to choose.

In the case of late abortions, the rule-utilitarian argument becomes less clear. At viability, an aborted child is in danger of suffering impaired health if it survives. A moral rule restricting abortions roughly from the time of viability might be justified by the risk to the happiness of the viable child from impaired health, combined with the increased emotional damage risked by the woman (who may not realize until afterward what her own response will be to late abortion).

Act Utilitarianism An act-utilitarian approach to abortion must consider all facets of each individual case. The pregnant woman's own interests are quite important, but *all* consequences must be considered. Although the *actual* net utility of a particular action determines its rightness, from the viewpoint of a person deliberating whether to abort, the *foreseeable* consequences are all-important. In most cases, it will not be possible to form any reasonable opinion about the future happiness of the potential child; the main exception is where, because of a genetic defect or other known circumstances, the child has a less than normal chance at a decent life. If the woman wants an early abortion, then the *foreseeable* consequences of abortion for her are positive. And so in many cases an act utilitarian will arrive at the moral decision to terminate pregnancy, for the *foreseeable* consequences will be a net gain in happiness.

Abortion after viability, of course, raises new questions and new foreseeable risks. For the act utilitarian, late abortions will probably be justified less frequently than would be early abortions, though there will certainly be cases in which even very late abortion will be accepted as justifiable.

Readings The problem case, *Roe* v. *Wade*, raises the general question of the right of women to terminate pregnancy. The legal right is grounded upon the constitutional right of privacy. But there continues to be controversy concerning both the legal and the moral issues at stake.

The selection from Roger Wertheimer sets out the natural-law position against abortion. In the complete essay, Wertheimer argues that the abortion controversy is irresolvable. In the passages presented here, Wertheimer elucidates the conservative view that from conception the new human life has the moral status of a human being protected under the principle that prohibits killing the innocent.

The selection from Mary Anne Warren is neo-Kantian in its emphasis upon consciousness and the developed capacity of reasoning as criteria for "humanity in the moral sense." She argues that the fetus is not a member of the moral community, and that women have a moral right to terminate pregnancy under all conditions.

The selection from Laura Purdy and Michael Tooley offers a utilitarian defense of the woman's right to choose abortion. After explaining the benefits of allowing abortion, they argue that the fetus has no right to life since it lacks the capacity for self-consciousness.

Notes

[1] *Roe* v. *Wade*, 410 U.S. 113, 93 S. Ct. 705 (1973).

[2] St. Thomas Aquinas, *Summa Theologica*, I–II, Q. 96, trans. Anton Pegis, *The Basic Writings of Saint Thomas Aquinas* (New York: Random House, 1945).

[3] Baruch Brody, *Abortion and the Sanctity of Human Life* (Cambridge, Mass.: MIT Press, 1975), chap. 3.

[4] Daniel Callahan, "Abortion: The New Ruling," in *The Problem of Abortion*, ed. Joel Feinberg (Belmont, Calif.: Wadsworth, 1973), p. 195.

[5] See John Finnis, "The Rights and Wrongs of Abortion," *Philosophy and Public Affairs* 2 (1973): 117–45.

⁶ Judith Jarvis Thomson, "A Defense of Abortion," *Philosophy and Public Affairs* 1 (1971): 47–66.

⁷ For a contemporary statement of this view, see Alan Donagan, *The Theory of Morality* (Chicago, Ill.: University of Chicago Press, 1977), pp. 82–83 and 168–71.

⁸ John Rawls, *A Theory of Justice* (Cambridge, Mass.: Harvard University Press, 1971), p. 128.

Bibliography on Abortion

Brody, Baruch. *Abortion and the Sanctity of Human Life: A Philosophical View.* Cambridge, Mass.: MIT Press, 1975.

Callahan, Daniel. *Abortion: Law, Choice, and Morality.* New York: Macmillan, 1970.

Feinberg, Joel. "Abortion." In *Matters of Life and Death*, edited by Tom Regan. New York: Random House, 1980.

_____, ed. *The Problem of Abortion.* Belmont, Calif.: Wadsworth, 1973.

Finnis, John. "The Rights and Wrongs of Abortion: A Reply to Judith Thomson." *Philosophy and Public Affairs* 2 (1973): 117–45.

Foot, Philippa. "The Problem of Abortion and the Doctrine of the Double Effect." *Oxford Review*, no. 5 (1967).

Grisez, Germain G. *Abortion: The Myths, the Realities and the Arguments.* New York: Corpus Books, 1970.

Hare, R. M. "Abortion and the Golden Rule." *Philosophy and Public Affairs* 4 (1975): 201–22.

Manier, Edward, Liu, William, and Solomon, David, eds. *Abortion.* Notre Dame, Ind.: University of Notre Dame Press, 1977.

Noonan, John T., Jr. *A Private Choice.* New York: Free Press, 1979.

_____, ed. *The Morality of Abortion: Legal and Historical Perspectives.* Cambridge, Mass.: Harvard University Press, 1970.

Perkins, Robert L., ed. *Abortion.* Cambridge, Mass.: Schenkman, 1975.

Ramsey, Paul. "The Morality of Abortion." In *Moral Problems*, edited by James Rachels. New York: Harper & Row, 1975.

Sumner, L. W. *Abortion and Moral Theory.* Princeton, N.J.: Princeton University Press, 1981.

Thomson, Judith Jarvis. "A Defense of Abortion." *Philosophy and Public Affairs* 1 (1971): 47–66.

_____. "Rights and Deaths." *Philosophy and Public Affairs* 2 (1973): 146–59.

Tooley, Michael. "Abortion and Infanticide." *Philosophy and Public Affairs* 2 (1972): 37–65.

Problem Case

Roe v. Wade, 410 U.S. 113 (1973)

Under the fictitious name of Jane Roe, an unmarried pregnant woman challenged the constitutionality of the Texas criminal statutes that restricted abortions to cases in which the life of the woman was endangered by continuing the pregnancy. Jane Roe's life was not endangered by the pregnancy. She claimed that the Texas statutes unconstitutionally prevented her from obtaining a safe, legal abortion.

The majority opinion of the United States Supreme Court held that the constitutional right of privacy "is broad enough to encompass a woman's decision whether or not to terminate her pregnancy." The fetus is not *legally* a person "in the whole sense." After the first three months of pregnancy, states may regulate abortion in order to safeguard the woman's health and to maintain medical standards; during the last three months of pregnancy, states *may* protect fetal life, though not at the expense of the life *or health* of the woman.

Should the United States Constitution be changed either to protect the rights of the fetus directly, or to allow the states to recriminalize abortion? Morally, is the fetus a person?

ROGER WERTHEIMER
UNDERSTANDING THE CONSERVATIVE ARGUMENT

The defense of the extreme conservative position, as normally stated by Catholics, runs as follows. The key premise is that a human fetus is a human being, not a partial or potential one, but a full-fledged, actualized human life. Given that premise, the entire conservative position unfolds with a simple, relentless logic, every principle of which would be endorsed by any sensible liberal. Suppose human embryos are human beings. Their innocence is beyond question, so nothing could justify our destroying them except, perhaps, the necessity of saving some other innocent human life. That is, since similar cases must be treated in similar ways, some consideration would justify the abortion of a prenatal child if and only if a comparable consideration would justify the killing of a postnatal child.

This is a serious and troubling argument posing an objection in principle to abortion. It is the *only* such argument. . . . Once the Catholic premise is granted, a liberal could reasonably dissent on only three side issues, none of which is a necessary or essential feature of conservatism.

It should be unmistakably obvious what the Catholic position is. Yet, and this deserves heavy emphasis, liberals seem not to understand it, for their arguments are almost invariably infelicitous. The Catholic defense of the status quo is left unfazed, even untouched, by the standard liberal critique that consists of an inventory of the calamitous effects of our abortion laws on mother and child, on family, and on society in general. Of course, were it not for those effects we would feel no press to be rid of the laws—nor any *need* to retain them. That inventory does present a conclusive rebuttal of any of the piddling objections conservatives often toss in

Roger Wertheimer, "Understanding the Abortion Argument," *Philosophy and Public Affairs*, 1, no. 1 (Fall 1971). Copyright © 1971 by Princeton University Press. Excerpts reprinted by permission. The original essay explains the various main positions in the abortion controversy. In the excerpts presented here, Wertheimer is describing the views of conservatives, but he is not himself advocating that position.

for good measure. But still, the precise, scientific tabulations of grief do not add up to an argument here, for sometimes pain, no matter how considerable and how undesirable, may not be avoidable, may not stem from some injustice. I do not intend to understate that pain; the tragedies brought on by unwanted children are plentiful and serious—but so too are those brought on by unwanted parents, yet few liberals would legalize parricide as the final solution to the massive social problem of the permanently visiting parent who drains his children's financial and emotional resources. In the Church's view, these cases are fully analogous: the fetus is as much a human life as is the parent; they share the same moral status. Either can be a source of abiding anguish and hardship for the other—and sometimes there may be no escape. In this, our world, some people get stuck with the care of others, and sometimes there may be no way of getting unstuck, at least no just and decent way. Taking the other person's life is not such a way. . . .

Now, why do liberals, even the cleverest ones, so consistently fail to make contact with the Catholic challenge? After all, as I have made plain, once premised that the fetus is a person, the entire conservative position recites the common sense of any moral man. The liberal's failure is, I suggest, due to that premise, not to some Jesuitical subtlety in the reasoning. It is the liberal's imagination, not his intellect, that is boggled. He doesn't know how to respond to the argument, because he cannot *make sense* of that premise. To him, it is not simply false, but wildly, madly false; it is nonsense, totally unintelligible, literally unbelievable. Just look at an embryo. It is an amorphous speck of apparently coagulated protoplasm. It has no eyes or ears, no head at all. It can't walk or talk; you can't dress it or wash it. Why, it doesn't even qualify as a Barbie doll, and yet millions of people call it a human being, just like one of us. It's as though someone were to look at an acorn and call it an oak tree, or, better, it's as though someone squirted a paint tube at a canvas and called the outcome a painting, a work of art—and people believed him. The whole thing is precisely that mad—and just that sane. The liberal is befuddled by the conservative's argument, just as Giotto would be were he to assess a Pollock production as a *painting*. If the premises make no sense, then neither will the rest of the argument, except as an exercise in abstract logic—and that is, I think, the only way in which liberals do understand the conservative argument. . . .

. . . But, discomforting though it may be, people, and not just Catholics, can and sometimes do agree on all the facts about embryos and still disagree as to whether they are persons. Indeed, apparently people can agree on *every* fact and still disagree on whether it is a fact that embryos are human beings. So now one might begin to wonder: What sort of fact is it?

I hasten to add that not only can both parties agree on the scientific facts, they need not disagree on any supernatural facts either. The situation here is *not* comparable to that in which a man stands before what looks for all the world like some fermented grape juice and a biscuit and calls it the blood and body of someone who died and decomposed a couple of millennia ago. The conservative claim does not presuppose that we are invested with a soul, some sort of divine substance, at or shortly after our conception. No doubt it helps to have one's mind befogged by visions of holy hocus-pocus, but it's not necessary, since some unmuddled atheists endorse a demythologized Catholic view. Moreover, since ensoulment is an unverifiable occurrence, the theologian dates it either by means of some revelation—which, by the way, the Church does not (though some of its parishioners may accept the humanity of embryos on the Church's say-so)—or by means of the same scientifically acceptable data by which his atheistical counterpart gauges the emergence of an unbesouled human life (e.g., that at such and such a time the organism is capable of independent life, or is motile, or assumes human form, or possesses its complete genetic makeup).

The religious position derives its plausibility from independent secular considerations. It serves as an expression of them, not as a substitute for them. In brief, here as elsewhere, talk about souls involves an unnecessary shuffle. Yet, though unnecessary, admittedly it is not without effect, for such conceptions color our perceptions and attitudes toward the world and thereby give sense and substance to certain arguments whose secular translations lack appeal. . . .

The liberal dates hominization from birth or viability. The choice of either stage is explicable by reference to some obvious considerations. At birth the child leaves its own private space and enters the public world. He becomes an active member of the community, a physically separate and distinct individual. He begins to act and behave like a human being, not just move as he did in the womb. And he can be looked at and acted upon and interacted with. He has needs and wants independent from those of his mother. And so on. On the other hand, someone may say viability is the crucial point, because it is then that the child has the capacity to do all those things it does at birth; the sole difference is a quite inessential one of geography. . . .

. . . Quickening—that is, when the mother first *feels* the fetus move —could be used, because that clearly serves as a sign of life. Liberal detractors point out that the fetus moves long before the mother feels it, and biologically it is a living organism long before that. But such objections overlook the connections between our concept of a person and our concept of an agent, something that can act. It's not to be wondered at that quickening should seem a dramatic moment, especially to the mother who receives the fetus' signal that it *can now move on its own*.

Similarly, liberals always misplace the attractions of fertilization as the critical date when they try to argue that if you go back that far, you could just as well call the sperm or the egg a human being. But people call the zygote a human life not just because it contains the DNA blueprint which determines the physical development of the organism from then on, and not just because of the potential inherent in it, but also because it and it alone can claim to be the beginning of the spatio-temporal-causal chain of the physical object that is a human body. And though I think the abortion controversy throws doubt on the claim that bodily continuity is the *sole* criterion of personal identity, I think the attractions of that philosophical thesis are of a piece with the attractions of fertilization as the point marking the start of a person. Given our conceptual framework, one can't go back further. Neither the sperm nor the egg could be, by itself, a human being, any more than an atom of sodium or an atom of chlorine could by itself properly be called salt. One proof of this is that *no one* is in the least inclined to call a sperm or an egg a human life, a fact acknowledged by the liberal's very argument, which has the form of a *reductio ad absurdum*. At one time people were so inclined, but only because they thought the sperm merely triggered the development of the egg and hence the egg was a human being, or they thought that the egg was merely the seedbed for the male seed and thus the sperm was a human being. . . .

The conservative points, and keeps pointing, to the similarities between each set of successive stages of fetal development, instead of pointing, as the liberal does, to the gross differences between widely separated stages. Each step of his argument is persuasive, but if this were all there was to it, his total argument would be no more compelling than one which traded on the fuzziness of the boundaries of baldness and the arbitrariness of any sharp line of demarcation to conclude that Richard M. Nixon is glabrous. If this were the whole conservative argument, then it would be open to the liberal's *reductio* argument, which says that if you go back as far as the zygote, the sperm and the egg must also be called persons. But in fact the conservative can stop at the zygote; fertilization does seem to be a nonarbitrary point marking the inception of a particular object, a human body. That is, the conservative has *independent* reasons for picking the date of conception, just like the liberal who picks the date of birth or viability, and unlike the sophist who concludes that Nixon is bald.

But we still don't have the whole conservative argument, for on the basis of what has been said so far the conservative should also call an acorn an oak tree, but he doesn't, and the reason he uses is that, as regards a human life, it would be *morally* arbitrary to use any date other than that of conception. That is, he can ask liberals to name the earliest stage at which they are willing to call the organism a human being, something which may not be killed for any reason short of saving some other human life. The conservative will then take the stage of development immediately preceding the one the liberals choose and challenge them to point to a difference between the two stages, a difference that is a morally relevant difference, a difference that would justify the massive moral and legal difference of allowing us to kill the creature at the earlier stage while prohibiting that same act at the succeeding stage.

Suppose the liberal picks the date of birth. Yet a newborn infant is only a fetus that has suffered a change of address and some physiological changes like respiration. A neonate delivered in its twenty-fifth week lies in an incubator physically less well developed and no more independent than a normal fetus in its thirty-seventh week in the womb. What difference is there that justifies calling that neonate a person, but not that fetus? What difference is there that can be used to justify killing the prenatal child where it would be wrong to kill the postnatal child?

Or suppose the liberal uses the date of viability. But the viability of a fetus is its capacity to survive outside the mother, and *that* is totally relative to the state of the available medical technology. At present the law dates viability from the twenty-eighth week, but so late a date is now without any medical justification. In principle, eventually the fetus may be deliverable at any time, perhaps even at conception. The problems this poses for liberals are obvious, and in fact one finds that either a liberal doesn't understand what viability really is, so that he takes it to be necessarily linked to the later fetal stages; or he is an extreme liberal in disguise, who is playing along with the first kind of liberal for political purposes; or he has abandoned the viability criterion and is madly scurrying about in search of some other factor in the late fetal stages which might serve as a nonarbitrary cutoff point. For example, in recent years some liberals have been purveying pious nonsense about the developing cerebral cortex in the third trimester and its relation to consciousness. But I am inclined to suppose that the conservative is right, that going back stage by stage from the infant to the zygote one will not find any differences between successive stages significant enough to bear the enormous moral burden of allowing wholesale slaughter at the earlier stage while categorically denying that permission at the next stage.

It needs to be stressed here that we are talking about life and death on a colossal scale. It has been estimated that thirty million abortions are performed yearly, one million in the United States alone. So the situation contrasts sharply with that in which a society selects a date like the eighteenth or twenty-first birthday on which to confer certain legal rights, for the social costs of using a less arbitrary measure of maturity can reasonably be held to outweigh any injustices involved in the present system. Even the choice of a birthday for military conscription, a morally ambiguous practice anyway, is not comparable for obvious reasons.

The full power and persuasiveness of the conservative argument is still not revealed until we uncover its similarities to and connections with any of the dialectical devices that have been used to widen a man's recognition of his fellowship with all the members of his biological species, regardless of their race or sex or nationality or religion or lineage or social class. To be sure, not every discriminatory injustice based on such arbitrary and morally irrelevant features as race or sex has been rationalized on the grounds that the victim is not a full-fledged human being. Still, it is a matter of record that men of good will have often failed to recognize that a certain class of fellow creatures were really human beings just like themselves. . . .

In brief, when seen in its totality the conservative's argument *is* the liberal's argument turned completely inside out. While the liberal stresses the differences between disparate stages, the conservative stresses the resemblances between consecutive stages. The liberal asks, "What has a zygote got that is valuable?" and the conservative answers, "Nothing, but it's a human being, so it is wrong to abort it." Then the conservative asks, "What does a fetus lack that an infant has that is so valuable?" and the liberal answers, "Nothing, but it's a fetus, not a human being, so it is all right to abort it." The arguments are equally strong and equally weak, for they are the *same* argument, an argument that can be pointed in either of two directions. The argument does not itself point in either direction: it is *we* who must point it, and *we* who are led by it. If you are led in one direction rather than the other, that is not because of logic, but because you respond in a certain way to certain facts.

Recall that the arguments are usually formulated in the interrogative, not the indicative, mood. Though the answers are supposed to be absolutely obvious, they are not comfortably assertible. Why? Because an assertion is a truth claim which invites a request for a proof, but here any assertible proof presupposes premises which beg the question. If one may speak of proof here, it can lie only in the audience's response, in their acceptance of the answer and of its obviousness. The questions convince by leading us to appreciate familiar facts. The conclusion is validated not through assertible presuppositions, but through our acknowledgment that the questions are *rhetorical*. You might say that the conclusion is our seeing a certain aspect: e.g., we see the embryo as a human being. But this seems an unduly provocative description of the situation, for what is at issue is whether such an aspect is there to be seen. . . .

MARY ANNE WARREN
THE MORAL STATUS OF ABORTION

DEFINING THE MORAL COMMUNITY

Can it be established that genetic humanity is sufficient for moral humanity? I think that there are very good reasons for not defining the moral community in this way. I would like to suggest an alternative way of defining the moral community, which I will argue for only to the extent of explaining why it is, or should be, self-evident. The suggestion is simply that the moral community consists of all and only *people,* rather than all and only human beings;[1] and probably the best way of demonstrating its self-evidence is by considering the concept of personhood, to see what sorts of entity are and are not persons, and what the decision that a being is or is not a person implies about its moral rights.

From Mary Anne Warren, "On the Moral and Legal Status of Abortion," *The Monist* 57 (1973): 54–61. Reprinted from *The Monist,* Vol. 57, No. 1, with the permission of the author and the publisher.

What characteristics entitle an entity to be considered a person? This is obviously not the place to attempt a complete analysis of the concept of personhood, but we do not need such a fully adequate analysis just to determine whether and why a fetus is or isn't a person. All we need is a rough and approximate list of the most basic criteria of personhood, and some idea of which, or how many, of these an entity must satisfy in order to properly be considered a person.

In searching for such criteria, it is useful to look beyond the set of people with whom we are acquainted, and ask how we would decide whether a totally alien being was a person or not. (For we have no right to assume that genetic humanity is necessary for personhood.) Imagine a space traveler who lands on an unknown planet and encounters a race of beings utterly unlike any he has ever seen or heard of. If he wants to be sure of behaving morally toward these beings, he has to somehow decide whether they are people, and hence have full moral rights, or whether they are the sort of thing which he need not feel guilty about treating as, for example, a source of food.

How should he go about making this decision? If he has some anthropological background, he might look for such things as religion, art, and the manufacturing of tools, weapons, or shelters, since these factors have been used to distinguish our human from our prehuman ancestors, in what seems to be closer to the moral than the genetic sense of 'human.' And no doubt he would be right to consider the presence of such factors as good evidence that the alien beings were people, and morally human. It would, however, be overly anthropocentric of him to take the absence of these things as adequate evidence that they were not, since we can imagine people who have progressed beyond, or evolved without ever developing, these cultural characteristics.

I suggest that the traits which are most central to the concept of personhood, or humanity in the moral sense, are, very roughly, the following:

1. consciousness (of objects and events external and/or internal to the being), and in particular the capacity to feel pain;

2. reasoning (the *developed* capacity to solve new and relatively complex problems);

3. self-motivated activity (activity which is relatively independent of either genetic or direct external control);

4. the capacity to communicate, by whatever means, messages of an indefinite variety of types, that is, not just with an indefinite number of possible contents, but on indefinitely many possible topics;

5. the presence of self-concepts, and self-awareness, either individual or racial, or both.

Admittedly, there are apt to be a great many problems involved in formulating precise definitions of these criteria, let alone in developing universally valid behavioral criteria for deciding when they apply. But I will assume that both we and our explorer know approximately what (1)–(5) mean, and that he is also able to determine whether or not they apply. How, then, should he use his findings to decide whether or not the alien beings are people? We needn't suppose that an entity must have *all* of these attributes to be properly considered a person; (1) and (2) alone may well be sufficient for personhood, and quite probably (1)–(3) are sufficient. Neither do we need to insist that any one of these criteria is *necessary* for personhood, although once again (1) and (2) look like fairly good candidates for necessary conditions, as does (3), if 'activity' is construed so as to include the activity of reasoning.

All we need to claim, to demonstrate that a fetus is not a person, is that any being which satisfied *none* of (1)–(5) is certainly not a person. I consider this claim to be so obvious that I think anyone who denied it, and claimed that a being which satisfied none of (1)–(5) was a person all the same, would thereby demonstrate that he had no notion at all of what a person is—perhaps because he had confused the concept of a person with that of genetic humanity. If the opponents of abortion were to deny the appropriateness of these five criteria, I do not know what further arguments would convince them. We would probably have to admit that our conceptual schemes were indeed irreconcilably different, and that our dispute could not be settled objectively.

I do not expect this to happen, however, since I think that the concept of a person is one which is very nearly universal (to people), and that it is common to both proabortionists and antiabortionists, even though neither group has fully realized the relevance of this concept to the resolution of their dispute. Furthermore, I think that on reflection even the antiabortionists ought to agree not only that (1)–(5) are central to the concept of personhood, but also that it is a part of this concept that all and only people have full moral rights. The concept of a person is in part a moral concept; once we have admitted that x is a person we have recognized, even if we have not agreed to respect, x's right to be treated as a member of the moral community. It is true that the claim that x is a *human being* is more commonly voiced as part of an appeal to treat x decently than is the claim that x is a person, but this is either because 'human being' is here used in the sense which implies personhood, or because the genetic and moral senses of 'human' have been confused.

Now if (1)–(5) are indeed the primary criteria of personhood, then it is clear that genetic humanity is neither necessary nor sufficient for establishing that an entity is a person. Some human beings are not people, and there may well be people who are not human beings. A man or woman whose consciousness has been permanently obliterated but who remains alive is a human being which is no longer a person; defective human beings, with no appreciable mental capacity, are not and presumably never will be people; and a fetus is a human being which is not yet a person, and which therefore cannot coherently be said to have full moral rights. Citizens of the next century should be prepared to recognize highly advanced, self-aware robots or computers, should such be developed, and intelligent inhabitants of other worlds, should such be found, as people in the fullest sense, and to respect their moral rights. But to ascribe full moral rights to an entity which is not a person is as absurd as to ascribe moral obligations and responsibilities to such an entity.

FETAL DEVELOPMENT AND THE RIGHT TO LIFE

Two problems arise in the application of these suggestions for the definition of the moral community to the determination of the precise moral status of a human fetus. Given that the paradigm example of a person is a normal adult human being, then (1) How like this paradigm, in particular how far advanced since conception, does a human being need to be before it begins to have a right to life by virtue, not of being fully a person as of yet, but of being *like* a person? and (2) To what extent, if any, does the fact that a fetus has the *potential* for becoming a person endow it with some of the same rights? Each of these questions requires some comment.

In answering the first question, we need not attempt a detailed consideration of the moral rights of organisms which are not developed enough, aware enough, intelligent enough, etc., to be considered people, but which resemble people in some respects. It does seem reasonable to suggest that the more like a person, in the relevant respects, a being is, the stronger is the case for regarding it as having a right to life, and indeed the stronger its right to life is. Thus we ought to take seriously the suggestion that, insofar as "the human individual develops biologically in a continuous fashion . . . the rights of a human person might develop in the same way."[2] But we must keep in mind that the attributes which are relevant in determining whether or not an entity is enough like a person to be regarded as having some of the same moral rights are no different from those which are relevant to determining whether or not it is fully a person —i.e., are no different from (1)–(5)—and that being genetically human, or having recognizably human facial and other physical features, or detectable brain activity, or the capacity to survive outside the uterus, are simply not among these relevant attributes.

Thus it is clear that even though a seven- or eight-month fetus has features which make it apt to arouse in us almost the same powerful protective instinct as is commonly aroused by a small infant, nevertheless it is not significantly more personlike than is a very small embryo. It is *somewhat* more personlike; it can apparently feel and respond to pain, and it may even have a rudimentary form of consciousness, insofar as its brain is quite active. Nevertheless, it seems safe to say that it is not fully conscious, in the way that an infant of a few months is, and that it cannot reason, or communicate messages of indefinitely many sorts, does not engage in self-motivated activity, and has no self-awareness. Thus, in the *relevant* respects, a fetus, even a fully developed one, is considerably less personlike than is the average mature mammal, indeed the average fish. And I think that a rational person must conclude that if the right to life of a fetus is to be based upon its resemblance to a person, then it cannot be said to have any more right to life than, let us say, a newborn guppy (which also seems to be capable of feeling pain), and that a right of that magnitude could never override a woman's right to obtain an abortion, at any stage of her pregnancy.

There may, of course, be other arguments in favor of placing legal limits upon the stage of pregnancy in which an abortion may be performed. Given the relative safety of the new techniques of artificially inducing labor during the third trimester, the danger to the woman's life or health is no longer such an argument. Neither is the fact that people tend to respond to the thought of abortion in the later stages of pregnancy with emotional repulsion, since mere emotional responses cannot take the place of moral reasoning in determining what ought to be permitted. Nor, finally, is the frequently heard argument that legalizing abortion, especially late in the pregnancy, may erode the level of respect for human life, leading, perhaps, to an increase in unjustified euthanasia and other crimes. For this threat, if it is a threat, can be better met by educating people to the kinds of moral distinctions which we are making here than by limiting access to abortion (which limitation may, in its disregard for the rights of women, be just as damaging to the level of respect for human rights).

Thus, since the fact that even a fully developed fetus is not personlike enough to have any significant right to life on the basis of its personlikeness shows that no legal restrictions upon the stage of pregnancy in which an abortion may be performed can be justified on the grounds that we should protect the rights of the older fetus; and since there is no other apparent justification for such restrictions, we may conclude that they are entirely unjustified. Whether or not it would be *indecent* (whatever that means) for a woman in her seventh month to obtain an abortion just to avoid having to postpone a trip to Europe, it would not, in itself, be *immoral*, and therefore it ought to be permitted.

POTENTIAL PERSONHOOD AND THE RIGHT TO LIFE

We have seen that a fetus does not resemble a person in any way which can support the claim that it has even some of the same rights. But what about its *potential*, the fact that if nurtured and allowed to develop naturally it will very probably become a person? Doesn't that alone give it at least some right to life? It is hard to deny that the fact that an entity is a potential person is a strong prima facie reason for not destroying it; but we need not conclude from this that a potential person has a right to life, by virtue of that potential. It may be that our feeling that it is better, other things being equal, not to destroy a potential person is better explained by the fact that potential people are still (felt to be) an invaluable resource, not to be lightly squandered. Surely, if every speck of dust were a potential person, we would be much less apt to conclude that every potential person has a right to become actual.

Still, we do not need to insist that a potential person has no right to life whatever. There may well be something immoral, and not just imprudent, about wantonly destroying potential people, when doing so isn't necessary to protect anyone's rights. But even if a potential person does have some prima facie right to life, such a right could not possibly outweigh the right of a woman to obtain an abortion, since the rights of any actual person invariably outweigh those of any potential person, whenever the two conflict. Since this may not be immediately obvious in the case of a human fetus, let us look at another case.

Suppose that our space explorer falls into the hands of an alien culture, whose scientists decide to create a few hundred thousand or more human beings, by breaking his body into its component cells, and using these to create fully developed human beings, with, of course, his genetic code. We may imagine that each of these newly created men will have all of the original man's abilities, skills, knowledge, and so on, and also have an individual self-concept, in short that each of them will be a bona fide (though hardly unique) person. Imagine that the whole project will take only seconds, and that its chances of success are extremely high, and that our explorer knows all of this, and also knows that these people will be treated fairly. I maintain that in such a situation he would have every right to escape if he could, and thus to deprive all of these potential people of their potential lives; for his right to life outweighs all of theirs together, in spite of the fact that they are all genetically human, all innocent, and all have a very high probability of becoming people very soon, if only he refrains from acting.

Indeed, I think he would have a right to escape even if it were not his life which the alien scientists planned to take, but only a year of his freedom, or, indeed, only a day. Nor would he be obligated to stay if he had gotten captured (thus bringing all these people-potentials into existence) because of his own carelessness, or even if he had done so deliberately, knowing the consequences. Regardless of how he got captured, he is not morally obligated to remain in captivity for *any* period of time for the sake of permitting any number of potential people to come into actuality, so great is the margin by which one actual person's right to liberty outweighs whatever right to life even a hundred thousand potential people have. And it seems reasonable to conclude that the rights of a woman will outweigh by a similar margin whatever right to life a fetus may have by virtue of its potential personhood.

Thus, neither a fetus's resemblance to a person, nor its potential for becoming a person provides any basis whatever for the claim that it has any significant right to life. Consequently, a woman's right to protect her health, happiness, freedom, and even her life,[3] by terminating an unwanted pregnancy, will always override whatever right to life it may be appropriate to ascribe to a fetus, even a fully developed one. And thus, in the absence of any overwhelming social need for every possible child, the laws which restrict the right to obtain an abortion, or limit the period of pregnancy during which an abortion may be performed, are a wholly unjustified violation of a woman's most basic moral and constitutional rights.

Notes

[1] From here on, we will use 'human' to mean genetically human, since the moral sense seems closely connected to, and perhaps derived from, the assumption that genetic humanity is sufficient for membership in the moral community.

[2] Thomas L. Hayes, "A Biological View," *Commonweal*, 85 (March 17, 1967), 677–78; quoted by Daniel Callahan, in *Abortion: Law, Choice, and Morality* (London: Macmillan & Co., 1970).

[3] That is, insofar as the death rate, for the woman, is higher for childbirth than for early abortion.

LAURA PURDY AND MICHAEL TOOLEY
IS ABORTION MURDER?

This essay deals with the morality of abortion. We shall argue that abortion is morally unobjectionable, and that society benefits if abortion is available on demand. We begin by setting out a preliminary case in support of the practice of abortion. . . . We conclude by considering what properties something needs in order to have a serious right to life, and we show that a human fetus does not possess those properties. Thus since there is no moral objection to abortion, the practice must be viewed as both permissible and desirable, in the light of the advantages outlined in the first section of our paper.

PRELIMINARY CONSIDERATIONS IN SUPPORT OF ABORTION

One way of approaching the abortion question is to envision two possible societies, one where strict anti-abortion laws are in force, the other where abortion is unrestricted. In imagining these two societies, we suppose that all other factors are the same, and that the societies otherwise resemble the United States in their social arrangements.

To flesh out these images, we must make some empirical assumptions, which philosophers are no more qualified to evaluate than is the ordinary educated individual, since it is not the main business of philosophy to ascertain facts. However, such assumptions cannot be avoided in moral and political philosophy, unless one is uninterested in the outcomes of various

From Laura Purdy and Michael Tooley, "Is Abortion Murder?" *Abortion: Pro and Con*, edited by Robert L. Perkins (Cambridge, Mass.: Schenkman, 1974), pp. 129–36, 144–48. Reprinted by permission.

courses of action. About the facts relevant to the issues discussed in this section there is room for disagreement, for we are dependent upon sciences that are as yet incomplete and upon common sense. But while the accuracy of the following pictures is contingent upon future investigation, the major features of the pictures seem plausible, in the light of present knowledge and theory.

The first society is much like that which has existed in the United States up until the present, where abortion has been generally unavailable, either because of restrictive legislation or because of de facto unobtainability. The second society is very different. In it, abortion is freely available. We contend that, as a result, individuals in that society suffer less unhappiness than those in the first society.

Let us consider, in concrete terms, why this is the case. First of all, men and women in our second world can enjoy sex more, since anxiety regarding contraceptive failure will no longer exist. Moreover, pregnancies can be timed so that no child is neglected, reducing stress on all concerned. As a result, couples can plan on temporary or permanent childlessness when necessary or desirable to achieve life goals. In addition, if pregnancy threatens the health—either physical or mental—of the mother, or of other parties, or unduly strains the marriage, it can be safely terminated. Last, and most important perhaps, illegal abortions, now a significant factor in the maternal death rate, can be replaced by legal abortions, thus saving the lives of very many women.

That abortion on demand would reduce frustration and unhappiness among the young is equally evident. When abortion is readily available we can prevent the birth of babies who would otherwise enter the world with gross physical or mental abnormalities and who would face short and unhappy lives. We can also ensure that only wanted children will be born. Since parents who sincerely desire a child are more apt to provide for its physical, intellectual, and emotional needs, it is probable that children will be better cared for than at present. This change should be especially significant in light of our growing awareness of the problem of child abuse.

It also seems reasonable to believe that members of society who do not belong to families availing themselves of abortion will benefit. It is generally frustrated and unhappy individuals who turn to crime, violent or otherwise. Happy people, if not necessarily constructive citizens, are at least not destructive ones. Thus readily available abortions, by eliminating sources of frustration and unhappiness, should improve the social environment for everyone. Secondly, abortion, by making childbearing completely voluntary, will help keep the population in check. The importance of this with respect to education and the environment, and thus the impact upon the general quality of life, need not be labored.

It seems reasonable to conclude then, on the basis of our present knowledge, that the second society will be much happier than the first. At this point two questions arise. The first is empirical: ''Is abortion on demand in fact the *best* way to satisfy the needs and desires of members of society? Mightn't some third type of society be superior to both of the possibilities we have so far considered, as measured in terms of the happiness of its members?'' The second is moral: ''Even if members of the second society are on the whole happier than members of the first, does it follow that the second society is morally preferable to the first? Are there not other factors that should be taken into account, such as the rights of the unborn, that tell in favor of the first society?'' . . .

The issue, then, is this. May there not be alternative social arrangements, not involving abortion, that would result in even greater happiness? Those who are wary of the practice of abortion on demand sometimes suggest that the same ends can be achieved as follows. First, society should ensure that everyone has access to safe and completely reliable methods of contraception. Secondly, there should be legislation to cope with the social welfare problems that are created or aggravated by unwanted or defective children.

This alternative presupposes the existence of a foolproof contraceptive having no undesirable side effects. At present no such device exists. It is true that if a perfect method of contraception were developed, it would dissolve much of the abortion problem. However, at least two problems would remain. First, pregnancy, even though initially desired, sometimes has a serious negative effect upon the mother or other people. We will still need abortion to handle cases of this sort. Secondly, some fetuses turn out to be grossly deformed, or otherwise seriously defective. If abortion is not available, what is likely to happen to such defective children? Proper care is expensive, and if the societies we are envisaging do resemble the present day United States, then we know that to do the job adequately will be thought to impose too great a sacrifice upon parents and taxpayers. This fact cannot be swept under the rug; it must enter any realistic assessment of the available options. As the real alternative to abortion here, the defective person will face life in an uncaring environment, where physical needs will be only barely met, and where emotional needs will generally go unfulfilled. Only if drastic changes in social legislation were to occur would such individuals have the opportunity to lead a protected life and to develop fully their potentialities. Thus it is not possible to achieve, by contraception and social legislation, all of the benefits that can be realized by abortion.

We must now consider two important objections to our position. The first is that in evaluating the happiness of society, one should take into account the happiness of the fetus, and we have failed to do this. We have considered only the happiness of other members of society. So that, while abortion may increase the happiness of these other members, it certainly does not satisfy the fetus's desires and so contribute to its happiness.

Our response to this is that it is a mistake to attribute to a fetus a significant range of desires. A fetus may have a few very rudimentary desires, such as a desire not to feel pain, but it is incapable of having most of the desires that adult humans can have.

ow can we support this claim that a fetus is capable of having only
elementary desires? Perhaps the place to start is by drawing a distinc-
between having a desire for some state, and being programmed to act
s to increase the likelihood that the state in question will be attained.
s, imagine a machine constructed so that when its batteries run down,
arches for an electrical outlet to recharge its batteries. The machine is
grammed to behave in ways that tend to bring about certain states, but
could not literally speak of the machine having a *desire* to recharge its
eries. Similarly, imagine a more complex machine that can ''recog-
'' certain situations as threats to its survival, and take action that de-
es the likelihood of its being destroyed. Even if such a machine were
ble of a wide range of complex and effective survival behavior, it
d not make sense to speak of it having a desire for continued exist-
Moreover, all plant behavior and that of lower animals provide other
ples in which there is complex programmed behavior directed toward
goal, but where the organism has no corresponding desire.

What, then, is required before one can attribute desires to something?
ur view is that first, it is not possible to attribute desires to something
unless it is capable of *consciousness*. So if a machine is not conscious, one
cannot attribute any desires to it, no matter how sophisticated its behavior.
Second, the *specific* desires a thing can have are limited by the concepts it
possesses. The justification for this claim is as follows. The fundamental
way of describing a given desire is as a desire that a certain proposition be
true. But one cannot desire that a certain proposition be true unless one
understands it, and since one cannot understand it without possessing the
concepts involved in it, it follows that the desires one can have are limited
by the concepts one possesses.

A slightly different way of developing this point is this: if something is
to have any desires at all, it must possess consciousness. But to have a specific desire it is not enough to be conscious and to be disposed to bring
about certain states. The migration of birds, for example, enables them to
achieve a certain end, and it certainly seems likely that they are to some extent conscious. Yet it is implausible to attribute to them a desire for those
states that their migratory behavior makes possible. What is needed is a
specific connection between consciousness and the goal towards which the
behavior is directed. One speaks of a desire only where the organism is
capable of recognizing that its behavior is directed towards certain ends:
where the organism is incapable of being aware of the object of its behavior, one does not attribute the corresponding desire to it. To be aware of a
certain state as the aim of one's behavior presupposes that one possesses
concepts that can be employed to characterize that state.

Given this account of the conditions an organism must satisfy if it is
to have desires, the justification for our claim that a fetus has at best extremely simple desires should be clear. In the early stages of the development of a human organism it has no mental life at all, i.e., no consciousness, and hence no desires. At later stages, it is reasonable to think that

the fetus has some sensations, but its mental life is still very limited.
if one compares, say, a human fetus with a chimpanzee fetus, there a
grounds for holding that the mental life of the former is signific
richer than that of the latter. This means that one should not attribu
sires to a human fetus which one would be unwilling to attribute
chimpanzee fetus. The upshot is that one cannot consistently obje
abortion in the case of humans, on the grounds that the destruction o
fetus violates some desires that the fetus has, unless one would also o
to abortion in the case of chimpanzees.

Moreover, there seem to be no grounds for attributing complex d
to fetuses, human or otherwise. In particular, it seems absurd to attr
to any fetus a desire for continued existence, since to have such a de
would have to have a conception of what it is to be a continuing subj
experiences and other mental states.

Are there any desires that a fetus has which might be violated by
tion? It appears reasonable to say that fetuses can feel pleasure and
Thus abortion might violate a fetus's desire to avoid pain. As it is cert
undesirable to inflict suffering upon any living organism, abortion shou.
be carried out so as to inflict as little pain as possible upon the fetus. If thi
is done, we do not think that the fetus has any desires that are violated by
abortion.

To sum up, our response to the first objection is this: we certainly
agree that in choosing policies and institutions, one should take into account everyone affected. So in particular, if the fetus had desires which
were adversely affected by abortion, it would be unfair not to take those
desires into account. But we have argued that, as a matter of fact, the fetus
is incapable of having desires that will go unsatisfied if it is destroyed, providing that action is carried out painlessly.

This brings us to the second objection. It involves the suggestion that
while the consequences of isolated acts of abortion do benefit society, this
would not be true if abortion were to become a *generally accepted practice*. It is precisely the latter issue that one is interested in.

It has often been suggested that general acceptance of abortion would
have disastrous consequences; however, no convincing evidence has been
offered in support of this contention. Antiabortionists usually attempt to
sway unreflective people with vague claims that abortion will lead to the
"denigration of humanity," or to an "erosion of respect for the sanctity of
life." Such emotion-laden appeals are in the same intellectual category as
politicians' rhetoric about patriotism and the family. Both are designed to
encourage unthinking acceptance of a position that would fare ill if exposed
to impartial, rational scrutiny.

It is possible, however, to divest the claim of its illicit emotional appeal.
When this is done, the underlying suggestion appears to be that if one permits the killing of some humans, viz., fetuses, then respect for human life
will decrease, so that other classes of humans, such as the handicapped
and the elderly, become candidates for elimination. But this conclusion

rests upon intellectual and moral confusion. Specifically, it rests upon a failure to get clear about the conditions something must satisfy if it is to have a serious right to life. To advocate abortion is *not* to suggest that one allow violations of one's moral principles when it happens to be socially convenient. The proabortionist's position is that the *fundamental* principle involved here is that it is seriously wrong to kill, not human beings, but *persons*. If it is seriously wrong to kill a human being it is *because* he is a person, not because he is a human being. And our contention is that fetuses are not persons, but only *potential* persons. Once one realizes that it is persons who have a right to life, and that abortion is morally unobjectionable because fetuses are not persons, there is no danger that one will conclude that it is morally acceptable to kill other humans, such as handicapped and elderly ones, who are persons. When the moral principles relevant to abortion are clear, it is apparent that general acceptance of the practice should not have any undesirable consequences of the sort envisioned by the antiabortionist.

This completes our defense of the claim that where abortion is viewed as morally permissible and is available on demand, people are happier than they would otherwise be. We can now proceed to consider the views of those who hold that abortion should be prohibited even if it is the case that to do so will result in significant frustration and unhappiness. Most antiabortionists feel that there are moral considerations involved in the issue of abortion that far outweigh considerations of human happiness. In view of what is at stake, this is not a claim to be lightly advanced. By lobbying for the prohibition of abortion, the antiabortionist is in effect assuming responsibility for the consequences of those actions. As we have emphasized above, these consequences are deeply disturbing. If antiabortionists prohibit abortion, they will be responsible for untold human misery. They will be responsible for lessened enjoyment of sex; for frustration caused by inconvenient pregnancies and childbearing; for ill health, either physical or mental, of mothers or other persons; for deaths of women resulting from pregnancies and illegal abortions; for child abuse; for crimes committed by frustrated or improperly socialized individuals; and for the stunted life of everyone if overpopulation seriously curbs our freedoms or lowers the quality of life. The ardent antiabortionist must shoulder the burden of responsibility for these things since, had he acted otherwise, they would not have existed. What considerations, then, can the antiabortionist point to that outweigh the suffering produced by the prohibition of abortion?

In reply to the accusation that the responsibility for this catalogue of woes lies on his shoulders, the antiabortionist will argue that these evils are necessary in order to avoid a much greater evil. Fetuses have a right to life. They have a right to be born and to have the opportunity to become adults. To destroy them by abortion is seriously wrong, and in comparison with it the miseries enumerated above pale into insignificance. Fetuses are human beings, and to kill a human being is murder. . . .

WHEN DOES AN ORGANISM HAVE A RIGHT TO LIFE?

. . . Our view is as follows: an organism can have a right to life only if it now possesses, or possessed at some time in the past, the capacity to have a desire for continued existence. An organism cannot satisfy this requirement unless it is a person, that is, a continuing subject of experiences and other mental states, and unless it has the capacity for self-consciousness—where an organism is self-conscious only if it recognizes that it is itself a person.

The basis for our contention is the claim that there is a conceptual connection between, on the one hand, the rights an individual can have and the circumstances under which they can be violated, and, on the other, the desires he can have. A right is something that can be violated and, in general, to violate an individual's right to something is to frustrate the corresponding desire. Suppose, for example, that someone owns a car. Then you are under a *prima facie* obligation not to take it from him. However, the obligation is not unconditional: if he does not care whether you drive off with his car, then *prima facie* you do not violate his right by doing so.

A precise formulation of the conceptual connection in question would require considerable care. The most important point is that violation of an individual's right to something does not always involve thwarting a *present* desire, that is, a desire that exists at the same time as the action that violates the right. Sometimes the violation of a right involves thwarting a *past* desire. The most dramatic illustration is provided by the rights of dead persons, since here the individual whose right is being transgressed no longer exists. A more common example is that of people who are temporarily unconscious. When a person is unconscious, he does not have any desires. Yet his rights can certainly be infringed upon. This presents no problem when one takes past desires into account. The reason that it is wrong to kill a temporarily unconscious adult is that in the period before he became unconscious, he had a desire to go on living—a desire which it is possible to satisfy.

Violation of an individual's right may also involve frustrating a *future* desire. The most vivid example of this is the case of rights of future generations. Most people would hold that for those living today to use up all of the world's resources would violate the rights of future individuals. Here, as in the case of the rights of a dead person, the violation of an individual's rights occurs at a time when the individual does not even exist.

However, it is very important to notice that what is relevant are the desires that individuals will *actually have* at some time in the future. The desires that individuals would have *if* they were to exist at certain times at which, as a matter of fact, they will not exist, are not relevant. . . . Rights of future generations provide . . . an example. Suppose we know with certainty that no future generation will ever exist. Then there is no objection to using up the world's resources now. But if one were obliged to take

into account the desires future individuals would have if they
exist, it would be wrong to use up the world's resources.

A complete account of the connection between rights and
would also have to take into consideration unusual cases, where an
vidual is in an emotionally unbalanced state, or where a person's de
have been affected by lack of relevant information, or by his being s
jected to abnormal physiological or psychological factors. We shall ign
these, and confine ourselves to paradigm cases of violations of an indivi
ual's rights. When this is done, we can say that first, an individual canno
have a right to something unless there can be actions that would violate it.
Second, an action cannot violate an individual's right to something unless
it wrongs him by depriving him of the thing in question. And thirdly, an
action can wrong an individual by depriving him of something only if it
violates his desire for that thing. The desire is generally a present desire,
but it may be a past or future desire. It follows that a person cannot have a
right to something unless he is at some time capable of having the corresponding desire.

Let us now apply this to the case of the right to life. The expression
"right to life" misleads one into thinking that the right concerns the continued existence of a biological organism. The following example shows
that this interpretation is inadequate. Suppose that we could completely
reprogram an adult human so that it has (apparent) memories, beliefs, desires, and personality traits radically different from those associated with it
before the reprogramming. (Billy Graham is reprogrammed as a replica of
Bertrand Russell.) In such a case, however beneficial the change might be,
it is true that *someone* has been destroyed, that someone's right to life has
been violated, even though no biological organism has been killed. So the
right to life cannot be construed as merely the right of a biological organism to continue to exist.

How then can the right in question be more accurately described? A
natural suggestion is that the expression "right to life" refers to the right
of a person—a subject of experiences and other mental states—to continue
to exist. However, this interpretation begs the question against certain
possible positions. It might be that while persons have a right to continue
to exist, so do other things that are only potentially persons. A right to life
on this view would be either the right of a person to continue to exist or the
right of something that is only potentially a person to become a person.

We concluded above that something cannot have a specific right unless
it is capable at some time of having the corresponding desire. It follows
from this together with the more accurate analysis of the right to life that
something cannot have a right to life unless it is capable at some time
either of having a desire to continue to exist as a person, or of having a desire to become a person. If something has not been capable of having
either of these desires in the past, and is not now capable, then if it is now
destroyed, it will never have possessed the capacity in question. Hence an

organism cannot have a right to life unless it is now capable, or was capable at some time in the past, of having a desire to continue to exist as a person or a desire to become a person.

But recall now the discussion of desires [above]. We showed that one's desires are limited by the concepts one possesses. Therefore one cannot have a desire to continue to exist as a person or a desire to become a person unless one has the concept of a person. The question we must now ask is whether something that is not itself a person could have the concept of such an entity. It seems plausible to hold that it could not. This means that something that is not a person cannot have a desire to become a person. Hence the right to life is confined to persons.

This brings us to our final requirement: an organism cannot have a right to life unless it is capable of self-consciousness, where an organism is self-conscious only if it recognizes that it is itself a continuing subject of experiences and other mental states. To justify this requirement, let us ask whether a person can fail to recognize that it is a person. If the answer were negative, it would follow from the requirement just established that an organism cannot have a right to life unless it possesses self-consciousness.

It is unclear, however, that something necessarily possesses self-consciousness if it is a person. Perhaps a person might fail to notice this fact about himself. Even if this is possible, it seems reasonable to believe that if something is a person, then it is *ipso facto capable* of acquiring the concept of a person, and of recognizing that it is itself a person. Thus even if something can have a right to life without having been self-conscious, it appears that it cannot have such a right without ever having possessed the capacity for self-consciousness.

Thus, the psychological characteristics that bestow a right to life upon an organism are these: it must be a person, capable of self-consciousness, of envisaging a future for itself, and of having desires about its own future states. . . .

The issue of abortion thus ceases to be puzzling. A human fetus does not have a right to life because it does not have the capacity for self-consciousness: it cannot conceive of itself as a continuing subject of experiences; it cannot envisage a future for itself, nor have desires about such a future. A fetus is not a person, but only a potential person. Hence there is no moral objection to abortion. To prohibit it is to inflict unjustified suffering and death upon society.

chapter 5

*E*uthanasia

INTRODUCTION

Historically, the term *euthanasia* has referred to an easy or good death. But it was also often used to mean the active killing of a person for that person's own good, especially to relieve suffering. The definition of the term has now been extended to include the withdrawal or withholding of life-prolonging medical treatment. The latter is frequently called *passive* euthanasia and the former *active* euthanasia. Euthanasia is distinguished from other types of killing by its motive, namely, a concern for the good of the "victim." A murderer intends harm to the victim, but one who commits euthanasia wishes to end another's life because one thinks that the person would be better off dead.

A couple of factors have made euthanasia a recent topic of wide concern. One factor is that people now die of different causes than they did in the past. The causes of death have changed radically during this century. In the United States in 1900 infectious diseases accounted for 60 percent of nonfetal deaths, excluding accidents and suicide; due to the development of vaccines, antibiotics, and better sterilization procedures in 1970 they accounted for fewer than 5 percent.[1] People are much more likely to die in old age of such chronic illnesses as cancer. With these chronic, debilitating diseases, death may come only at the end of a long, painful, and demoralizing process. A second factor is the development of medical technology. With artificial respirators, dialysis, and other technology, people—both adults and children—can now be kept alive when formerly they would have died.

Euthanasia can be accomplished in several ways and in different circumstances. These must be kept distinct, because some people believe they are ethically different. Besides distinguishing between active and passive euthanasia, one can also distinguish between euthanasia that is voluntary and euthanasia that is not. If the victim is rationally competent and voluntarily requests or consents to euthanasia, then it is voluntary; otherwise it is not. However, one also must distinguish between two forms of euthanasia that is not voluntary. In *involuntary euthanasia,* the victim is

147

rationally competent and refuses to consent; in *nonvoluntary euthanasia,* the victim is not rationally competent to make a choice. Thus one can speak of six types of euthanasia: (1) voluntary passive euthanasia; (2) voluntary active euthanasia; (3) involuntary passive euthanasia; (4) involuntary active euthanasia; (5) nonvoluntary passive euthanasia, and (6) nonvoluntary active euthanasia. It is possible, for each type of euthanasia, to hold that some or all instances are wrong, permissible, or obligatory. The following discussion will focus on the first two types and then briefly will consider the types of euthanasia that are not voluntary.

Voluntary Passive Euthanasia   In voluntary passive euthanasia, it is assumed that the victim is rationally competent and consents to or requests being allowed to die by the withholding or withdrawal of life-prolonging treatment. Each of the theories will judge the acceptability or inacceptability of this type according to its own tenets. The central premise of a *natural-law* view is that life is a basic good. This premise derives from Aquinas's view that all beings act toward self-preservation, which shows that life is a good.[2] Any act directly contrary to the good of human life is wrong. If one chooses to act on a proposal or plan that intentionally includes someone's death, the act is wrong. One can intend a death either directly as an end, as in the murdering of one's enemy, or as a means, as in the killing of oneself to avoid pain.

Since intending a person's death is wrong, whether one actively brings about the death or fails to prevent death is irrelevant. Seen this way, if one fails to provide intravenous fluids to a person so that he dies of dehydration, one has intended his death and acted wrongly. But although it is wrong to intentionally bring about someone's death, one need not do everything possible to keep oneself or another alive. If the means necessary to preserve life are unduly burdensome, one need not use them. For example, during the Middle Ages, if persons were advised to move from the seashore to the mountains for their health, they were not ethically required to do so. In refusing or withholding means of prolonging life that are burdensome, one is not intending death. One's intention is simply to avoid an excessive burden rather than to bring about death, for one's intention also will be fulfilled if the person lives. Today, when the permissibility of omitting burdensome means is considered, the terms ordinary and extraordinary means will often be used. *Ordinary means* are those that do not impose a sufficient burden to make the failure to use them permissible. *Extraordinary means* are all those that are not ordinary, that is, which are so burdensome that withholding them is permissible. In contemporary medical practice, for example, artificial respirators and heart transplants are understood as extraordinary means, whereas antibiotics for pneumonia or intravenous fluids to prevent dehydration are ordinary means.

To sum up, according to natural-law theory, allowing someone to die is wrong if the intention includes that person's death either as an end or as a means. Extraordinary means of prolonging life need not be employed, provided the intention is merely to avoid their burden rather than to bring about death.

The fundamental premise of a *natural-rights* position is that everyone has a right to life. Traditionally, the right to life is understood as the right not to be killed by others. It has not encompassed positive acts by one person to prolong another's life, as for example, by saving someone from drowning. Consequently, withholding or withdrawing life-prolonging treatment does not violate the right to life and so is permissible.

The *Kantian* tradition is not clear about the permissibility of allowing a person to die. Although Kant clearly holds that suicide is wrong, many commentators believe that his theory does not imply suicide is always wrong. Even if suicide is wrong, it does not follow that refusing life-prolonging treatment is wrong. It probably depends upon the reason a person refuses the treatment. Even though Kant believed suicide is wrong, he did not think it necessarily wrong to place oneself in a position in which death would almost certainly result. He, therefore, found acceptable dying to save one's country, or even killing oneself if one might be a danger to others, as for example, if one contracted incurable rabies.[3] Kant rejected suicide because it destroys the subject of morality, which is the rational will.[4] Refusing treatment that would incapacitate one's reason would not destroy but preserve the rational will and so seems permissible according to Kant's own rationale.

A *contractarian* view would almost certainly permit compliance with a person's rational, voluntary request to be allowed to die. Rational contractors will presumably choose a system incorporating a maximum liberty compatible with the assurance of a like liberty for others. The liberty to choose one's medical treatment is an application of the basic freedom of bodily integrity protected by the laws of assault and battery. Individual liberties, however, may be limited to better secure the overall system of liberty. A contractor might fear that the liberty to decide for oneself whether treatment should be withheld could be threatened by the withholding of treatment in cases when the victim did not voluntarily consent. Although this consideration might lead contractors to permit the withholding of treatment only under stringent conditions to guarantee the voluntariness and rationality of consent, it would not lead them to forbid the withholding of treatment upon a voluntary request.

Finally, *utilitarianism* generally permits people to die voluntarily. A consenting victim has judged that his prolonged life would be miserable, so withholding treatment and allowing him to die avoids misery and, as far as the victim is concerned, has more utility than prolonging his life. However, act utilitarians might decide that, in some cases, continued life-prolonging treatment, despite the victim's request to be allowed to die, would be permissible or even obligatory. They might argue that, although competent, the victim was mistaken in his perception of the utility of prolonging his life. They might also argue that the benefits to others would outweigh the continued suffering of the victim. For example, experiments on the victim might help prevent the occurrence of the disease in others or alleviate their suffering.

Voluntary Active Euthanasia   While theories that do not permit allowing persons to die voluntarily are unlikely to permit the active killing of them, theories that do permit voluntary death also may not permit active euthanasia. Whereas *natural-law* views usually will permit a person to die by the omission of extraordinary treatment, almost all active killing is forbidden. (In killing, one usually chooses a plan that intends death.) Nonetheless, some conduct that will cause death is permissible. Many natural-law theorists adopt the doctrine of double effect. The doctrine of double effect holds that an action having both a good and bad effect is permissible if (1) the bad effect is not intended as a means or as an end; and (2) the good effect outweighs the bad.[5] Condition 1 is the crucial one, for it guarantees that death is not intended. The doctrine of double effect gives little scope for euthanasia. Although it permits, for example, giving drugs to alleviate pain even if the side effect might be to shorten a person's life, it does not justify injecting a lethal dose of morphine.

The central question asked in the *natural-rights* tradition is whether the right not to be killed can be waived. One must distinguish between the inalienability of a right and its unwaivability. Consider the property right to one's car, which includes a right that others not use it. One may waive that right for particular people, for example, by letting a friend use it for an afternoon. However, one retains one's property right to the car. One alienates one's right to the car if one sells it and thus surrenders one's entire right to it. An inalienable right not to be killed could thus still be waivable. In one natural-rights view, which is basically that of John Locke, one cannot waive one's right not to be killed, because life is a gift from God and people are, in effect, God's property. Curiously, in this view, the right to life really is already alienated, inasmuch as it is God's right rather than one's own. If one considers individuals the full possessors of their right to life, then the right can be waived and voluntary active killing is permissible.

A *Kantian* view of active killing depends on whether Kant is correct about suicide. If suicide is wrong, then with a few possible exceptions noted earlier, active euthanasia is wrong. By the universal law of nature test, a person could not rationally will a universal maxim that he be killed. Consequently, no one else could will a universal law permitting him to kill the victim, for were he in the victim's position, he could not rationally will the universal law. Similarly, by the doctrine of ends, if a person would not be treating himself as an end in willing his death, neither would someone else. In short, active euthanasia always depends on whether it is permissible that the individual will he be killed.

A very prevalent justification for active killing stems from the Kantian tradition. It emphasizes the autonomy of rational agents. To respect that autonomy, a competent person must be free to choose life or death. As it is permissible for a competent person to exercise his autonomy to choose death, it is also permissible for another to kill him if he rationally and voluntarily chooses it. This argument does not, however, establish that medical personnel or anyone else has an obligation to kill a person who so requests it.

Although *contractarians* would certainly hold a principle generally forbidding the killing of others, they might allow an exception if the person rationally and voluntarily requested to be killed. To allow for such a death might maximize liberty and benefit people suffering intolerable conditions who might thus be classified as among the least advantaged persons. Contractors would insist that the person voluntarily request that he killed, for otherwise a significant freedom would be infringed. Moreover, they would require that, allowing for people's differing conceptions of a good life, the decision be rational. One would want to be protected from decisions one might make in an irrational state of mind or even from irrational decisions made when in a normal state of mind. How, precisely, another person is to decide whether one's decision is rational given one's conception of the good is not completely clear. Contractors would wish to balance assurance that the decision was rational with the claim to freedom, but no clear, explicit formula for so doing is evident.

Finally, *utilitarian* theory implies that no intrinsic moral difference exists between actively killing and allowing to die. Here it clearly and sharply differs from the natural-law tradition. The latter emphasizes whether death is intended, but for the utilitarian the intention makes no difference as long as the utility of the consequences is the same. Indeed, in some cases, utilitarian considerations clearly favor active killing. If, for instance, allowing a person to die will result in great pain during the lengthy process of dying, then painless killing is preferable. Generally, to decide whether the dying process will be so painful as to render actively killing a person preferable, one should be guided by the patient's wishes. If the patient requests only that he be allowed to die, then he has decided that the process of dying will not be so bad as to render active killing more useful for him. Sometimes a utilitarian may decide that a person is mistaken as to which method will have the highest utility for him. Rule utilitarians might differ from act utilitarians, for they might believe that accepting a rule against killing with an exception permitting actively killing people upon their request would have worse consequences than not allowing that exception. It might significantly decrease people's respect for life and thus lead to other undesirable consequences. However, few rule utilitarians would be so persuaded by this argument as to forbid active euthanasia, although they might have fairly stringent conditions as to the circumstances in which it is permissible.

Involuntary and Nonvoluntary Euthanasia   If voluntary euthanasia is prohibited by a theory so, of course, is euthanasia that is not voluntary. For some theories, voluntariness is crucial to the permissibility of euthanasia. In *natural-law* theory, however, the voluntariness of euthanasia is irrelevant to its permissibility. As it is the intention of causing death rather than its voluntariness that is crucial, it can be permissible to kill or to allow someone to die who cannot consent to it. Extraordinary treatment may be withheld from, or medicines shortening life as a side effect may be administered to, incompetent adults or infants and perhaps even competent persons who refuse to consent, although it is difficult to conceive of an acceptable example of the latter.

In the *natural-rights* tradition, involuntary active euthanasia is always wrong. The right not to be killed is certainly violated if the victim does not consent, no matter what the reason. The only possible exception to the wrongness of active involuntary euthanasia would be if the person were a threat to someone else's life, even innocently so.[6] However, in that case, the reason for the killing would be self-defense, not the well-being of the victim, so it would not even be appropriately classified as euthanasia. As no right to life-prolonging treatment exists, withholding it is permissible whether the person is incompetent or is competent and requests its continuation.

Likewise, in the *Kantian* tradition involuntary euthanasia of competent persons is wrong. If a competent patient wants treatment, one could not will withholding it were one in the patient's condition. The permissibility of nonvoluntary euthanasia is somewhat more difficult to determine. The problem is that the Kantian view is not clear about the status that should be accorded to nonrational persons. Morality is founded on, and holds for, rational wills. In one interpretation, all human beings have an underlying rational self, so they must all be treated as ends. In another interpretation, only beings manifesting rationality must be treated as ends. The former position seems to be the better interpretation of Kant. According to it, nonvoluntary euthanasia is permissible if, and only if, a rational person in the victim's position could consistently will his death. Finally, the neo-Kantian argument from autonomy for voluntary euthanasia cannot be extended to support involuntary euthanasia, for such euthanasia clearly denies a person's autonomy. Nor can nonvoluntary euthanasia with substituted consent be considered an exercise of the victim's autonomy, even if it respects the victim's expressed wishes before becoming incompetent.

Although *contractarians* emphasize the importance of voluntariness for the permissibility of euthanasia, they might permit some euthanasia that is not voluntary. Contractarians would not agree to involuntary euthanasia, for it permits someone to end another's life against his will. However, they might well agree to a principle permitting nonvoluntary euthanasia. For example, contractarians would have no reason to prohibit euthanasia of the irreversibly comatose. If comatose, people have no opportunity to enjoy the primary goods or to achieve their conception of the good. Generalizing from this, contractors would probably agree to nonvoluntary euthanasia for anyone incapable of significantly achieving any plausible conception of the good.

Finally, although *utilitarians* have good reason to be cautious about euthanasia that is not voluntary, they do not prohibit it in all cases. Act and rule utilitarians usually will differ in their thinking about involuntary euthanasia. In either view, the fact that a person wants to live is evidence of the utility to him or her of continued life. However, the utility of continued life to the individual must be weighed against its utility to others. Suppose that in order to live a few more weeks, someone wants a very expensive treatment, for example, an artificial heart costing $200,000. The cost, and other burdens, on relatives and others might outweigh the utility to the patient. Accepting a rule limiting the amount of resources a person could consume in prolonging his life might have more utility than accepting a rule without such a limit, so a rule utilitarian might agree to this limit. But an act utilitarian would go further. Suppose a person's continued life would be a financial and emotional strain on his family, and if he died his kidneys and eyes could be transplanted to others. The utility to others of euthanasia might well outweigh the utility of continued life to the person. Rule utilitarians probably would not accept a rule permitting euthanasia in such cases. If a rule permitting involuntary euthanasia were accepted, then everyone would be afraid that should they become seriously ill a physician or someone else might judge that there would be more utility in their dying. A rule prohibiting euthanasia in such situations would produce less unhappiness and so more utility, everything considered.

Act utilitarians would permit nonvoluntary euthanasia whenever its utility was greater than that of the person's continued life. The first and most important consideration would be the happiness the victim might expect from continued life. If the person was likely to suffer great pain and never recover, then his life would have net disutility for him. If he were likely to recover and have an enjoyable life, or have an enjoyable life even if he did not fully recover, then his life would have net utility for him, and euthanasia could be justified only if the benefits to others from his death outweighed those to him from continued life. For the reasons given above, a rule utilitarian would probably limit the permissibility of nonvoluntary euthanasia to situations in which continued life would have net disutility for the victim.

Readings The problem case is an unusual one. Most discussions of euthanasia assume that the victim has a terminal illness. The victim in this case does not and can expect to live for an indefinite period. Moreover, he has all his mental faculties (another factor many writers think is significant). Nonetheless, he requests to be allowed to die, because he still faces a long period of painful treatment and will be physically incapacitated afterward, although the extent of physical incapacitation is uncertain. The reader should consider whether it would make any difference if the person requested to be killed instead of merely to be allowed to die.

The selection from Germain Grisez and Joseph Boyle, Jr., represents the natural-law tradition. They argue that every act of killing is wrong but that not every deadly deed is killing. Active euthanasia as a form of killing is wrong regardless of its voluntariness. Allowing a person to die, as long as it involves acting on a proposal encompassing a person's death as an end or as a means, is also wrong. Although they do not use the doctrine of double effect, according to their theory, it is permissible to provide medicines that may shorten life, if the proposal one acts on does not include the person's death as a means or as an end. Finally, they distinguish between ordinary and extraordinary means and argue that it is permissible to refuse or not to provide treatment by extraordinary means.

The selection by Bertram and Elsie Bandman is in the Kantian and contractarian tradition, although it is not clearly an argument of either type. They agree with Rawls that justice has primacy over utility. Moreover, they argue on the basis of freedom, or autonomy, that people have a right to die as well as to live. By considering four hypothetical cases, they bring out possible conflicts between Kantian and utilitarian reasons for euthanasia, and they propose a principle to decide between them on the basis of the number and importance of the rights involved. They argue that euthanasia which is not voluntary is always wrong.

The selection by Richard Brandt represents the utilitarian tradition. Brandt does not directly apply the ideal moral code theory discussed in Chapter 3. In this paper he confines himself to considerations that would show a principle about killing to be acceptable to most people and thus coincide with their intuitions. The attentive reader will note that most of the arguments are concerned to show that limiting a principle about the wrongness of killing would increase happiness. From this perspective, Brandt is arguing that the principle he supports will have more utility than would another form of the principle.

Brandt considers a principle about the *prima facie* wrongness of killing. By this, he essentially means that killing prohibited by the principle is wrong unless considerations based on another rule or principle support the killing and outweigh the considerations against it. The primary considerations about killing, he argues, are the preferences of the victim and whether the killing will be an injury (produce negative utility for the victim). He concludes that it is *prima facie* wrong to terminate a person's life if it would be an injury to him or if he does not wish his life terminated. It is not, however, *prima facie* wrong if the termination would not be an injury or if it would be a positive benefit.

Notes

[1] U. S. Department of Commerce, Bureau of the Census, *Historical Statistics of the United States*, Bicentennial Edition (Washington, D.C.: U. S. Government Printing Office, 1975), vol. 1, p. 58.

[2] St. Thomas Aquinas, *Summa Theologica*, trans. Anton Pegis, *The Basic Writings of Saint Thomas Aquinas* (New York: Random House, 1945), I-II, Question 94, Article 2.

[3] Immanuel Kant, *The Doctrine of Virtue*, trans. Mary J. Gregor (New York: Harper & Row, 1964), p. 86; Akademie, p. 423.

[4] Ibid., p. 85; Akademie, pp. 422–23.

[5] Edwin F. Healey, S.J., *Medical Ethics* (Chicago, Ill.: Loyola University Press, 1956), p. 98; Norman St. John-Stevas, *Life, Death, and the Law* (Cleveland, O.: World, Meridian Books, 1961), p. 190; John C. Ford, S.J., "The Morality of Obliteration Bombing," in *War and Morality*, ed. Richard A. Wasserstrom (Belmont, Calif.: Wadsworth, 1970), p. 26.

[6] Robert Nozick, *Anarchy, State, and Utopia* (New York: Basic Books, 1974), pp. 34–35.

Bibliography on Euthanasia

Bayles, Michael D., and High, Dallas M., eds. *Medical Treatment of the Dying: Moral Issues*. Boston: G. K. Hall and Schenkman, 1978.

Behnke, John A., and Bok, Sissela, eds. *The Dilemmas of Euthanasia*. Garden City, N.Y.: Doubleday, Anchor Books, 1975.

Feinberg, Joel. "Voluntary Euthanasia and the Inalienable Right to Life." *Philosophy & Public Affairs* 7 (1978): 93–123.

Foot, Philippa. "Euthanasia." *Philosophy & Public Affairs* 6 (1977): 85–112.

Glover, Jonathan. *Causing Death and Saving Lives*. New York: Penguin, 1977.

Keyserlingk, Edward W. *Sanctity of Life or Quality of Life*. Protection of Life Series. Ottawa: Law Reform Commission of Canada, 1979.

Kluge, Eike-Henner W. *The Ethics of Deliberate Death*. Port Washington, N.Y.: Kennikat Press, 1981.

Kohl, Marvin. *The Morality of Killing*. New York: Humanities Press, 1974.

————, ed. *Beneficent Euthanasia*. Buffalo, N.Y.: Prometheus Books, 1975.

Ladd, John, ed. *Ethical Issues Relating to Life and Death*. New York: Oxford University Press, 1979.

McCloskey, H. J. "The Right to Life." *Mind* 84 (1975): 403–25.

McCormick, Richard A., S.J. "To Save or Let Die: The Dilemma of Modern Medicine." *Journal of the American Medical Association* 229 (1974): 172–76.

Rachels, James. "Euthanasia." In *Matters of Life and Death: New Introductory Essays in Moral Philosophy*, edited by Tom Regan, pp. 28–66. New York: Random House, 1980.

Veatch, Robert M. *Death, Dying and the Biological Revolution*. New Haven, Conn.: Yale University Press, 1976.

Woods, John. *Engineered Death*. Ottawa: University of Ottawa Press, 1978.

Zaner, Richard M., ed. "Appraisals." *The Journal of Medicine and Philosophy* 4 (September 1979).

Problem Case

The Texas Burn Victim

An unmarried, twenty-six-year-old former military jet pilot was severely burned in an accident, when he and his father set off an explosion of propane gas from a leaky pipeline as they started their car. The father was killed, and the young man sustained second- and third-degree burns over two-thirds of his body. Both eyes were blinded. After nine months of treatment, one eye had been removed, the tips of his fingers had been amputated, his hands were useless, and his body was infected in many places. To treat the infections, he was given a painful daily bath in a pool of antiseptic solution. There was some chance that partial sight might be restored to one eye and that some mobility be gained for his hands.

Ever since the accident, although he had accepted treatment, the man had stated that he did not want to live. After nine months, he refused permission for further surgery on his hands and insisted that he be permitted to leave the hospital to go home to die. Despite his protests,

See "Case Studies in Bioethics: A Demand to Die," *Hastings Center Report* 5 (June 1975): 9–10, 47.

the bathings were continued. The physicians called in a psychiatrist to treat what they considered to be the man's irrational depression. They wanted to have him judged incompetent and a guardian appointed to give permission for treatments. However, the psychiatrist determined that the man was quite rational. Should the man be permitted to refuse further treatment, because he does not want to live as a blind and crippled person?

GERMAIN GRISEZ AND JOSEPH M. BOYLE, JR.
EUTHANASIA

THE MORALITY OF KILLING: GENERAL CONSIDERATIONS

In the strict sense one kills a person when, having considered bringing about a person's death as something one could do, one commits oneself to doing it by adopting this proposal instead of some alternative and by undertaking to execute it. By definition killing in the strict sense is an action contrary to the good of life. The adoption of a proposal to bring about someone's death is incompatible with respect for this good. Thus every act which is an act of killing in the strict sense is immoral. No additional circumstance or condition can remove this immorality.

This definition and moral characterization of killing in the strict sense make no distinction between intent to kill, attempt to kill, and the consummation of the undertaking by successful execution. These distinctions, which are legally significant, are morally irrelevant. If one commits oneself to realizing a certain state of affairs, by the commitment one constitutes oneself as a certain type of person. If one commits oneself to killing a person, one constitutes oneself a murderer. This remains true even if one is prevented from attempting to execute one's purpose—for example, if someone else kills the intended victim first. Even more obviously it remains true if one attempts to execute one's purpose but fails—for example, if one shoots to kill but misses the intended victim.

Although everything which is an act of killing in the strict sense is immoral, not every deadly deed is an act of killing in this sense. . . . Some deadly deeds carry out a consciously projected design, but the performance is not the execution of a proposal adopted by the actor's choice to bring about the death of a human individual. . . . In what follows we call this type of performance a "deadly deed" to distinguish it from a killing in the strict sense.

Finally, there are other cases of causing death, such as some killing in self-defense, which are neither killing in the strict sense nor deadly deeds as here defined. The proposal adopted or the consciously projected design

From Germain Grisez and Joseph M. Boyle, Jr., *Life and Death with Liberty and Justice: A Contribution to the Euthanasia Debate* (Notre Dame, Ind.: University of Notre Dame Press, 1979), pp. 393–94, 412–19. Copyright 1979, University of Notre Dame Press, Notre Dame, Indiana 46556.

carried out by persons defending themselves might not extend beyond incapacitating the attacker, but this can result in the attacker's death if the only available and adequate means to incapacitate the attacker also will result in mortal wounds.

Deadly deeds and death-causing behavior which are not killing in the strict sense might or might not be immoral. The fact that killing in the strict sense always is immoral does not mean that other acts which result in someone's death are morally acceptable or less immoral than killing in the strict sense. What is distinctive about deadly deeds and death-causing behavior is that their morality is not settled by the kinds of acts they are, whereas the morality of killing in the strict sense is settled by the kind of act it is.

Of course, ordinary language, which heavily relies upon observable behavior in classifying acts, does not embody the distinctions we have made. Thus, to evaluate the morality of various classes of acts which result in death, we begin from the ordinary conceptions of these acts which are described by ordinary language and then apply our analysis to the morally significant distinctions in the subject matter.

It is worth noticing that our approach here would be quite impossible in the law, where actions must be determined by factors about which evidence is possible. But morality is not primarily a matter of making judgments about actions, still less a matter of one person judging the actions of another. Rather, morality is a matter of shaping one's own life toward its fullness. Hence, distinctions which individuals can respect or ignore in the hidden depths of their own consciences can be extremely important to morality, although totally unrealistic as instruments of social control, and so wholly irrelevant to the law. . . .

ACTIVE EUTHANASIA: VOLUNTARY AND NONVOLUNTARY

Considering matters from a moral point of view and from the side of the one whose life is to be ended, voluntary euthanasia is not significantly different from other cases of suicide. The proposal is to bring about death as a means to ending suffering. This proposal, if adopted and executed, is an instance of killing in the strict sense. It can never be morally justified.

Of course, a person who is in severe pain and who seeks death to escape it is likely to have mitigated responsibility or even to be drawn into acceptance without a deliberate choice, just as is the case with others whose suffering drives them to a deadly deed against themselves.

However, if an individual plans to seek euthanasia and arranges for it well in advance of the time of suffering, then the possibility that the demand for death is not an expression of deliberate choice is greatly lessened. The conditions which from the point of view of proponents of euthanasia are optimum for making a decision about the matter are precisely the conditions in which the decision is likely to be a morally unjustifiable act of killing in the strict sense.

Considering voluntary euthanasia from the point of view of the person who would carry out the killing, matters seem no better from a moral viewpoint. The performance can hardly fail to be an execution of a deliberate choice; the one carrying out the killing can hardly be driven to it, nor can anyone in the present culture accept the duty unquestioningly.

Of course, when a family member kills a relative under the present legal conditions, there is considerable likelihood that pressures of emotion are an important factor, and there is a possibility that no act of killing is done. But we are now thinking of the moral responsibility of someone who would carry out requested euthanasia if the practice were legalized, through acting by deliberate choice and perhaps in a professional capacity.

It might be objected that not everyone believes that human life itself is a basic good. Perhaps this belief is sincere. In such a case individuals seeking euthanasia and those providing this service would be doing nothing immoral by deliberate choice, for they would be acting upon a sincere belief, even if this belief is mistaken. After all, people are responsible, not for what they actually do, but for what they sincerely believe they are doing. How can one consider immoral the acts of those who seek or provide beneficent euthanasia in acting upon the conviction that human life is merely an instrumental good?

Our first response to this objection is that we are concerned here, not to judge anyone, but only to clarify sound guidelines for morally responsible deliberation and choice. We have argued . . . against the instrumentalist view of human life. If it is false, then those who shape their lives on this false assumption at the least are seriously mistaken about a matter of basic human concern. This mistake can hardly fail to lead to serious consequences for their attitudes and behavior toward other persons in many instances in which life is at stake.

But a further response to this objection is needed. The insight that human life is a basic good of persons is not a matter of empirical fact; it is a principle of practical reasoning. This principle underlies large areas of everyone's rational behavior. It is not easy to be mistaken about the inherent goodness of life, its inviolability, its worthiness of respect in every instance without exception. Somewhere there must be moral responsibility for a bias which hides and distorts so fundamental a truth.

This responsibility might be in an individual's own previous immoral choices. The opinion that life is not a basic good which deserves respect might be an effect of personal rationalization. Then again there is a tendency for this false opinion to attain the status of a climate of opinion by the formation of a social or cultural bias against human life. Here those who form opinion, shape the law, provide what ought to be scholarly reflection upon morality, and so on are the morally responsible agents of the moral blindness of others.

Nonvoluntary euthanasia also clearly proposes death as a treatment of choice. The act hardly can fail to be killing in the strict sense. And in addition to the violation of the good of life, the rights of those to be killed also will be violated—for example, by denial to them of equal protection of the laws. Nonvoluntary euthanasia would violate both life and justice.

On our analysis abortion is a subclass of nonvoluntary euthanasia. It is especially complicated, since in the case of abortion there are instances in which the child's death results from some act which is not itself the execution of a proposal that the child should die. In cases in which the retarded, the insane, the senile, or others would be terminated by nonvoluntary euthanasia it is difficult to think of circumstances in which their deaths would be caused otherwise than by the carrying out of the proposal that they should die, on the rationalization that their lives are not worth living and that they will be better off dead.

It will be objected that some who carried out nonvoluntary euthanasia —or who now promote it—might be motivated by genuine sympathy for others. We do not deny this possibility, although we suspect that the movement for euthanasia would have little political power were it not also motivated by the desire to get rid of the burden of unwanted people.

The important point is that sympathy, like other emotions, can lead to grossly immoral acts. Not all immorality is explicit egoism and self-indulgence. By sympathy one is identified with another psychologically, just as by patriotism one is identified with one's country, by racism with one's race, and so on. These emotions are morally neutral in themselves. They do permit one, however, to act immorally while to seem not to act out of self-interest. Sympathy together with a fanatical attachment to the good of avoiding pain and suffering can lead to grossly immoral violations of the good of life and rights of others in the ultimate form of paternalism: the killing of people for their own good.

Like all forms of paternalism, beneficent euthanasia would involve the arrogant presumption that one can determine on the basis of one's own scheme of values what is best for others who might well not share that scheme. And like all forms of paternalism which become institutionalized, beneficent euthanasia could easily become a mask for intentional injustices toward those whose lives were "kindly" extinguished—extinguished in the interests of others or society at large.

OMISSIONS, KILLING, AND LETTING DIE

The preceding treatment has been concerned with instances in which people bring about death by an outward performance. We now turn to a consideration of cases in which individuals refuse treatment for themselves or others, or withhold treatment, or fail or neglect to give it. To apply the moral theory which we articulated . . . to such cases we must first say something about omissions.

If people act when they carry out a proposal which they have adopted by choice, certain cases of outward nonperformance must count as human actions. One can adopt a proposal and carry it out by deliberately not causing or preventing something which one could cause or prevent. One's choice not to cause or prevent something can be a way of realizing a state of affairs one considers somehow desirable. For example, one might adopt the proposal to protest against a government policy permitting the use of public funds for abortion by not paying certain taxes. In this case one aims to realize a desired state of affairs by means of nonconformance with the demands of the law. The nonconformance need involve no outward performance at all.

Omissions of this type—those in which one undertakes to realize a proposed state of affairs by not causing or preventing something—are very important for understanding the morality of withholding treatment from dying patients, refusing treatment proposed for oneself, and in general letting people die.

On the analysis of this sort of omission which we just now stated it clearly is possible to kill in the strict sense by deliberately letting someone die. If one adopts the proposal to bring about a person's death and realizes this proposal by not behaving as one otherwise would behave, then one is committed to the state of affairs which includes the person's death. This commitment, although carried out by a nonperformance, is morally speaking an act of killing. It involves the adoption and execution of a proposal contrary to the basic good of human life. Thus, any case in which one chooses the proposal that a person die and on this basis allows the person to die is necessarily immoral.

For example, if a child is born suffering from various defects and if the physicians and parents decide that the child, the family, and society will all be better off if the burdens entailed by the child's continued life are forestalled by its death, and if they therefore adopt the proposal not to perform a simple operation, which otherwise would be done, so that the child will die, then the parents and physicians morally speaking kill the child—"kill" in the strict sense clarified at the beginning of this chapter. The fact that there is no blood spilled, no poison injected, that the death certificate can honestly show that the child has died from complications arising from its defective condition—none of this is morally relevant. The moral act is no different from any other moral act of murder.

The same thing will be true in every instance in which a judgment is made that someone—whether oneself or another—would be better off dead, the proposal to bring about death by not causing or preventing something is considered and adopted, and this proposal is executed by outward nonperformance of behavior which one otherwise might have attempted.

Moreover, it must be noticed that hastening death is bringing about death; no one lives forever, and so all killing merely hastens death. The essential factor from a moral point of view is, not whether a person killed already is dying, but whether one's performance or omission executes a proposal that one bring about the state of affairs which includes the person's being dead when one thinks that otherwise they might be alive.

It is worth noting that one's adopting a proposal to bring about a person's death does not require that one regard the person's death as desirable in itself, or that one will be pleased when it occurs. One might regret that a patient is suffering from a painful and mortal disease; one might wish that a retarded, insane, or senile person were normal and vigorously healthy. One might feel deep compassion for the person to be killed; one might be very reluctant to kill the person; one might feel very sad when the person dies. Nevertheless, if one adopts a proposal to hasten death—for example, by injecting an overdose of opiates—one does an act of killing in the strict sense. The commitment contrary to the good of life is made, although it is made in a situation in which alternatives lack much of their ordinary appeal, and although it is made with great sadness and executed with great regret.

This point is not too difficult to grasp in cases of action which involves an outward performance. But the same thing is just as true when the proposed method of killing is by not causing or preventing something. The murderous quality of an omission can more easily be overlooked or rationalized, however, due to confusion between the adoption of the proposal and the emotional situation and wishes which accompany the adoption of the proposal.

One killing by omission in a case of this sort both wants and does not want dead the person who is to be killed. The wanting is the voluntary adoption of the proposal that the person be dead; this is what is morally determinative. The not-wanting is in the wishes that things might be otherwise, the feeling of sadness and so forth with which the chosen means to the desired good—for example, release from suffering—are brought about.[1] . . .

NONTREATMENT AND REFUSAL OF TREATMENT

The fundamental point about these omissions is that one can omit to do some good or prevent some evil without adopting any proposal which either is opposed to the good or embraces (as means) the evil whose occurrence one accepts. This possibility is most obviously instantiated when one must forgo doing a certain good or preventing a certain evil because one has a duty, incompatible with doing the good or preventing the evil, to do some other good or prevent some other evil.

For example, in an emergency situation in which many people are seriously injured and the medical resources—including time and personnel—are limited, those making decisions must choose to treat some and put off the treatment of others, perhaps with fatal consequences to those not treated first. The nontreatment of those who are not treated is deliberate; even their deaths might be foreseen as an inevitable consequence and knowingly accepted when the decision to treat others is made. Yet plainly the nontreatment of those who are not treated need involve no proposal that these people should die or die more quickly than they otherwise would. Provided there is no partiality or other breach of faith with those not treated, the execution of a proposal to save others does not embrace the death of those who die, and no immorality is done.

In the preceding example there is a certain lack of choice, in that the situation itself prohibits one from treating everyone. There are other situations in which someone forgoes doing something good because of the opportunity to do something else which also is good but incompatible with the adoption and execution of the first proposal. This situation arises whenever there is a choice between alternatives, any of which can be adopted without moral fault. It can arise in a specific case in which one and only one alternative would involve acting to save a person's life.

For example, physicians can refuse to accept additional patients, even though they know that their refusal will lead to a patient's earlier death, without proposing that the patient die. Physicians might simply be choosing to limit their practice at a level which permits them to take reasonable care of their children's personal needs, of their own health, their religious duties, and other legitimate concerns.

Obviously there are limits. Physicians who refuse occasionally to interrupt their recreation to tend to a severe medical emergency might not be in violation of medical ethics or any specific duty, but any person with a proper level of dedication will be generous with time and talents in the service of others, and all who are fair-minded will do to others as they would wish others to do to them and to their own loved ones. In other words, the golden rule sets a very important moral limit beyond which an upright person will not go in omitting to serve the needs of others. To violate this limit is just as immoral—and can show just as vicious a disposition —as to violate the good of life by killing in the strict sense.

There is another type of reason for forgoing doing good which involves no disrespect for the good which would be realized by the action. One might notice that doing the action good in itself will in fact bring about many undesirable consequences. And one might choose not to adopt the proposal to do the good in order to avoid accepting these various bad consequences. This situation is exemplified in a very important way in many instances in which potentially life-prolonging treatment is refused, withheld, or withdrawn—even in the case of a patient who is not dying— because of the expected disadvantages of accepting, carrying out, or continuing treatment.

In chapter nine we have articulated grounds on which someone might reasonably consider treatment undesirable: if the treatment is experimental or risky, if it would be painful or otherwise experienced negatively, if it would interfere with activities or experiences the patient might otherwise enjoy, if it would conflict with some moral or religious principle to which the patient adheres, if it would be psychologically repugnant to the patient, or if the financial or other impact of the treatment upon other persons would constitute a compelling reason to refuse treatment.

The moral legitimacy of refusing treatment in some cases on some such grounds certainly was part of what Pius XII was indicating by his famous distinction between ordinary and extraordinary means of treatment. The Pope defined "extraordinary means" as ones which involve a "great burden," and he allowed that one could morally forgo the use of extraordinary means.[2]

The conception of extraordinary means clearly is abused, however, when the proposal is to bring about death by the omission of treatment, and the difficulties of the treatment are pointed to by way of rationalizing the murderous act. If it is decided that a person would be better off dead and that treatment which would be given to another will be withheld because of the poor quality of the life to be preserved, then the focus in decision is not upon the means and its disadvantageous consequences. Rather, what is feared is that the means would be effective, that life would be preserved, and that the life itself and its consequences would be a burden.

Moreover, even when treatment is refused, withheld, or withdrawn because of an objection to the means—and without the adopting of a proposal to bring about death—there still can be a serious moral failing.

A person who refuses lifesaving or life-prolonging treatment, not on a suicidal proposal but because of great repugnance for the treatment itself, might have an obligation to maintain life longer in order to fulfill duties toward others.

For example, someone on dialysis might wish to give up the treatment because of the difficulties it involves, and some persons in this situation could discontinue treatment and accept death without moral fault. But a parent with children in need of continued care, a professional person with grave responsibilities, and many other persons who can prolong their lives at considerable sacrifice to themselves are morally bound to do so, even by this extraordinary means, because they have accepted duties which others are entitled to have fulfilled, and persons who love the goods as one ought will faithfully fulfill duties toward others at considerable cost to themselves.

Similarly, if one refuses, withholds, or withdraws lifesaving or life-prolonging treatment for another because of the grave burdens entailed by such treatment, the burdens must be grave indeed. This is especially clear in cases in which the patient is not dying—for example, cases of defective infants. One must be quite sure, at the least, that with no suicidal proposal one would in the patient's place not wish the treatment. Otherwise, one accepts moral responsibility for a very grave wrong toward the patient. . . .

Again, people can omit treatment as part of a project to cause death without becoming morally guilty of killing in the strict sense because the project is not the proposal upon which they act. Consider, for instance, the situation of nurses who are trained—perhaps too strictly—to follow the orders of physicians. If parents and physicians conspire in the killing of a defective infant by starving it to death, and if the physicians order that neither food nor fluids are to be given the infant, a nurse might not think of disobeying. In such cases nurses do not make themselves parties to the conspiracy. Their fault, if fault it is, is in their too uncritical acceptance of the domination of their own proper sphere of activity by physicians, even when physicians no longer act in the interest of the patient and in the service of life.

Notes

[1] See Gerald Hughes, "Killing and Letting Die," *The Month* 236 (1975): 43–44.

[2] Pius XII, "The Prolongation of Life," *The Pope Speaks* 4 (1957–1958): 395–96 (*AAS*, 49 [1957], pp. 1027–33 at 1030).

BERTRAM AND ELSIE BANDMAN
RIGHTS, JUSTICE, AND EUTHANASIA

THE RIGHT TO DECIDE TO LIVE OR DIE

We wish to suggest an amended corollary to H. L. A. Hart's justly famous thesis that "if there are any moral rights at all, it follows that there is at least one natural right, the equal right of all men to be free."[1] Our amended corollary is that if there are any moral rights at all, there is at least one prior right founded on justice—the equal right of all persons to be free to decide to live or die. Such a prior moral right, we shall argue, is moreover one whose claims are nearly incontestable and can only be overridden under extraordinary circumstances (a) favoring the continuation of a person's life and (b) involving the least injustice. The type of exception to be noted is justified only on the grounds that it provides the least injustice to everyone's otherwise inviolably equal right to be free.

The equal right to be free to decide to live or die, we hold, is based largely on John Rawls' point that "to respect persons is to recognize that they possess an inviolability founded on justice that even the welfare of society as a whole cannot override."[2] We demur, ever so slightly, however, to Rawls' implication that "the welfare of society as a whole" makes no morally just claim. There is also justice in being on the side of "the welfare of society as a whole." A conflict between moral rights and claims involving difficult choices calls for a just procedure to effect the least possible injustice, which does not, however, override the claims of justice. That is, justice, as "the first virtue of social institutions,"[3] cannot be overturned in principle; only in some of the circumstances of its application is a just claim ever overridden, but always and only by some other just claim. But justice and just claims are never morally overriden by injustice or by unjust claims, only by those that effect the least injustice. According to Rawls, with whom we agree on this point, "the interests requiring the violation of justice have no value. Having no merit in the first place, they cannot override its claims.[4]

This article first appeared in *Beneficent Euthanasia*, edited by Marvin Kohl, published by Prometheus Books, Buffalo, N.Y., and is reprinted by permission.

THE RIGHT TO BE FREE TO DECIDE TO LIVE OR DIE

But first this explication of what it means to have the prior right to be free to decide to live or die.

A corollary of the right to be free is the right to live. One cannot be free if one is not alive. Almost no one wants to die. There is such a thing as living well, but not dying well. Almost no one to whom beneficent euthanasia applies wants to die. Justice is connected to what a person wants.[5] The first moral right, if there is one, is the equal right to be free. And this freedom involves the freedom to live as unimpaired, as uninjured, and as long as possible.

To die is to lose whatever freedom one has. The moral right to be free, if there is any moral right at all, implies the equal right to be free to live. One cannot exercise freedom in death. . . .

. . . If everyone has an equal right to be free, this entails the equal right to be free to live as well and as long as possible. The only way to exercise such a right is to be put in a corresponding position to *claim* it.

A just society is here distinguishable from one that is unjust. An unjust society makes no provision for the physically weak and infirm to have their moral rights respected and recognized and put into effect. A just society is one that respects a person's inviolable right to be free even if he is in no position to make the needed physical movements to assume and safeguard his rights. Others protect but do not usurp or assume the right to live of the debilitated person.

. . . A just society utilizes its resources to respect the wishes of its people, young and old, and does more to prevent and also to attempt to cure fatal diseases than does an unjust society. A just society places its priorities on values that make possible the long and good life equally for everyone.

Even those who welcome death seldom do so in the belief that death is another phase of a better life rather than the end of life.

Notwithstanding such a desire, the requirement to respect a person's autonomy implies that a person is capable of being rational, that he is adequately informed and freely gives consent, and that he alone has not only the equal moral right to be free to live but also that he has, ultimately and finally, the equal right to be free to decide to live or die.

As bad as death is to most persons who want to live, the right of a person to decide includes the last decision for which one may be free, to decide to die, "to end it all" in Hamlet's phrase. Only the patient has the moral right to decide the question of his death; and to assure that his right to live or die shall be respected, restrictive conditions accompany those who would, with his consent, terminate his life.

To decide to live or die counts among the chief performances one could possibly be engaged in. They involve a person's being. The right of a person to be free to live or die is accordingly *first person*, not second or third person.

According to Stanley Benn, "If one is a person, he can't legitimately be a subject of consequentialist arguments that wholly exclude his interests; he has a right to have his own events taken into account."[6] One's own moral right to live or die is not someone else's to decide. Proxies decide for the "incompetent, infant or aged, but to do so violates the sanctity of a person."[7]

But even for a person, the right to die is not as high a priority right as the right to live, because a consequence of the exercise of the right to die is the final elimination of a person's freedom. A person who chooses to die cannot take back his decision after it has been acted on. So safeguards are needed to assure that the desire to die is the firm conviction of the patient.

There may even be extenuating circumstances in which the prolonged suffering of a person may have beneficial consequences that enhance other persons' possibilities of living. The right to live outweighs the right to die. So, in a pinch where the lives of others depend on overruling a person's right to die, his right to die justly gives way to their prior right to live.

But the converse is not ordinarily just. Sacrificing a person's life to save others is not necessarily just. It may be done, it may be necessary, but necessity is not morality. It is only moral if it is the least unjust thing to do. Would sacrificing one life to save others be the least unjust thing to do in some circumstances?[8] If so, it would be the moral thing to do. But the following priorities must be recognized within the right to decide to live or die: (1) a person's right to decide to live or die overrides anyone else's right to decide for that person; (2) a person's right to live overrides another person's right to die; (3) in a situation involving two or more persons' rights to live or die, taking 1 and 2 into consideration, the least injustice overrides anyone's right to live or die—that is, the equal rights of several persons to live outweighs one person's right to live.

Least injustice can be explained as follows. Every person has the equal right to be free to decide to live or die. Justice as the *equal* right to be free and to be treated fairly and impartially means that a person's right to be free is made less equal if unjust exception is taken to 1 and 2. And, in 3, everyone's equal right to live (assuming that all rights are at least partly derived from needs) means that in a "catastrophe case" the equal rights of several persons to live overrides one person's equal right to live. The sacrifice of one's life in certain emergency situations to save the lives of many may constitute the least injustice. A fireman may sense that the least evil and also the least injustice is in his risking his life, or an elderly person in a life raft may sense that the least injustice is in giving up his life.[9] On the other hand, the person in a life raft who is best qualified to guide it to safety ought, on the grounds of the survival of the majority, to be the last to sacrifice himself.

The point is that the least injustice in life-and-death cases consists in an equal consideration of every person's need to live.[10] The reason for 3 is that in a "catastrophe case"[11] one person's equal right to be free to live or die may be overridden by another person's right to live if it results in the least injustice. Killing a person is morally wrong unless it can be shown that killing that person effects the least injustice in a given situation.[12] At any rate, as a matter of moral priority, only after settling the question of whether or under what conditions to permit beneficent euthanasia does the question of having to administer beneficent euthanasia arise. But under no circumstances is killing a person with "mercy" or "kindness," inducing a "a good death," or effecting "death with dignity" without recognition of the recipient's rights morally desirable. Are these expressions even logically free of a category mistake?[13] . . .

SOME EXAMPLES

Hypothetical Case 1: (A₁) Mr. Black, a gifted pathologist, can cure a disease that will save others' lives but is himself cancer-ridden and wants to die. Black is still functioning but would rather die. According to A₁ Black has a right to die.

(B₁) There is an overriding reason to deny Black the right to die. If Black were not gifted, B₁'s response would be that Black has the right to die. But B₁ appeals to Black's capacity to help others. That is, Black, although painfully suffering from an incurable disease, is the only one who knows how to cure his disease, which will extinguish life in his community.

Does Black in this instance have the incontestable right to decide to live or die? If commonsense moral intuitions are consulted, one might, in this instance, invoke B₁'s argument, thus restricting Black's right to decide. What happened to Black's inviolable right?

Hypothetical Case 2: (A₂) Mr. Blue, cancer ridden, wants to live, but his family is seriously inconvenienced by the cost of Blue's care. The family finances are depleted. Yet, according to A₂ Blue has the right to live.

(B₂) Blue's right to live is overridden by his family's needs and claims. Blue is a drain on the family finances, which effectively prevents his four sons from going to college. Moreover, the physician believes that Blue will be a drag on society and that he would be better off dead than living in a public home at the taxpayers' expense. According to B₂ Blue will only become a burden to society and so his right to live is overridden by the greater needs of society.

A₂ says that Blue was not only deprived of his right to live but that his right to decide whether to live or die also was *violated.* On the contrary, B₂ says, it was Blue's family that suffered the most. Blue no longer had the right to decide, and even if he did, it was overruled by the needs, claims, and interests of his family and of society.

One's sense of justice this time seems to favor A₂'s side, perceiving that Blue's right to decide to live or die was violated. Moreover, favoring A₂ accords with Blue's equal right to be free to decide whether to live or die. So, although there may be a problem, which we will consider, in resolving the case 1 conflict, there seems to be no problem of consistency or explanation in case 2; for the decision favoring A₂ is consistent with Blue's prior right to decide to live or die.

Hypothetical Case 3: (A_3) Let us next imagine the following: Mrs. Green, a woman of wealth and an accomplished pianist, has twins, each of whom needs an immediate kidney transplant to live. She is the only available donor. She has heart trouble and an operation would risk her life. There is a 50 percent chance of her dying in surgery, but if she dies in surgery, then both kidneys may be transplanted and both children can be saved. According to A_3 her children have a right to live, but not at the risk of her life. Her right to live overrides their right.

(B_3) Mrs. Green's twins have a right to live, either of whom can do so only if she gives up a kidney for either child, possibly by drawing lots. Better to risk one life, Mrs. Green's, and save at least one of the twins. If Mrs. Green dies during surgery, then both children will live. In either case, her risk means that two people will live in good health. If she refuses, she lives, but both sons will die. To B_3 it is two lives to one in any case. Therefore, the right of at least one son to live overrides the right of the mother to refuse to take a 50 percent risk.

Case 2 offered us little difficulty; case 3 is indeed difficult to judge. Here Mrs. Green, in exercising her right to live or die, chooses to live, which overrides the right to die. But Mrs. Green's right to live—more precisely, her right to refuse to risk her life for the sake of saving the life of at least one other person in a pinch case—is overridden by her twins' rights to live because it is the least unjust thing to do in the situation.[14] This appeal will also subsequently be defended.

Hypothetical Case 4: (A_4) Brown, aged sixteen, the brilliant only child of professional parents, suffers from advanced leukemia, following years of painful drug administration, radiation, transfusions, and hospitalizations. He has seen other children die of the same illness and can no longer bear the painful process of the disease and wishes to die. A_4 holds that Brown has the right to die. The doctor's prognosis coincides with the boy's. He sees no point in prolonging a painful and hopeless process.

(B_4) Brown's parents are heartbroken. They are able to supply every possible means of medical assistance and care to prolong his life and keep hoping for a remission or the discovery of a lifesaving drug, despite the obvious terminal phase of their son's illness. They want him to live. According to B_4 Brown's right to decide to die is overridden by his parents' wishes.

A_4 overrides B_4 because Brown's right to be free to decide to live or die outweighs the preferences of his parents and even Brown's right to prefer death to life, which although a lower priority than the right to life is in accord with Brown's prior right to decide. Case 4 is different from case 1 in that Brown, unlike Black, does not have the lives of others depending on his continuing to live. So Brown has the equal moral right to decide to die. In Black's case that right is not equal since others' lives depend on Black. In case 2 Blue's right to live overrides his family's concerns with serious financial difficulty; nor does the inconvenience to society count. And unlike the Green case, Blue's right involves no pinch or "either/or," as Black's case does. According to the principles of justice so far developed, in cases 1 and 3, B's argument overrides A's; and in cases 2 and 4 A's argument overrides B's. . . .

PRINCIPLES

A appeals to a modified deontological or Kantian view that bases all action on exceptionless principles. B appeals to utilitarian consequentialist principles, which are concerned with maximizing flourishing and minimizing the total amount of pain and has been called the "aggregative principle."[15] A appeals to a principle K: Every person without exception has the equal moral right to be free. Therefore, treat every person with respect and justice as an end, never as a means to be sacrificed without his consent for the convenience, welfare, or the lives of others.[16] B, however, appeals to a principle U: Always maximize happiness and flourishing for everyone without regard for the rights of any given person and minimize the total amount of suffering in the world. Regarding euthanasia, maximize kindness and minimize cruelty.

In case 1 our moral intuitions, it seems, favor B_1. But does this mean that Black has no right to decide whether to live or die? He has, but his right is overridden by appeal to U, which coincides with the priority of life over death. In case 2 A's appeal to K coincides with everyone's equal right to be free to decide to live or die, and with Blue's right to live, which has priority over financial inconvenience to Blue's family. In case 3, Mrs. Green's right to live without risking her life is overridden by appealing to U, which maximizes the saving of life. In case 4, Brown's right to decide is not overridden by the rights of others, in this case the preferences of his family. Black (case 1) and Brown (case 4) want euthanasia. Black's right is overridden by the equal right of others to live. This is not so with Brown, who has the right to have his life ended. Case 4 clearly rules in favor of beneficent euthanasia, whereas case 1 rules against it. So, even one's right to end life is not sacrosanct. Blue and Green (cases 2 and 3) both want to live. Blue's right involves no other person's equal right to live and so his right overrides his family's financial concerns. Case 2 accordingly clearly rules in favor of Blue and reveals in this type of case the strength of K over U.

But on what basis do we decide to favor B in case 3? Gertrude Ezorsky tells us in a similar connection that in dire cases of this sort—"catastrophic cases" or "pinch cases"—one appeals to a compromise principle "to referee the outcome."[17] We accordingly appeal in a pinch case to the following principle, KU: Consider happiness, flourishing, pleasure, and pain, but do the least injustice possible. Hence, Mrs. Green's right to live and not to risk her life is overridden, but by appeal to the compromise principle KU.

Appeal to KU gives the equal rights of Mrs. Green's twins a moral edge over Mrs. Green's right not to risk her life. In case 1, in conjunction with the principles of justice stated initially, appeal to U suffices to decide between Black's desire to die and the needs of those whose lives depend on his staying alive. If there is doubt about whether to appeal to U or to K, appeal to KU, being closest to our initial principles, settles the issue in favor of those who need help to live that only Black can give.

In case 2, in conjunction with our initial principles, appeal to K is also sufficient. Again, if a doubt arises, further appeal to KU settles the question in favor of Blue's right to live. Finally, in cases 3 and 4, appeal to U and K, respectively, settles the matter. But, if a doubt arises, appeal to KU in Green's case favors the saving of more lives and in Brown's case favors his right to live or die over the preferences of others. Consequently, wherever a doubt arises, one may appeal finally to KU to decide any of the four cases. But what is the basis for appeal to KU?

FULLY INFORMED AND FREELY GIVEN CONSENT

. . . What about "permanent-coma" or "vegetable" cases or severely brain-damaged and paralyzed infants? We do not think that the killing of any person without his fully informed and freely given consent is ever just, and moreover, we do not think that unjust killing is ever beneficent. . . .

We hold with Rawls that "the priority of justice is accounted for by holding that the interests requiring the violation of justice have no value. Having no merit in the first place, they cannot override its claims."[18] "With the principles of . . . justice, the aims of benevolence and the requirements of respect are both undefined. . . . Once justice is on hand, the ideas of respect and human dignity [acquire] . . . a more definite meaning. . . . Thus, to respect persons is to recognize that they possess an inviolability founded on justice that even the welfare of society as a whole cannot override. The loss of freedom for some is not made right by a greater welfare enjoyed by others."[19]

Our point is that the just termination of a person's life does not consist in disregarding his rights. Just and beneficent euthanasia entails full disclosure and freely given consent. Otherwise, it is neither just nor beneficent, but killing of another kind. Kindness alone will not do. A master may be kind to his slaves, but that makes no difference because slavery itself is without dignity and respect. . . .

One may be kind to animals and put them to death kindly without informing them or obtaining their consent. But respecting a person's right to decide to live or die involves his and only his fully and freely given *consent*. No amount of kindness or benevolence can ever justify depriving a person of his right to consent or to refuse to have his life medically terminated.

One argument that is made for beneficent euthanasia is the appeal to "dying with dignity." There is no dignity, however, if there is either coercion or absence of informed and freely given consent. Thus, "dying with dignity" rules out coercion. Respecting the rights of a patient is more important than involuntarily terminating a patient's life with kindness or compassion to assure that he dies in peace. A kind, compassionate, or peaceful death is neither beneficent nor just if it implies a patient's loss of his right to be free to decide.

THE RIGHT TO DIE IS LIMITED AND HEDGED ROUND WITH RESTRICTIONS

A way to keep the "wedge" from applying is to restrict the conditions for justifying euthanasia. Conditions for justified euthanasia are the fully informed and freely given consent of the recipient.

These conditions can be overridden only if prolonging a person's life (or risking it) against his will results in saving the lives of others (as in cases 1 and 3). Otherwise a person's will cannot be overridden (as in cases 2 and 4).

Everyone has an *equal* moral right to decide to live or die, and one person's right to decide is *not equal* to that of others if their lives depend on overriding his right. That was one reason for appealing to KU in a pinch case such as 1 or 3. Extraneous family financial factors (case 2) or family preferences (case 4) do not carry moral weight against every person's equal right to decide. Where there is a conflict, the right to live overrides the right to die (as in case 1); and if there is a conflict between two or more people's equal rights to live, two or more equal rights outweigh one person's equal right (as in case 3). Only with such exceptions to restrict euthanasia does one provide the least injustice in pinch cases, thereby safeguarding the beneficence of euthanasia.

Even a rational and just society occasionally calls on a person to perform the supererogatory and heroic acts of living with unbearable pain or of risking one's life (as in cases 1 and 3) for the good of others. There are otherwise no rational grounds for weakening restrictions against justified euthanasia. A society that compels people to make premature life or death decisions may foreclose alternatives for improving and lengthening life and is, to that extent, cruel and unjust for not assuring every person's equal right to be free; for if a person is free, he will ordinarily choose to live. . . .

Notes

[1] H. L. A. Hart, "Are There Any Natural Rights?" in A. I. Melden, ed., *Human Rights* (Belmont, Calif.: Wadsworth, 1970), p. 61.

[2] J. Rawls, *A Theory of Justice* (Cambridge, Mass.: Harvard Univ. Press, 1971), p. 586.

[3] *Ibid.*, p. 3.

[4] *Ibid.*, p. 31.

[5] Cf. Philippa Foot, "Moral Beliefs," *Proceedings of the Aristotelian Society* (1958), p. 104.

[6] See also S. Benn, "Abortion, Infanticide, and Respect for Persons," in J. Feinberg, ed., *The Problem of Abortion* (Belmont, Calif.: Wadsworth, 1973), p. 103.

[7] It may not only be individual persons who have rights in a just scheme. Animals, too, may have rights, but the question of animal rights is not resolved here. It is assumed that at least persons have moral rights.

⁸ Louise Horowitz posed this ingenious example. A and B need a kidney transplant. C is dying. Killing C may help A or B, not both. Should the doctor kill C to save A? We hold that a person's right to be free to decide to live (or die) should have absolute priority over anyone else's (for example, the doctor's) right to kill one person in order to save another person.

⁹ For a further discussion of need in relation to justice, see A. D. Woozley, "Injustice," *American Philosophy Quarterly*, Monograph No. 7 (1973), pp. 109–112, especially p. 114.

¹⁰ Marvin Kohl in *The Morality of Killing* (New York: Humanities Press, 1974), pp. 27–28, recounts an example in Hersey's novel *The Wall* where an innocent, crying child is killed by a resistance leader to save ninety people from being found and killed by the Nazis. We contend that this is an example of the least unjust thing to do. That is, if ninety persons had been massacred to avoid killing one innocent person a greater injustice would have been done. See also Rawls, p. 4.

¹¹ See G. Ezorsky, "The Ethics of Punishment," in G. Ezorsky, ed., *Philosophical Perspectives on Punishment* (Albany, N.Y.: State Univ. of New York Press, 1971), pp. xx–xxii.

¹² The right to decide to live or die, as with any moral right, is founded on justice. Even cruelty, torture, rape, incest, killing without consent, since they violate a person's rights, are unjust. Whenever rights are invoked as violated, questions of justice or injustice arise. Injustice, moreover, is morally wrong. Cf. Kohl, *The Morality of Killing*, pp. 13–14; also pp. 28 and 35.

¹³ See Paul Ramsey, "Indignity of 'Death with Dignity,'" *Studies*, Hastings Center, 2:2 (May 1974), p. 48.

¹⁴ One may call this the "double effect." In a pinch or massacre case, one has to do an evil in order to do good. One has to settle for the least injustice.

¹⁵ These principles are adapted from Ezorsky, p. xxi.

¹⁶ K is action based on exceptionless principles. We interpret K, however, without Kant's prohibition against suicide. Our reason is that anyone suffering intractable pain, with the resulting disinclination to live based on the reality of imminent death, could rationally universalize the class of self-willed deaths under such conditions without implying the conclusion that the whole human race should, therefore, commit suicide. Cf. also H. J. Paton, *The Categorical Imperative* (Chicago: Univ. of Chicago Press, 1948), p. 172. Regarding A₃ Kant held that man only has an imperfect duty to help others. See H. J. Paton, *The Moral Law,* Hutchinson, 1948, p. 31.

¹⁷ G. Ezorsky, pp. xxi and xxii.

¹⁸ Rawls, p. 31.

¹⁹ *Ibid.*, p. 586.

RICHARD BRANDT
A MORAL PRINCIPLE ABOUT KILLING

One of the Ten Commandments states: "Thou shalt not kill." The commandment does not supply an object for the verb, but the traditional Catholic view has been that the proper object of the verb is "innocent human beings" (except in cases of extreme necessity), where "innocent" is

This article first appeared in *Beneficent Euthanasia,* edited by Marvin Kohl, published by Prometheus Books, Buffalo, N.Y., and is reprinted by permission.

taken to exclude persons convicted of a capital crime or engaged in an unjust assault aimed at killing, such as members of the armed forces of a country prosecuting an unjust war. Thus construed, the prohibition is taken to extend to suicide and abortion. (There is a qualification: that we are not to count cases in which the death is not wanted for itself or intended as a *means* to a goal that is wanted for itself, provided that in either case the aim of the act is the avoidance of some evil greater than the death of the person.) Can this view that all killing of innocent human beings is morally wrong be defended, and if not, what alternative principle can be?

This question is one the ground rules for answering which are far from a matter of agreement. I should myself be content if a principle were identified that could be shown to be one that would be included in any moral system that rational and benevolent persons would support for a society in which they expected to live. Apparently others would not be so content; so in what follows I shall simply aim to make some observations that I hope will identify a principle with which the consciences of intelligent people will be comfortable. I believe the rough principle I will suggest is also one that would belong to the moral system rational and benevolent people would want for their society.

Let us begin by reflecting on what it is to kill. The first thing to notice is that *kill* is a biological term. For example, a weed may be killed by being sprayed with a chemical. The verb *kill* involves essentially the broad notion of death—the change from the state of being biologically alive to the state of being dead. It is beyond my powers to give any general characterization of this transition, and it may be impossible to give one. If there is one, it is one that human beings, flies, and ferns all share; and to kill is in some sense to bring that transition about. The next thing to notice is that at least human beings do not live forever, and hence killing a human being at a given time must be construed as *advancing the date* of its death, or as *shortening its life*. Thus it may be brought about that the termination of the life of a person occurs at the time t instead of at the time $t + k$. Killing is thus shortening the span of organic life of something.

There is a third thing to notice about *kill*. It is a term of causal agency and has roots in the legal tradition. As such, it involves complications. For instance, suppose I push a boulder down a mountainside, aiming it at a person X and it indeed strikes X, and he is dead after impact and not before (and not from a coincidental heart attack); in that case we would say that I killed X. On the other hand, suppose I tell Y that X is in bed with Y's wife, and Y hurries to the scene, discovers them, and shoots X to death; in that case, although the unfolding of events from my action may be as much a matter of causal law as the path of the boulder, we should *not* say that I killed X. Fortunately, for the purpose of principles of the morally right, we can sidestep such complications. For suppose I am choosing whether to do A or B (where one or the other of these "acts" may be construed as essentially *inaction*—for example, *not* doing what I know is the one thing that will *prevent* someone's death); then it is enough if I know, or have reason to think it highly probable, that were I to do A, a state of the world including the death of some person or persons would ensue, whereas were I to do B, a state of the world of some specified different sort would ensue. If a moral principle will tell me in this case whether I am to do A or B, that is all I need. It could be that a moral principle would tell me that I am absolutely never to perform any action A, such that were I to do it the death of some innocent human being would ensue, provided there is some alternative action I might perform, such that were I to do it no such death would ensue.

It is helpful, I think, to reformulate the traditional Catholic view in a way that preserves the spirit and intent of that view (although some philosophers would disagree with this assessment) and at the same time avoids some conceptions that are both vague and more appropriate to a principle about when a person is morally blameworthy for doing something than to a principle about what a person ought morally to do. The terminology I use goes back, in philosophical literature, to a phrase introduced by W. D. Ross, but the conception is quite familiar. The alternative proposal is that there is a *strong prima facie obligation* not to kill any human being except in justifiable self-defense; in the sense (of prima facie) that it is morally *wrong* to kill any human being except in justifiable self-defense *unless* there is an even stronger prima facie moral obligation to do something that cannot be done without killing. (The term *innocent* can now be omitted, since if a person is not innocent, there may be a stronger moral obligation that can only be discharged by killing him; and this change is to the good since it is not obvious that we have no prima facie obligation to avoid killing people even if they are not innocent.) This formulation has the result that sometimes, to decide what is morally right, we have to compare the stringencies of conflicting moral obligations—and that is an elusive business; but the other formulation either conceals the same problem by putting it in another place, or else leads to objectionable implications. (Consider one implication of the traditional formulation, for a party of spelunkers in a cave by the oceanside. It is found that a rising tide is bringing water into the cave and all will be drowned unless they escape at once. Unfortunately, the first man to try to squeeze through the exit is fat and gets wedged inextricably in the opening, with his head inside the cave. Somebody in the party has a stick of dynamite. Either they blast the fat man out, killing him, or all of them, including him, will drown. The traditional formulation leads to the conclusion that all must drown.)

Let us then consider the principle: "There is a strong prima facie moral obligation not to kill any human being except in justifiable self-defense." I do not believe we want to accept this principle without further qualification; indeed, its status seems not to be that of a basic principle at all, but derivative from some more-basic principles. W. D. Ross listed what he thought were the main basic prima facie moral obligations; it is noteworthy that he listed a prima facie duty not to *cause injury*, but he did not include an obligation not to kill. Presumably this was no oversight. He might have thought that killing a human being is always an injury, so that the additional listing of an obligation not to kill would be redundant; but he might also have thought that killing is sometimes *not* an injury and that it is prima facie obligatory not to kill only when, and because, so doing would injure a sentient being.

What might be a noninjurious killing? If I come upon a cat that has been mangled but not quite killed by several dogs and is writhing in pain, and I pull myself together and put it out of its misery, I have killed the cat but surely not *injured* it. I do not injure something by relieving its pain. If someone is being tortured and roasted to death and I know he wishes nothing more than a merciful termination of life, I have not injured him if I shoot him; I have done him a favor. In general, it seems I have not injured a person if I treat him in a way in which he would want me to treat him if he were fully rational, or in a way to which he would be indifferent if he were fully rational. (I do not think that terminating the life of a human fetus in the third month is an injury; I admit this view requires discussion.[1])

Consider another type of killing that is not an injury. Consider the case of a human being who has become unconscious and will not, it is known, regain consciousness. He is in a hospital and is being kept alive only through expensive supportive measures. Is there a strong prima facie moral obligation not to withdraw these measures and not to take positive steps to terminate his life? It seems obvious that if he is on the only kidney machine and its use could *save* the life of another person, who could lead a normal life after temporary use, it would be wrong not to take him off. Is there an obligation to continue, or not to terminate, if there is no countering obligation? I would think not, with an exception to be mentioned; and this coincides with the fact that he is *beyond* injury. There is also not an obligation *not* to preserve his life, say, in order to have his organs available for use when they are needed.

There seems, however, to be another morally relevant consideration in such a case—knowledge of the patient's own wishes when he was conscious and in possession of his faculties. Suppose he had feared such an eventuality and prepared a sworn statement requesting his doctor to terminate his life at once in such circumstances. Now, if it is morally obligatory to some degree to carry out a person's wishes for disposal of his body and possessions after his death, it would seem to be equally morally obligatory to respect his wishes in case he becomes a "vegetable." In the event of the existence of such a document, I would think that if he can no longer be injured we are free to withdraw life-sustaining measures and also to take positive steps to terminate life—and are even morally bound, prima facie, to do so. (If, however, the patient had prepared a document directing that his body be preserved alive as long as possible in such circumstances, then there would be a prima facie obligation *not* to cease life-sustaining measures and not to terminate. It would seem obvious, however, that such an obligation would fall far short of giving the patient the right to continued use of a kidney machine when its use by another could save that person's

life.) Some persons would not hesitate to discontinue life-sustaining procedures in such a situation, but would balk at more positive measures. But
the hesitation to use more positive procedures, which veterinarians employ
frequently with animals, is surely nothing but squeamishness; if a person
is in the state described, there can be no injury to him in positive termination more than or less than that in allowing him to wither by withdrawing
life-supportive procedures.

If I am right in my analysis of this case, we must phrase our basic principle about killing in such a way as to take into account (1) whether the killing
would be an injury and (2) the person's own wishes and directives. And
perhaps, more important, any moral principle about killing must be viewed
simply as an implicate of more basic principles about these matters.

Let us look for corroboration of this proposal to how we feel about another type of case, one in which termination would be of positive benefit
to the agent. Let us suppose that a patient has a terminal illness and is in
severe pain, subject only to brief remissions, with no prospect of any event
that could make his life good, either in the short or long term. It might
seem that here, with the patient in severe pain, at least life-supportive
measures should be discontinued, or positive termination adopted. But I
do not think we would accept this inference, for in this situation the patient, let us suppose, has his preferences and is able to express them. The
patient may have strong religious convictions and prefer to go on living despite the pain; if so, surely there is a prima facie moral obligation not positively to terminate his life. Even if, as seemingly in this case, the situation
is one in which it would be *rational* for the agent, from the point of view
of his own welfare, to direct the termination of his life,[2] it seems that if he
(irrationally) does the opposite, there is a prima facie moral obligation not
to terminate and some prima facie obligation to sustain it. Evidently a person's own expressed wishes have moral force. (I believe, however, that we
think a person's expressed wishes have *less* moral force when we think the
wishes are irrational.)

What is the effect, in this case, if the patient himself expresses a preference for termination and would, if he were given the means, terminate
his own existence? Is there a prima facie obligation to sustain his life—and
pain—against his will? Surely not. Or is there an obligation *not* to take
positive measures to terminate his life immediately, thereby saving the patient much discomfort? Again, surely not. What possible reason could be
offered to justify the claim that the answer is affirmative, beyond theological ones about God's will and our being bound to stay alive at His pleasure? The only argument I can think of is that there is some consideration
of public policy, to the effect that a recognition of such moral permission
might lead to abuses or to some other detriment to society in the long run.
Such an argument does seem weak.

It might be questioned whether a patient's request should be honored,
if made at a time when he is in pain, on the grounds that it is not rational.
(The physician may be in a position to see, however, that the patient is

quite right about his prospects and that his personal welfare would be maximized by termination.) It might also be questioned whether a patient's formal declaration, written earlier, requesting termination if he were ever in his present circumstances, should be honored, on the grounds that at the earlier time he did not know what it would be like to be in his present situation. It would seem odd, however, if *no* circumstances are identifiable in which a patient's request for termination is deemed to have moral force, when his request *not* to terminate is thought morally weighty in the same circumstances, even when this request is clearly irrational. I think we may ignore such arguments and hold that, in a situation in which it is rational for a person to choose termination of his life, his expressed wish is morally definitive and removes both the obligation to sustain life and the obligation not to terminate.

Indeed, there is a question whether or not in these circumstances a physician has not a moral obligation at least to withdraw life-supporting measures, and perhaps positively to terminate life. At least there seems to be a general moral obligation to render assistance when a person is in need, when it can be given at small cost to oneself, and when it is requested. The obligation is the stronger when one happens to be the only person in a position to receive such a request or to know about the situation. Furthermore, the physician has acquired a special obligation if there has been a long-standing personal relationship with the patient—just as a friend or relative has special obligations. But since we are discussing not the possible obligation to terminate but the obligation *not* to terminate, I shall not pursue this issue.

The patient's own expression of preference or consent, then, seems to be weighty. But suppose he is unable to express his preference; suppose that his terminal disease not only causes him great pain but has attacked his brain in such a way that he is incapable of thought and of rational speech. May the physician, then, after consultation, take matters into his own hands? We often think we know what is best for another, but we think one person should not make decisions for another. Just as we must respect the decision of a person who has decided after careful reflection that he wants to commit suicide, so we must not take the liberty of deciding to bring another's life to a close contrary to his wishes. So what may be done? Must a person suffer simply because he cannot express consent? There is evidence that can be gathered about what conclusions a person would draw if he were in a state to draw and express them. The patient's friends will have some recollection of things he has said in the past, of his values and general ethical views. Just as we can have good reason to think, for example, that he would vote Democratic if voting for president in a certain year, so we can have good reason to think he would take a certain stand about the termination of his own life in various circumstances. We can know of some persons who because of their religious views would want to keep on living until natural processes bring their lives to a close. About others we can know that they decidedly would not take this view. We can also know what would be the *rational* choice for them to make, and our knowledge of this can be *evidence* about what they would request if they were able. There are, of course, practical complications in the mechanics of a review board of some kind making a determination of this sort, but they are hardly insurmountable.

I wish to consider one other type of case, that of a person who, say, has had a stroke and is leading, and for some time can continue to lead, a life that is comfortable but one on a very low level, *and* who has antecedently requested that his life be terminated if he comes, incurably, into such a situation. May he then be terminated? In this case, unlike the others, there are probably ongoing pleasant experiences, perhaps on the level of some animals, that seem to be a good thing. One can hardly say that *injury* is being done such a person by keeping him alive; and one might say that some slight injury is being done him by terminating his existence. There is a real problem here. Can the (slight) goodness of these experiences stand against the weight of an earlier firm declaration requesting that life be terminated in a situation of hopeless senility? There is no *injury* in keeping the person alive despite his request, but there seems something *indecent* about keeping a mind alive after a severe stroke, when we know quite well that, could he have anticipated it, his own action would have been to terminate his life. I think that the person's own request should be honored; it should be if a person's expressed preferences have as much moral weight as I think they should have.

What general conclusions are warranted by the preceding discussion? I shall emphasize two. First, there is a prima facie obligation *not* to terminate a person's existence when this would injure him (except in cases of self-defense or of senility of a person whose known wish is to be terminated in such a condition) *or* if he wishes not to be terminated. Second, there is *not* a prima facie obligation not to terminate when there would be *no* injury, or when there would be a positive benefit (release from pain) in so doing, provided the patient has not declared himself otherwise or there is evidence that his wishes are to that effect. Obviously there are two things that are decisive for the morality of terminating a person's life: whether so doing would be an *injury* and whether it conforms to what is known of his *preferences*.

I remarked at the outset that I would be content with some moral principles if it could be made out that rational persons would want those principles incorporated in the consciences of a group among whom they were to live. It is obvious why rational persons would want these principles. They would want injury avoided both because they would not wish others to injure them and because, if they are benevolent, they would not wish others injured. Moreover, they would want weight given to a person's own known preferences. Rational people do want the decision about the termination of their lives, where that is possible; for they would be uncomfortable if they thought it possible that others would be free to terminate their lives without consent. The threat of serious illness is bad enough without that prospect. On the other hand, this discomfort would be removed if they knew that termination would not be undertaken on their behalf without their explicit consent, except after a careful inquiry had been made, both into whether termination would constitute an injury and whether they would request termination under the circumstances if they were in a position to do so.

If I am right in all this, then it appears that killing a person is not something that is just prima facie wrong *in itself*; it is wrong roughly only if and because it is an *injury* of someone, or if and because it is contrary to the *known preferences* of someone. It would seem that a principle about the prima facie wrongness of killing is *derivative* from principles about when we are prima facie obligated not to injure and when we are prima facie obligated to respect a person's wishes, at least about what happens to his own body. I do not, however, have any suggestions for a general statement of principles of this latter sort.

Notes

[1] See my "The Morality of Abortion" in *The Monist*, 56 (1972), pp. 503–26; and, in revised form, in *Ethics and Population*, ed. Michael D. Bayles (Cambridge, Mass.: Schenkman, 1976).

[2] See my "The Morality and Rationality of Suicide," in James Rachels, ed., *Moral Problems*, 3rd ed. (New York: Harper & Row, 1979); and, in revised form, in E. S. Shneidman, ed., *Suicidology: Current Developments* (New York: Grune and Stratton, 1975), pp. 378–99.

chapter 6

*P*unishment and the Death Penalty

INTRODUCTION

During the last two decades, punishment has been a topic of much philosophical and public discussion. One reason for this interest has been the movement in the English-speaking world toward elimination of the death penalty. In 1965 the British Parliament abolished the death penalty for a trial period of five years. At the end of that time, it was permanently eliminated. In 1972 the U.S. Supreme Court declared unconstitutional the death penalty provisions of the Georgia state law and by implication those of most other states.[1] In 1976 the Canadian Parliament abolished the death penalty, although controversy still surrounds the issue, with various groups arguing for its reimposition. That same year the U.S. Supreme Court refused to declare all use of the death penalty to be unconstitutionally cruel and unusual punishment.[2] The Court left the issue up to the state legislatures, which may, but need not, impose the death penalty.

The issue of the death penalty is part of a larger controversy surrounding criminal punishment. During the late 1960s and early 1970s, as the crime rate in the United States increased rapidly, views of punishment and imprisonment changed. In the early 1960s rehabilitation was the dominant ideal. Many people claimed that criminals were suffering from psychological problems and that effective psychological therapy would rehabilitate them. But as the results of various experiments in group therapy for criminals came in, many people became disillusioned with rehabilitation. Community treatment then became popular. Imprisonment, it was argued, does not deter criminals; indeed, many persons become more criminal as a result of their imprisonment. Treating people in local communities, it was thought, would be both cheaper and more effective in preventing future crime. Subsequently, some have become disillusioned with community treatment because it did not decrease the rate of offenders who committed further crimes. Many now recommend a return to the imposition of a fixed punishment for crimes. This confusion about punishment is not due simply to a lack of empirical evidence about what works best but also stems from disagreement about what punishment is to accomplish. It is at this point that the ethical principles of just punishment become involved.

The ethics of punishment involves a number of issues. (1) What is the definition of punishment? How is punishment different from compulsory treatment? Is, for example, compulsory treatment for heroin or alcohol dependency punishment, or is it a form of treatment akin to compulsory inoculation against communicable diseases? (2) What is the justifying aim of punishment? Punishment involves the imposition of such undesirable conditions as death, physical pain (flogging), or deprivation of liberty, which normally it is ethically wrong to impose on others. Consequently, punishment requires some aim that will ethically justify it. (3) Who should be punished? Should the insane and young teenagers be punished, or should they be excused from punishment due to their mental disability or age? (4) How much should people be punished for various criminal acts? In particular, should the death penalty ever be imposed? This chapter will focus on issues (2) and (4). A theory of the justifying aim of punishment usually will also have implications for issues (3) and (4).

The Aim of Punishment Interestingly, despite the variety of ethical theories, views of punishment tend to reduce to two, with some mixed views. One view is *retributivism*, that wrongdoing deserves punishment in proportion to the wrong done. The other view is *deterrence*, that in order to deter wrongdoing punishment may be justified. These two views are most explicit in Kantian and utilitarian theory, but one should also understand why other ethical theories tend to one or the other of these views of the justifying aim of punishment.

Aquinas's *natural-law* theory combines both retributivist and deterrence considerations. Principles of natural law prescribe that humans live in society and avoid conduct detrimental to the good of society.[3] Justice is a habit of rendering each person his due.[4] Good things are due to those who act rightly, and evil things to those who act wrongly.[5] Some people are prone to wrongful conduct, and human punishment serves to deter them from it and thus to protect others. As habits are developed by doing, punishment can also enable the wrongdoers to become habituated to acting rightly.[6] The aim of human (as opposed to divine) punishment is to deter people from wronging others in society.

According to *natural-rights* theory, the aim of punishment is to protect people's rights.[7] In the state of nature, each person has the right to punish a transgression of the natural rights of anyone. This system of punishment is unsatisfactory, because there is no settled law, no impartial judge to decide disputes, and no assured power to impose punishment. Consequently, people form a civil society and establish a government to remedy these defects of the state of nature.[8] Although the aim of punishment is to protect rights, its imposition will appear to deprive the wrongdoer of his natural rights. It is not immediately clear whose rights should prevail.

John Locke resolved this puzzle by the *doctrine of forfeiture,* which states that in commiting a wrong, the wrongdoer in effect declares war on society and thus forfeits his rights.[9]

The natural-rights theory essentially adopts a deterrence view of punishment. As the aim of punishment is to protect the rights of others, to be justified punishment must deter the wrongdoer and others from future crimes. A problem with the natural-rights approach is the doctrine of forfeiture. Does a wrongdoer forfeit all his rights? Modern practice implies that he does not; criminals have rights, for example, to fair trials and not to be tortured. But if only specific rights are forfeited, how can one tell which right or rights are forfeited by the commission of a particular crime?

Kant's theory generates a strong form of retributivism. Deterrence is clearly ruled out as a justification of punishment, because it involves using a person as a mere means to the good of others. Justice and the law of the state are confined to duties for which legislation is possible.[10] Duties that require a particular motive are excluded, because legislation can concern only external conduct. The law of justice is to "act externally in such a way that the free use of your will is compatible with the freedom of everyone according to universal law."[11] Coercion to enforce duties of justice is justifiable, because it counteracts their violation. Consequently, state laws may prescribe coercive punishment. The principle of equality, however, is necessary for the imposition of punishment, for otherwise one person would be treated worse than another; no one could will such a universal law. Equality requires the principle of *lex talionis,* an eye for an eye and a tooth for a tooth.

Kant's retributive theory of punishment involves two principles: (1) justice requires that punishment be imposed if, and only if, a person has committed a wrong; and (2) the punishment must be equal to the wrong. Kant's theory is a strong form of retributivism, because justice requires that wrongdoers be punished and any consideration of the good that might come from punishment is excluded. The most serious objection to Kant's theory is that it requires punishment even when no good will result. In such cases, punishment appears to cause pointless suffering.

A *contractarian* theory of punishment is apt to present a weak form of retributivism.[12] Contractors will support a system of legal justice for approximately the same reasons Locke thought the state was justified. Thus, a system of legal justice will be expected to impartially decide disputes and to enforce those fundamental principles of justice which are so important that everyone benefits by their enforcement. The principle of liberty entails that punishment be imposed only if the defendant could have avoided committing the crime. Without that limitation, the liberty of people would be restricted, for they would be punished for unavoidable conduct. To secure maximum liberty, contractors would also prohibit punishing the innocent. As the aim of punishment is to enforce principles of justice, contractors would require punishment to be proportional to the wrong done, understood as the importance of the duty violated and the culpability of the wrongdoer. Finally, as contractors wish as much freedom and as little suffering as possible, they would accept a principle of effectiveness and economy of punishment. Only the smallest punishment needed to ensure compliance with duties should be imposed.

This view is called *weak retributivism* for several reasons. First, unlike Kant's view, it does not require that wrongdoers be punished. The doing of a wrong only makes punishment permissible; punishment of an innocent person is not permissible. Second, instead of requiring that punishment be equal to the wrong done, it requires only that punishment be proportional to the wrong done. Third, by the principle of effectiveness and economy it leaves room for considerations of the good that punishment might do. This last feature is crucial. The first two considerations would not justify punishment, for the permissibility of punishment fails to provide a reason for punishing. It is permissible for the reader to go to a movie, but the permissibility of so doing does not provide a reason for doing it. The principle of effectiveness and economy provides a reason to impose punishment, namely, to deter wrongdoing.

Weak retributivism takes deterrence to be the justifying aim of punishment but restricts pursuit of that aim by other principles of justice. It thus avoids imposing punishment when no good will result. Although the principle of proportionality seems more flexible than Kant's principle of *lex talionis,* there are problems with it. The principle of proportionality requires that both crimes and punishments be ranked from the most serious to the least serious. However, it is not clear how one can thus rank crimes. Supposedly, one should consider both the harm done and the mental state in which the person acted, whether, for instance, he acted with intention or only with disregard of a serious risk of harm. But how can these two items be put together? Is intentionally beating a person (battery) more or less serious than killing a person by disregarding a serious risk of death (manslaughter)?

The importance of these restrictions of justice upon pursuit of deterrence, no matter how difficult they are to formulate, becomes clear when one examines a pure deterrence view, such as that held by act utilitarians.

Act utilitarianism justifies punishment (as it does any other act) if, and only if, its net utility is at least as great as that of any alternative act the agent could perform in the situation. Generally, as punishment itself is unpleasant, it cannot be justified unless the prevention of crime will avoid greater unhappiness. Bentham put the point concisely when he wrote, "All punishment in itself is evil. Upon the principle of utility, if it ought at all to be admitted, it ought only to be admitted in as far as it promises to exclude some greater evil."[13]

Utilitarians usually recognize three (and sometimes four) ways in which punishment can prevent greater unhappiness. First, punishment can be a specific deterrent, that is, deter the person punished from committing crimes in the future. Second, punishment can serve as a general deterrent, that is, deter other persons from committing crimes for fear of being similarly punished. Third, punishment can serve to incapacitate the person punished and thus prevent him or her from committing other crimes. While they are imprisoned, for example, criminals will not be able to commit most crimes. Fourth, punishment can serve to reform a criminal so that he or she will not want to commit crimes in the future. This consideration differs from specific deterrence only by the motive—fear, or lack of desire—a punished person has for refraining from future crime.

The principle of utility implies several restrictions upon punishment. Punishment should not be imposed if it would involve more unhappiness that it would prevent. Nor should it be imposed if it would not deter; for example, if the harm were caused by accident. Neither the offender nor others can be deterred from causing harm by accident. Furthermore, the punishment ought to be as light as possible, while still assuring the prevention of future unhappiness. A greater punishment than necessary would have less net utility. Sometimes a lesser punishment should be imposed even if it would result in more crime, because the unhappiness avoided by using the lesser punishment will be greater than that which would be caused by a few more crimes. Finally, punishments that are more severe should be reserved for more serious crimes. Were all crimes to be punished in the same way, people would have no reason to commit lesser rather than more serious crimes.

The act-utilitarian deterrence view confronts a number of objections. Perhaps the most serious is that it might justify punishing an innocent person. Critics have imagined various situations in which punishing an innocent person might have more net utility than not punishing him. For example, suppose the police have been unable to apprehend the perpetrator of a rash of crimes and other people are now committing similar crimes because they think they can get away with them. Much crime might be prevented if some innocent person were to be tried, convicted, and punished for the original crimes. Similarly, a prosecutor might have evidence that a particular defendant is innocent of the crime with which he is charged but know that he is guilty of other crimes for which he cannot be convicted. Suppressing the evidence and allowing the person to be convicted of the crime of which he is innocent might have more net utility than not doing so. Another objection is that utilitarianism might justify too severe a punishment. Alcohol-impaired drivers cause more deaths than do murderers. A punishment of life imprisonment for vehicular homicide while drunk might save many lives and be justified according to a utilitarian theory, although critics would find the punishment too harsh.

Utilitarians, of course, reply to these objections as they do to others (see Chapter 3) by denying that their theory has these implications or by maintaining that conventional views are incorrect. Still, the objections show why many people think the principles of retributivism are important. They exclude punishing the innocent and retain some proportionality between the punishment and the crime.

Punishment is one area in which *rule utilitarianism* is often thought to be a significant improvement over act utilitarianism. Rule utilitarianism shares act utilitarianism's emphasis upon deterrence and incapacitation. However, acceptance of a rule that would permit the punishment of innocent people or would allow a punishment disproportionate to the crime would probably not have as much utility as acceptance of one that did not permit so punishing. Acceptance of rules permitting such punishment would cause people to fear that they might be framed or punished excessively. Moreover, punishment might lose much of its deterrent effect, because citizens often would not know whether the person punished had indeed committed the crime charged or had been framed. Although some critics of rule utilitarianism argue that it would not prohibit absolutely all punishment of the innocent,[14] most critics recognize that it would do so except in the most extreme cases. Rule utilitarianism, however, might support very severe punishment for such crimes as vehicular homicide while drunk.

The Death Penalty   Arguments about the death penalty concern the amount or kind of punishment appropriate for particular crimes. For *natural-law* and *natural-rights* theories, a particular problem with the death penalty stems from their emphasis upon the injunction not to kill and the right to life. Aquinas's natural-law theory leaves room for one to adopt either a retributivist or deterrence view in determining the appropriate amount of punishment. The natural law prescribes only that wrongdoers be punished, not the amount of punishment appropriate to each crime.[15] Natural-law theorists might adopt a retributivist view that what is due a wrongdoer should be equal to the wrong done, thereby justifying, for example, the death penalty for murder. Or, they might adopt a deterrence view that state punishment is to protect society and to enable people to live together. Aquinas appears to have adopted a form of deterrence. He argued for the permissibility of the death penalty by an analogy with surgery in which a part of the body is removed to protect the rest. Likewise, Aquinas claimed, the state may order the execution of a person who is dangerous to the community.[16] For Locke, the forfeiture of rights legitimates the death penalty. Since the criminal must forfeit his right to life, the death penalty is permissible. However, as the aim of punishment is to protect rights, one must ask whether the death penalty is a more effective deterrent than would be life imprisonment.

Only the strong *Kantian* retributivist view requires the death penalty. If one person deliberately kills another without justification or excuse, then the only equal punishment is death. Kant's retributivism does not clearly require the death penalty for crimes other than homicide. The death penalty, for instance, does not seem to be an equal punishment for kidnapping in which the victim is released unharmed. In such a case, imprisonment would seem to be the most appropriate punishment, since it implies a loss of liberty equal to that committed in kidnapping. Nor does the death penalty appear appropriate for rape. The crime of rape, however, points out a severe difficulty with Kant's principle, because, for most crimes, one cannot inflict an equal punishment on the wrongdoer. For example, theft is often committed by poor people, who lack sufficient property for it to be possible to deprive them of an amount equal to what they stole, although one might require them to work to compensate the victims. This is one of the chief reasons for preferring the principle of proportionality to that of equality (*lex talionis*).

Insofar as the weak retributivism of the *contractarian* view rests on deterrence, its justification of the death penalty will depend upon whether it is understood as an effective and economical deterrent. Although it does not necessarily exclude the death penalty,[17] contractarianism does provide the basis for one strong argument against it. The weak retributivist view prohibits punishment of the innocent. In the imperfect justice of criminal trials, innocent persons have been mistakenly convicted of capital crimes. If the death penalty is imposed, no opportunity exists to later rectify the mistake. If, however, life imprisonment is imposed and the conviction is later discovered to have been mistaken, the person can be released. Although a person cannot have the time spent in prison returned to him, he can be compensated and thus avoid the full punishment that was to be imposed. Many people, therefore, argue that the death penalty should be abolished in order to avoid, as far as possible, irrevocably punishing the innocent.

The whole argument about the death penalty for *utilitarians* rests upon its deterrent effect. If it is understood as a significantly stronger deterrent than is life imprisonment, it is justified. But even a deterrence view will not justify the death penalty whenever it is a greater deterrent than would be life imprisonment. Suppose that for every 100 executions only 1 murder is prevented that would not be prevented by life imprisonment. Then with the death penalty 100 lives would be lost and 1 saved, which is a net loss of 99 lives. However, it does not follow that for a utilitarian to justify the death penalty at least one murder must be prevented for each execution. The increased unhappiness from practice of the death penalty is the difference between the unhappiness of execution and that of life in prison. This difference is probably not as great as that between life and death for an innocent victim. Consequently, according to a utilitarian theory, the lives of those convicted of serious crimes will probably not weigh as heavily as will those of potential victims.

It should now be clear why contemporary debate over the death penalty focuses upon its deterrent effect versus that of life imprisonment. Only the strong Kantian retributivist view makes this irrelevant. As far as most theories are concerned, to be justified, the death penalty must deter more crime than would life imprisonment. Whether it does so is an empirical question that is not easily settled. Obtaining evidence about the relative deterrent effects of the death penalty and life imprisonment faces a number of problems. First, one cannot directly determine how many crimes are prevented by the death penalty or by life imprisonment. Second, one cannot determine how many, if any, crimes occurred because criminals were not deterred by life imprisonment but would have been by the death penalty. Third, the death penalty was not suddenly eliminated in any country but more or less withered away. The rate and number of executions declined for years before it was abolished. Moreover, it may take years before its absence is fully absorbed by society. Even if it did deter, the crime rate might not change immediately after its abolition. So one cannot simply compare crime rates before and after abolition. Fourth, the evidence and statistics gathered generally have focused upon the death penalty as punishment for homicide. However, the effectiveness of the death penalty might vary for different types of murders. People who commit unpremeditated murder are probably less likely to be deterred by the death penalty than are others.

Finally, one other argument about the death penalty has been prevalent. In practice, critics argue, the death penalty is imposed unfairly. More poor and minority people receive the death penalty than do middle- and upper-class white people. The death penalty should be abolished, in this view, because it is unfairly applied. Defenders of the death penalty reply that this problem is not specific to the death penalty but endemic to the entire criminal justice system. The remedy, they suggest, is to make the whole criminal justice system more impartial, not to remove the death penalty.

Readings   The problem case sets out the facts of *Gregg* v. *Georgia*, a case in which the U.S. Supreme Court upheld a Georgia law imposing the death penalty. One should not take the case as typical, for a large proportion of murders occur within families—spouses or other relatives killing in the passion of dispute. However, it does typify the kind of case in which many people believe the death penalty is appropriate.

The selection from Sir William Blackstone represents the natural-law and natural-rights tradition. Blackstone was an eighteenth-century English lawyer, and his *Commentaries,* which at the time were the main exposition of the law, became the basis of much nineteenth-century law and introduced much of natural-law and natural-rights theory into the common law. Blackstone asserts that the state's right to punish stems from the right to punish held by individuals in a state of nature. Unlike Locke, he does not mention forfeiture of rights as a basis for punishing but instead relies upon the consent of citizens to a society with penal laws. He suggests that for most crimes violating natural law, the right to use the death penalty comes from God. For crimes that violate only civil law, he essentially relies upon a deterrence argument. This excerpt concludes with his cautionary remarks about the proliferation of capital crimes in Britain—saying that over 160 at the time (1769) are punishable by death. A significant decrease in capital crimes occurred in the nineteenth century, in large part due to the adoption of utilitarian deterrence considerations.

The selection from Kant provides his account of the strong retributivist view. Kant argues for the *lex (jus) talionis* as the only appropriate principle and as one that requires the imposition of punishment. The categorical imperative justifies an action only if everyone can will the universal law it implies, yet it seems no criminal could will his own punishment. Kant argues that the criminal does not will his own punishment. Rather his rational self (*homo noumenon*) wills the system of laws that involves the punishment which is imposed upon his sensible self (*homo phaenonmenon*). As a rational person, even the criminal is able to *will* the law by which he is punished, although as a person with desires, he does not *desire* his own punishment.

The final selection by former U.S. Attorney General Ramsey Clark provides a largely utilitarian argument against the death penalty. Indeed, Clark argues that the death penalty is counterproductive. It fails to deter; other prisoners and guards are adversely affected; fewer guilty persons are convicted; innocent people are executed; and the penalty is imposed in a discriminatory way.

Notes

¹ *Furman* v. *Georgia*, 408 U.S. 238 (1972).

² *Gregg* v. *Georgia*, 428 U.S. 153 (1976).

³ *Summa Theologica*, 1–11, Q. 94, a. 2.

⁴ Ibid., 11–11, Q. 58, a. 1.

⁵ *Summa Contra Gentiles*, chap. 145, 4.

⁶ *Summa Theologica*, 1–11. Q. 95, a. 1.

⁷ John Locke, *Second Treatise of Government*, chap. 2, sec. 7.

⁸ Ibid., chap. 9, secs. 124–26.

⁹ Ibid., chap. 4, sec. 23; chap. 15, sec. 172.

¹⁰ Immanuel Kant, *Metaphysical Elements of Justice*, trans. John Ladd (Indianapolis, Ind.: Bobbs-Merrill, 1965), p. 45; Akademie, p. 239.

¹¹ Ibid., p. 34; Akademie, p. 231.

¹² See David A. J. Richards, *The Moral Criticism of Law* (Encino, Calif.: Dickenson, 1977), pp. 235–46.

¹³ Jeremy Bentham, *An Introduction to the Principles of Morals and Legislation* (New York: Hafner, 1948), p. 170 (chap. 13, 2).

¹⁴ See Alan Donagan, "Is There a Credible Form of Utilitarianism?" in *Contemporary Utilitarianism*, ed. Michael D. Bayles (Garden City, N.Y.: Doubleday, Anchor Books, 1968), pp. 187–202.

¹⁵ *Summa Theologica*, 1–11, Q. 95, a. 2.

¹⁶ Ibid., 11–11, Q. 64, a. 2; *Summa Contra Gentiles*, chap. 146, 5.

¹⁷ Richards, *Moral Criticism of Law*, p. 254.

Bibliography on Punishment and the Death Penalty

Acton, H. B., ed. *The Philosophy of Punishment*. New York: St. Martin's Press, 1969.

Bedau, Hugo Adam. "Capital Punishment." In *Matters of Life and Death*, edited by Tom Regan. New York: Random House, 1980.

———, ed. *The Death Penalty in America*. 3rd ed. New York: Oxford University Press, 1982.

Berns, Walter. *For Capital Punishment*. New York: Basic Books, 1979.

Ezorsky, Gertrude, ed. *Philosophical Perspectives on Punishment*. Albany, N.Y.: SUNY Press, 1972.

Feinberg, Joel, and Gross, Hyman, eds. *Punishment: Selected Readings*. Belmont, Calif.: Dickenson, 1975.

Furman v. *Georgia*, 408 U.S. 238 (1972).

Gerber, Rudolph J., and McAnany, Patrick D., eds. *Contemporary Punishment*. Notre Dame, Ind.: University of Notre Dame Press, 1972.

Goldinger, Milton, ed. *Punishment and Human Rights*. Cambridge, Mass.: Schenkman, 1974.

Gregg v. *Georgia*, 428 U.S. 153 (1976).

Hart, Herbert L. A. *Punishment and Responsibility*. New York: Oxford University Press, 1968.

Honderich, Ted. *Punishment: The Supposed Justifications*. Baltimore, Md.: Penguin, 1969.

Leiser, Burton M. *Liberty, Justice, and Morals*. 2d ed. New York: Macmillan, 1979. Chapters 6–8.

Murphy, Jeffric G. *Retribution, Justice, and Therapy*. Dordrecht: D. Reidel, 1979.

_____, ed. *Punishment and Rehabilitation*. Belmont, Calif.: Wadsworth, 1973.

Pincoffs, Edmund. *The Rationale of Legal Punishment*. New York: Humanities Press, 1966.

Richards, David A. J. *The Moral Criticism of Law*. Encino, Calif.: Dickenson, 1977. Chapter 6.

Symposium. "Crime and Punishment." *The Monist* 63 (1980): 135–257.

van den Haag, Ernest. *Punishing Criminals*. New York: Basic Books, 1978.

von Hirsch, Andrew. *Doing Justice: The Choice of Punishments*. New York: Hill and Wang, 1976.

Problem Case
Gregg v. Georgia, 428 U.S. 153 (1976)

Tony Gregg and Floyd Allen were hitchhiking when they were picked up by Fred Simmons and Bob Moore. Another hitchhiker was picked up later and then dropped off. Simmons and Moore briefly left the car while stopped for a rest. Gregg told Allen that they were going to rob Simmons and Moore. As Simmons and Moore came back, Gregg fired at them and they fell. He then went up and shot each of them in the head, robbed their corpses, and drove away with Allen. After they were arrested, Allen described the events as above. Gregg first admitted that the account was accurate, then later denied it. He claimed Simmons had attacked him and that he had killed the two men in self-defense. The jury found Gregg guilty of two counts of murder, and then determined that the murders were committed during the commission of two other capital felonies and for the purpose of robbery. Is it permissible to execute Gregg?

SIR WILLIAM BLACKSTONE
NATURE OF PUNISHMENTS

. . . I proceed, in the next place, to consider the general nature of *punishments,* which are evils or inconveniences consequent upon crimes and misdemeanors; being devised, denounced, and inflicted by human laws, in consequence of disobedience or misbehavior in those, to regulate whose conduct such laws were respectively made. . . .

. . . The right to punish. It is clear that the right of punishing crimes against the law of nature, as murder and the like, is in a state of mere nature vested in every individual. For it must be vested in somebody; otherwise the laws of nature would be vain and fruitless, if none were empowered to put them in execution; and if that power is vested in any *one,* it must also be vested in *all* mankind, since all are by nature equal. Whereof the first murderer, Cain, was so sensible, that we find him expressing his apprehensions that *whoever* should find him would slay him. In a state of society this right is transferred from individuals to the sovereign power; whereby men are prevented from being judges in their own causes, which is one of the evils that civil government was intended to remedy. Whatever power, therefore, individuals had of punishing offenses against the law of nature, that is now vested in the magistrate alone, who bears the sword of justice by the consent of the whole community. . . .

As to offenses merely against the laws of society, which are only *mala prohibita,* and not *mala in se,* the temporal magistrate is also empowered to inflict coercive penalties for such transgressions; and this by the consent of individuals, who, in forming societies, did either tacitly or expressly invest the sovereign power with the right of making laws, and of enforcing obedience to them when made, by exercising, upon their non-observance, severities adequate to the evil. The lawfulness, therefore, of punishing such criminals is founded upon this principle, that the law by which they suffer was made by their own consent; it is a part of the original contract into which they entered when first they engaged in society; it was calculated for, and has long contributed to their own security.

This right, therefore, being thus conferred by universal consent, gives to the state exactly the same power, and no more, over all its members as each individual member had naturally over himself or others. Which has occasioned some to doubt how far a human legislature ought to inflict capital punishments for *positive* offenses, offenses against the municipal law only, and not against the law of nature; since no individual has, naturally, a power of inflicting death upon himself or others for actions in themselves indifferent. With regard to offenses *mala in se,* capital punishments are, in some instances, inflicted by the immediate *command* of God himself to all mankind; as in the case of murder, by the precept delivered to Noah, their common ancestor and representative, "whoso sheddeth man's blood,

From Sir William Blackstone, *Commentaries on the Laws of England* (1769).

by man shall his blood be shed.'' In other instances they are inflicted after the *example* of the Creator, in his positive code of laws for the regulation of the Jewish republic; as in the case of the crime against nature. But they are sometimes inflicted without such express warrant or example, at the will and discretion of the human legislature; as for forgery, for theft, and sometimes for offenses of a lighter kind. Of these we are principally to speak; as these crimes are, none of them, offenses against natural, but only against social rights, not even theft itself, unless it be accompanied with violence to one's house or person; all others being an infringement of that right of property which, as we have formerly seen, owes its origin not to the law of nature, but merely to civil society.

The practice of inflicting capital punishments for offenses of human institution is thus justified by that great and good man, Sir Matthew Hale: "When offenses grow enormous, frequent, and dangerous to a kingdom or state, destructive or highly pernicious to civil societies, and to the great insecurity and danger of the kingdom or its inhabitants, severe punishment, and even death itself, is necessary to be annexed to laws in many cases by the prudence of lawgivers." It is, therefore, the enormity, or dangerous tendency, of the crime that alone can warrant any earthly legislature in putting him to death that commits it. It is not its frequency only, or the difficulty of otherwise preventing it, that will excuse our attempting to prevent it by a wanton effusion of human blood. For, though the end of punishment is to deter men from offending, it never can follow from thence that it is lawful to deter them at any rate and by any means, since there may be unlawful methods of enforcing obedience even to the justest laws. Every humane legislator will be, therefore, extremely cautious of establishing laws that inflict the penalty of death, especially for slight offenses, or such as are merely positive. He will expect a better reason for his so doing than that loose one which generally is given, that it is found by former experience that no lighter penalty will be effectual. For is it found, upon further experience, that capital punishments are more effectual? Was the vast territory of all the Russias worse regulated under the late Empress Elizabeth than under her more sanguinary predecessors? Is it now, under Catharine II, less civilized, less social, less secure? And yet we are assured that neither of these illustrious princesses have, throughout their whole administration, inflicted the penalty of death; and the latter has, upon full persuasion of its being useless, nay, even pernicious, given orders for abolishing it entirely throughout her extensive dominions. But, indeed, were capital punishments proved by experience to be a sure and effectual remedy, that would not prove the necessity (upon which the justice and propriety depend) of inflicting them upon all occasions when other expedients fail. I fear this reasoning would extend a great deal too far. For instance, the damage done to our public roads by loaded wagons is universally allowed, and many laws have been made to prevent it, none of which have hitherto proved effectual. But it does not, therefore, follow that it would be just for the legislature to inflict death upon every obstinate carrier who defeats or eludes the provisions of former statutes. Where the evil to be prevented is not adequate to the violence of the preventive, a sovereign that thinks seriously can never justify such a law to the dictates of conscience and humanity. To shed the blood of our fellow-creature is a matter that requires the greatest deliberation and the fullest conviction of our own authority; for life is the immediate gift of God to man, which neither he can resign, nor can it be taken from him, unless by the command or permission of Him who gave it; either expressly revealed, or collected from the laws of nature or society by clear and indisputable demonstration.

I would not be understood to *deny* the right of the legislature in any country to enforce its own laws by the death of the transgressor, though persons of some abilities have *doubted* it; but only to suggest a few hints for the consideration of such as are, or may hereafter become, legislators. When a question arises whether death may be lawfully inflicted for this or that transgression, the wisdom of the laws must decide it; and to this public judgment or decision all private judgments must submit; else there is an end of the first principle of all society and government. The guilt of blood, if any, must lie at their doors who misinterpret the extent of their warrant, and not at the doors of the subject, who is bound to receive the interpretations that are given by the sovereign power.

The object of punishment. As to the *end* or final cause of human punishments. This is not by way of atonement or expiation for the crime committed; for that must be left to the just determination of the Supreme Being; but as a precaution against future offenses of the same kind. This is effected three ways: either by the amendment of the offender himself; for which purpose all corporeal punishments, fines, and temporary exile or imprisonment are inflicted: or by deterring others, by the dread of his example, from offending in the like way . . . ; which gives rise to all ignominious punishments, and to such executions of justice as are open and public: or, lastly, by depriving the party injuring of the power to do future mischief; which is effected by either putting him to death, or condemning him to perpetual confinement, slavery, or exile. The same one end, of preventing future crimes, is endeavored to be answered by each of these three species of punishment. The public gains equal security, whether the offender himself be amended by wholesome correction, or whether he be disabled from doing any further harm; and if the penalty fails of both these effects, as it may do, still the terror of his example remains as a warning to other citizens. The method, however, of inflicting punishment ought always to be proportioned to the particular purpose it is meant to serve, and by no means to exceed it; therefore the pains of death, and perpetual disability by exile, slavery, or imprisonment, ought never to be inflicted but when the offender appears incorrigible; which may be collected either from a repetition of minuter offenses, or from the perpetration of some one crime of deep malignity, which of itself demonstrates a disposition without hope or probability of amendment; and in such cases it would be cruelty to the public to defer the punishment of such a criminal till he had an opportunity of repeating, perhaps, the worst of villainies.

The degree of punishment. . . . The quantity of punishment can never be absolutely determined by any standing invariable rule; but it must be left to the arbitration of the legislature to inflict such penalties as are warranted by the laws of nature and society, and such as appear to be the best calculated to answer the end of precaution against future offenses.

Hence it will be evident that what some have so highly extolled for its equity, the *lex talionis,* or law of retaliation, can never be in all cases an adequate or permanent rule of punishment. In some cases, indeed, it seems to be dictated by natural reason; as in the case of conspiracies to do an injury, or false accusation of the innocent; to which we may add that law of the Jews and Egyptians, mentioned by Josephus and Diodorus Siculus, that whoever, without sufficient cause, was found with any mortal poison in his custody, should himself be obliged to take it. But, in general, the difference of persons, place, time, provocation, or other circumstances, may enhance or mitigate the offense; and in such cases retaliation can never be a proper measure of justice. If a nobleman strikes a peasant, all mankind will see that if a court of justice awards a return of the blow, it is more than a just compensation. On the other hand, retaliation may sometimes be too easy a sentence; as, if a man maliciously should put out the remaining eye of him who had lost one before, it is too slight a punishment for the maimer to lose only one of his; and therefore the law of the Locrians, which demanded an eye for an eye, was in this instance judiciously altered by decreeing, in imitation of Solon's laws, that he who struck out the eye of a one-eyed man should lose both his own in return. Besides, there are very many crimes that will in no shape admit of these penalties, without manifest absurdity and wickedness. Theft can not be punished by theft, defamation by defamation, forgery by forgery, adultery by adultery, and the like. And we may add, that those instances wherein retaliation appears to be used, even by the Divine authority, do not really proceed upon the rule of exact retribution, by doing to the criminal the same hurt he has done to his neighbor, and no more; but this correspondence between the crime and punishment is barely a consequence from some other principle. Death is ordered to be punished with death: not because one is equivalent to the other, for that would be expiation, and not punishment. Nor is death always an equivalent for death: the execution of a needy, decrepit assassin is a poor satisfaction for the murder of a nobleman in the bloom of his youth, and full enjoyment of his friends, his honors, and his fortune. But the reason upon which this sentence is grounded seems to be, that this is the highest penalty that man can inflict, and tends most to the security of mankind, by removing one murderer from the earth, and setting a dreadful example to deter others: so that even this grand instance proceeds upon other principles than those of retaliation. And truly, if any measure of punishment is to be taken from the damage sustained by the sufferer, the punishment ought rather to exceed than equal the injury, since it seems contrary to reason and equity that the guilty (if convicted) should suffer no more than the innocent has done before him; especially as the suffering of the innocent is past and irrevocable, that of the guilty is future, contingent, and liable to be escaped or evaded. With regard, indeed, to crimes that are incomplete, which consist merely in the intention, and are not yet carried into act, as conspiracies and the like, the innocent has a chance to frustrate or avoid the villainy, as the conspirator has also a chance to escape his punishment: and this may be one reason why the *lex talionis* is more proper to be inflicted, if at all, for crimes that consist in intention, than for such as are carried into act. It seems, indeed, consonant to natural reason, and has therefore been adopted as a maxim by several theoretical writers, that the punishment due to the crime of which one falsely accuses another, should be inflicted on the perjured informer. Accordingly, when it was once attempted to introduce into England the law of retaliation, it was intended as a punishment for such only as preferred malicious accusations against others; it being enacted by statute . . . that such as preferred any suggestions to the king's great council should put in sureties of taliation, that is, to incur the same pain that the other should have had in case the suggestion were found untrue. But, after one year's experience, this punishment of taliation was rejected, and imprisonment adopted in its stead. . . .

Lastly: as a conclusion to the whole, we may observe, that punishments of unreasonable severity, especially when indiscriminately inflicted, have less effect in preventing crimes, and amending the manners of a people, than such as are more merciful in general, yet properly intermixed with due distinctions of severity. . . .

It is, moreover, absurd and impolitic to apply the same punishments to crimes of different malignity. A multitude of sanguinary laws (besides the doubt that may be entertained concerning the right of making them) do likewise prove a manifest defect either in the wisdom of the legislative, or the strength of the executive power. It is a kind of quackery in government, and argues a want of solid skill, to apply the same universal remedy, the *ultimum supplicium,* to every case of difficulty. It is, it must be owned, much *easier* to extirpate than to amend mankind: yet that magistrate must be esteemed both a weak and a cruel surgeon who cuts off every limb which, through ignorance or indolence, he will not attempt to cure. It has been, therefore, ingeniously proposed that in every state a scale of crimes should be formed, with a corresponding scale of punishments, descending from the greatest to the least; but if that be too romantic an idea, yet at least a wise legislator will mark the principal divisions, and not assign penalties of the first degree to offenses of an inferior rank. Where men see no distinction made in the nature and gradations of punishment, the generality will be led to conclude there is no distinction in the guilt. Thus, in France, the punishment of robbery, either with or without murder, is the same; hence it is that though, perhaps, they are therefore subject to fewer robberies, yet they never rob but they also murder. In China, murderers are cut to pieces, and robbers not; hence in that country they never murder on the highway, though they often rob. And in England, besides the additional terrors of a speedy execution, and a subsequent exposure or dissection, robbers have a hope of transportation, which seldom is extended to murderers. This has the same effect here as in China, in preventing frequent assassination and slaughter.

Yet, though in this instance we may glory in the wisdom of the English law, we shall find it more difficult to justify the frequency of capital punishment to be found therein, inflicted (perhaps inattentively) by a multitude of successive independent statutes upon crimes very different in their natures. It is a melancholy truth that, among the variety of actions which men are daily liable to commit, no less than a hundred and sixty have been declared, by act of Parliament, to be felonies without benefit of clergy; or, in other words, to be worthy of instant death. So dreadful a list, instead of diminishing, increases the number of offenders. The injured, through compassion, will often forbear to prosecute; juries, through compassion, will sometimes forget their oaths, and either acquit the guilty or mitigate the nature of the offense; and judges, through compassion, will respite one half of the convicts, and recommend them to the royal mercy. Among so many chances of escaping, the needy and hardened offender overlooks the multitude that suffer; he boldly engages in some desperate attempt, to relieve his wants or supply his vices; and if, unexpectedly, the hand of justice overtakes him, he deems himself peculiarly unfortunate in falling at last a sacrifice to those laws which long impunity has taught him to contemn.

IMMANUEL KANT
THE RIGHT TO PUNISH

The right to punish contained in the penal law [*das Strafrecht*] is the right that the magistrate has to inflict pain on a subject in consequence of his having committed a crime. It follows that the suzerain of the state cannot himself be punished; we can only remove ourselves from his jurisdiction. A transgression of the public law that makes him who commits it unfit to be a citizen is called either simply a crime (*crimen*) or a public crime (*crimen publicum*). [If, however, we call it a public crime, then we can use the term "crime" generically to include both private and public crimes.][1] The first (a private crime) is brought before a civil court, and the second (a public crime), before a criminal court. Embezzlement, that is, misappropriation of money or wares entrusted in commerce, and fraud in buying and selling, if perpetrated before the eyes of the party who suffers, are private crimes. On the other hand, counterfeiting money or bills of exchange, theft, robbery, and similar acts are public crimes, because through them the commonwealth and not just a single individual is exposed to danger. These crimes may be divided into those of a base character (*indolis abjectae*) and those of a violent character (*indolis violentae*).

From Immanuel Kant, *The Metaphysical Elements of Justice: Part I of the Metaphysics of Morals*, trans. John Ladd (Indianapolis, Ind.: Bobbs-Merrill, 1965), pp. 99–106. Reprinted by permission.

Judicial punishment (*poena forensis*) is entirely distinct from natural punishment (*poena naturalis*). In natural punishment, vice punishes itself, and this fact is not taken into consideration by the legislator. Judicial punishment can never be used merely as a means to promote some other good for the criminal himself or for civil society, but instead it must in all cases be imposed on him only on the ground that he has committed a crime; for a human being can never be manipulated merely as a means to the purposes of someone else and can never be confused with the objects of the Law of things [*Sachenrecht*]. His innate personality [that is, his right as a person] protects him against such treatment, even though he may indeed be condemned to lose his civil personality. He must first be found to be deserving of punishment before any consideration is given to the utility of this punishment for himself or for his fellow citizens. The law concerning punishment is a categorical imperative, and woe to him who rummages around in the winding paths of a theory of happiness looking for some advantage to be gained by releasing the criminal from punishment or by reducing the amount of it—in keeping with the Pharisaic motto: "It is better that one man should die than that the whole people should perish." If legal justice perishes, then it is no longer worth while for men to remain alive on this earth. If this is so, what should one think of the proposal to permit a criminal who has been condemned to death to remain alive, if, after consenting to allow dangerous experiments to be made on him, he happily survives such experiments and if doctors thereby obtain new information that benefits the community? Any court of justice would repudiate such a proposal with scorn if it were suggested by a medical college, for [legal] justice ceases to be justice if it can be bought for a price.

What kind and what degree of punishment does public legal justice adopt as its principle and standard? None other than the principle of equality (illustrated by the pointer on the scales of justice), that is, the principle of not treating one side more favorably than the other. Accordingly, any undeserved evil that you inflict on someone else among the people is one that you do to yourself. If you vilify him, you vilify yourself; if you steal from him, you steal from yourself; if you kill him, you kill yourself. Only the Law of retribution (*jus talionis*) can determine exactly the kind and degree of punishment; it must be well understood, however, that this determination [must be made] in the chambers of a court of justice (and not in your private judgment). All other standards fluctuate back and forth and, because extraneous considerations are mixed with them, they cannot be compatible with the principle of pure and strict legal justice.

Now, it might seem that the existence of class distinctions would not allow for the [application of the] retributive principle of returning like for like. Nevertheless, even though these class distinctions may not make it possible to apply this principle to the letter, it can still always remain applicable in its effects if regard is had to the special sensibilities of the higher classes. Thus, for example, the imposition of a fine for a verbal injury has no proportionality to the original injury, for someone who has a good deal of money can easily afford to make insults whenever he wishes. On the other hand, the humiliation of the pride of such an offender comes much closer to equaling an injury done to the honor of the person offended; thus the judgment and Law might require the offender, not only to make a public apology to the offended person, but also at the same time to kiss his hand, even though he be socially inferior. Similarly, if a man of a higher class has violently attacked an innocent citizen who is socially inferior to him, he may be condemned, not only to apologize, but to undergo solitary and painful confinement, because by this means, in addition to the discomfort suffered, the pride of the offender will be painfully affected, and thus his humiliation will compensate for the offense as like for like.

But what is meant by the statement: "If you steal from him, you steal from yourself"? Inasmuch as someone steals, he makes the ownership of everyone else insecure, and hence he robs himself (in accordance with the Law of retribution) of the security of any possible ownership. He has nothing and can also acquire nothing, but he still wants to live, and this is not possible unless others provide him with nourishment. But, because the state will not support him gratis, he must let the state have his labor at any kind of work it may wish to use him for (convict labor), and so he becomes a slave, either for a certain period of time or indefinitely, as the case may be.

If, however, he has committed a murder, he must die. In this case, there is no substitute that will satisfy the requirements of legal justice. There is no sameness of kind between death and remaining alive even under the most miserable conditions, and consequently there is also no equality between the crime and the retribution unless the criminal is judicially condemned and put to death. But the death of the criminal must be kept entirely free of any maltreatment that would make an abomination of the humanity residing in the person suffering it. Even if a civil society were to dissolve itself by common agreement of all its members (for example, if the people inhabiting an island decided to separate and disperse themselves around the world), the last murderer remaining in prison must first be executed, so that everyone will duly receive what his actions are worth and so that the bloodguilt thereof will not be fixed on the people because they failed to insist on carrying out the punishment; for if they fail to do so, they may be regarded as accomplices in this public violation of legal justice.

Furthermore, it is possible for punishment to be equal in accordance with the strict Law of retribution only if the judge pronounces the death sentence. This is clear because only in this way will the death sentence be pronounced on all criminals in proportion to their inner viciousness (even if the crime involved is not murder, but some other crime against the state that can be expiated only by death). To illustrate this point, let us consider a situation, like the last Scottish rebellion, in which the participants are motivated by varying purposes, just as in that rebellion some believed that they were only fulfilling their obligations to the house of Stuart (like

Balmerino and others),[2] and others, in contrast, were pursuing their own private interests. Suppose that the highest court were to pronounce as follows: Each person shall have the freedom to choose between death and penal servitude. I say that a man of honor would choose death and that the knave would choose servitude. This is implied by the nature of human character, because the first recognizes something that he prizes more highly than life itself, namely, honor, whereas the second thinks that a life covered with disgrace is still better than not being alive at all (*animam praeferre pudori*).[3] The first is without doubt less deserving of punishment than the other, and so, if they are both condemned to die, they will be punished exactly in proportion [to their inner viciousness]; the first will be punished mildly in terms of his kind of sensibility, and the second will be punished severely in terms of his kind of sensibility. On the other hand, if both were condemned to penal servitude, the first would be punished too severely and the second too mildly for their baseness. Thus, even in sentences imposed on a number of criminals united in a plot, the best equalizer before the bar of public legal justice is death.

It may also be pointed out that no one has ever heard of anyone condemned to death on account of murder who complained that he was getting too much [punishment] and therefore was being treated unjustly; everyone would laugh in his face if he were to make such a statement. Indeed, otherwise we would have to assume that, although the treatment accorded the criminal is not unjust according to the law, the legislative authority still is not authorized to decree this kind of punishment and that, if it does so, it comes into contradiction with itself.

Anyone who is a murderer—that is, has committed a murder, commanded one, or taken part in one—must suffer death. This is what [legal] justice as the Idea of the judicial authority wills in accordance with universal laws that are grounded a priori. The number of accomplices (*correi*) in such a deed might, however, be so large that the state would soon approach the condition of having no more subjects if it were to rid itself of these criminals, and this would lead to its dissolution and a return to the state of nature, which is much worse, because it would be a state of affairs without any external legal justice whatsoever. Since a sovereign will want to avoid such consequences and, above all, will want to avoid adversely affecting the feelings of the people by the spectacle of such butchery, he must have it within his power in case of necessity (*casus necessitatis*) to assume the role of judge and to pronounce a judgment that, instead of imposing the death penalty on the criminals, assigns some other punishment that will make the preservation of the mass of the people possible, such as, for example, deportation. Such a course of action would not come under a public law, but would be an executive decree [*Machtspruch*], that is, an act based on the right of majesty, which, as an act of reprieve, can be exercised only in individual cases.

In opposition to this view, the Marquis of Beccaria,[4] moved by sympathetic sentimentality and an affectation of humanitarianism, has asserted that all capital punishment is illegitimate. He argues that it could not be contained in the original civil contract, inasmuch as this would imply that every one of the people has agreed to forfeit his life if he murders another (of the people); but such an agreement would be impossible, for no one can dispose of his own life.

No one suffers punishment because he has willed the punishment, but because he has willed a punishable action. If what happens to someone is also willed by him, it cannot be a punishment. Accordingly, it is impossible to will to be punished. To say, "I will to be punished if I murder someone," can mean nothing more than, "I submit myself along with everyone else to those laws which, if there are any criminals among the people, will naturally include penal laws." In my role as colegislator making the penal law, I cannot be the same person who, as subject, is punished by the law; for, as a subject who is also a criminal, I cannot have a voice in legislation. (The legislator is holy.) When, therefore, I enact a penal law against myself as a criminal it is the pure juridical legislative reason (*homo noumenon*) in me that submits myself to the penal law as a person capable of committing a crime, that is, as another person (*homo phaenomenon*) along with all the others in the civil union who submit themselves to this law. In other words, it is not the people (considered as individuals) who dictate the death penalty, but the court (public legal justice); that is, someone other than the criminal. The social contract does not include the promise to permit oneself to be punished and thus to dispose of oneself and of one's life, because, if the only ground that authorizes the punishment of an evildoer were a promise that expresses his willingness to be punished, then it would have to be left up to him to find himself liable to punishment, and the criminal would be his own judge. The chief error contained in this sophistry . . . consists in the confusion of the criminal's own judgment (which one must necessarily attribute to his reason) that he must forfeit his life with a resolution of the Will to take his own life. The result is that the execution of the Law and the adjudication thereof are represented as united in the same person.

Notes

[1] [Natorp and Cassirer agree that there is something wrong with the sentence following this one. Either a sentence has been omitted or the sentence in question has been misplaced. Kant's meaning is, however, perfectly clear, and I have inserted a sentence to provide the transition.]

[2] [Arthur Elphinstone, Sixth Baron Balmerino (1688–1746), participated in the Jacobite rebellion that attempted to put Prince Charles Edward Stuart on the British throne. He was captured, tried, found guilty, and beheaded. He is said to have acted throughout with great constancy and courage.]

[3] ["To prefer life to honor"—Juvenal, *Satire* 8. 83.] . . .

[4] [Cesare Bonesana, Marquis di Beccaria (1738–1794), Italian publicist. His *Dei delitti e delle pene* (1764) (*On Crimes and Punishments,* trans. Henry Paolucci, "The Library of Liberal Arts," No. 107 [New York: The Liberal Arts Press, 1963]) was widely read and had great influence on the reform of the penal codes of various European states.]

RAMSEY CLARK
THE DEATH PENALTY

History shows that the death penalty has been unjustly imposed—innocents have been killed by the state, effective rehabilitation has been impaired, judicial administration has suffered—and crime has not been deterred. Our emotions may cry for vengeance in the wake of a horrible crime, but we know that killing the criminal cannot undo the crime, will not prevent similar crimes by others, does not benefit the victim, destroys human life, and brutalizes society. If we are to still violence, we must cherish life. Executions cheapen life.

The major argument for capital punishment today is the belief that fear of death will keep people from committing serious crimes. But most studies of the death penalty have concluded with Professor Thorsten Sellin that "it has failed as a deterrent." A comprehensive United Nations report found that abolition of the death penalty has no effect on murder rates. With or without capital punishment, murder rates are much the same.

Why should we expect a deterrent value? Do we really believe most capital crimes are rational acts? Are they not more often committed on impulse—in a moment of passion—without thought of gain or loss? Only extreme fear of punishment—so emotionally severe that basic instincts are cowed—can deter unpremeditated crime. It is, after all, meditation before the act that may cause a person aware of the risks and consequences of being caught to refrain from prohibited conduct.

Premeditated crime, in the view of scholarship on the subject, is committed by people who believe they will not be caught. They do not really weigh the penalty. If this is so, the best deterrent for premeditated crime is to give potential offenders cause to believe they will be caught and proven guilty. Swift apprehension, effective prosecution and quick conviction will do this. When these are achieved, people can see that in fact they are paying society's price. Professionally trained police, the application of science and technology to criminal justice, successful prosecution and speedy trials can thus prevent violence—while capital punishment only makes crime a more deadly game.

The hardened criminal, devoid of human compassion, will not be deterred by the fear of death or severe punishment. He lives among the springs of American violence, where sudden death is no stranger. Society must protect itself by rehabilitating him or isolating him. To seek some public satisfaction from his execution will only brutalize others.

George Bernard Shaw believed, "Murder and capital punishment are not opposites that cancel one another, but similars that breed their kind." His view has scientific basis. The death penalty is observed by many psy-

From "The Death Penalty and Reverence for Life," *Crime in America: Observations on Its Nature, Causes, Prevention and Control.* Copyright © 1970 by Ramsey Clark. Reprinted by permission of Simon & Schuster, a Division of Gulf & Western Corporation.

chologists to be an incentive for some mentally unstable persons to commit capital crimes. Recognizing the high correlation between murder and emotional disturbance, as well as a psychotic compulsion to gain notoriety, to shock sensitive people and to injure oneself, they see the death penalty as a cause of serious crime. Unquestionably, it has this effect on some. Just as arson, assassination, murder and rape inspire others who hear of them to consider and sometimes commit similar crimes, the news of executions affects mentally disturbed people, who have been known to emulate the offenses of the condemned. . . .

The death penalty causes violence in many ways. The effect of executions on other inmates in a prison where the condemned wait to die is devastating. The "big houses," major penitentiaries where the executions usually occur, frequently confine several thousand men. They are the most dangerous offenders convicted of crime, many deeply disturbed emotionally. Inmates there are constantly aware of the men on death row. Seeing them wait month after month, they wonder what kind of people we are. What kind of game this is we play—as if society were a giant cat and the condemned man a mouse to be toyed with before being killed. Even when prisoners who have lived in the presence of the condemned are released—and nearly all are—we know most will be convicted of crime again, because we fail to give them a chance. For how many of those later released has the final image before pulling the trigger of a pistol pointed at a police officer been the eyes of the men on death row and the thought, not me?

The impact of the death penalty on other prisoners has several dimensions. In *Soul on Ice,* Eldridge Cleaver described the many handicaps of clergyman working in prison, concluding, "Besides, men of the cloth who work in prison have an ineradicable stigma attached to them in the eyes of convicts because they escort condemned men into the gas chamber."

Wardens and guards are deeply affected by death row. The ugly details —the last meal, clothing that will not retain poisonous gas, the frequent failures on first attempt, the fear that a last-minute commutation may come too late, working with warm flesh that knows it is about to die—are not pleasant experiences. The roll of wardens who have spoken out strongly against capital punishment is long. It includes Clinton Duffy of San Quentin, James Johnston of Alcatraz, Lewis Lawes of Sing Sing and John Ryan of Milan. They know the inhumanity of the death penalty and the effect of executions on the other men in their custody.

Capital punishment harms everything it touches. The impact of the death penalty on the administration of justice has been terribly damaging. Lawyers have long noted that hard cases make bad law. There are few cases harder than those which take a life. Justice Felix Frankfurter strongly opposed capital punishment for this reason. "When life is at hazard in a trial," he said, "it sensationalizes the whole thing almost unwittingly." He regarded the effect on juries, the bar, the public and the judiciary as "very bad." President Johnson's Crime Commission found that the emotion surrounding a capital case "destroys the fact-finding process." Realization of the consequences of error permeates the entire proceeding. A jury may acquit because of its fear of the death penalty when the evidence clearly establishes guilt of a serious crime. Justice Robert H. Jackson believed that appellate courts in capital cases "are tempted to strain the evidence and even, in close cases, the law, in order to give a doubtfully condemned man another chance."

Fear of mistake produces excruciating delays in executions. In the late 1960's there were more than four hundred persons on death row at all times. Most spent years in the shadow of death. Their ages ranged from fifteen to seventy. The unbearably long wait adds immeasurably to the inhumanity of capital punishment and, combined with the infrequency of actual execution, eliminates the one deterrent effect the penalty might otherwise be thought to have. The punishment is not only slow; it usually never comes.

In a 1961 study the American Bar Foundation found that long delays such as those in the Caryl Chessman case weaken public confidence in the law. This is an understatement born of self-interest. Such cases have disgusted millions. In a more outspoken vein, the President's Crime Commission noted: "The spectacle of men living on death row for years while their lawyers pursue appellate and collateral remedies, tarnishes our image of humane and expeditious justice."

We torture ourselves through delay, indecision and doubt because we do not really believe in taking human life. No one in the process feels comfortable with himself, or about his government. The resulting hesitation further heightens the harm of the penalty. This is part of the price of hypocrisy.

History is full of men who have opposed capital punishment. Because the death penalty is irrevocable, Lafayette vowed to oppose it until "the infallibility of human judgment" was demonstrated to him. Fear of error has caused many to oppose capital punishment. It should. Innocent persons have been executed. In addition, some incapable of knowing what they did—the mentally retarded and disturbed—have been sacrificed to our lust for punishment and vengeance. Judicial determination of mental competence, a prerequisite to a finding that a person is legally responsible for a criminal act, remains far from a precise science. The legal standards are neither clear nor sound, and the decisions are made in emotional contexts. But fear of a mistake, that the person was innocent or knew not what he did, ignores the greater reason for abolition. We must be humane.

Death has been visited in a discriminatory fashion. A small group of offenders selected by chance have been destroyed. Most who committed similar crimes were never caught. Nearly all of the persons caught and convicted of the same crimes for which a few were killed have been imprisoned—not executed. There are thousands of prisoners serving life sentences or less whose crimes were more inhumane than those of the men on death row.

The poor and the black have been the chief victims of the death penalty. Clarence Darrow observed that "from the beginning, a procession of the poor, the weak, the unfit, have gone through our jails and prisons to their deaths. They have been the victims." It is the poor, the sick, the ignorant, the powerless and the hated who are executed.

Racial discrimination is manifest from the bare statistics of capital punishment. Since we began keeping records in 1930, there have been 2,066 Negroes and only 1,751 white persons put to death. Negroes have been only one-eighth of our population. Hundreds of thousands of rapes have occurred in America since 1930, yet only 455 men have been executed for rape—and 405 of them were Negroes. There can be no rationalization or justification of such clear discrimination. It is outrageous public murder, illuminating our darkest racism.

Why must we kill? We are finally beginning to realize that crime is preventable and rehabilitation possible. The medical sciences, psychiatry, psychology, sociology, education, training and employment can prevent crime. Modern penology offers effective methods of protecting society. Pre-delinquency guidance and assistance, treatment centers, halfway houses and work release programs are evidence of the movement toward community programs that offer so much. They are the future of corrections. It is a sad commentary on how much we care that this wealthy nation spends 95 per cent of all funds for corrections on pure custody and only 5 per cent on hope—health services, education, employment and rehabilitation techniques—while still killing those who offend it the most.

If an offender cannot adapt to community programs, he can be retained in prison. If he is dangerous, he can be prevented from doing injury. Through employment in industries within the prison he can be productive. If he is unable or unwilling to work, he can still be treated kindly and allowed to live. Society can be fully protected. We no longer need to kill from fear.

Murderers, the persons for whom the death penalty is most frequently invoked, generally make well-behaved prisoners. They are rarely a threat to the safety of others. A study during the 1940's of 121 assaults with intent to kill in the prisons of twenty-seven states showed that only 10 were committed by prisoners serving life sentences for murder. There is nothing in prison experience to indicate that the death penalty would protect prison personnel from assaults by life-termers, whatever their earlier crime.

The death penalty is inconsistent with the purposes of modern penology. It deters rehabilitation. It is a disastrous substitute for the effort and money needed to develop correctional knowledge and skills.

Surely the abolition of the death penalty is a major milestone in the long road up from barbarism. There were times when self-preservation may have necessitated its imposition. Later, when food, clothing and shelter were scarce and often insufficient, inordinate sacrifices by the innocent would have been required to isolate dangerous persons from the public. Our civilization has no such excuse.

There is no justification for the death penalty. It demeans life. Its inhumanity raises basic questions about our institutions and our purpose as a people. Why must we kill? What do we fear? What do we accomplish besides our own embitterment? . . .

chapter 7

Sexual Ethics

INTRODUCTION

Are there *kinds* of sexual conduct that are *in themselves* wrong according to the principles of right conduct? All ethical theories condemn some kinds of conduct that include sexual aspects, such as rape; but the conduct is condemned as either a violation of individual rights, or as a serious harm to another person, rather than because of any *specifically sexual* characteristic of the conduct. Of course, sexual conduct can harm others in less serious ways, and sexual conduct can violate rights less central than the right to bodily security. Deception and emotional hurt are not uncommon in sexual relations between consenting adults. Just as in the case of rape, however, deceiving or hurting another is not a specifically *sexual* wrong.

The contemporary British philosopher Peter Winch has remarked that "the vulgar identification of morality with sexual morality certainly *is* vulgar; but it is a vulgarization of an important truth."[1] Indeed, many uses of the words "morality" and "morals" demonstrate this vulgar identification; when the question of someone's "morals" is raised, sexual conduct is usually what is being spoken about, rather than fairness or kindness. But why would a philosopher suggest that an important truth lies behind this vulgarization? Winch was calling attention to an important feature of the customs (*mores*) surrounding birth, death, and sexual relations: these customs are a focus for the sense of significance people find in their lives.

To understand the weight placed upon specifically sexual morality in many cultures, one must see the sexual mores as serving a larger structural role in the lives of people in that culture. A "good life" will have a shape partly determined by sexual relations and the social structures connected with sexual relations. The kinship system and the structure of the family will involve a view of what is right and wrong in sexual conduct. But in a pluralistic society in which sexual conduct increasingly has little structural role, the traditional sense of the importance of specifically sexual morality will seem irrational to many.

Traditional Sexual Morality Conventional sexual morality in Judaeo-Christian societies has condemned various kinds of sexual conduct outright,

204

regardless of any connection they might have with other kinds of moral wrong. This traditional sexual morality places sex within a structure of significance that makes sense of and gives credence to its prohibitions and requirements. The conventional prohibitions can be classified under the general categories of fornication and perversity. *Fornication* is sexual intercourse outside of marriage. *Perversity* is sexual intercourse which is not of the kind that can lead to reproduction; perverse sexual conduct may occur either within or outside of marriage. Examples of perverse sexual acts (as traditionally understood) include homosexual intercourse, oral copulation (whether homosexual or heterosexual), and masturbation. Traditional sexual morality permits only nonperverse (that is, "natural") sexual acts within marriage. Adultery is a double wrong, for it involves both fornication (a *sexual* immorality) and a serious violation of the promise of fidelity to the spouse.

Much of this traditional sexual morality is now in question. Even among those who retain the traditional view that homosexual intercourse is wrong, many no longer view all fornication as wrong, and few view masturbation as wrong. The traditional sexual morality sees all of its prohibitions as growing out of a single view of sexuality and its proper place as a structuring force in a good human life. But it is an important question whether selected elements of the traditional view can, with consistency, be salvaged by someone who cannot accept the entire view.

Natural Law   The traditional view of the proper place of sexuality in human life received its philosophical foundation in the theory of natural law. Saint Thomas Aquinas argued that just as there is a proper end or goal for human beings as such (rational activity), so there is a proper end for each separate human faculty, or part. Each action should aim at the proper end for actions of that kind. Sexuality is by nature directed toward the end of reproduction. Each act of copulation, therefore, should be open to the natural end of reproduction. This rules out "perverse" sexual acts, including, for instance, heterosexual intercourse in which the seed is intentionally diverted from its "natural" goal. Also, since by nature human infants need a long period of care and education, the specifically *human* characteristic of sexual morality demands that copulation be limited to sexual partners united in a marriage, which is understood as providing the educative context for any child born of the union. Thus fornication is immoral, because it fails to respect what is specifically human in sexuality, according to Aquinas.[2]

And so natural-law theorists see sexual acts as having an intrinsic significance, or meaning. The procreative significance, however, is not the only significance intrinsic to sexual acts. Natural-law theorists also recognize a *unitive* significance to intercourse, that is, sexual intimacy should aim not only at procreation but also at expressing and deepening the personal union between the partners. This personal union is a special kind of friendship, for it excludes all others from participation. There is no real conflict caused by this dual significance of sex. Since human procreation should be restricted to the context of marriage (so the offspring can be properly reared), both the procreative and the unitive significance of sex may be seen as pointing toward exclusivity in sexual relations. However, only monogamy is permissible, precisely because the unitive significance requires that neither men nor women be reduced to the status of reproductive tools. Polygamy is a form of exclusive union that perhaps serves the need to rear children as well as does monogamy, but the mutual exclusivity required by the unitive purpose of sexuality makes it unacceptable.

The main contemporary debate within natural-law theory concerns contraception. Some theorists argue that the unitive significance of sexual acts can be viewed as primary, and so artificial contraception within marriage can be justified. However, the official teaching of the Roman Catholic Church continues to be that artificial contraception constitutes a direct choice against procreation. Procreation is a fundamental good, according to the natural-law theory, and it is always wrong to choose an action that goes against a fundamental good when that good is directly at issue. (See Chapter 1.) This debate is likely to continue within natural-law theory, for the unitive significance of sexual acts has received increasing emphasis. This emphasis seems reasonable, for the natural-law tradition has always emphasized what is distinctively human as the key to right conduct. Only human beings can imbue sexual acts with the significance of union between two persons in exclusive friendship.

If the unitive significance of sex acts is primary, then exclusive homosexual partnerships may also be viewed as "natural." Traditional natural-law theory condemned homosexual acts as *in kind* unnatural, for they were not the kind of acts that could lead to reproduction. But there is another "natural" purpose of sex, indeed more specific to *human* nature than is reproduction. Homosexual partners may express and deepen their union as persons in sexual acts, and this union may be as exclusive and long-term as are heterosexual unions. Just as it is "natural" for human beings to engage in scientific inquiry (for humans are distinctively creatures who seek knowledge), so it can be argued that it is "natural" for a homosexual person to seek the same kind of personal and sexual union as a heterosexual person seeks. The word "natural" in natural-law theory has always permitted surprising applications. But just as artificial contraception remains illicit within official Roman Catholic teaching, so homosexual acts remain illicit even when they are part of an exclusive long-term union of persons in friendship.

Natural Rights   The natural-rights theorists replaced the natural sociality of human nature found in Aristotle and Aquinas with a view of human nature as consisting of an individualist, self-interested rationality. Natural sociality had formed an important element in the natural-law conception of sex, for the family had been viewed as a natural community, and sexual life was seen as a part of that communal existence. Procreation had been viewed as a fundamental human good, based on the animal nature that is included in human nature. But the individualist emphasis upon rights leaves no room for a specifically sexual morality. Procreation, and even living among others in society, becomes a mere tool to further individual self-interest. Each person is free to act as he chooses, as long as the rights of others are respected. In sexual conduct, deception and violence are wrong, for they violate the rights of others. Thus sex outside of marriage poses no *special* problems, if both parties agree to it. Solitary sex (for example, masturbation) is unproblematic, for there are no duties to self in natural-rights theory.

Sexual partners are seen as free, contracting individuals. Each has a duty to the other to keep the terms of the agreement; and so adultery usually will be wrong. However, the parties can release each other either from the marriage itself or even from specific expectations of fidelity (leaving them united in an "open marriage"). Within traditional sexual morality, permission from one's spouse to commit adultery is irrelevant. But for the natural-rights theorist, marriage is just another contractual relationship. (Open marriage would have shocked the early natural-rights theorists, but their theory of right conduct seems to justify such an arrangement.)

Kant Kant shared the particular views about sexual conduct found in the natural-law tradition. He even used natural-law arguments identifying procreation as the natural end of sexual acts.[3] In Kant's view, the marriage contract provides the only context in which each sexual partner can respect the person of the other as an "end-in-itself," for in marriage *each* has mutually given the whole self to the other. Outside of marriage, Kant views sexual intercourse as a use of each partner as a *mere* means to gratification by the other.

But a Kantian account of sexual morality might differ from Kant's own traditionalism. Respect for rational nature ("humanity") in one's own person and in the person of others need not be interpreted in Kant's distinctively legalistic way. The contemporary American philosopher Alan Donagan has argued that Kant and the natural-law tradition have been mistaken in condemning *all* "perverse" and nonmarital sexual acts. Donagan, however, argues that respect for rational humanity does have a specific sexual application—and thus that a sexual morality which merely refrains from such nonsexual wrongs as deception and violence is inadequate. Sexual acts can be wrong because of their "imaginative significance" for those participating. Even between consenting adults, sexual conduct can express contempt for one's own or another's humanity.[4] This neo-Kantian view shares with the natural-law tradition the view that sexual acts are intrinsically significant and that a specifically sexual morality is based upon that significance. Donagan, however, sees the significance of sexual acts as contextually determined, rather than determined once and for all by biology. But even Donagan observes that "the imaginative significance of a form of sexual activity cannot but be affected by its relation to the forms I have called 'non-deviant.'"[5]

Contractarianism What principles would a contractarian apply to sexual conduct? Behind the veil of ignorance that hides such details as one's own sexual preference and personal sexual psychology, rational contractors might reach a view comparable to the natural-rights position. In order to promote their own interests in case they happened to be homosexual (or unusual in some other way), the contractors would probably adopt the view that there is no specifically sexual morality. Only violence, deception, and other violations of the rights of others would be morally wrong. However, since self-respect is an important primary good that the contractors seek to maximize, there might be contractarian grounds for a moral principle of sexual conduct that prohibits symbolically degrading oneself or others even in fully consensual sexual conduct. Such a principle would accord with the Kantian basis of contractarianism. But perhaps the contractors would not adopt such a principle, since it might frustrate their own desires if, after the veil of ignorance is lifted, they find that they have deep sado-masochistic desires. There is a tension between the natural-rights and the Kantian elements of contractarian thought. Within the theory of institutional justice, the question of duties to respect oneself does not arise; but in a complete contractarian account of right conduct, duties to self might be specified, as might duties to respect others even in ways they themselves do not demand. Consensual sado-masochism could violate duties to self and others if a truly Kantian conception of personal dignity is included in contractarianism.

Act Utilitarianism   Utilitarianism has little room for a specifically sexual morality. Since actions are morally right to the extent that happiness or pleasure is maximized, sexual pleasure is on the credit side of the moral ledger for the utilitarian. All pleasure is intrinsically good. In the moral evaluation of sexual acts, all foreseeable consequences must be considered. An act utilitarian will evaluate each particular action, striving to maximize happiness. If there are no further consequences, pleasurable sexual acts will be morally right, regardless of what kind of acts are performed and regardless of the relationship between the parties. Unhappiness foreseeably caused by sexual acts must be subtracted from the pleasure (and other, more subtle, happiness consequent to sexual activity). If net happiness is greater than the net unhappiness foreseeably caused by alternative actions, then the sexual act is morally right. An act utilitarian will sometimes consider a particular sexual act wrong, because of the emotional distress that will be suffered by someone with traditional moral attitudes. However, it is not, for instance, that adultery or perversion is itself wrong but rather that the wrong is simply causing more unhappiness than happiness. So the act utilitarian has no specifically sexual morality.

Rule Utilitarianism   Rule utilitarians have more theoretical room for a specifically sexual morality. The conditions of society will determine whether there are specific utilitarian rules for sexual conduct. A rule utilitarian evaluates particular actions by applying rules, which in turn are justified by the utility of their acceptance. (See Chapter 3 for alternative formulations of rule utilitarianism.) Under certain social conditions, specific rules governing sexual conduct may have a high acceptance utility (that is, the acceptance of the rules may lead to greater net happiness than would the acceptance of alternative rules, or having *no* specific rules concerning sexual conduct). Without reliable methods of birth control, rules against casual fornication may perhaps have a utilitarian justification. Indeed, even further elements of traditional sexual morality might be given a rule-utilitarian justification within the context of earlier social and technological conditions.

Contemporary social conditions, however, leave little empirical ground for a rule-utilitarian justification of a specifically sexual morality. Birth control is now easy to obtain and reliable; early abortions (acceptable to utilitarians) are now a safe and legal second defense against unwanted pregnancy. And, perhaps most important, the background social system no longer requires that great importance be placed upon sexual conduct of specific kinds. Women are no longer dependent upon "finding the right man" in order to lead fulfilling lives, and there is thus less rationale for the traditional sexual morality related to the woman's need to protect her value as a potential wife. In contemporary society, there is great mobility in family roles and in personal relationships; sexual acts no longer lock a person into a long-term or permanent status as they once could.

However, even though a rule utilitarian is unlikely to justify rules specific to sexual conduct in contemporary society, there remains a rule-utilitarian justification for more general rules against violence, deception, and breaking promises. And, of course, there is always the fundamental utilitarian principle that happiness should be promoted and unhappiness avoided. These general moral principles will apply to sexual conduct as much as to conduct of any other sort. Since sexual conduct can be a source of great happiness and of great unhappiness, the utilitarian will consider it an important area of moral concern even if there is nothing morally special about it. However, specific *kinds* of sexual acts, such as fornication or perversity, will not be viewed as wrong in themselves.

Readings The problem case, *Pettit* v. *State Board of Education,* raises questions concerning both perversity and adultery. The actual legal case turned upon the right to privacy, a right central to the tradition of natural rights with its emphasis upon self-determination.

The selection from John Finnis is a natural-law defense of traditional sexual morality. He argues that the fundamental human good of procreation is inescapably at issue in sexual conduct and that both fornication and perversity are morally wrong. He also discusses the unitive significance of sexual intimacy and the respect for one's spouse this requires.

The selection from Sara Ruddick cannot be characterized as fitting simply into any one tradition. She elaborates a specific sexual morality based on the distinctive interpersonal communication of embodied self found in the best sexual experience. She rejects the natural-law condemnation of perversity. Ruddick applies the Kantian concept of respect for persons to "complete" sex, though in a way that would have surprised Kant.

Alan Goldman also defies neat classification. However, he expresses a theory of value with roots in utilitarianism. Goldman rejects even the moderate view that sex is better when a part of complex, interpersonal communication. Goldman's rejection of a specifically sexual morality links him to the natural-rights tradition, although he sees himself as Kantian.

Notes

[1] Peter Winch, "Understanding a Primitive Society," in *Rationality,* ed. Bryan Wilson (New York: Harper & Row, 1970), p. 110.

[2] See St. Thomas Aquinas, *On the Truth of the Catholic Faith*, trans. Vernon Bourke (New York: Doubleday, 1956), bk. 3, pt. 1.

[3] Immanuel Kant, *The Doctrine of Virtue*, trans. Mary Gregor (Philadelphia, Pa.: University of Pennsylvania Press, 1964), pp. 87–90.

[4] Alan Donagan, *The Theory of Morality* (Chicago, Ill.: University of Chicago Press, 1977), pp. 105–08.

[5] Ibid., p. 107.

Bibliography on Sexual Ethics

Anscombe, G. E. M. "Contraception and Chastity." In *Ethics and Population*, edited by Michael D. Bayles. Cambridge, Mass.: Schenkman, 1976.

Atkinson, Ronald. *Sexual Morality.* New York: Harcourt, Brace, 1966.

Baker, Robert, and Elliston, Frederick, eds. *Philosophy and Sex.* Buffalo, N.Y.: Prometheus Books, 1975.

Bertocci, Peter. *The Human Venture in Sex, Love and Marriage.* New York: Association Press, 1949.

_____. *Sex, Love, and the Person.* New York: Sheed and Ward, 1967.

Cohen, Carl. "Sex, Birth Control, and Human Life." *Ethics* 79 (1969): 251–62.

Curran, Charles E. "Homosexuality and Moral Theology: Methodological and Substantive Considerations." *The Thomist* 35 (1971): 447–81.

Gray, Robert. "Sex and Sexual Perversion." *Journal of Philosophy* 75 (1978): 189–99.

Kupfer, Joseph. "Sexual Perversion and the Good." *The Personalist* 59 (1978): 70–77.

McNeill, John J. *The Church and the Homosexual.* Kansas City, Mo.: Sheed, Andrews and McMeel, 1976.

Milhaven, John. "Thomas Aquinas on Sexual Pleasure." *Journal of Religious Ethics* 5 (1977): 157–81.

Moulton, Janice. "Sexual Behavior: Another Position." *Journal of Philosophy* 73 (1976): 537–46.

Nagel, Thomas. "Sexual Perversion." *Journal of Philosophy* 66 (1969): 5–17.

Noonan, John T., Jr. *Contraception.* Cambridge, Mass.: Harvard University Press, 1965.

Russell, Bertrand. *Marriage and Morals.* New York: Liveright, 1928.

_____. "Our Sexual Ethics." *The American Mercury* 38 (1936): 36–41.

Soble, Alan, ed. *Philosophy of Sex.* Totowa, N.J.: Rowman and Littlefield, 1980.

Toon, Mark. *The Philosophy of Sex According to St. Thomas Aquinas.* Catholic University of America Philosophical Studies, no. 56. Washington, D.C.: Catholic University of America, 1954.

Verene, D. P., ed. *Sexual Love and Western Morality: A Philosophical Anthology.* New York: Harper & Row, 1972.

Whiteley, Charles H., and Whiteley, W. M. *Sex and Morals.* New York: Basic Books, 1967.

Wilson, John. *Logic and Sexual Morality.* Baltimore, Md.: Penguin, 1956.

Problem Case

Pettit v. State Board of Education, 10 Cal. 3d 29; 109 Cal. Rptr. 665, 513 P.2d 889 (1973)

A married woman and her husband joined a private club in Los Angeles called The Swingers. An undercover policeman attended a private party during which Mrs. Pettit was observed in several acts of oral copulation with different men; there were other spectators when these acts took place. She was arrested, charged with oral copulation under the California Penal Code, and pleaded guilty (apparently in a plea bargain) to the lesser charge of outraging public decency. Mrs. Pettit was a teacher of retarded, elementary-school children in the public-school system. After disciplinary proceedings, her teaching credential was revoked on the grounds that her conduct involved moral turpitude and demonstrated her unfitness to teach. Mrs. Pettit petitioned the courts to order the State Board of Education to restore her teaching credential. The courts denied her request.

Was Mrs. Pettit's conduct at the party morally wrong? Does it make a moral difference that spectators were present? Is oral copulation morally wrong *in and of itself?*

JOHN M. FINNIS
NATURAL LAW AND UNNATURAL ACTS

Plato has situated the problem of sexual vice at the core of ethical speculation. In his great early dialogue, the *Gorgias,* in which he declares unequivocal 'war and battle' (cf. 447A) against the enlightened contemporary society, Plato has Socrates confront Callicles, the exponent of a pragmatic and egoistic hedonism. The crisis of their discussion, perhaps of the whole dialogue, is the question whether there are bad pleasures. Callicles maintains that the happy life consists in having many appetites which one can satisfy with enjoyment. Socrates asks whether a man is indeed happy who itches and wants to scratch, and can spend his life scratching. The question is vulgar and absurd, thinks Callicles; but he will not give way: a life of pleasurable scratching is a happy life. 'But suppose the itch were not confined to one's head. Must I go on with my questions? Think what you will answer, Callicles, if you are asked the questions which naturally follow. To bring the matter to a head—take the life of one who wallows in unnatural vices. . . . Isn't that shocking and shameful and miserable?' (494E). The question makes Callicles squirm. Socrates presses him: 'Can it be, my good friend, that good is not identical with enjoyment of *whatever* kind? If it is, the shocking things I hinted at just now must obviously follow, and

From John M. Finnis, "Natural Law and Unnatural Acts," *The Heythrop Journal* 2 (1970): 365–66, 379–87. Other sections of this article, not reproduced in this anthology, sketch a theory of natural law that the author has since elaborated in a book, *Natural Law and Natural Rights* (Oxford University Press, 1980). Reprinted by permission.

many other things as well' (495B). 'That's what you think, Socrates', re-torts Callicles—it is the classical retort to all ethical speculation and teaching. But in fact the back of Callicles's resistance has been broken.

The appeal of Socrates–Plato has not been to any ethical doctrine of natural law. It has been to Callicles's, and the reader's, confused, submerged but real grasp of what is good and what is a falling away, an aversion, a flight from good. Natural law is not a doctrine. It is one's permanent dynamic orientation towards an understanding grasp of the goods that can be realized by free choice, together with a bias (like the bias in one's 'speculation' towards raising questions that will lead one on from data to insight and from insight to judgement) towards actually making choices that are intelligibly (because intelligently) related to the goods which are understood to be attainable, or at stake, in one's situation. Now the jargon-laden sentence just uttered is a piece of speculation, theorizing, doctrine about natural law. But the point of all such theorizing can be little more than to uncover what is already available to everyone, submerged and confused, perhaps, but shaping everyone's practical attitudes and choices of what to do, what to love and what to respect. . . .

Sexual intercourse or interplay between the intelligent young:

> The idea that morality could enter into it is one I refuse to discuss—I find it so laughable. Sex is natural, wonderful, something to be shared, like a marvellous meal. I don't know when, or even if, I shall get married, so why should I wait indefinitely to enjoy it?[1]

How do some people respond to this rhetorical question (which I have taken, more or less at random, from an interview with an educated and respectable young woman in London, commenting on the decade or so since she gave up her virginity)?

The Dutch Catechism says:

> sexual intercourse . . . has by its very nature a definitive character. It implies that it is for good. If they surrender themselves to it, there is an inner change in the young man and the young woman. From then on they experience each other as husband and wife, and each act of union conjures up one to follow. This brings with it on the one hand the sense of being married, and on the other, the conflict of knowing that they are not married. And a step backwards—at any rate if a long period is involved—is only possible at the cost of profound inner tensions. From all these human reasons we can deduce God's will and law—that only married people should live together [p. 387].

Now it may be that this passage (as its context suggests) is concerned only with the psychology of engaged couples. In this case the apparent generality of the final deduction (I am assuming, to preserve the Christian sense of the Catechism, that 'live together' is a euphemism) is unwarranted (quite apart from the fact that the major premise of the deduction appears to be the negative, neo-utilitarian precept, 'Avoid inner tensions and conflicts'). And if the propositions preceding the deduction are concerned with young people generally—those contemplating not marriage but some years of contracepted (or in some way non-procreative) sexual play, before settling down to a serious and disciplined marriage in which adultery will be excluded or at any rate prudently moderated for the sake of the children and as a sign of the completeness of one's devotion to one's spouse— then I am afraid that this Catechism has nothing to say to (or about) such people. I am afraid it is not true to say that their sexual intercourse 'has by its very nature a definitive character' and 'implies that it is for good'. Our London girl and her partners could have a good laugh at the claim that 'they experience each other as husband and wife'! They *can* experience each other in this way, of course, and some do (often involuntarily), but they need not, and many do not: it is mainly a matter of what you make of it, and the avoidance of the risks which preachers put before you—unwanted children and hang-ups of one sort and another—is just a challenge to intelligence and an invitation to cultivate a dash of the worldly wisdom of moderation. One can even be prayerful about it, since apart from moderation, there seems to be in sexual play no moral implication that could come between God and me (except the *ipse dixit* of the Catechism).

The relevant Committee of the Lambeth Conference in 1958, addressing itself to young unmarried people, said:[2]

> The full giving and receiving of a whole person which sexual intercourse expresses is only possible within the assurance and protection of the faithful, life-long promise of each to the other, 'forsaking all others.'

This is well said. But the more relevant question is: Why should sexual intercourse be engaged in *only* in order to express a full giving and receiving? Why not to express . . . well, what we express in parties, in dancing, in dining out together, in comforting each other (just acquaintances) in times of stress . . . and so on? And if it is said that, *despite* one's intentions and the context, *the physical form of the act* 'has a definitive character' or 'expresses the full giving and receiving of a human person', then we must respond with two questions: (*i*) Really? What is it about the physical form of the act that has or bestows this extraordinary significance? (*ii*) Anyway, so what? After all, on no plausible ethical theory are we bound to respect the natural, given physical form of an act simply because it is its physical form. So why should we respect the 'natural significance' of that form (if the latter conception be granted)? At this point the Dutch and Lambeth seem to run out of breath. But more needs to be said.

We talk easily, these days, about the 'significance', for example the 'unitive significance' (*significatio unitatis*), of sexual intercourse. Now the English, 'unitive significance', rather more than the Latin, suggests that this act of physical union of bodies in some way has the meaning of bringing about a uniting of the partners, as if it had (perhaps in some realm of meanings) an effect. But the latter proposition, as it stands and as far as I understand it, seems to be false, for the reasons I have suggested. There seems no reason at all to accept that intercourse engaged in promiscuously, or as play or in sympathy or otherwise, need have any such effect. On the other hand, the Latin, *significatio unitatis*, rather suggests that intercourse expresses, is a symbol of, a union that already exists; and no doubt this is true: *ex hypothesi*, sexual intercourse is a union of bodies, and *as such* can express a common affection, a common playfulness, a common celebration, more vividly than dining out together . . . or dancing. It is 'something to be shared, like a marvellous meal'. But of course, *this* doesn't bear the load we want to put on the notion of *significatio unitatis*. Moreover, to say that intercourse 'has' this expressive sense or force obscures the fact that often intercourse actually expresses no more than a mutual taste for diversion, or a mutual *libido dominandi*.

What then is the source of the appeal and apparent plausibility of talk about the unitive significance of sexual intercourse? I think it is this: *granted* an ideal of a profound, life-long, exclusive, loving union between man and woman, then intercourse between these spouses is to be regarded as a very apt expression of their union, their common and exclusive project. And then one may wish to add, with the Lambeth Conference Committee again, that this apt expression is somehow made less apt (or perhaps is impossible?) unless 'the partners bring to each other a complete offering of self-hood unspoiled by any liaison'—hence 'pre-marital intercourse can never be right'.[3]

But before one leaps with relief to this conclusion, let us raise a few questions, not so much about the all-too-questionable assertion that casual sexual play 'spoils one's self-hood', but rather about the premise that intercourse is a peculiarly apt expression of the ideal of marriage. (*i*) Once more: What is it about intercourse, the union of bodies and members in *this* way (rather than that . . .), that makes it so apt an expression? (*ii*) Granted that this is the most apt expression of the ideal of marriage, does it follow that it is the only apt use of one's sexual powers? And even if it does follow, what is *morally* offensive about an inapt use of a physical capacity? (*iii*) More radically: What is the sense of the ideal of a profound, life-long, exclusive, loving union between one man and one woman?

This last question emerges, not out of a cheap cynicism, but from reflection on the meaning of friendship. It is self-evidently lovely for a person to go out from himself in friendship. *Bonum sui diffusivum* is the principle of a whole philosophical and theological civilization.[4] The mutual sharing of the good things of life is itself an unsurpassed good. So friendship does not rest satisfied with one friend, but seeks to extend itself to one's friend's friends, to widen the circle of love; it even dreams of a love of all men. For the union between one man and another man is deepened and strengthened, not weakened and dissipated, by its extension to other persons, the friends of my friends, sharing an ever-greater good, namely the ever-extending sharing of the goods open to man. Into this meditation on friendship erupts the peremptory demand that *one* friendship be exclusive and share its highest good with no one. Or rather, to reverse the challenge: into contemporary Christian rhapsodies about 'the couple' *we* (married people) must inject the blunt question: Why is it not perhaps vice, rather than virtue, to cultivate the exclusive life of the couple, and to reserve certain good things for *one* other person? No amount of praise of unity or of acts signifying unity will be an adequate response to this question: indeed, it will only increase the urgency of the question.

The only eligible answer to the question, I think, is that given in the terse and masterly summary of the Christian ideal of marriage which prefaces the analysis of that ideal in the encyclical *Humanae Vitae*.[5] It runs: 'By means of the reciprocal personal gift of self, proper and exclusive to them, husband and wife tend towards the communion of their beings in view of mutual personal perfection'—so far, an inadequate response, an apparently senseless closing-in of the couple against the world—'*in order to* [my emphasis] collaborate with God in the generation and education of new lives'— and there's the solution, the challenge to 'the couple' to find their mutually fulfilling communion and friendship not in an inexplicably exclusive cultivation of each other, but in a common pursuit, the pursuit of a good that *de facto* cannot be adequately realized otherwise than by a single-minded devotion to that good, by the *only* two people who can be *the* mother and *the* father of *that* child. Now to say this is not to draw any further conclusions (which would in fact be unwarranted)—such as that marriage should be entered upon primarily with the motive of having children, or that intercourse within marriage ought to be so motivated. No, the point is simply to issue a reminder about that dimension of sexuality which had not yet been mentioned, and to suggest in passing (because the emphasis of much modern catechetics seems to me profoundly awry) that what, in the last analysis, makes sense of the conditions of the marital enterprise, its stability and exclusiveness, is not the worthy and delightful sentiments of love and affection which invite one to marry, but the desire for and demands of a *procreative* community, a family.

However, to show that it is sensible to reserve a *complete and procreative self-giving* to the context of a stable and exclusive union is very far from showing that it is sensible to reserve *sexual intercourse* to that context. For a sexual movement, like any other bodily motion, has as a human action the meaning one gives it in context, and can be engaged in without any pretence that one is either establishing or expressing a stable and exclusive union.

The meaning one gives it—this meaning-giving is an act of choice. Now an intelligent choice to engage in sexual intercourse has to take into account a plain fact—not a 'meaning' so much as a biological fact of physical causality—*viz.* that intercourse may bring about procreation; that a child may be conceived; that intercourse is procreative (cause and effect, nothing more). One can accept this fact and to seek to capitalize on it, or one can ignore this fact and proceed regardless, or one can by simple means prevent the effect following from the cause. But in any case, one is willy nilly engaged, in sexual intercourse, with the basic human value of procreation. When I get into my car to drive home at night, I am not on a life-saving mission, but the causal potentialities of my activity bring me willy nilly within the range of the basic human value of life, and in terms of that value my actions can be characterized as sufficiently respectful of life, careless of life or wilfully violative of life, as the case may be. I am not bound to be always cultivating life, to be always cultivating God, or truth or social justice, or to be always procreating. But sometimes I find myself in (or bring myself within) situations which by their brute causal structure require of me an attention or a choice that will be adequately open to a basic value whose realization or violation is, by reason of that structure, at stake or in question in the situation. And then the call of reason reaching up towards the source of all intelligible good is to remain fully open to that basic intelligible good which now immediately confronts me.

From this point, and from no other, unfolds naturally the whole Christian understanding of the morality of sexual activity. Certainly, the Christian grasp of this basic value, procreation, is distinctively intense—*genitum non factum*—and what is demanded in procreation is not just its *esse* but its *bene esse*, not a spawning, but the bringing of the child into a community of love which will provide the substance of his education into a loving ability to realize all the human values. But this peculiarly intense grasp of the basic natural value does not distort or render peculiar or non-natural the development of the norm of *prudentia* in response to the call of the value. As always, the question is: What actions, by their causal structure, involve a choice adequately open to the basic values, and what actions involve, by their causal structure, a choice immediately against a basic value?

The Christian weighting of the value of procreation, as the value of procreation and education within a *communio personarum*, means that fornication, in which procreation may follow but not within an assured *communio personarum*, involves an inadequate openness to procreation (so understood). Nor can this conclusion be avoided by pointing to the fact that it is easy to exclude the possibility of procreation from fornication. For the choice to exclude the possibility of procreation while engaging in intercourse is always, and in an obvious and unambiguous way (which it requires no Christian weighting of the value of procreation to see), a choice directly and immediately against a basic value. (To this last remark it is perhaps unnecessary to add that taking steps to prevent procreation when one has or is about to bring oneself within the range of the procreative value by engaging in sexual intercourse is obviously very different from the policy of *not* bringing oneself fully within the range of the value at times when procreation might follow, but engaging in intercourse at other times within the framework of the procreative *communio personarum*.) And if a question is raised about solitary sexual acts or sexual intercourse *extra vas* (whether homo- or hetero-sexual), the Christian response, making explicit the confused natural sense of the question which

Plato was able to appeal to even in a Callicles, turns on the fact that all sexual activity involves an inchoate version, or perhaps a kind of reminder, of the procreative causal potency of 'full' sexual intercourse; this reminder or inchoate version brings a sensitive man sufficiently within the range of the procreative value for that value to make its ordinary imperious claim (like the other basic values) to a sufficient openness and respect towards it. And it is this sense of the symbolic relation of sexual movements to the value of procreation (understood as the rich familial *communio personarum*)[6] that makes the fornication of even the 'naturally' sterile seem, to the Christian, an inadequate openness to a basic good.

So, since the value of procreation, like other basic values, is a permanent and irreducible part of the structure of our will, of our thirst for the intelligible good, and since, like other basic values, its realization or rejection are permanent possibilities always implicit in certain of our situations, it is possible to see (given the vertical perspective towards the Good that can confront us in the immediate form of our choice) that some sexual acts are (as types of choice) always wrong because an inadequate response, or direct closure, to the basic procreative value that they put in question. By a trick of certain European languages, we call the more visibly non-procreative of these acts 'unnatural'; but whether the opposition or indifference to procreation as a value be visible or merely causal, symbolic or effective, all such acts are morally of a kind. If someone wishes to distinguish within the class, we must ask him to reflect: 'Think what you will answer, Callicles, if you are asked the questions which naturally follow . . . the shocking things I hinted at just now must obviously follow, and many other things as well.' . . .

. . . If you do engage in a sexual act of conjugal love you cannot escape its *de facto* corollary: the act is also procreative, either actually, or very possibly, or only barely possibly or (though this does not matter where contraception is in question) only by way of a physical structure reminiscent of its procreative potentialities. And the effect of this is that willy nilly you are forced to choose directly (in a straightforward sense when contracepting, and in more or less symbolic senses in other forms of sexual vice) for or against procreation in that act.

Why, then, is it not 'licit' to break the nexus between the contextual intention of the act (which concerns the *significatio unitatis*) and its causal structure (which confers the *significatio procreationis*)? There seems no sanctity in *de facto* connexions of this sort. I think the true reason why it can be said that *this* connexion should not be broken is that to attack either of the *significationes* is wrong in itself. It is wrong to force sexual attentions on one's spouse, indifferent to her state or her wishes—not for any special sexual reason, but because that is contrary to the demands of the basic value of friendship. It is wrong to choose directly against procreation in a context where procreation is immediately in question—again for the general reason that it is wrong to choose against any basic value in such a way. Both basic values which together come in question in sexual intercourse must be respected, not because they are together, but because each is inescapably in question. One could only break the connexion by rejecting one in favour of the other, and that would be wrong; but it would equally be wrong to engage in sexual activity which involved one in rejecting both together.

Finally, there is a secondary and derivative sense in which there is an indissoluble nexus between friendship and procreation in one's sexual activity. Each value demands respect *through* the other. If you choose to reject the procreative value in your act, your act is morally vitiated and so a poor thing to share with your friend—an inadequate response to the fundamental call of friendship, which is to be worthy of your friend and seek true goods for him. Conversely, if you reject the demands of friendship in your act, your act is an inadequate response to the value of procreation, the value which makes sense of the peculiarly exclusive form of friendship that marriage is.

Notes

1 See the *Daily Mail*, 23 September, 1969, 'Femail' section.
2 Report of the Committee on the Family in Contemporary Society, *The Lambeth Conference 1958* (London, 1958), 2, 156.
3 Loc. cit.
4 Cf. Per Erik Persson, *Sacra Doctrina: Reason and Revelation in Aquinas* (Oxford, 1970), pp. 132–8, on the difference between the neo-Platonist and Thomist worlds of thought, and the corresponding treatments of the tag, *bonum sui diffusivum*.
5 Para. 8.
6 It is this symbolic relation of intra-marital sexual acts to the value of procreation so understood that makes sense of marriage of the naturally sterile; their permanent and exclusive union honours the procreative community as a value they would wish to have devoted themselves to in common had they been able to effectively as well as symbolically.

SARA RUDDICK
BETTER SEX

It might be argued that there is no specifically sexual morality. We have, of course, become accustomed to speaking of sexual morality, but the "morality" of which we speak has a good deal to do with property, the division of labor, and male power, and little to do with our sexual lives. Sexual experiences, like experiences in driving automobiles, render us liable to specific moral situations. As drivers we must guard against infantile desires for revenge and excitement. As lovers we must guard against cruelty and betrayal, for we know sexual experiences provide special opportunities for

From Sara Ruddick, "Better Sex," in *Philosophy and Sex,* edited by Robert Baker and Frederick Elliston, published by Prometheus Books, Buffalo, N.Y. Copyright © 1975 by Sara L. Ruddick.

each. We drive soberly because, before we get into a car, we believe that it is wrong to be careless of life. We resist temptations to adultery because we believe it wrong to betray trust, whether it be a parent, a sexual partner, or a political colleague who is betrayed. As lovers and drivers we act on principles that are particular applications of general moral principles. Moreover, given the superstitions from which sexual experience has suffered, it is wise to free ourselves, as lovers, from any moral concerns, other than those we have as human beings. There is no specifically sexual morality, and none should be invented. Or so it might be argued.

When we examine our moral "intuitions," however, the analogy with driving fails us. Unburdened of *sexual* morality, we do not find it easy to apply general moral principles to our sexual lives. The "morally average" lover can be cruel, violate trust, and neglect social duties with less opprobrium precisely *because* he is a lover. Only political passions and psychological or physical deprivation serve as well as sexual desire to excuse what would otherwise be seriously and clearly immoral acts. (Occasionally, sexual desire is itself conceived of as a deprivation, an involuntary lust. And there is, of course, a tradition that sees sexual morality as a way of controlling those unable to be sexless: "It is better to marry than to burn.") Often, in our sexual lives, we neither flout nor simply apply general moral principles. Rather, the values of sexual experience themselves figure in the construction of moral dilemmas. The conflict between better sex (more complete, natural, and pleasurable sex acts) and, say, social duty is not seen as a conflict between the immoral and compulsive, on one hand, and the morally good, on the other, but as a conflict between alternative moral acts.

Our intuitions vary but at least they suggest we can use "good" sex as a positive weight on some moral balance. What is that weight? Why do we put it there? How do we, in the first place, evaluate sexual experiences? On reflection, should we endorse these evaluations? These are the questions whose answers should constitute a specifically sexual morality. . . .

A characteristic renders a sex act morally preferable to one without that characteristic if it gives, increases, or is instrumental in increasing the "benefit" of the act for the person engaging in it. Benefits can be classified as peremptory or optional. Peremptory benefits are experiences, relations, or objects that anyone who is neither irrational nor anhedonic will want so long as he wants anything at all. Optional benefits are experiences, relations, or objects that anyone, neither irrational nor anhedonic, will want so long as he will not thereby lose a peremptory benefit. There is widespread disagreement about which benefits are peremptory. Self-respect, love, and health are common examples of peremptory benefits. Arms, legs, and hands are probably optional benefits. A person still wanting a great deal might give up limbs, just as she would give up life, when mutilation or death is required by self-respect. As adults we are largely responsible for procuring our own benefits and greatly dependent on good fortune for success in doing so. However, the moral significance of benefits is most clearly seen not from the standpoint of the person procuring and enjoying them but from the standpoint of another *caring* person, for example, a lover, parent, or political leader responsible for procuring benefits for specific others. A benefit may then be described as an experience, relation, or object that anyone who properly cares for another is obliged to attempt to secure for him. Criteria for the virtue of care and for benefit are reciprocally determined, the virtue consisting in part in recognizing and attempting to secure benefits for the person cared for, the identification of benefit depending on its recognition by those already seen to be properly caring.

In talking of benefits I shall be looking at our sexual lives from the vantage point of hope, not of fear. The principal interlocutor may be considered to be a child asking what he should rightly and reasonably hope for in living, rather than a potential criminal questioning conventional restraints. The specific question the child may be imagined to ask can now be put: In what way is better sex beneficial or conducive to experiences or relations or objects that are beneficial?

A characteristic renders a sex act morally preferable to one without that characteristic if either the act is thereby more just or the act is thereby likely to make the person engaging in it more just. Justice includes giving others what is due them, taking no more than what is one's own, and giving and taking according to prevailing principles of fairness.

A characteristic renders a sex act morally preferable to one without that characteristic if because of the characteristic the act is more virtuous or more likely to lead to virtue. A virtue is a disposition to attempt, and an ability to succeed in, good acts—acts of justice, acts that express or produce excellence, and acts that yield benefits to oneself or others.

Sensual experiences give rise to sensations and experiences that are paradigms of what is pleasant. Hedonism, in both its psychological and ethical forms, has blinded us to the nature and to the benefits of sensual pleasure by overextending the word "pleasure" to cover anything enjoyable or even agreeable. The paradigmatic type of pleasure is sensual. Pleasure is a temporally extended, more or less intense quality of particular experiences. Pleasure is enjoyable independent of any function pleasurable activity fulfills. The infant who continues to suck well after he is nourished, expressing evident pleasure in doing so, gives us a demonstration of the nature of pleasure.[1] . . .

The completeness of a sexual act depends upon the *relation* of the participants to their own and each other's *desire*. A sex act is complete if each partner allows himself to be "taken over" by an active desire, which is desire not merely for the other's body but also for his active desire. Completeness is hard to characterize, though complete sex acts are at least as natural as any others—especially, it seems, among those people who take them casually and for granted. The notion of "completeness" (as I shall call it) has figured under various guises in the work of Sartre, Merleau-

Ponty, and more recently Thomas Nagel. "The being which desires is consciousness making itself body."[2] "What we try to possess, then, is not just a body, but a body brought to life by consciousness."[3] "It is important that the partner be aroused, and not merely aroused, but aroused by the awareness of one's desire."[4] . . .

The final characteristic of allegedly better sex acts is that they are "natural" rather than "perverted." The ground for classifying sexual acts as either natural or unnatural is that the former type serve or could serve the evolutionary and biological function of sexuality—namely, reproduction. "Natural" sexual desire has as its "object" living persons of the opposite sex, and in particular their postpubertal genitals. The "aim" of natural sexual desire—that is, the act that "naturally" completes it—is genital intercourse. Perverse sex acts are deviations from the natural object (for example, homosexuality, fetishism) or from the standard aim (for example, voyeurism, sadism). Among the variety of objects and aims of sexual desire, I can see no other ground for selecting some as natural, except that they are of the type that can lead to reproduction.[5] . . .

Some sex acts are, allegedly, better than others insofar as they are more pleasurable, complete, and natural. What is the moral significance of this evaluation? In answering this question, official sexual morality sometimes appeals to the social consequences of particular types of better sex acts. For example, since dominantly perverse organizations of sexual impulses limit reproduction, the merits of perversion depend upon the need to limit or increase population. Experience of sexual pleasure may be desirable if it promotes relaxation and communication in an acquisitive society, undesirable if it limits the desire to work or, in armies, to kill. The social consequences of complete sex have not received particular attention, because the quality of sexual experience has been of little interest to moralists. It might be found that those who had complete sexual relations were more cooperative, less amenable to political revolt. If so, complete sexual acts would be desirable in just and peaceable societies, undesirable in unjust societies requiring revolution.

The social desirability of types of sexual acts depends on particular social conditions and independent criteria of social desirability. It may be interesting and important to assess particular claims about the social desirability of sex acts, but this is not my concern. What is my concern is the extent to which we will allow our judgments of sexual worth to be influenced by social considerations. But this issue cannot even be raised until we have a better sense of sexual worth. . . .

What is the moral significance of the perversity of a sexual act? Next to none, so far as I can see. Though perverted sex may be "unnatural" both from an evolutionary and developmental perspective, there is no connection, inverse or correlative, between what is natural and what is good. Perverted sex is sometimes said to be less pleasurable than natural sex. We have little reason to believe that this claim is true and no clear idea of the

kind of evidence on which it would be based. In any case, to condemn perverse acts for lack of pleasure is to recognize the worth of pleasure, not of
naturalness. . . .

Complete sex consists in mutually embodied, mutually active, responsive desire. Embodiment, activity, and mutual responsiveness are instrumentally beneficial because they are conducive to our psychological well-
being, which is an intrinsic benefit. The alleged pathological consequences
of disembodiment are more specific and better documented than those of
perversity.[6] To dissociate oneself from one's actual body, either by creating
a delusory body or by rejecting the bodily, is to court a variety of ill effects,
ranging from self-disgust to diseases of the will, to faulty mental development, to the destruction of a recognizable "self," and finally to madness.
It is difficult to assess psychiatric claims outside their theoretical contexts,
but in this case I believe that they are justified. Relative embodiment is a
stable, *normal* condition that is not confined to cases of complete embodiment. But psychiatrists tell us that exceptional physical occasions of embodiment seem to be required in order to balance tendencies to reject or to
falsify the body. Sexual acts are not the only such occasions, but they do
provide an immersion of consciousness in the bodily, which is pleasurable
and especially conducive to correcting experiences of shame and disgust
that work toward disembodiment.

The mutual responsiveness of complete sex is also instrumentally beneficial. It satisfies a general desire to be recognized as a particular "real"
person and to make a difference to other particular "real" people. The
satisfaction of this desire in sexual experience is especially rewarding, its
thwarting especially cruel. Vulnerability is increased in complete sex by the
active desiring of the partners. When betrayal, or for that matter, tenderness or ecstasy, ensues, one cannot dissociate oneself from the desire with
which one identified and out of which one acted. The psychic danger is
real, as people who attempt to achieve a distance from their desires could
tell us. But the cost of distance is as evident as its gains. Passivity in respect
to one's own sexual desire not only limits sexual pleasure but, more seriously, limits the extent to which the experience of sexual pleasure can be
included as an experience of a coherent person. With passivity comes a
kind of irresponsibility in which one can hide from one's desire, even from
one's pleasure, "playing" seducer or victim, tease or savior. Active sexual
desiring in complete sex acts affords an especially threatening but also
especially happy occasion to relinquish these and similar roles. To the extent that the roles confuse and confound our intimate relations, the benefit from relinquishing them in our sexual acts, or the loss from adhering to
them then, is especially poignant.

In addition to being beneficial, complete sex acts are morally superior
for three reasons. They tend to resolve tensions fundamental to moral life;
they are conducive to emotions that, if they become stable and dominant,
are in turn conducive to the virtue of loving; and they involve a pre-
eminently moral virtue—respect for persons.

In one of its aspects, morality is opposed to the private and untamed. Morality is "civilization," social and regulating; desire is "discontent" resisting the regulation. Obligation, rather than benefit, is the notion central to morality so conceived, and the virtues required of a moral person are directed to preserving right relations and social order. Both the insistence on natural sex and the encouragement of complete sex can be looked upon as attempts to make sexual desire more amenable to regulation. But whereas the regulation of perverted desires is extrinsic to them, those of completeness modify the desires themselves. The desiring sensual body that in our social lives we may laugh away or disown becomes our "self" and enters into a social relation. Narcissism and altruism are satisfied in complete sex acts in which one gives what one receives by receiving it. Social and private "selves" are unified in an act in which impersonal, spontaneous impulses govern an action that is responsive to a particular person. For this to be true we must surmount our social "roles" as well as our sexual "techniques," though we incorporate rather than surmount our social selves. We must also surmount regulations imposed in the name of naturalness if our desires are to be spontaneously expressed. Honestly spontaneous first love gives us back our private desiring selves while allowing us to see the desiring self of another. Mutually responding partners confirm each other's desires and declare them good. Such occasions, when we are "moral" without cost, help reconcile us to our moral being and to the usual mutual exclusion between our social and private lives.

The connection between sex and certain emotions—particularly love, jealousy, fear, and anger—is as evident as it is obscure. Complete sex acts seem more likely than incomplete pleasurable ones to lead toward affection and away from fear and anger, since any guilt and shame will be extrinsic to the act and meliorated by it. It is clear that we need not feel for someone any affection beyond that required (if any is) simply to participate with him in a complete sex act. However, it is equally clear that sexual pleasure, especially as experienced in complete sex acts, is conducive to many feelings—gratitude, tenderness, pride, appreciation, dependency, and others. These feelings magnify their object who occasioned them, making him unique among men. When these magnifying feelings become stable and habitual they are conducive to love—not universal love, of course, but love of a particular sexual partner. However, even "selfish" love is a virtue, a disposition to care for someone as her interests and demands would dictate. Neither the best sex nor the best love require each other, but they go together more often than reason would expect—often enough to count the virtue of loving as one of the rewards of the capacity for sexual pleasure exercised in complete sex acts. . . .

Finally, as Sartre has suggested, complete sex acts preserve a respect for persons. Each person remains conscious and responsible, a "subject" rather than a depersonalized, will-less, or manipulated "object." Each actively desires that the other likewise remain a "subject." Respect for persons is a central virtue when matters of justice and obligation are at issue.

Insofar as we can speak of respect for persons in complete sex acts, there are different, often contrary requirements of respect. Respect for persons, typically and in sex acts, requires that *actual present* partners participate, partners whose desires are recognized and endorsed. Respect for persons typically requires taking a distance from both one's own demands and those of others. But in sex acts the demands of desire take over, and equal distance is replaced by mutual responsiveness. Respect typically requires refusing to treat another person merely as a means to fulfilling demands. In sex acts, another person is so clearly a means to satisfaction that she is always on the verge of becoming merely a means ("intercourse counterfeits masturbation"). In complete sex acts, instrumentality vanishes only because it is mutual and mutually desired. Respect requires encouraging, or at least protecting, the autonomy of another. In complete sex, autonomy of will is recruited by desire, and freedom from others is replaced by frank dependence on another person's desire. Again the respect consists in the reciprocity of desiring dependence, which bypasses rather than violates autonomy.

Despite the radical differences between respect for persons in the usual moral contexts and respect for persons in sex acts, it is not, I think, a mere play on words to talk of respect in the latter case. When, in any sort of intercourse, persons are respected, their desires are not only, in fair measure, fulfilled. In addition, their desires are active and determine, in fair measure, the form of intercourse and the manner and condition of desire's satisfaction. These conditions are not only met in sexual intercourse when it is characterized by completeness; they come close to defining completeness.

Sartre is not alone in believing that just because the condition of completeness involves respect for persons, complete sex is impossible. Completeness is surely threatened by pervasive tendencies to fantasy, to possessiveness, and to varieties of a sadomasochistic desire. But a complete sex act, as I see it, does not involve an heroic restraint on our sexual impulses. Rather, a complete sex act is a normal mode of sexual activity expressing the natural structure and impulses of sexual desire.

While complete sex is morally superior because it involves respect for persons, incomplete sex acts do not necessarily involve immoral disrespect for persons. They may, depending upon the desires and expectations of the partners; but they may involve neither respect nor disrespect. Masturbation, for example, allows only the limited completeness of embodiment and often fails of that. But masturbation only rarely involves disrespect to anyone. Even the respect of the allegedly desirable sleeping woman may not be violated if she is unknowingly involved in a sex act. Disrespect, though likely, may be obviated by her sensibilities and expectations that she has previously expressed and her partner has understood. Sex acts provide one context in which respect for persons can be expressed. That context is important both because our sexual lives are of such importance to us and because they are so liable to injury because of the experience and the fear of the experience of disrespect. But many complete sex acts in which respect is maintained makes other casual and incomplete sex acts unthreatening. In this case a goodly number of swallows can make a summer.

In sum, then, complete sex acts are superior to incomplete ones. First, they are, whatever their effects, better than various kinds of incomplete sex acts because they involve a kind of "respect for persons" in acts that are otherwise prone to violation of respect for, and often to violence to, persons. Second, complete sex acts are good because they are good for us. They are conducive to some fairly clearly defined kinds of psychological well-being that are beneficial. They are conducive to moral well-being because they relieve tensions that arise in our attempts to be moral and because they encourage the development of particular virtues.

To say that complete sex acts are preferable to incomplete ones is not to court a new puritanism. There are many kinds and degrees of incompleteness. Incomplete sex acts may not involve a disrespect for persons. Complete sex acts only *tend* to be good for us, and the realization of these tendencies depends upon individual lives and circumstances of sexual activity. The proper object of sexual desire is sexual pleasure. It would be a foolish ambition indeed to limit one's sexual acts to those in which completeness was likely. Any sexual act that is pleasurable is prima facie good, though the more incomplete it is—the more private, essentially autoerotic, unresponsive, unembodied, passive, or imposed—the more likely it is to be harmful to someone.

There are many questions we have neglected to consider because we have not been sufficiently attentive to the quality of sexual lives. For example, we know little about the ways of achieving better sex. When we must choose between inferior sex and abstinence, how and when will our choice of inferior sex damage our capacity for better sex? Does, for example, the repeated experience of controlled sexual disembodiment ("desire which takes over will take you too far") that we urge (or used to urge) on adolescents damage their capacity for complete sex? The answers to this and similar questions are not obvious, though unfounded opinions are always ready at hand.

Some of the traditional sexual vices might be condemned on the ground that they are inimical to better sex. Obscenity, or repeated public exposure to sexual acts, might impair our capacity for pleasure or for response to desire. Promiscuity might undercut the tendency of complete sex acts to promote emotions that magnify their object. Other of the traditional sexual vices are neither inimical nor conducive to better sex, but are condemned because of conflicting nonsexual benefits and obligations. For example, infidelity qua infidelity neither secures nor prevents better sex. The obligations of fidelity have many sources, one of which may be a past history of shared complete sex acts, a history that included promises of exclusive intimacy. Such past promises are as apt to conflict with as to accord with a current demand for better sex. I have said nothing about how such a conflict would be settled. I hope I have shown that where the possibility of better sex conflicts with obligations and other benefits, we have a *moral dilemma,* not just an occasion for moral self-discipline.

The pursuit of more pleasurable and more complete sex acts is, among many moral activities, distinguished not for its exigencies but for its rewards. Since our sexual lives are so important to us, and since, whatever our history and our hopes, we are sexual beings, this pursuit rightly engages our moral reflection. It should not be relegated to the immoral, nor to the "merely" prudent.

Notes

[1] The example is from Sigmund Freud, *Three Essays on Sexuality,* standard ed., vol. 7 (London: Hogarth, 1963), p. 182.

[2] Jean-Paul Sartre, *Being and Nothingness,* tr. Hazel E. Barnes (New York: Philosophical Library, 1956), p. 389.

[3] Merleau-Ponty, *Phenomenology of Perception,* tr. Colin Smith (London: Routledge & Kegan Paul, 1962), p. 167.

[4] Thomas Nagel, "Sexual Perversion," *The Journal of Philosophy* 66, no. 1 (January 16, 1969): 13.

[5] See, in support of this point, Sigmund Freud, *Introductory Lectures on Psychoanalysis,* standard ed., vol. 26 (London: Hogarth, 1963), chaps. 20, 21.

[6] See, for example, R. D. Laing, *The Divided Self* (Baltimore: Pelican Books, 1965).

ALAN H. GOLDMAN
PLAIN SEX

I shall suggest here that sex continues to be misrepresented in recent writings, at least in philosophical writings, and I shall criticize the predominant form of analysis which I term "means-end analysis." Such conceptions attribute a necessary external goal or purpose to sexual activity, whether it be reproduction, the expression of love, simple communication, or interpersonal awareness. They analyze sexual activity as a means to one of these ends, implying that sexual desire is a desire to reproduce, to love or be loved, or to communicate with others. All definitions of this type suggest false views of the relation of sex to perversion and morality by implying that sex which does not fit one of these models or fulfill one of these functions is in some way deviant or incomplete.

The alternative, simpler analysis with which I will begin is that sexual desire is desire for contact with another person's body and for the pleasure which such contact produces; sexual activity is activity which tends to fulfill such desire of the agent. Whereas Aristotle and Butler were correct in

Alan H. Goldman, "Plain Sex," *Philosophy and Public Affairs,* vol. 6, no. 3 (Spring 1977). Copyright © 1977 by Princeton University Press. Excerpts reprinted by permission.

holding that pleasure is normally a byproduct rather than a goal of purposeful action, in the case of sex this is not so clear. The desire for another's body is, principally among other things, the desire for the pleasure that physical contact brings. On the other hand, it is not a desire for a particular sensation detachable from its causal context, a sensation which can be derived in other ways. This definition in terms of the general goal of sexual desire appears preferable to an attempt to more explicitly list or define specific sexual activities, for many activities such as kissing, embracing, massaging, or holding hands may or may not be sexual, depending upon the context and more specifically upon the purposes, needs, or desires into which such activities fit. The generality of the definition also represents a refusal (common in recent psychological texts) to overemphasize orgasm as the goal of sexual desire or genital sex as the only norm of sexual activity (this will be hedged slightly in the discussion of perversion below).

Central to the definition is the fact that the goal of sexual desire and activity is the physical contact itself, rather than something else which this contact might express. By contrast, what I term "means-end analyses" posit ends which I take to be extraneous to plain sex, and they view sex as a means to these ends. Their fault lies not in defining sex in terms of its general goal, but in seeing plain sex as merely a means to other separable ends. I term these "means-end analyses" for convenience, although "means-separable-end analyses," while too cumbersome, might be more fully explanatory. The desire for physical contact with another person is a minimal criterion for (normal) sexual desire, but is both necessary and sufficient to qualify normal desire as sexual. Of course, we may want to express other feelings through sexual acts in various contexts; but without the desire for the physical contact in and for itself, or when it is sought for other reasons, activities in which contact is involved are not predominantly sexual. Furthermore, the desire for physical contact in itself, without the wish to express affection or other feelings through it, is sufficient to render sexual the activity of the agent which fulfills it. Various activities with this goal alone, such as kissing and caressing in certain contexts, qualify as sexual even without the presence of genital symptoms of sexual excitement. The latter are not therefore necessary criteria for sexual activity.

This initial analysis may seem to some either over- or underinclusive. It might seem too broad in leading us to interpret physical contact as sexual desire in activities such as football and other contact sports. In these cases, however, the desire is not for contact with another body per se, it is not directed toward a particular person for that purpose, and it is not the goal of the activity—the goal is winning or exercising or knocking someone down or displaying one's prowess. If the desire is purely for contact with another specific person's body, then to interpret it as sexual does not seem an exaggeration. A slightly more difficult case is that of a baby's desire to be cuddled and our natural response in wanting to cuddle it. In the case of the baby, the desire may be simply for the physical contact, for the pleasure of the caresses. If so, we may characterize this desire, especially in keeping with Freudian theory, as sexual or protosexual. It will differ nevertheless from full-fledged sexual desire in being more amorphous, not directed outward toward another specific person's body. It may also be that what the infant unconsciously desires is not physical contact per se but signs of affection, tenderness, or security, in which case we have further reason for hesitating to characterize its wants as clearly sexual. The intent of our response to the baby is often the showing of affection, not the pure physical contact, so that our definition in terms of action which fulfills sexual desire *on the part of the agent* does not capture such actions, whatever we say of the baby. (If it is intuitive to characterize our response as sexual as well, there is clearly no problem here for my analysis.) The same can be said of signs of affection (or in some cultures polite greeting) among men or women: these certainly need not be homosexual when the intent is only to show friendship, something extrinsic to plain sex although valuable when added to it.

Our definition of sex in terms of the desire for physical contact may appear too narrow in that a person's personality, not merely her or his body, may be sexually attractive to another, and in that looking or conversing in a certain way can be sexual in a given context without bodily contact. Nevertheless, it is not the contents of one's thoughts per se that are sexually appealing, but one's personality as embodied in certain manners of behavior. Furthermore, if a person is sexually attracted by another's personality, he or she will desire not just further conversation, but actual sexual contact. While looking at or conversing with someone can be interpreted as sexual in given contexts it is so when intended as preliminary to, and hence parasitic upon, elemental sexual interest. Voyeurism or viewing a pornographic movie qualifies as a sexual activity, but only as an imaginative substitute for the real thing (otherwise a deviation from the norm as expressed in our definition). The same is true of masturbation as a sexual activity without a partner.

That the initial definition indicates at least an ingredient of sexual desire and activity is too obvious to argue. We all know what sex is, at least in obvious cases, and do not need philosophers to tell us. My preliminary analysis is meant to serve as a contrast to what sex is not, at least, not necessarily. I concentrate upon the physically manifested desire for another's body, and I take as central the immersion in the physical aspect of one's own existence and attention to the physical embodiment of the other. One may derive pleasure in a sex act from expressing certain feelings to one's partner or from awareness of the attitude of one's partner, but sexual desire is essentially desire for physical contact itself: it is a bodily desire for the body of another that dominates our mental life for more or less brief periods. Traditional writings were correct to emphasize the purely physical or animal aspect of sex; they were wrong only in condemning it. This characterization of sex as an intensely pleasurable physical activity and acute physical desire may seem to some to capture only its barest level. But it is worth distinguishing and focusing upon this least common denominator in order to avoid the false views of sexual morality and perversion which emerge from thinking that sex is essentially something else.

I

We may turn then to what sex is not, to the arguments regarding supposed conceptual connections between sex and other activities which it is necessary to conceptually distinguish. The most comprehensible attempt to build an extraneous purpose into the sex act identifies that purpose as reproduction, its primary biological function. While this may be "nature's" purpose, it certainly need not be ours (the analogy with eating, while sometimes overworked, is pertinent here). While this identification may once have had a rational basis which also grounded the identification of the value and morality of sex with that applicable to reproduction and childrearing, the development of contraception rendered the connection weak. Methods of contraception are by now so familiar and so widely used that it is not necessary to dwell upon the changes wrought by these developments in the concept of sex itself and in a rational sexual ethic dependent upon that concept. In the past, the ever present possibility of children rendered the concepts of sex and sexual morality different from those required at present. There may be good reasons, if the presence and care of both mother and father are beneficial to children, for restricting reproduction to marriage. Insofar as society has a legitimate role in protecting children's interests, it may be justified in giving marriage a legal status, although this question is complicated by the fact (among others) that children born to single mothers deserve no penalties. In any case, the point here is simply that these questions are irrelevant at the present time to those regarding the morality of sex and its potential social regulation. (Further connections with marriage will be discussed below.)

It is obvious that the desire for sex is not necessarily a desire to reproduce, that the psychological manifestation has become, if it were not always, distinct from its biological roots. There are many parallels, as previously mentioned, with other natural functions. The pleasures of eating and exercising are to a large extent independent of their roles in nourishment or health (as the junk-food industry discovered with a vengeance). Despite the obvious parallel with sex, there is still a tendency for many to think that sex acts which can be reproductive are, if not more moral or less immoral, at least more natural. These categories of morality and "naturalness," or normality, are not to be identified with each other, as will be argued below, and neither is applicable to sex by virtue of its connection to reproduction. The tendency to identify reproduction as the conceptually connected end of sex is most prevalent now in the pronouncements of the Catholic church. There the assumed analysis is clearly tied to a restrictive sexual morality according to which acts become immoral and unnatural when they are not oriented towards reproduction, a morality which has independent roots in the Christian sexual ethic as it derives from Paul.

However, the means-end analysis fails to generate a consistent sexual ethic: homosexual and oral-genital sex is condemned while kissing or caressing, acts equally unlikely to lead in themselves to fertilization, even when properly characterized as sexual according to our definition, are not.

II

Before discussing further relations of means-end analyses to false or inconsistent sexual ethics and concepts of perversion, I turn to other examples of these analyses. One common position views sex as essentially an expression of love or affection between the partners. It is generally recognized that there are other types of love besides sexual, but sex itself is taken as an expression of one type, sometimes termed "romantic" love. Various factors again ought to weaken this identification. First, there are other types of love besides that which it is appropriate to express sexually, and "romantic" love itself can be expressed in many other ways. I am not denying that sex can take on heightened value and meaning when it becomes a vehicle for the expression of feelings of love or tenderness, but so can many other usually mundane activities such as getting up early to make breakfast on Sunday, cleaning the house, and so on. Second, sex itself can be used to communicate many other emotions besides love, and, as I will argue below, can communicate nothing in particular and still be good sex.

On a deeper level, an internal tension is bound to result from an identification of sex, which I have described as a physical-psychological desire, with love as a long-term, deep emotional relationship between two individuals. As this type of relationship, love is permanent, at least in intent, and more or less exclusive. A normal person cannot deeply love more than a few individuals even in a lifetime. We may be suspicious that those who attempt or claim to love many love them weakly if at all. Yet, fleeting sexual desire can arise in relation to a variety of other individuals one finds sexually attractive. It may even be, as some have claimed, that sexual desire in humans naturally seeks variety, while this is obviously false of love. For this reason, monogamous sex, even if justified, almost always represents a sacrifice or the exercise of self-control on the part of the spouses, while monogamous love generally does not. There is no such thing as casual love in the sense in which I intend the term "love." It may occasionally happen that a spouse falls deeply in love with someone else (especially when sex is conceived in terms of love), but this is relatively rare in comparison to passing sexual desires for others; and while the former often indicates a weakness or fault in the marriage relation, the latter does not.

If love is indeed more exclusive in its objects than is sexual desire, this explains why those who view sex as essentially an expression of love would again tend to hold a repressive or restrictive sexual ethic. As in the case of reproduction, there may be good reasons for reserving the total commitment of deep love to the context of marriage and family—the normal personality may not withstand additional divisions of ultimate commitment and allegiance. There is no question that marriage itself is best sustained by a deep relation of love and affection; and even if love is not naturally monogamous, the benefits of family units to children provide additional reason to avoid serious commitments elsewhere which weaken family ties. It can be argued similarly that monogamous sex strengthens families by restricting and at the same time guaranteeing an outlet for sexual desire in marriage. But there is more force to the argument that recognition of a clear distinction between sex and love in society would help avoid disastrous marriages which result from adolescent confusion of the two when sexual desire is mistaken for permanent love, and would weaken damaging jealousies which arise in marriages in relation to passing sexual desires. The love and affection of a sound marriage certainly differs from the adolescent romantic variety, which is often a mere substitute for sex in the context of a repressive sexual ethic.

In fact, the restrictive sexual ethic tied to the means-end analysis in terms of love again has failed to be consistent. At least, it has not been applied consistently, but forms part of the double standard which has curtailed the freedom of women. It is predictable in light of this history that some women would now advocate using sex as another kind of means, as a political weapon or as a way to increase unjustly denied power and freedom. The inconsistency in the sexual ethic typically attached to the sex-love analysis, according to which it has generally been taken with a grain of salt when applied to men, is simply another example of the impossibility of tailoring a plausible moral theory in this area to a conception of sex which builds in conceptually extraneous factors.

I am not suggesting here that sex ought never to be connected with love or that it is not a more significant and valuable activity when it is. Nor am I denying that individuals need love as much as sex and perhaps emotionally need at least one complete relationship which encompasses both. Just as sex can express love and take on heightened significance when it does, so love is often naturally accompanied by an intermittent desire for sex. But again love is accompanied appropriately by desires for other shared activities as well. What makes the desire for sex seem more intimately connected with love is the intimacy which is seen to be a natural feature of mutual sex acts. Like love, sex is held to lay one bare psychologically as well as physically. Sex is unquestionably intimate, but beyond that the psychological toll often attached may be a function of the restrictive sexual ethic itself, rather than a legitimate apology for it. The intimacy involved in love is psychologically consuming in a generally healthy way, while the psychological tolls of sexual relations, often including embarrassment as a correlate of intimacy, are too often the result of artificial sexual ethics and taboos. The intimacy involved in both love and sex is insufficient in any case in light of previous points to render a means-end analysis in these terms appropriate. . . .

III

. . . The attempts to brand forms of sex outside the idealized models as immoral or perverted fail to achieve consistency with intuitions that they themselves do not directly question. The reproductive model brands oral-genital sex a deviation, but cannot account for kissing or holding hands; the communication account holds voyeurism to be perverted but cannot accommodate sex acts without much conscious thought or seductive non-physical foreplay; the sex-love model makes most sexual desire seem degrading or base. The first and last condemn extra-marital sex on the sound but irrelevant grounds that reproduction and deep commitment are best confined to family contexts. The romanticization of sex and the confusion of sexual desire with love operate in both directions: sex outside the context of romantic love is repressed; once it is repressed, partners become more difficult to find and sex becomes romanticized further, out of proportion to its real value for the individual.

What all these analyses share in addition to a common form is accordance with and perhaps derivation from the Platonic-Christian moral tradition, according to which the animal or purely physical element of humans is the source of immorality, and plain sex in the sense I defined it is an expression of this element, hence in itself to be condemned. All the analyses examined seem to seek a distance from sexual desire itself in attempting to extend it conceptually beyond the physical. The love and communication analyses seek refinement or intellectualization of the desire; plain physical sex becomes vulgar, and too straightforward sexual encounters without an aura of respectable cerebral communicative content are to be avoided. Solomon explicitly argues that sex cannot be a "mere" appetite, his argument being that if it were, subway exhibitionism and other vulgar forms would be pleasing.[1] This fails to recognize that sexual desire can be focused or selective at the same time as being physical. Lower animals are not attracted by every other member of their species, either. Rancid food forced down one's throat is not pleasing, but that certainly fails to show that hunger is not a physical appetite. Sexual desire lets us know that we are physical beings and, indeed, animals; this is why traditional Platonic morality is so thorough in its condemnation. Means-end analyses continue to reflect this tradition, sometimes unwittingly. They show that in conceptualizing sex it is still difficult, despite years of so-called revolution in this area, to free ourselves from the lingering suspicion that plain sex as physical desire is an expression of our "lower selves," that yielding to our animal natures is subhuman or vulgar.

IV

Having criticized these analyses for the sexual ethics and concepts of perversion they imply, it remains to contrast my account along these lines. To the question of what morality might be implied by my analysis, the answer is that there are no moral implications whatever. Any analysis of sex which imputes a moral character to sex acts in themselves is wrong for that reason. There is no morality intrinsic to sex, although general moral rules apply to the treatment of others in sex acts as they apply to all human relations. We can speak of a sexual ethic as we can speak of a business ethic, without implying that business in itself is either moral or immoral or that special rules are required to judge business practices which are not derived from rules that apply elsewhere as well. Sex is not in itself a moral category, although like business it invariably places us into relations with others in which moral rules apply. It gives us opportunity to do what is otherwise recognized as wrong, to harm others, deceive them or manipulate them against their wills. Just as the fact that an act is sexual in itself never renders it wrong or adds to its wrongness if it is wrong on other grounds (sexual acts towards minors are wrong on other grounds, as will be argued below), so no wrong act is to be excused because done from a sexual motive. If a "crime of passion" is to be excused, it would have to be on grounds of temporary insanity rather than sexual context (whether insanity does constitute a legitimate excuse for certain actions is too big a topic to argue here). Sexual motives are among others which may become deranged, and the fact that they are sexual has no bearing in itself on the moral character, whether negative or exculpatory, of the actions deriving from them. Whatever might be true of war, it is certainly not the case that all's fair in love or sex.

Our first conclusion regarding morality and sex is therefore that no conduct otherwise immoral should be excused because it is sexual conduct, and nothing in sex is immoral unless condemned by rules which apply elsewhere as well. The last clause requires further clarification. Sexual conduct can be governed by particular rules relating only to sex itself. But these precepts must be implied by general moral rules when these are applied to specific sexual relations or types of conduct. The same is true of rules of fair business, ethical medicine, or courtesy in driving a car. In the latter case, particular acts on the road may be reprehensible, such as tailgating or passing on the right, which seem to bear no resemblance as actions to any outside the context of highway safety. Nevertheless their immorality derives from the fact that they place others in danger, a circumstance which, when avoidable, is to be condemned in any context. This structure of general and specifically applicable rules describes a reasonable sexual ethic as well. To take an extreme case, rape is always a sexual act and it is always immoral. A rule against rape can therefore be considered an obvious part of sexual morality which has no bearing on nonsexual conduct. But the immorality of rape derives from its being an extreme violation of a person's body, of the right not to be humiliated, and of the general moral prohibition against using other persons against their wills, not from the fact that it is a sexual act.

The application elsewhere of general moral rules to sexual conduct is further complicated by the fact that it will be relative to the particular desires and preferences of one's partner (these may be influenced by and hence in some sense include misguided beliefs about sexual morality itself). This means that there will be fewer specific rules in the area of sexual ethics than in other areas of conduct, such as driving cars, where the relativity of preference is irrelevant to the prohibition of objectively dangerous conduct. More reliance will have to be placed upon the general moral rule, which in this area holds simply that the preferences, desires, and interests of one's partner or potential partner ought to be taken into account. This rule is certainly not specifically formulated to govern sexual relations; it is a form of the central principle of morality itself. But when applied to sex, it prohibits certain actions, such as molestation of children, which cannot be categorized as violations of the rule without at the same time being classified as sexual. I believe this last case is the closest we can come to an action which is wrong *because* it is sexual, but even here its wrongness is better characterized as deriving from the detrimental effects such behavior can have on the future emotional and sexual life of the naive victims, and from the fact that such behavior therefore involves manipulation of innocent persons without regard for their interests. Hence, this case also involves violation of a general moral rule which applies elsewhere as well.

Aside from faulty conceptual analyses of sex and the influence of the Platonic moral tradition, there are two more plausible reasons for thinking that there are moral dimensions intrinsic to sex acts per se. The first is that such acts are normally intensely pleasurable. According to a hedonistic, utilitarian moral theory they therefore should be at least prima facie morally right, rather than morally neutral in themselves. To me this seems incorrect and reflects unfavorably on the ethical theory in question. The pleasure intrinsic to sex acts is a good, but not, it seems to me, a good with much positive moral significance. Certainly I can have no duty to pursue such pleasure myself, and while it may be nice to give pleasure of any form to others, there is no ethical requirement to do so, given my right over my own body. The exception relates to the context of sex acts themselves, when one partner derives pleasure from the other and ought to return the favor. This duty to reciprocate takes us out of the domain of hedonistic utilitarianism, however, and into a Kantian moral framework, the central principles of which call for just such reciprocity in human relations. Since independent moral judgments regarding sexual activities constitute one area in which ethical theories are to be tested, these observations indicate here, as I believe others indicate elsewhere, the fertility of the Kantian, as opposed to the utilitarian, principle in reconstructing reasoned moral consciousness.

It may appear from this alternative Kantian viewpoint that sexual acts must be at least prima facie wrong in themselves. This is because they invariably involve at different stages the manipulation of one's partner for one's own pleasure, which might appear to be prohibited on the formulation of Kant's principle which holds that one ought not to treat another as a means to such private ends. A more realistic rendering of this formulation, however, one which recognizes its intended equivalence to the first universalizability principle, admits no such absolute prohibition. Many human relations, most economic transactions for example, involve using other individuals for personal benefit. These relations are immoral only when they are one-sided, when the benefits are not mutual, or when the transactions are not freely and rationally endorsed by all parties. The same holds true of sexual acts. The central principle governing them is the Kantian demand for reciprocity in sexual relations. In order to comply with the second formulation of the categorical imperative, one must recognize the subjectivity of one's partner. . . . Even in an act which by its nature "objectifies" the other, one recognizes a partner as a subject with demands and desires by yielding to those desires, by allowing oneself to be a sexual object as well, by giving pleasure or ensuring that the pleasures of the acts are mutual. It is this kind of reciprocity which forms the basis for morality in sex, which distinguishes right acts from wrong in this area as in others. (Of course, prior to sex acts one must gauge their effects upon potential partners and take these longer range interests into account.)

Note

[1] Robert Solomon, "Sex and Perversion," *Philosophy & Sex,* ed. R. Baker & F. Elliston (Buffalo: Prometheus, 1975), p. 285.

chapter *8*

Pornography and Censorship

INTRODUCTION

Pornography and censorship raise complex questions of ethics, politics, and law. Many people find pornography morally outrageous, while others see nothing ethically wrong with it. A majority of a U.S. commission examining obscenity and pornography in 1970 recommended repeal of legislation prohibiting the sale of obscene and pornographic materials to consenting adults but with continued criminal regulation of its sale and display to minors.[1] Then President Nixon rejected the commission's report.

For the last twenty-five years, the U.S. Supreme Court has struggled with the constitutionality of laws prohibiting the sale of obscene materials. The central question is whether the First Amendment guarantees of freedom of speech and press bar such regulation. The issue of obscenity reveals fundamental differences of opinion on the court. The leading case is *Roth* v. *United States*.[2] The most important aspect of this decision was the holding that because it is utterly without redeeming social importance, obscenity is not protected by the First Amendment. This holding set the ground for many subsequent arguments about the definition of obscenity and whether particular materials fell within the definition. The *Roth* test for obscenity of materials was "whether to the average person, applying contemporary community standards, the dominant theme of the material taken as a whole appeals to prurient interest."[3] During the ensuing years, the court made minor modifications in this test, the most important being that the prosecution must prove that the material is utterly without redeeming social value. During this period, most of the justices watched a large number of movies in order to decide whether the definition applied to them. Justice Black, however, refused, because he adamantly maintained that the First Amendment protects even obscene material from prohibition. The difficulties in defining obscenity and applying a test to particular materials led one justice to remark that although he could not define hard-core pornography, he could recognize it when he saw it.

Finally, in 1973 the Court seemed to arrive at a temporary resolution

236

of the problem. In *Miller* v. *State of California*[4] Chief Justice Burger announced a revised test of obscenity. The fundamental test is "(a) whether 'the average person, applying contemporary community standards,' would find that the work, taken as a whole, appeals to the prurient interest, (b) whether the work depicts or describes, in a patently offensive way, sexual conduct specifically defined by the applicable state law, and (c) whether the work, taken as a whole, lacks serious literary, artistic, political, or scientific value."[5] The important differences between this test and the previous *Roth* test are (1) that the work need not be "utterly without redeeming social importance"; and (2) that the community standards to be applied are those of the local community and not the nation. This decision has generated much controversy.

Pornography and obscenity raise a number of distinct issues. First, there is the problem of defining terms. The Supreme Court has restricted its definition of obscenity to sexual matters, but many believe that some forms of violence are also obscene. Moreover, not all pornography need be considered obscene. Several members of the Supreme Court have held that only hard-core pornography is obscene. Several ethical issues can be distinguished. One might ask whether the content itself of obscene or pornographic materials is unethical. If one decides that it is, then one might ask whether it is unethical (wrong) to produce, distribute, or view such materials. One could hold that producing or selling pornographic materials is wrong but that perceiving them is not. If producing and distributing pornography is unethical, should the law prohibit such conduct? Not all immoral conduct is or should be illegal. To decide this matter, one must determine the grounds for criminal legislation.

At least four different principles might be relevant to legislation against pornography and obscenity. Each of these principles presents a kind of reason for making conduct illegal. A particular principle need not apply to justify making conduct illegal; and if a principle does apply, one still might choose to maintain the legality of the conduct. The principles are as follows: (1) the *harm principle* states that conduct may be prohibited if it might cause harm to others; (2) the *legal moralist principle* states that conduct may be prohibited if it is immoral; (3) the *offense principle* states that conduct may be prohibited if it might cause offense to others; and (4) the *paternalist principle* states that conduct may be prohibited to prevent persons from harming themselves. In considering whether the production and distribution of obscene and pornographic materials should be illegal, one must first determine which principles are appropriate for legislation and then apply them to obscene and pornographic materials.

Although the U.S. Commission on Obscenity and Pornography was not explicit about its principles, it seems to have adopted the harm, offense, and restricted paternalist principles. The commission recommended allowing obscene materials to be sold to adults primarily because it did not believe viewing the materials would lead people to harm others. The recommended restrictions upon the sale of such materials to children rested partly on paternalistic grounds as well as on a desire to aid parents in controlling children's access to materials. Finally, the commission's recommendation that public displays of obscene and pornographic materials be regulated is primarily designed to prevent persons giving offense to others.

Ethical and Political Perspectives   The following discussion will concentrate on the ethical and political nature of pornography and its censorship by punishment for production and distribution. The definitional issue is not addressed. Further, it is assumed that censorship will involve punishment for conduct rather than prior restraint. The latter involves review and prohibition of materials prior to distribution. Although most Canadian provinces censor movies prior to their distribution, prior restraint is almost always unconstitutional in the United States. The censorship board of the province of Ontario has been the subject of much controversy in recent years due to its stipulation of cuts in acclaimed movies and to charges of pressure being put on its members. While reforms made in the board in 1981 may alleviate political pressures, they probably will not eliminate criticism of the board's decisions.

In the traditional *natural-law* view, since sexual intercourse is permissible only within heterosexual marriage, the content of most pornographic materials portraying sexual intercourse will be judged as wrong conduct. Producing and distributing such materials, of course, is also wrong, because it encourages immoral ideas and conduct. One, however, must distinguish the discussion of such conduct from the portrayal of it in an appealing manner. But in the natural-law view, even viewing obscene pornographic materials is apt to be wrongful, because doing so appeals to interests and desires that are wrongful (perhaps unnatural) and should not be satisfied or promoted.

Society is a natural organization of individuals to promote the common good. Classically, promoting the common good has included the morality of the community's members. If pornography and obscenity are immoral, then the state may, subject to other considerations, regulate or prohibit it for the common good. A minimalist natural-law view would only subject the political process and law to certain basic standards of morality that could not be violated. It might permit obscenity and pornography. However, this minimalist view comes close to a natural-rights approach.

A *natural-rights* view holds conduct to be wrong only if it violates the rights of others. Sexual conduct between consenting adults does not violate people's rights and so is not wrongful. This statement will hold if the theory contains a broad natural right to freedom. However, to determine that conduct is not wrong does not settle the issue of its ethical character. Some conduct is not good—is something one ought not to do—even though it is not wrong. Thus, perhaps one should not engage in some sexual conduct even though it does not violate anyone's rights. Also, in the natural-rights view, portrayals of brutality and violence (including nonconsensual sexual conduct) depict wrongful conduct.

But even if content is judged unethical, it does not follow that producing, distributing, and perceiving it are. A natural right to freedom of speech (and press) would likely imply that producing and distributing obscene and pornographic materials are within an individual's rights. Similarly, a right to freedom would allow individuals to perceive such materials. One might hold that a right to freedom allows individuals to view obscene materials in the privacy of their own home but does not allow their production and dissemination. The Supreme Court, which in interpreting the First Amendment has engaged in reasoning similar to that a natural-rights theorist might use, has held that private possession of obscene materials is a constitutionally protected right to freedom or privacy.[6]

States and governments are not permitted to abridge people's natural rights. Consequently, determining the rights with respect to obscenity and pornography also partly settles the political-legal questions of legislation prohibiting it. If producing and distributing pornography and obscenity are within an individual's natural rights, then the state cannot prohibit those activities unless they violate more important rights of others. If those activities are not within the scope of natural rights, then the state perhaps may prohibit them; it may certainly do so if they violate the rights of others. Public displays of obscenity raise the issue of a natural right not to be offended. If such a right exists, then not only may governments prohibit public displays of obscenity, but failure to do so would permit people's rights to be violated. As the state primarily exists to protect and enforce natural rights, the government should then act against public indecency.

It is not completely clear what a *Kantian* view of pornography entails. By the law of nature formula, portrayals of sexual conduct between consenting adults are likely to be of ethically permissible conduct. As long as the partners are consenting, one could will the conduct to be a universal law of nature, even were the roles reversed. However, as in the natural-rights view, the content of pornography would be immoral if one of the parties did not consent; this applies as well to all violence, not just sexual violence. By the formula of treating humanity as an end, it is less clear that content displaying consensual sexual conduct is ethically permissible. Even though a party consents, one (or both) partners might view the other merely as a means to sexual gratification. However, Kant viewed marriage essentially as a contract for the mutual exclusive use of each other's genitals.[7] Nonmarital relationships for mutual sexual gratification might not be wrong but be only short-term contracts. If so, then nonmarital relationships between consenting adults would be ethically permissible, for the mutual short-term contract would mean that each person was also treated as an end.

The ethical nature of the content of pornography and obscenity, for a Kantian, probably determines the morality of its production and distribution. Given that the content is unethical, then one could not rationally will its production and distribution nor could one be treating humanity as an end in so doing. Producing and distributing unethical material does not respect humanity, for it encourages people to enjoy unethical conduct.

The fact that unethical conduct is merely portrayed does not seem to make a difference.

In the political realm, Kant held that the law should not be concerned with whether people act from respect for the moral law; instead, it should be restricted to behavior. The universal law of justice governing legislation is to "act externally in such a way that free use of your will is compatible with the freedom of everyone according to a universal law."[8] Violations of this principle may be punished. Hence, if the production and distribution of pornography are immoral, they come under the universal law of justice and are an appropriate subject for state prohibition. Indeed, Kant himself obeyed a government edict prohibiting him from publishing further on religion, although some people have noted that he had by then published about everything he had to say.

A *contractarian* approach to pornography, obscenity, and censorship primarily involves the equal-liberties principle. An equal right to the greatest equal liberties compatible with like liberties for all includes the freedom of speech and other forms of communication. The rights involved relate to both the individual as a speaker and as a member of the audience. To preserve equal liberties, captive audiences, for instance, unforewarned passers-by, should not be subjected to obtrusive and unwanted speech. The content of obscenity, appropriately defined, can be seen as unethical, because it involves abuse of bodily or personal functions that are demeaning and disgusting to the person involved.[9] Of course, by this view not all pornography will be judged obscene. But if the depicted act is obscene, this guaranteees that its communication is also wrong.[10] Thus, both obscene acts and communications will be understood as having unethical content. They are or depict conduct demeaning and disgusting, because it violates the standards of the individuals involved. Furthermore, purveyors and consumers of pornographic materials might hold standards by which the conduct would not be considered wrong and, therefore, might be expressing a pornographic view of life. Since obscenity can be communicated, it is included in the liberty of free speech. Rational contractors behind the veil of ignorance would not prohibit the communication of ideas involving different standards, because they would not know which standards they might hold. As the principles of justice restrict what the majority may do to protect and promote its standards, the equal-liberty principle implies that obscenity and pornography should not be legally prohibited. This conclusion is subject to two qualifications. First, it does not apply to children, because the liberty principle does not apply to them because they lack full rationality.[11] Second, it does not imply that laws may not be passed prohibiting public displays of obscenity, for such displays infringe upon each person's liberty of choice as to what will be viewed.[12]

Utilitarians have rarely discussed the ethical as opposed to the political-legal aspect of pornography and obscenity. From a *utilitarian* ethical point of view, it is tempting to conclude that the content as well as the production and distribution of pornographic and obscene materials are permissible so long as they do not harm anyone. However, that is not the appropriate *act-utilitarian* test. To be permissible, acts must produce at least as much net utility as any other acts the agents could perform in the given situation. No matter what sexual thrills and delights are expressed by the actors in pornographic films (often excluding the males), other conduct might produce more net utility. This conclusion becomes more plausible if one considers the producers and distributors of such materials. Thus, by act utilitarian-reasoning, possibly the content, and probably the production and distribution, of obscene and pornographic materials might be wrong.

This conclusion is less likely to be reached by a *rule utilitarian*. The content of pornographic and obscene materials would be unethical only if they portrayed conduct violating a set of rules the adoption of which would have as much net utility as any other. Such a moral code is unlikely to contain a rule prohibiting consensual sexual conduct (what is the utility in that!). However, it would almost certainly prohibit violence and non-consensual sexual conduct. Whether it would also contain a rule prohibiting the production and distribution of materials depicting such conduct is another matter. Generally, such a code is unlikely to prohibit conduct unless it causes net disutility; otherwise the psychological, and other, costs required to support the rule would not be worthwhile. Thus, in a rule-utilitarian view, the production and distribution of obscene and pornographic materials are less likely to be wrong than in an act-utilitarian view.

The differences between act and rule utilitarianism usually vanish when one considers the legal prohibition of obscenity and pornography. As the act of legislating creates a rule, in most situations evaluation of the act is tantamount to evaluation of the rule. Historically, most utilitarian discussions of obscenity and pornography legislation derive from John Stuart Mill's *On Liberty*. Mill generally held that only the harm principle provides an acceptable basis for legislation. He rejected the legal moralist principle and accepted paternalism only for children.[13] At one place in the book, he appeared to accept the offense principle for certain public conduct.[14]

Much recent discussion of pornography and obscenity has (perhaps unwittingly) assumed the correctness of Mill's position. Thus most discussion has focused on whether obscenity and pornography influence those who view it to commit acts harmful to others. Even the newer defenders of laws against obscenity appear to assume that it may be prohibited only if it results in harm to others; they have merely broadened the scope of harm and looked for more subtle ways in which obscenity might bring it about.[15] Many defenders of laws against obscenity probably do not believe that only the harm principle (and perhaps the offense principle) may justify legislation. They implicitly hold the legal-moralist principle. At least the argument would take on a quite different complexion were the legal-moralist principle used. Proponents of censorship would not need to show harm results but only that the conduct is immoral.

Readings The problem case presents a rather novel situation in that it does not deal with obscene and pornographic movies and books. Indeed, the case does not even involve material that would be considered obscene by usual constitutional standards. Instead, it involves the public broadcasting of language offensive to some people during the time children normally listen to the radio. This case should be kept in mind while reading the other selections, in order best to consider just how this case differs from those involving obscene and pornographic films at an adult theater. Consider, too, whether these differences are relevant to the ethical and political-legal questions.

The selection by Harry Clor largely represents a natural-law view of the justifiability of legal prohibition of obscenity, including portrayals of violence and death. He argues that all societies have public moral standards concerning the sensual aspects of life. If such standards are essential (and natural?) for societies, then censorship can support them by reducing corrupting influences and upholding authoritative standards. Further, he argues, merely punishing indecency without censorship would require greater penalties than those extant, or society would have to lower its standards.

The selection by Ann Garry both represents a Kantian view and raises the question of whether pornography is antifeminist. Garry argues that the content of pornography is unethical because it portrays women in a way that violates the Kantian principle of respect for persons. Garry is concerned only with the morality of pornography, particularly its content, and does not consider whether it should be legally prohibited. She generally assumes that it is not.

In the final selection, Joel Feinberg discusses Mill's view about the legal prohibition of obscenity and pornography. After distinguishing harm from offense, he argues that a restricted offense principle can be used to justify prohibition of public offensive conduct but not books and films, because individuals have a free choice to read or view them.

Notes

[1] U.S. Commission on Obscenity and Pornography, *The Report of the Commission on Obscenity and Pornography* (New York: Bantam, 1970).

[2] 354 U.S. 476 (1957).

[3] Ibid., 489.

[4] 413 U.S. 15 (1973).

[5] Ibid., 24.

[6] *Stanley* v. *Georgia*, 394 U.S. 557 (1969).

[7] Immanuel Kant, *The Philosophy of Law*, trans. W. Hastie (Edinburgh: T. & T. Clark, 1887), p. 110.

[8] Immanuel Kant, *The Metaphysical Elements of Justice*, trans. John Ladd (Indianapolis, Ind.: Bobbs-Merrill, 1965), p. 35; Akademie, p. 231.

[9] David A. J. Richards, *The Moral Criticism of Law* (Encino, Calif.: Dickenson, 1977), p. 61. This book contains an excellent, lengthy contractarian analysis of obscenity and pornography, pp. 56–77.

[10] Ibid., p. 66.
[11] Ibid., p. 72.
[12] Ibid., p. 73.
[13] *On Liberty*, ed. Currin V. Shields (Indianapolis, Ind.: Bobbs-Merrill, 1956), p. 13.
[14] Ibid., p. 119.
[15] See Fred R. Berger, "Pornography, Sex, and Censorship," in *Today's Moral Problems*, ed. Richard A. Wasserstrom, 2d ed. (New York: Macmillan, 1979), pp. 337–58.

Bibliography on Pornography and Censorship

Bayles, Michael D. "Comments: Offensive Conduct and the Law." In *Issues in Law and Morality*, edited by Norman S. Care and Thomas K. Trelogan, pp. 111–26. Cleveland: The Press of Case Western Reserve University, 1973.

Berns, Walter. "Pornography vs. Democracy: The Case for Censorship." *The Public Interest* 22 (Winter 1971): 3–24.

Clor, Harry M. *Obscenity and Public Morality: Censorship in a Liberal Society*. Chicago, Ill.: University of Chicago Press, 1969.

Dyal, Robert A. "Is Pornography Good for You?" *Southwestern Journal of Philosophy* 7 (1976): 95–118.

Feinberg, Joel "'Harmless Immoralities' and Offensive Nuisances," and "Reply." In *Issues in Law and Morality*, edited by Norman S. Care and Thomas K. Trelogan, pp. 83–109 and 127–40, respectively. Cleveland: The Press of Case Western Reserve University, 1973.

————. "Pornography and the Criminal Law." *University of Pittsburgh Law Review* 40 (1979): 567–604.

Goldstein, Michael J., and Kant, Harold S. *Pornography and Sexual Deviance*. Berkeley, Calif.: University of California Press, 1973.

Hart, Harold A., ed. *Censorship: For and Against*. New York: Hart Publishing, 1971.

Kristol, Irving. "Pornography, Obscenity and the Case for Censorship." *New York Times Magazine*, March 28, 1971, pp. 24ff.

Leiser, Burton M. *Liberty, Justice, and Morals: Contemporary Value Conflicts*. 2d ed. New York: Macmillan, 1979. Chapter 5.

Miller v. *State of California*, 413 U.S. 15 (1973).

Paris Adult Theatre I v. *Slayton*, 413 U.S. 49 (1973).

Report of the Committee on Obscenity and Film Censorship. Home office. London: Her Majesty's Stationery Office, 1979.

Richards, David A. J. *The Moral Criticism of Law*. Encino, Calif.: Dickenson, 1977. Pages 56–77.

United States Commission on Obscenity and Pornography. *The Report of the Commission on Obscenity and Pornography*. New York: Bantam Books, 1970.

Problem Case

FCC v. Pacifica Foundation, 438 U.S. 726 (1978)

Mr. Justice Stevens delivered the opinion of the Court (Parts I, II, III, and IV-C) and an opinion in which The Chief Justice and Mr. Justice Rehnquist joined (Parts IV-A and IV-B).

This case requires that we decide whether the Federal Communications

Commission has any power to regulate a radio broadcast that is indecent but not obscene.

A satiric humorist named George Carlin recorded a 12-minute monologue entitled "Filthy Words" before a live audience in a California theater. He began by referring to his thoughts about "the words you couldn't say on the public, ah, airwaves, um, the ones you definitely wouldn't say, ever." He proceeded to list those words and repeat them over and over again in a variety of colloquialisms. The transcript of the recording, which is appended to this opinion, indicates frequent laughter from the audience.

At about 2 o'clock in the afternoon on Tuesday, October 30, 1973, a New York radio station owned by respondent, Pacifica Foundation, broadcast the "Filthy Words" monologue. A few weeks later a man, who stated that he had heard the broadcast while driving with his young son, wrote a letter complaining to the Commission. He stated that, although he could perhaps understand the "record's being sold for private use, I certainly cannot understand the broadcast of same over the air that, supposedly, you control."

The complaint was forwarded to the station for comment. In its response, Pacifica explained that the monologue had been played during a program about contemporary society's attitude toward language and that immediately before its broadcast listeners had been advised that it included "sensitive language which might be regarded as offensive to some." Pacifica characterized George Carlin as a "significant social satirist" who "like Twain and Sahl before him, examines the language of ordinary people. . . . Carlin is not mouthing obscenities, he is merely using words to satirize as harmless and essentially silly our attitudes towards those words." Pacifica stated that it was not aware of any other complaints about the broadcast.

On February 21, 1975, the Commission issued a Declaratory Order granting the complaint and holding that Pacifica "could have been the subject of administrative sanctions." 56 FCC2d 94, 99 (1975). The Commission did not impose formal sanctions, but it did state that the order would be "associated with the station's license file, and in the event that subsequent complaints are received, the Commission will then decide whether it should utilize any of the available sanctions it has been granted by Congress."

HARRY M. CLOR
LAW, VIRTUE, AND SEX

It is often observed that standards of morality and immorality, obscenity and non-obscenity, differ widely from culture to culture. In some societies kissing in public is prohibited, while in others public acts of coitus are per-

From Harry M. Clor, *Obscenity and Public Morality: Censorship in a Liberal Society* (Chicago, Ill.: University of Chicago Press, 1969). Reprinted by permission of the University of Chicago Press. © 1969 by the University of Chicago.

formed as religious ceremonies.[1] But, as anthropologist Margaret Mead observes, "every known human society exercises some explicit censorship over behavior relating to the human body, especially as that behavior involves or may involve sex."[2] There is no known society in which matters relating to sex and the human body are left wholly unregulated. And there is no known society in which the regulation of these things is left wholly to individuals or to spontaneous social activity.

The proper treatment of the physical or sensual side of life is a crucial and universal social problem. Says Mead: "Society has two problems—how to keep sex activity out of forbidden channels that will endanger the bodies and souls of others or the orderly co-operative processes of social life, *and* how to keep it flowing reliably in those channels where it is necessary if children are to be conceived and reared in homes where father and mother are tied together by the requisite amount of sexual interest"[3] (italics in original).

All human societies deal with these matters in essentially the same way: they establish public moral standards which are made binding on their members. These standards dictate what sexual acts may be performed and with whom, they establish the distinction between physical acts which may be done in public and those which may be done only in private; and they govern to some extent permissible verbal expression about such matters. My point here is twofold: (1) these standards have the character of *public* standards—they are imposed by society as such; and (2) these standards have the character of *moral* standards—violation of them is supposed to be attended by the appropriate feelings of guilt, shame, or disgust.

Why do we need to have public standards of decency? The issues which are the subject of such standards are highly perplexing and disturbing to the great majority of mankind. They concern the control and direction of powerful passions, the determination of the proper relation between the physical, social, and spiritual sides of life, and the moral judgments which are implicit in such terms as "higher" and "lower." No man (or very few) can resolve these problems alone, on the basis of his own private reasoning. Nor can he resolve them on the basis of a spontaneous "free exchange of ideas" with others. Therefore, we will always require some authoritative pronouncements on such subjects as: the proper character of the family, the nature of the marriage bond, the duties and rights of married persons, the human meaning of sex and its relation to love, and the extent to which the human body and its various functions should be revealed or concealed in public. In matters so problematic, men rely upon guidance from the community in which they live. They need public standards.

But why should public moral standards require the support of law? Why can we not rely for their promulgation and maintenance upon society or the community?

Whatever may be the case in primitive communities, in civilized communities "society" is not an autonomous self-regulating entity. Society does not resolve its problems autonomously without authoritative direction. In civilized times it is the political community which most effectively represents the common ends and interests of society, and the political community characteristically acts by means of law. Indeed in the absence of the political community and its laws, it would be most difficult to locate, amid the complex diversities which characterize modern life, anything deserving the name of "the society" or "the community."

Society as such cannot censor morals. Strictly speaking, society as such cannot make decisions and act purposively. Thus, when it is said that "censorship should be the proper activity of the community rather than the law," this can reasonably mean only that the contemporary public opinion should do it, the family should do it, or the church should do it. It is not to be denied that these can be influential agencies promoting moral restraint or ethical training. But are they alone capable of performing the community's civilizing and moralizing functions? And can they perform these functions without the support of law?

If public opinion is to be a moral influence, from whence is public opinion to receive its moral guidance? It is well known that on particular issues—the "issues of the day"—public opinion is often unstable, uncertain, and transitory. Ill-defined feelings and half-formed attitudes tend to become public opinion when positions are taken by influential persons—including statesmen, lawmakers, and judges. The formation of public opinion is profoundly influenced by actions or positions taken in government and by laws—past, present, and prospective.

There is a more stable and more continuous "underlying" public opinion. Such opinion has more than one source, but surely one of its most important sources is to be found in tradition and customs which have been supported by (if not engendered by) the fundamental laws and principles of the country. Continuing public attitudes on many subjects (e.g., the rights of private property) may be traced in this manner to the Constitution and to the attitudes and decisions of such political men as Alexander Hamilton and John Marshall.

I dwell upon these commonplaces only in order to make the point that public opinion cannot be relied upon as if it were a self-dependent moral agent. The long-term or underlying public attitudes are what they are largely because of the context of social and political traditions in which they are formed. The public looks, in part, to the country's customs and laws for ethical and intellectual guidance. If there is now a body of public attitudes in support of moral decency, this must be, to a large extent, because there have been positions taken in the past in support of moral decency—positions resulting in or fostered by law. One may at least wonder what contemporary attitudes on moral matters would be if there had been no such decisions and no such laws.

Like the various public opinions, the family is but a part of civil society and is subject to the influences predominant therein. It would not be reasonable to expect "the home" to produce morally decent children if indecency prevailed in the society around it. The education promoted in the home could not withstand the influence of the surrounding moral environment, nor could the family as an institution avoid the effects of such an environment. For instance, the institution of monogamous marriage as we know it presupposes and requires some commitment to sexual fidelity. This is not to say that any lapse whatever from this commitment must be regarded as a "sin" which destroys a marriage. But, at least, there must be a belief in the obligation of faithfulness and efforts to live up to that obligation, if the family is to have the significance and perform the tasks which traditionally belong to it in our society. If, in the community at large, the commitment to fidelity as a norm were replaced by radical promiscuity, monogamy could not long retain its character. And the new institution, whatever moral training it might provide, could hardly continue to be a teacher of sexual fidelity. The family is not an autonomous social force capable of independently generating and sustaining values.

Traditionally, religious institutions have been such a source of values. For a number of reasons, they no longer have the political stature, the social influence, or the moral authority to perform for the community the civilizing functions which it requires.[4] The churches can teach morality, and they can lend their support to social movements concerned with morality, but they cannot be relied upon as a predominant influence upon character in modern society.

It is quite true that the social agencies under consideration are those most directly concerned with the promotion of virtue or decency. But inquiry shows that their success or failure is dependent upon factors or forces in society at large which they do not control.

The community, then, cannot rely solely upon public opinion, the family, and the church to promulgate and maintain its public morality. These agencies can shape the values which prevail in society, but, to a greater extent, they are shaped by these values.

Therefore, it must be a task of modern government and law to support and promote the public morality upon which a good social life depends. Censorship can serve this end in two ways: (1) by preventing or reducing some of the most corrupt influences and (2) by holding up an authoritative standard for the guidance of opinions and judgment.

Legitimate censorship is not designed to prevent the circulation of all literature which might have an immoral influence. It aims primarily at the most vicious materials. And it seeks, not directly to shape mind and character, but to contain some of those influences in modern society which shape mind and character in harmful ways. The effects of censorship upon these influences are not confined to the specific books or motion pictures which the censor condemns. Its more significant effects are those of deterrence. Publishers are deterred from publishing, and authors from writing, materials which cannot legally be circulated. Thus the results of legal censorship consist not in the confiscation of the relatively few obscene publications which the censor catches, but in the general reduction in the circulation of materials of that kind.

Laws against obscene publications may have a more subtle and, perhaps, more profound consequence. Such laws announce a moral decision
of the community arrived at and issued through its official organs. They
assert, in effect, that the organized community draws a line between the
decent and the indecent, the permissible and the impermissible. Individuals may, of course, step over the line, but they are made aware that the
community is committed to a distinction between what is right and what is
not. In the long run this awareness must have an effect upon the moral attitudes and values of most people.

The coercive and preventing functions of censorship are thus supplemented by its hortatory and educative functions. Or perhaps it would be
more correct to say that the latter are supplemented by the former. Liber-
tarian authors are inclined to speak as if punishment were the heart of all
legal censorship. They are inclined to refer to censorship exclusively as
"the legal enforcement of morality." But there are some forms of censorship which do not involve criminal proceedings and need not involve any
punishment at all. This is the case when the law employs purely administrative or civil proceedings for the condemnation or confiscation of obscene
materials. Here the purveyor will receive no legal penalties unless he defies
the orders of a court. And when the criminal law is used, punishment and
the threat of punishment, while serving as a deterrent to specific acts
against morality, are subordinate means to the larger educative ends. By
its willingness to punish some violations of its morality, the community indicates that it is serious about that morality. Conceivably, a community
could officially promulgate ethical standards without the slightest efforts
to use coercion in support of them. It is all too likely that such standards
would not be taken with sufficient seriousness by those most in need of
guidance. Willingness to use coercion in their support is surely a prime in-
dicator of the significance which society attaches to its various principles
and purposes.[5] We do not know of any political community which has relied upon simple promulgation and exhortation for the implementation of
its principles.

Laws against obscenity or other forms of vice serve to render community standards authoritative. They can also serve to clarify and define such
standards. One need not presuppose that there would be no criteria of decency whatever in the absence of legislation. Individuals and groups do,
obviously, have moral attitudes and values which they have not received
from government. But attitudes and values which arise in "society" tend
often to be vague, over-general, and contradictory. Individuals and social
groups do not easily succeed in establishing the precise applications and
limits of those general principles they hold in common. These principles,
then, seldom constitute a clear and agreed-upon boundary line between
decent and indecent activity. The law contributes to the drawing of
boundary lines by its definition of such terms as "obscenity." The law
thus helps to transform indistinct, indefinite, and personal moral feelings
into public standards.

In the absence of public norms thus established, social attitudes (or public opinion) may remain ill-defined, inconclusive, and ineffectual. Or, they may vacillate between extremes of moral indifference and moralistic zealotry. As legal censorship is relaxed, the private standards of many citizens may also be relaxed. Other citizens may be aroused to replace legal censorship with a form of censorship considerably more repressive. Many authors have observed that as legal censorship is restricted the censorship activities of private groups tend often to increase. And these groups can be far less discriminating in their moral and aesthetic judgments than is the law.

Communal standards, properly formulated, promulgated, and enforced, will inhibit the emergence—and perhaps prevent the ascendancy—of immoderate or unreasonable private standards. A public moral philosophy, supported in part by law, can profoundly affect the dispositions and opinions by which social life is shaped. It can encourage civil or reasonable dispositions and opinions, and it can discourage those which are uncivil or unreasonable.

Can it be truly said that the organized community has no right to be thus concerned with the minds of citizens, with their "inner lives"? And can it be reasonably said that the operations of law must be strictly confined to overt antisocial conduct or to considerations of peace and security?

I have presented arguments showing that the political community cannot be indifferent to the moral values and the moral character of its members and why it cannot rely simply upon nonpolitical institutions to sustain values and character at a moral level consistent with its needs. Public standards are required, and private agencies cannot be confidently relied upon to provide them. In the absence of legal and political support, the capacity of such agencies to provide a communal morality would depend upon the many diverse influences—economic, social, psychological, and intellectual—which make them what they are. If civil society requires certain virtues in its members, it cannot afford to leave this to the determination of fortuitous circumstances and chance influences.

Of course, the law can punish indecent acts. This is the policy recommended to it by opponents of censorship—you may punish wrongful conduct, but you must never do anything involving the slightest degree of coercion to influence men's values or the character of their private lives. But the threat of legal coercion will not sufficiently deter indecent acts when little attention has been given to the conditions which breed indecent men. If the law must restrain immoral conduct, then it cannot be indifferent to the influences which break down moral standards, weakening their hold upon conduct. If political society were to adopt a policy of legal coercion plus moral indifference, if it would seek by coercion to prevent immoral conduct while remaining neutral toward immoral character, two possible results are predictable. The penalties for bad conduct would have to be considerably increased; the coercive functions of the law would have to be made more effective. Or, the categories of punishable acts would have to be considerably reduced; society would have to lower its standards of conduct. If society is interested in the prevention of acts contrary to its moral standards, then it is neither reasonable nor safe to require it to wait until the acts have been done or are about to be done. A community with a large number of vicious citizens will have to control them by force—or the effort to control them will have to be abandoned.

Long before such a state of affairs is reached, the community is deeply interested in the morality of its citizens. Civilized social life requires not only that men observe certain decencies, but also that they believe in them. And political life requires not only that men perform certain duties, but also that they believe in them. The political education of every nation testifies to this communal interest in the minds, dispositions, and beliefs of its citizens.

These considerations are not less compelling when applied to the sensual or the sexual side of life. Every community must devote its attention to the discipline and direction of powerful natural impulses. Every social order must endeavor to give the sensual side of life its due while preventing undue or excessive preoccupation with it. The minds and energies of citizens must be available for the long-range pursuits and higher ends of the community. This requires socially imposed restraints upon the indulgence of the passions and, also, socially imposed standards and values concerning the indulgence of the passions. Since the community cannot be indifferent to what its members do about the physical side of life, it cannot be wholly indifferent to what they feel and believe about it. Censorship of some kind or degree is implicit in these propositions.

Notes

[1] Weston La Barre, "Obscenity: An Anthropological Appraisal," *Law and Contemporary Problems,* 20 (Autumn, 1955): 533–43.

[2] Margaret Mead, "Sex and Censorship in Contemporary Society," *New World Writing* (New York: The New American Library of World Literature, 1953), p. 7.

[3] Ibid., p. 11.

[4] For a substantiation of this proposition presented from a point of view quite different from that of this essay, see Harvey Cox, *The Secular Society* (New York: Macmillan Co., 1965).

[5] H. L. A. Hart reports the following assertions of a nineteenth-century Royal Commission on capital punishment: "The fact that men are hanged for murder is one great reason why murder is considered so dreadful a crime.'" Hart is not impressed with this proposition, but he does not refute it. See *Law, Liberty and Morality* (New York: Vintage Books, 1966), p. 58.

ANN GARRY
PORNOGRAPHY AND RESPECT FOR WOMEN

The second argument I consider is that pornography is morally objectionable not because it leads people to show disrespect for women, but because pornography itself exemplifies and recommends behavior which violates the moral principle to respect persons. The content of pornography is
what one objects to. It treats women as mere sex objects "to be exploited
and manipulated" and degrades the role and status of women. In order to
evaluate this argument I first clarify what it would mean for pornography
itself to treat someone as a sex object in a degrading manner. I then deal
with three issues which are central to the discussion of pornography and
respect for women: how "losing respect" for a woman is connected with
treating her as a sex object, what is wrong with treating someone as a sex
object, and why it is worse to treat women rather than men as sex objects. I
argue that today the content of pornography is sometimes in violation of
the moral principle to respect persons. . . .

To many people, including [Susan] Brownmiller and some other feminists, it appears to be an obvious truth that pornography treats people,
especially women, as sex objects in a degrading manner. And if we omit
'in a degrading manner,' it seems hard to disagree: how could pornography not treat people as sex objects?

First, is it permissible to talk about either the content of pornography
or pornography itself degrading people or treating people as sex objects? It
is not difficult to find examples of degrading content in which women are
treated as sex objects. There are unnamed movies conveying the message
that all women really want to be raped, so don't believe them when they
struggle against you. By portraying women in this manner, the content of
the movie degrades women. Degrading women is morally objectionable.
Seeing the movie need not cause anyone to imitate the behavior shown.
We can call the content degrading to women because of the character of
the behavior and attitudes it recommends. The same kind of point can be
made about films (books, or TV commercials) with other kinds of degrading, thus morally objectionable, content, for example, racist messages.

The next step in the argument is to infer that because the content or
message of pornography is morally objectionable, we can call pornography
itself morally objectionable. Support for this step can be found in an analogy. If a person takes every opportunity to recommend that men rape
women, we would think not only that his recommendation is immoral but
that he is immoral too. The objection to making the inference from that
which is recommended to that which recommends in the case of pornography is that we ascribe such predicates as 'immoral' differently to people
than to objects such as films, books, and so on. A film which is the vehicle

From Ann Garry, "Pornography and Respect for Women," published by *Social Theory and Practice* 4
(1978): 395–421, Tallahassee, Florida. Reprinted by permission.

for an objectionable message is still an object independent of its message, its director, its producer, those who act in it, and those who respond to it. Hence one cannot make an unsupported inference from "the content of the film is morally objectionable" to "the film is morally objectionable." Because the central points in this paper do not depend on pornography itself (in addition to its content) being morally objectionable, I will not try to support this inference. The question about the relation of the content to the work itself is, of course, extremely interesting; but in part because I cannot decide which side of the argument is more persuasive, I will pass.[1] Certainly one appropriate way to evaluate pornography is in terms of the moral features of its content. If a pornographic film exemplifies and recommends attitudes or behavior which are morally objectionable, then its content is morally objectionable.

Let us turn to the first of the remaining three questions about respect and sex objects: what is the connection between losing respect for a woman and treating her as a sex object? Some people who have lived through the era in which women were taught to worry about men "losing respect" for them if they engaged in sex in inappropriate circumstances, find it troublesome or at least amusing that feminists, supposedly "liberated" women, are outraged at being treated as sex objects, either by pornography or in any other way. The apparent alignment between feminists and traditionally "proper" women need not surprise us when we look at it more closely.

The respect which men traditionally believed they had for women, hence which they could lose, is not a general respect for persons as autonomous beings, nor is it respect that is earned because of one's personal merits or achievements. It is respect that is an outgrowth of the "double standard." Women are to be respected because they are more pure, delicate, and fragile than men, have more refined sensibilities, and so on. Because some women clearly do not have these qualities, thus do not deserve respect, women must be divided into two groups—the good ones on the pedestal and the bad ones who have fallen from it. One's mother, grandmother, Sunday school teacher, and usually one's wife are "good" women. The appropriate behavior to express respect for good women would be, for example, not swearing or telling dirty jokes in front of them, giving them seats on buses, and other "chivalrous" acts. This sort of respect for good women is that which adolescent boys in back seats of cars used to "promise" not to lose. Note that men define, display, and lose this kind of respect. If women lose respect for women, it is not typically loss of respect for (other) women as a class, but loss of self-respect.

It has now become commonplace to acknowledge that although a place on the pedestal might have advantages over a place in the "gutter" beneath it, a place on the pedestal is not at all equal to the place occupied by other people, that is, men. "Respect" for those on the pedestal was not respect for whole, full-fledged people, but for a special class of inferior beings.

If someone makes two traditional assumptions—that (at least some) sex is dirty and that women fall into two classes, good and bad—it is easy to see how this person might think that pornography could lead people to lose respect for women or that pornography is itself disrespectful to women.[2] Pornography describes or shows women engaging in activities which are inappropriate for good women to engage in, or at least inappropriate for them to be seen by strangers engaging in. If one sees these women as symbolic representatives of all women, then all women fall from grace with these women. This fall is possible, I believe, because the "respect" men had for women was not genuine wholehearted respect for full-fledged human beings, but half-hearted respect for lesser beings some of whom they felt the need to glorify and purify.[3] It is easy to fall from a pedestal. Can we imagine 41% of men and 46% of women answering "yes" to the question, "Do movies showing men engaging in violent acts lead people to lose respect for men?"

Two interesting asymmetries appear. The first is that it is more difficult to lose respect for men as a class (men with power, typically Anglo men) than it is to lose respect for women or ethnic minorities as a class. Anglo men whose behavior warrants disrespect are more likely to be seen as exceptional cases than are women or minorities (whose "transgressions" may be far less serious). Think of the following: women are temptresses; Blacks cheat the welfare system; Italians are gangsters; but the men of the Nixon administration are exceptions—Anglo men as a class did not lose respect because of Watergate and related scandals.

The second asymmetry concerns the active and passive roles of the sexes. Men are seen in the active role. If men lose respect for women because of something "evil" done by women (such as appearing in pornography) the fear is that men will then do harm to women, not that women will do harm to men. Whereas if women lose respect for male politicians because of Watergate the fear is still that male politicians will do harm, not that women will do harm to male politicians. This asymmetry might be a result of one way in which our society thinks of sex as bad—as harm men do to women (or to the person playing a female role, for example, in a homosexual rape). Robert Baker calls attention to this point in " 'Pricks' and 'Chicks': A Plea for 'Persons.' "[4] Our slang words for sexual intercourse, 'fuck', 'screw', or older words such as 'take' or 'have' not only can mean harm but traditionally have taken a male subject and a female object. The active male screws, harms, the passive female. A "bad" woman only tempts men to hurt her further.

One can understand why one's proper grandmother would not want men to see pornography or lose respect for women. But feminists reject these "proper" assumptions: there are not good and bad classes of women and sex is not dirty (though many people believe it is). Why then are feminists angry at women's being treated as sex objects, and some feminists opposed to pornography?

The answer is that feminists as well as proper grandparents are concerned with respect. However, there are differences. A feminist's distinction between treating a woman as a full-fledged person and treating her as merely a sex object does not correspond to the good-bad woman distinction. In the latter distinction "good" and "bad" are properties applicable to groups of women. On the feminist view, all women really are full-fledged people, it is just that some are treated as sex objects and perhaps think of themselves as sex objects. A further difference is that although "bad" women correspond to those who have been thought to deserve to be treated as sex objects, good women have not corresponded to full-fledged people: only men have been full-fledged people. Given the feminist's distinction, she has no difficulty at all saying that pornography treats women as sex objects, not as full-fledged people. She can object morally to pornography or anything else treating women as sex objects.

One might wonder whether any objection to being treated as a sex object implies that the person objecting still believes, deep down, that sex is dirty. I don't think so. Several other possibilities emerge. First, even if I believe intellectually and emotionally that sex is healthy, I might object to being treated *only* as a sex object, in the same spirit that I would object to being treated only as a maker of chocolate chip cookies or as a tennis partner—only a few of my talents are being valued. Second, perhaps I feel that sex is healthy, but it is apparent to me that you think it is dirty; so I don't want you to treat me as a sex object. Third, being treated as any kind of object, not just a sex object, has an unappealing ring to it. I would rather be a partner (sexual or otherwise) than an object.

Fourth, and more plausible than the first three, is Robert Baker's view mentioned above. Both (i) our traditional double standard of sexual behavior for men and women and (ii) the linguistic evidence that we connect the concept of sex with the concept of harm, point to what is wrong with treating women as sex objects. As I said earlier, in their traditional uses, 'fuck' and 'screw' have taken a male subject, a female object, and have had at least two meanings: harm and have sexual intercourse with. (In addition, a prick is a man who harms people ruthlessly; and a motherfucker is so low that he would do something very harmful to his own dear mother.)[5] Because in our culture we connect sex with harm that men do to women and think of the female role in sex as that of harmed object, we can see that to treat a woman as a sex object is automatically to treat her as less than fully human. To say this does not imply that no healthy sexual relationships exist; nor does it say anything about individual men's conscious intentions to degrade women by desiring them sexually (though no doubt some men have these intentions). It is merely to make a point about the concepts embodied in our language.

Psychoanalytic support for the connection between sex and harm comes from Robert J. Stoller. Stoller thinks that sexual excitement is linked with a wish to harm someone (and at least a whisper of hostility). The key process of sexual excitement can be seen as dehumanization (fetishization) in fantasy of the desired person. He speculates that this is true in some degree of everyone, men and women, with "normal" or "perverted" activities and fantasies.[6]

Thinking of sex objects as harmed objects enables us to explain some of the first three reasons why one wouldn't want to be treated as a sex object. (1) I may object to being treated only as a tennis partner, but being a tennis partner is not connected in our culture with being a harmed object. (2) I may not think that sex is dirty and that I would be a harmed object; I may not know what your view is; but what bothers me is that this is the view embodied in our language and culture.

Awareness of the connection between sex and harm helps us to explain other interesting points. Women are angry about being treated as sex objects in situations or roles in which they do not intend to be thought of in that manner, for example, serving on a committee or attending a discussion. It is not merely that a sexual role is inappropriate for the circumstances, it is thought to be a less fully human role than the one in which they intended to function.

Finally, the sex-harm connection makes it clear why it is worse to treat women as sex objects than to treat men as sex objects, and why some men have had difficulty understanding women's anger about the matter. It is more difficult for heterosexual men than for women to assume the role of "harmed object" in sex; for men have the concept of themselves as sexual agents, not as passive objects. This is also related to the point I made earlier about the difference in the solidity of respect for men and for women: respect for women is more fragile. Although there are exceptions, it is generally harder to degrade men sexually or nonsexually than to degrade women. Men and women have grown up with different patterns of self-respect and expectations about the extent to which they will be respected and the extent to which they deserve respect or degradation. The man who doesn't understand why women do not want to be treated as sex objects (because he'd sure like to be) would not think of himself as being harmed by that treatment: a woman might. Pornography, probably more than any other contemporary institution, succeeds in treating men as sex objects.

Having seen that the connection between sex and harm helps to explain both what is wrong with treating someone as a sex object and why it is worse to treat a woman in this way, I want to use the sex-harm connection to try to resolve a dispute about pornography and women. Recall Brownmiller's view that pornography is "the undiluted essence of antifemale propaganda" whose purpose is to degrade women.[7] Some people object to Brownmiller by saying that since pornography treats both men and women as sex objects for the purpose of arousing the viewer, it is not sexist, not antifemale, not designed to degrade women. It just happens that degrading women arouses some men. How can the dispute be resolved?

Suppose we were to rate the content of all pornography from most morally objectionable to least morally objectionable. Among the most objectionable would be the most degrading, for example, "snuff" films or movies which recommend that men rape women, molest children and puppies, and treat nonmasochists very sadistically. Next we would find a large number of cases, probably most pornography, which are not quite so blatantly offensive. In these cases it is relevant to appeal to the analysis of sex objects given above. As long as sex is connected with harm done to women, it will be very difficult not to see pornography as degrading to women. We can agree with Brownmiller's opponent that pornography treats men as sex objects, too, but maintain that this is only pseudo-equality: such treatment is still more degrading to women.

In addition, pornography often exemplifies the active-passive, harmer-harmed object roles in a very obvious way. Because pornography today is male oriented and supposed to make a profit, the content is designed to appeal to male fantasies. Judging from the content of the most popular legally available pornography, male fantasies still run along the lines of stereotypical sex roles and, if Stoller is right, include elements of hostility. In many cases the women's purpose is to cater to male desires, to service the man or men. Her own pleasure is rarely emphasized for its own sake; she is merely allowed a little heavy breathing, perhaps in order to show her dependence on the great male "lover" who produces her pleasure. In addition, women are clearly made into passive objects in still photographs showing only close-ups of their genitals. Even in movies which are marketed to appeal to heterosexual couples, such as "Behind the Green Door," the woman is passive and undemanding (and in this case kidnapped and hypnotized as well). Although there are many kinds of specialty magazines and films for different sexual tastes, very little in contemporary pornography goes against traditional sex roles. There is certainly no significant attempt to replace the harmer-harmed distinction with anything more positive and healthy. There are, of course, stag movies in which men are treated sadistically by women; but this is an attempt to turn the tables on degradation, not a positive improvement. . . .

Notes

[1] In order to help one determine which position one feels inclined to take, consider the following statement: It is morally objectionable to write, make, sell, act in, use, and enjoy pornography; in addition, the content of pornography is immoral; however, pornography itself is not morally objectionable. If this seems extremely problematic, then one might well be satisfied with the claim that pornography is degrading because its content is.

[2] The traditional meaning of 'lose respect for women' was evidently the one assumed in the Abelson survey cited by the Presidential Commission. No explanation of its meaning is given in reporting the study. See H. Abelson et al., "National Survey of Public Attitudes toward and Experience with Erotic Materials," Tech. Report, Volume 6, 1–137.

[3] Many feminists point this out. One of the most accessible references is Shulamith Firestone, The Dialectic of Sex: The Case for the Feminist Revolution (New York: Morrow, 1970); see especially 128–32.

[4] In Richard Wasserstrom, ed., Today's Moral Problems (New York: Macmillan, 1975), 152–71. See 167–71.

⁵ Baker, 168–69.

⁶ "Sexual Excitement." *Archives of General Psychiatry* 33 (August 1976): 899–909, especially 903. The extent to which Stoller sees men and women in different positions with respect to harm and hostility is not clear. He often treats men and women alike, but in *Perversion: The Erotic Form of Hatred* (New York: Pantheon Books, 1975), 89–91, he calls attention to differences between men and women, especially regarding their response to pornography, lack of understanding by men of women's sexuality, and so forth. Given that Stoller finds hostility to be an essential element in male-oriented pornography and given that women have not responded readily to it, one can think of possibilities for women's sexuality; their hostility might follow a different scenario; they might not be as hostile, and so on.

⁷ Susan Brownmiller, *Against Our Will: Men, Women and Rape* (New York: Simon and Schuster, 1975), 394.

JOEL FEINBERG
HARM, OFFENSE, AND OBSCENITY

Whatever else we believe about freedom, most of us believe it is something to be praised, or so luminously a Thing of Value that it is beyond praise. What is it that makes freedom a good thing? Some say that freedom is good in itself quite apart from its consequences. On the other hand, James Fitzjames Stephen wrote that ". . . the question whether liberty is a good or a bad thing appears as irrational as the question whether fire is a good or a bad thing."¹ Freedom, according to Stephen, is good (when it is good) only because of what it does, not because of what it is.

It would be impossible to demonstrate that freedom is good for its own sake, and indeed, this proposition is far from self-evident. Still, Stephen's analogy to fire seems an injustice to freedom. Fire has no constant and virtually invariant effects that tend to make it, on balance, a good thing whenever and wherever it occurs, and bad only when its subsequent remoter effects are so evil as to counterbalance its direct and immediate ones. Thus, a fire in one's bed while one is sleeping is dreadful because its effects are evil, but a fire under the pot on the stove is splendid because it makes possible a hot cup of coffee when one wants it. The direct effect of fire in these and all other cases is to oxidize material objects and raise the temperature in its immediate environment; but *these* effects, from the point of view of human interests, and considered just in themselves, are neither good nor bad.

Freedom has seemed to most writers quite different in this respect. When a free man violates his neighbor's interests, then his freedom, having been put to bad use, was, on balance, a bad thing, but unlike the fire in the bed, it was not an unalloyed evil. Whatever the harmful consequences of freedom in a given case, there is always a direct effect on the

From Joel Feinberg, *Social Philosophy* (Englewood Cliffs, N.J.: Prentice-Hall, 1973), pp. 20–22, 28–29, 33–34, 41–45. © 1973. Reprinted by permission of Prentice-Hall, Inc., Englewood Cliffs, New Jersey.

person of its possessor which must be counted a positive good. Coercion may prevent great evils, and be wholly justified on that account, but it always has its price. Coercion may be on balance a great gain, but its direct effects always, or nearly always, constitute a definite loss. If this is true, there is always a *presumption* in favor of freedom, even though it can in some cases be overridden by more powerful reasons on the other side.

The presumption in favor of freedom is usually said to rest on freedom's essential role in the development of traits of intellect and character which constitute the good of individuals and are centrally important means to the progress of societies. One consensus argument, attributable with minor variations to Von Humboldt, Mill, Hobhouse, and many others, goes roughly as follows. The highest good for man is neither enjoyment nor passive contentment, but rather a dynamic process of growth and self-realization. This can be called "happiness" if we mean by that term what the Greeks did, namely, "The exercise of vital powers along lines of excellence in a life affording them scope."[2] The highest social good is then the greatest possible amount of individual self-realization and (assuming that different persons are inclined by their natures in different ways) the resultant diversity and fullness of life. Self-realization consists in the actualization of certain uniquely human potentialities, the bringing to full development of certain powers and abilities. This in turn requires constant practice in making difficult choices among alternative hypotheses, policies, and actions —and the more difficult the better. John Stuart Mill explained why:

> The human faculties of perception, judgment, discriminative feeling, mental activity, and even moral preference are exercised only in making a choice. He who does anything because it is the custom makes no choice. He gains no practice either in discerning or in desiring what is best. The mental and moral, like the muscular, powers are improved only by being used.[3]

In short, one does not realize what is best in oneself when social pressures to conform to custom lead one mindlessly along. Even more clearly, one's growth will be stunted when one is given no choice in the first place, either because of being kept in ignorance or because one is terrorized by the wielders of bayonets.

Freedom to decide on one's own while fully informed of the facts thus tends to promote the good of the person who exercises it, even if it permits him to make foolish or dangerous mistakes. Mill added to this argument the citation of numerous social benefits that redound indirectly but uniformly to those who grant freedom as well as those who exercise it. We all profit from the fruits of genius, he maintained, and genius, since it often involves doggedness and eccentricity, is likely to flourish only where coercive pressures toward conformity are absent. Moreover, social progress is more likely to occur where there is free criticism of prevailing ways and adventurous experiments in living. Finally, true understanding of human nature requires freedom, since without liberty there will be little diversity, and without diversity *all* aspects of the human condition will be ascribed to fixed nature rather than to the workings of a particular culture.

Such are the grounds for holding that there is always a presumption in favor of freedom, that whenever we are faced with an option between forcing a person to do something and letting him decide on his own whether or not to do it, other things being equal, we should always opt for the latter. If a strong general presumption for freedom has been established, the burden of proof rests on the shoulders of the advocate of coercion, and the philosopher's task will be to state the conditions under which the presumption can be overridden. . . .

The relation of offensiveness to harmfulness can be treated in much the same way as that of hurtfulness to harmfulness. The following points can be made of both:

1. Some harms do not offend (as some do not hurt).

2. All offenses (like all hurts) are harms, inasmuch as all men have an interest in not being offended or hurt,

3. Some offenses (like some hurts) are symptoms or consequences of prior or concurrent harms.

4. Some offenses (like some hurts) are causes of subsequent harms: in the case of extreme hurt, harm to health; in the case of extreme offense, harm from provoked ill will or violence. These subsequent harms are harms of a different order, i.e., violations of interests other than the interest in not being hurt or offended.

5. Some offenses, like some hurts, are "harmless," i.e., do not lead to any *further* harm (violations of any interests other than the interest in not being hurt or offended).

6. Although offense and hurt are in themselves harms, they are harms of a relatively trivial kind (unless they are of sufficient magnitude to violate interests in health and peace).

Partly because of points 5 and 6, many writers use the word "harm" in a sense that is much narrower than "the invasion of any interest." In this narrower sense, harm is distinguished from and even contrasted with "mere offense." Some distinguish "harm to one's interests" from "offense to one's feelings" (as if there were no interest in unoffended feelings). This is a permissible, even useful, way of talking, if we agree that offensiveness as such is strictly speaking a kind of harm, but harm of such a trivial kind that it cannot by itself ever counterbalance the direct and immediate harm caused by coercion. One should appreciate how radical the harm principle is when interpreted in the strict and narrow way that excludes mere offensiveness as a relevant sort of harm. Both the British Wolfenden Report and the American Model Penal Code, for example, recognize "harmless" offensiveness as a ground for preventive coercion in some circumstances. . . . For clarity and convenience only, I shall stipulate then that "offensiveness as such" is a proposed ground for coercion distinct from harm of the sort required by the harm principle (narrowly interpreted), so that "the offense principle" can be treated as an independent principle in its own right.

Offensive behavior is such in virtue of its capacity to induce in others any of a large miscellany of mental states that have little in common except that they are unpleasant, uncomfortable, or disliked. These states do not necessarily "hurt," as do sorrow and distress. Rather the relation between them and hurt is analogous to that between physical unpleasantness and pain, for there is also a great miscellany of unpleasant but not painful bodily states—itches, shocks, and discomforts—that have little in common except that they don't hurt but are nevertheless universally disliked. Among the main sorts of "harmless but disliked" *mental* states are irritating sensations (e.g., bad smells, cacophony, clashing colors), disgust, shocked moral sensibilities, and shameful embarrassment. . . .

. . . One might hold that restriction of one person's liberty can be justified:

1. To prevent harm to others, either
    a. injury to individual persons (*The Private Harm Principle*), or
    b. impairment of institutional practices that are in the public interest (*The Public Harm Principle*);

2. To prevent offense to others (*The Offense Principle*);

3. To prevent harm to self (*Legal Paternalism*);

4. To prevent or punish sin, i.e., to "enforce morality as such" (*Legal Moralism*);

5. To benefit the self (*Extreme Paternalism*);

6. To benefit others (*The Welfare Principle*).

The liberty-limiting principles on this list are best understood as stating neither necessary nor sufficient conditions for justified coercion, but rather specifications of the *kinds* of reasons that are always relevant or acceptable in support of proposed coercion, even though in a given case they may not be conclusive. Each principle states that interference might be permissible *if* (but not *only if*) a certain condition is satisfied. Hence the principles are not mutually exclusive; it is possible to hold two or more of them at once, even all of them together, and it is possible to deny all of them. Moreover, the principles cannot be construed as stating sufficient conditions for legitimate interference with liberty, for even though the principle is satisfied in a given case, the general presumption against coercion might not be outweighed. The harm principle, for example, does not justify state interference to prevent a tiny bit of inconsequential harm. Prevention of minor harm always counts in favor of proposals (as in a legislature) to restrict liberty, but in a given instance it might not count *enough* to outweigh the general presumption against interference, or it might be outweighed by the prospect of practical difficulties in enforcing the law, excessive costs, and forfeitures of privacy. A liberty-limiting principle states considerations that are always good reasons for coercion, though neither exclusively nor, in every case, decisively good reasons. . . .

Up to this point we have considered the harm and offense principles together in order to determine whether between them they are sufficient to regulate conventional immoralities, or whether they need help from a further independent principle, legal moralism. Morals offenses were treated as essentially private so that the offense principle could not be stretched to apply to them. Obscene literature and pornographic displays would appear to be quite different in this respect. Both are materials deliberately published for the eyes of others, and their existence can bring partisans of the unsupplemented harm principle into direct conflict with those who endorse *both* the harm and offense principles.

In its untechnical, prelegal sense, the word "obscenity" refers to material dealing with nudity, sex, or excretion in an offensive manner. Such material becomes obscene in the legal sense when, because of its offensiveness or for some other reason [this question had best be left open in the definition], it is or ought to be without legal protection. The legal definition then incorporates the everyday sense, and essential to both is the requirement that the material be *offensive*. An item may offend one person and not another. "Obscenity," if it is to avoid this subjective relativity, must involve an interpersonal objective sense of "offensive." Material must be offensive by prevailing community standards that are public and well known, or be such that it is apt to offend virtually everyone.

Not all material that is generally offensive need also be harmful in any sense recognized by the harm principle. It is partly an empirical question whether reading or witnessing obscene material causes social harm; reliable evidence, even of a statistical kind, of causal connections between obscenity and antisocial behavior is extremely hard to find.[4] In the absence of clear and decisive evidence of harmfulness, the American Civil Liberties Union insists that the offensiveness of obscene material cannot be a sufficient ground for its repression:

> . . . the question in a case involving obscenity, just as in every case involving an attempted restriction upon free speech, is whether the words or pictures are used in such circumstances and are of such a nature as to create a clear and present danger that they will bring about a substantial evil that the state has a right to prevent. . . . We believe that under the current state of knowledge, there is grossly insufficient evidence to show that obscenity brings about *any* substantive evil.[5]

The A.C.L.U. argument employs *only* the harm principle among liberty-limiting principles, and treats literature, drama, and painting as forms of expression subject to the same rules as expressions of opinion. In respect to both types of expression, "every act of deciding what should be barred carries with it a danger to the community."[6] The suppression itself is an evil to the author who is squelched. The power to censor and punish involves risks that socially valuable material will be repressed along with the "filth." The overall effect of suppression, the A.C.L.U. concludes, is almost certainly to discourage nonconformist and eccentric expression generally. In order to override these serious risks, there must be in a given case an even more clear and present danger that the obscene material, if not squelched, will cause even greater harm; such countervailing evidence is never forthcoming. (If such evidence were to accumulate, the A.C.L.U. would be perfectly willing to change its position on obscenity.)

The A.C.L.U. stand on obscenity seems clearly to be the position dictated by the unsupplemented harm principle and its corollary, the clear and present danger test. Is there any reason at this point to introduce the offense principle into the discussion? Unhappily, we may be forced to if we are to do justice to all of our particular intuitions in the most harmonious way. Consider an example suggested by Professor Schwartz. By the provisions of the new Model Penal Code, he writes, "a rich homosexual may not use a billboard on Times Square to promulgate to the general populace the techniques and pleasures of sodomy."[7] If the notion of "harm" is restricted to its narrow sense, that is, contrasted with "offense," it will be hard to reconstruct a rationale for this prohibition based on the harm principle. There is unlikely to be evidence that a lurid and obscene public poster in Times Square would create a clear and present danger of injury to those who fail to avert their eyes in time as they come blinking out of the subway stations. Yet it will be surpassingly difficult for even the most dedicated liberal to advocate freedom of expression in a case of this kind. Hence, if we are to justify coercion in this case, we will likely be driven, however reluctantly, to the offense principle.

There is good reason to be "reluctant" to embrace the offense principle until driven to it by an example like the above. People take perfectly genuine offense at many socially useful or harmless activities, from commercial advertisements to inane chatter. Moreover, widespread irrational prejudices can lead people to be disgusted, shocked, even morally repelled by perfectly innocent activities, and we should be loath to permit their groundless repugnance to override the innocence. The offense principle, therefore, must be formulated very precisely and applied in accordance with carefully formulated standards so as not to open the door to wholesale and intuitively unwarranted repression. At the very least we should require that the prohibited conduct or material be of the sort apt to offend almost everybody, and not just some shifting majority or special interest group.

It is instructive to note that a strictly drawn offense principle would not only justify prohibition of conduct and pictured conduct that is in its inherent character repellent, but also conduct and pictured conduct that is inoffensive in itself but offensive in inappropriate circumstances. I have in mind so-called indecencies such as public nudity. One can imagine an advocate of the unsupplemented harm principle arguing against the public nudity prohibition on the grounds that the sight of a naked body does no one any harm, and the state has no right to impose standards of dress or undress on private citizens. How one chooses to dress, after all, is a form of self-expression. If we do not permit the state to bar clashing colors or bizarre hair styles, by what right does it prohibit total undress? Perhaps the sight of naked people could at first lead to riots or other forms of anti-social behavior, but that is precisely the sort of contingency for which we have police. If we don't take away a person's right of free speech for the reason that its exercise may lead others to misbehave, we cannot in consistency deny his right to dress or undress as he chooses for the same reason.

There may be no answering this challenge on its own ground, but the offense principle provides a ready rationale for the nudity prohibition. The sight of nude bodies in public places is for almost everyone acutely *embarrassing*. Part of the explanation no doubt rests on the fact that nudity has an irresistible power to draw the eye and focus the thoughts on matters that are normally repressed. The conflict between these attracting and repressing forces is exciting, upsetting, and anxiety-producing. In some persons it will create at best a kind of painful turmoil, and at worst that experience of exposure to oneself of "peculiarly sensitive, intimate, vulnerable aspects of the self"[8] which is called *shame*. "One's feeling is involuntarily exposed openly in one's face; one is uncovered . . . taken by surprise . . . made a fool of."[9] The result is not mere "offense," but a kind of psychic jolt that in many normal people can be a painful wound. Even those of us who are better able to control our feelings might well resent the *nuisance* of having to do so.

If we are to accept the offense principle as a supplement to the harm principle, we must accept two corollaries which stand in relation to it similarly to the way in which the clear and present danger test stands to the harm principle. The first, the *standard of universality*, has already been touched upon. For the offensiveness (disgust, embarrassment, outraged sensibilities, or shame) to be sufficient to warrant coercion, it should be the reaction that could be expected from almost any person chosen at random from the nation as a whole, regardless of sect, faction, race, age, or sex. The second is the *standard of reasonable avoidability*. No one has a right to protection from the state against offensive experiences if he can effectively avoid those experiences with no unreasonable effort or inconvenience. If a nude person enters a public bus and takes a seat near the front, there may be no effective way for other patrons to avoid intensely shameful embarrassment (or other insupportable feelings) short of leaving the bus, which would be an unreasonable inconvenience. Similarly, obscene remarks over a loudspeaker, homosexual billboards in Times Square, and pornographic handbills thrust into the hands of passing pedestrians all fail to be reasonably avoidable.

On the other hand, the offense principle, properly qualified, can give no warrant to the suppression of *books* on the grounds of obscenity. When printed words hide decorously behind covers of books sitting passively on bookstore shelves, their offensiveness is easily avoided. The contrary view is no doubt encouraged by the common comparison of obscenity with "smut," "filth," or "dirt." This in turn suggests an analogy to nuisance law, which governs cases where certain activities create loud noises or terrible odors offensive to neighbors, and "the courts must weigh the gravity of the nuisance [substitute "offense"] to the neighbors against the social utility [substitute "redeeming social value"] of the defendant's conduct.[10] There is, however, one vitiating disanalogy in this comparison. In the case of "dirty books" the offense is easily avoidable. There is nothing like the evil smell of rancid garbage oozing right out through the covers of a book. When an "obscene" book sits on a shelf, who is there to be offended? Those who want to read it for the sake of erotic stimulation presumably will not be offended (or else they wouldn't read it); and those who choose not to read it will have no experience by which to be offended. If its covers are too decorous, some innocents may browse through it by mistake and be offended by what they find, but they need only close the book to escape the offense. Even this offense, minimal as it is, could be completely avoided by prior consultation of trusted book reviewers. I conclude that there are no sufficient grounds derived either from the harm or offense principles for suppressing obscene literature, unless that ground be the protection of children; but I can think of no reason why restrictions on sales to children cannot work as well for printed materials as they do for cigarettes and whiskey.

Notes

[1] James Fitzjames Stephen, *Liberty, Equality, Fraternity* (London: 1873), p. 48.

[2] See Edith Hamilton, *The Greek Way* (New York: W. W. Norton & Company, Inc., 1942), pp. 35ff.

[3] John Stuart Mill, *On Liberty* (New York: Liberal Arts Press, 1956), p. 71.

[4] There have been some studies made, but the results have been inconclusive. See the *Report of the Federal Commission on Obscenity and Pornography* (New York: Bantam Books, 1970), pp. 169–308.

[5] *Obscenity and Censorship* (Pamphlet published by the American Civil Liberties Union, New York, March, 1963), p. 7.

[6] *Obscenity and Censorship*, p. 4.

[7] Louis B. Schwartz, "Morals Offenses and the Model Penal Code," *Columbia Law Review*, LXIII (1963), 680.

[8] Helen Merrill Lynd, *On Shame and the Search for Identity* (New York: Science Editions, Inc., 1961), p. 33.

[9] Lynd, *On Shame and the Search for Identity*, p. 32.

[10] William L. Prosser, *Handbook of the Law of Torts* (St. Paul: West Publishing, 1955), p. 411.

chapter 9

Equality of the Sexes

INTRODUCTION

The last two decades have seen both a rebirth and a transformation of the women's movement. During the early decades of the twentieth century, the movement focused on political rights, especially the right to vote. Many thought that once women had the right to vote, they would secure full equality with men. The Great Depression and World War II diverted people's attention to those problems, but by the 1960s it was plain that the right to vote had not brought about the full equality of the sexes that many had desired and expected. Moreover, the black civil-rights movement raised people's consciousness about the status and treatment of other groups. The similarities and differences between discrimination on grounds of race and discrimination on grounds of sex are complex and sometimes subtle.[1] Nonetheless, the civil-rights movement provided impetus to the modern women's movement.

During the last decade or so, various issues relating to equality between the sexes have risen to public attention and often have been the center of constitutional controversies. Perhaps the first issue to come to the fore was hiring and payment practices. Women (and men) are often discriminated against in hiring; some occupations have traditionally been female or male—women, for instance, have been confined to elementary-school teaching and nursing, men to truck driving. Many studies showed that even when women were hired, they received less pay than did men for the same work. A more recent controversy concerns pension payments. Many women spend part or all of their lives as housewives and yet are not entitled to social-security benefits on the basis of that work. In private pension plans, as women on average live longer than men, their monthly benefits are lower than those for men of a similar age, who have made equivalent contributions. Some think that even though sexual equality is an ideal, such statistical differences between sexes are legitimate bases for differential treatment, while others believe that such a system is discriminatory, because it cannot be shown that any particular woman will live so long as to draw more in benefits than she contributed.

265

Considerable concern has been expressed about equality in sports. In the past, male collegiate and high-school sports have been more heavily funded and brought in more revenues that did female sports. New rules have been adopted to require more equal funding. Such programs, however, are still predicated upon separate sports or teams for males and females. Frequent disagreements have arisen from the desire of females to participate in Little League baseball or to join previously all-male hockey and wrestling teams.

The question of sexual equality should be broken into at least two parts. First, one should ask what the ideal of the relations between the sexes should be. Should they be treated differently? People who say yes sometimes disagree about the ways in which they should be. The historical model, patriarchy, has been for males to have the superior positions in society, but a few societies have been matriarchies ruled by women. Even those who agree that the sexes should be equal sometimes disagree as to what that means. One vision is a complete blending of feminine and masculine characteristics in each person, while another vision is to allow individuals to develop in various ways so that some are feminine, some masculine, and others various blends. (Keep in mind that feminine and masculine characteristics are not necessarily tied to female and male sex, although most people with feminine characteristics will be female and those with masculine characteristics will be male.)

Second, one must consider what social programs and methods are appropriate to achieve or maintain the ideal. Should children be socialized into different gender roles? Should women (and blacks) be given preference in hiring or admission to graduate or professional schools over equally or even better academically qualified white males? This last question pertains to *affirmative action* (preferential treatment, reverse discrimination). This issue has resulted in significant Supreme Court decisions about the meaning of equal protection.[2] Disregarding the constitutional aspects, it also raises significant questions about the appropriate ethical concept of equality.

Philosophers have discussed equality of the sexes on and off since Plato, in the *Republic*, made the then radical proposal that males and females be equal members of the guardian class.[3] Philosophical support for equality of the sexes was short-lived, as Plato's student, Aristotle, thought women were by nature inferior to men. To the extent philosophers discussed or thought about the matter, implicitly if not explicitly, Aristotle's view remained dominant for 2,000 years. Philosophical denigration of women reached its zenith in Schopenhauer's essay "On Women."[4] At about the same time, however, John Stuart Mill published *On the Subjection of Women*, an eloquent argument for legal and social equality of the sexes.

The Ideal   According to *natural-law* views, the ideal relations between the sexes depend upon their natural inclinations. If males and females are naturally inclined toward different social activities, then society should recognize and support these inclinations. If females have a nurturing inclination, then they should not act contrary to it but should follow it by raising children. If males have natural inclinations to conduct that women do not have, then they should be encouraged to act on them.

Much controversy surrounds the empirical question of whether the sexes have differing natural inclinations. Some people believe that genetic-based hormonal differences produce inclinations to different types of behaviors, although others deny that there is any sex-linked inclination to one type of conduct rather than another. The latter maintain that any differences between the sexes evident in society are socially rather than genetically or naturally induced. People holding a natural-law view can, depending upon their reading of the evidence, hold any substantive position regarding the relations between the sexes. Nevertheless, the more prevalent view of natural-law theorists is that males are better suited for more aggressive leadership roles in society. This position can be and is reversed by a few writers who maintain that because women are more inclined to loving and nurturing and are genetically stronger, they are superior to men.[5]

A *natural-rights* view easily lends itself to sexual equality. No matter how chauvinistic the classical natural-rights theorists were personally, they held that natural rights pertain to people simply in virtue of their being human. As the basis of natural rights is humanity, not male humanity, people of both sexes possess the same rights. One should not too quickly conclude that natural or human rights would not support any differences between the sexes. Some alleged human rights, such as the right to paid maternity leave, might seem to be restricted to one sex. However, these rights might be specific instances of more general rights, such as paid leave for parental duties.

The human right to freedom, understood as autonomy or self-determination, seems to support sexual equality. If women (and men) have a natural right to self-determination, then both socialization to gender roles and denial of opportunities on the basis of sex seem to violate that right.[6] Yet one might argue that socialization (or at least some forms of it) does not deprive a person of freedom and autonomy; socialization is necessary for a person to fully develop one's personality, especially one's desires and preferences. In short, self-determination or freedom pertains to the availability of options that one can choose if one wants to, and the shaping of preferences and desires does not eliminate these options. To sustain this argument, however, one needs to distinguish between those ways of shaping preferences, such as brainwashing, that do limit freedom and those that do not.

A *Kantian* view also seems to imply sexual equality as the ideal. By the formula of the law of nature, it is doubtful one could will a maxim involving sexual discrimination to be a universal law, especially were the positions reversed. The formula of humanity requires that one not treat humanity as a mere means. The relevant condition is humanity, not male humanity. However, neither formula excludes all distinctions on the basis of sex. For example, choosing a male rather than a female to portray Julius Caesar in a school play might be willed by a person even were she excluded because of sex. The principle of women and children being given first place in the lifeboats might be admitted by the formula of humanity because it seems to treat women as ends and not mere means. However, no harmful distinction on the basis of sex would respect humanity, or be capable of being willed were positions reversed.

By the very way moral principles are determined, *contractarian* views seem to prohibit sexual discrimination. As rational contractors are to choose moral principles behind the veil of ignorance, they will not know to which sex they belong. Consequently, they do not appear to have a basis for choosing principles that discriminate between the sexes. This appearance, however, could be deceiving. Contractors also have general knowledge about science and societies. Suppose it were established that the sexes had different dispositions suiting them for different social activities. Then a rational contractor might have good reason to favor some principles providing incentives for members of the sexes to pursue alternative careers and goals. Yet if the dispositions and talents were only statistically different, some members of each sex might be better at activities usually best performed by members of the other sex. Consequently, a rational contractor would not favor any principles that prohibited members of one sex from occupying positions usually best fulfilled by members of the other sex.

Instead of addressing the problem from the position of an original contractor, one might contend that contractors would simply adopt the principles of justice Rawls argues for: equal liberties, fair equality of opportunity, and the difference principles. Considerations of equality between the sexes arise only after these principles have been adopted. To distinguish between persons on the basis of sex violates either the equal basic liberties or the fair equality of opportunity principles.

One of the classic arguments for equality of the sexes is John Stuart Mill's *utilitarian* defense of equality. In *On the Subjection of Women,* Mill argues for perfect equality between the sexes.[7] He devotes a large portion of the book to refuting arguments that women are incapable of various tasks, claiming that part of their previous lack of achievement is attributable to their socialization. He rejects arguments for the natural superiority of males. No adequate basis exists for such a conclusion, he contends, as no society has ever actually tried a system of thoroughgoing equality. In the end, Mill claims, both women and men would benefit from equality; women would be spared the frustration and unhappiness of their subordinate position, and men would benefit, along with the whole society, from the use of women's previously wasted talents. Mill, however, does not anticipate an equal mix of men and women in all occupations and activities, because he thinks the majority of women are likely to prefer childbearing and raising and so not be as fully employed in the economy.[8]

Two further points need to be noted about a utilitarian approach to equality of the sexes. First, not all considerations need point toward equality. Were evidence produced that the sexes have different inclinations, so that socializing all for similar rather than distinct activities would produce more frustration, then a utilitarian would have a reason to favor socialization for different roles. Second, the distinction between act and rule utilitarianism is not relevant at the level of the ideal. The ideal concerns the relationship that will yield the most happiness and is thus independent of whether one uses it to evaluate acts or rules.

The Method: Affirmative Action   The adage that the end does not justify the means is shared, in one interpretation or another, by all ethical theories. Whatever ideal one pursues, some means to it are not ethically acceptable. Even utilitarians reject means that produce more unhappiness than the ideal would provide. Although questions of means arise whatever ideal one holds, the following discussion assumes the ideal of sexual equality and is restricted to the ethics of only one means of reaching it— *affirmative action*. Many interpretations or meanings can be given to affirmative action. It can mean simply making a special effort to seek out and consider hiring members of particular groups— blacks, women, and other minorities. It can also include preferring members of these groups to nonmembers when both are equally qualified on other grounds. Or it can include preferring members of these minority groups despite the fact that they are less well qualified on other relevant grounds than are nonmembers. Only the last version, which can be called *strong affirmative action*, will be considered here.

Natural-law, natural-rights, Kantian, and contractarian theories are unlikely to support strong affirmative action, unless it is by principles of compensation or reparation. The basic problem with strong affirmative action is its treatment of those (white males) over whom women, blacks, and others would be preferred. Preference for group members seems to violate the natural rights of nonmembers. It fails to treat nonmembers as ends in themselves; would not be acceptable were one in their position; and violates nonmembers' rights to equal liberty and fair equality of opportunity. However, if strong affirmative action is compensation or reparation to women or blacks for past wrongs done to them, then these views might permit it. A problem with any such justification of strong affirmative action is that those who would effectively make the reparations, or provide the compensation, are probably not those who have committed the wrongs. Furthermore, those who would benefit most from reparation are probably not those who have been most harmed.

This criticism might be met in either of two ways. First, it could be argued that whether or not they participated in it, all members of the historically favored group have in fact benefited from the previous discrimination. Consequently, they would not be as well off as they are had it not been for past injustices. They are only being required to surrender unjust gains. A contractarian could add that the inequalities involved in preferential treatment will be to the advantage of the least advantaged, although the difference principle is normally subject to the fair equality of opportunity principle. Second, the criticism could be acknowledged and it be recommended that older white males make sacrifices so that younger males will not bear the entire burden.[9]

Another common argument to support strong affirmative action available on these theories is that the usual criteria for evaluating candidates for jobs and graduate or professional schools are biased. For example, intelligence and aptitude tests are often said to be biased against minorities. If the traditional criteria are biased, then preference for women and others corrects for biases and results in selection of those best qualified.

A final argument available on these theories is to question assumptions about the functions of positions. For example, it might be said that the function of a university professor is not simply to teach and to write scholarly papers but also to serve as a role model for students. In this light, being a woman or black is relevant to a university professor's job, for a woman or black will provide a role model for persons currently lacking many such role models. Consequently, to consider a person's sex or race is not to consider an irrelevant factor, any more than it would be in selecting someone to play Julius Caesar. This argument can easily slip into a utilitarian argument for strong affirmative action on the ground that it will effectively promote equality. Utilitarian arguments are not usually open to persons holding natural-law, natural-rights, Kantian, and contractarian theories. Natural rights and equal liberties are not to be sacrificed for utility.

For *utilitarians*, compensation and reparation are not really relevant. The crucial issue for a utilitarian is what method most effectively brings about the ideal condition or equality. Instead of worrying about the rights of persons (white males) excluded by affirmative action, a utilitarian will be concerned chiefly with whether its net utility is greater than that of alternative methods of bringing about equality. Its net utility primarily depends upon the unhappiness it brings to those who lose versus the happiness it brings to those who gain. Of special significance is whether the gain is illusory. For example, it is sometimes said that a woman (or black) hired under strong affirmative action will not know, nor will others know, whether she was hired because she was the most competent or because she is a woman. This can create much unhappiness for the person hired. Yet providing people such help might end discrimination sooner and thus bring about more happiness for more people. A utilitarian will never forget the unhappiness and misery sexual and racial discrimination produces, as well as the benefits that would accrue to everyone from making use of the previously unused talents of women and blacks.

Act utilitarians will examine each case in light of the above and other considerations to decide whether strong affirmative action is appropriate to it. If act utilitarians believe that, say, a particular department especially needs a woman or black (perhaps to serve as a role model), they will weigh that heavily. In the case of another university department that already has several female and black faculty members, they might believe strong affirmative action to be less appropriate. The extent to which they will weigh a candidate's being female or black will depend upon how effectively hiring a female or black in that job will promote equality.

A *rule utilitarian* has a more difficult task. Adopting a rule of strong affirmative action might promote discrimination as an ideal. That is, the best rule for society in the short-term might not be the best in the long-term. Of course, one could adopt one rule for the short-term and another later on, but the possible cost might be that people would receive mixed signals as to what the ideal situation is. In effect, this problem is a variation on that of choosing the rule which would be best if everyone adhered to it but that is not if they do not. (See Chapter 3.) With affirmative action, the best rule for today might not be the best one for later when equality had been generally achieved.

Readings   The problem case is taken from one of the earliest Supreme Court cases raising the issue of sexual equality. Michigan law prohibited women being licensed bartenders in cities of more than 50,000 people, unless they were a wife or daughter of the male owner of an establishment. The issue was whether equal protection of the laws required that women be licensed on the same basis as men. In addition to arguments of legislative discretion, those favoring the law might argue that women would be unable to control unruly customers and so could not adequately perform the tasks of the position. The Supreme Court upheld the Michigan law, but in 1971 the California Supreme Court declared a similar law contrary to a provision of the California State Constitution that explicitly bans sex discrimination.[10]

In "The Inevitability of Patriarchy," Steven Goldberg argues for sexual inequality on largely natural-law grounds. Goldberg believes that sex-based hormonal differences make males more aggressive and thus more properly suited for, that is, more likely to achieve, leadership positions in modern societies. In one interpretation, Goldberg does not provide a standard natural-law argument, for he claims that male dominance is inevitable. If it is inevitable, no ethical issue is raised, for it cannot be avoided. However, Goldberg also argues that people will be happier and the social good achieved if people are socialized to different roles. Although this may sound like a utilitarian argument, it is closer to the natural-law tradition. The natural-law tradition determines the good for human individuals and society on the basis of natural inclinations, and Goldberg certainly rests his argument on natural (genetic) inclinations and claims that society should conform to, not frustrate, those inclinations.

Bernard Boxill argues on largely contractarian grounds against the assimilationist ideal of sexual blindness. According to this ideal, sex differences would matter no more than do differences of eye color. However, Boxill contends, to achieve it is too costly. Such valuable unalienated activities as ballet dancing and various sports would have to be eliminated.

This, in turn, would eliminate opportunities to gain self-esteem. Moreover, he contends that assimilation is not necessary for equality of opportunity and sacrifices equality of respect.

In the final selection, Joyce Trebilcot discusses two forms of androgynism. She distinguishes between *monoandrogynism,* in which each individual has a similar mixture of feminine and masculine characteristics, and *polyandrogynism,* in which people variously exhibit feminine or masculine characteristics or various mixtures of them. On largely utilitarian grounds, she argues that polyandrogynism is preferable. Monoandrogynism may produce frustration if people are by inclination predominantly feminine or masculine, and the ideal mix cannot be determined unless people have a free choice to express their preferences.

These three readings not only present three different arguments about the ideal relations between the sexes, they also exhibit distinct ideals. Goldberg foresees as inevitable a society in which males predominate in leadership positions. Boxill argues for a society in which sex differences exist but neither sex dominates the other. Trebilcot presents a similar but distinct ideal in which differences exist but sex is not the basis for them. A fourth view, not advocated, would eliminate social and personal differences of sex or gender.

Notes

[1] See Laurence Thomas and B. C. Postow, "Symposium on Sexism and Racism," *Ethics* 90 (1980): 239–56.

[2] *Regents of the University of California* v. *Bakke,* 98 S. Ct. 3140 (1978).

[3] For an excellent collection of materials on the view of women in the history of philosophy, see Martha Lee Osborne, ed., *Woman in Western Thought* (New York: Random House, 1979).

[4] In ibid., pp. 212–21.

[5] See Ashley Montagu, "The Natural Superiority of Women," in ibid., pp. 221–28.

[6] See Sharon Bishop Hill, "Self-Determination and Autonomy," in *Today's Moral Problems,* ed. Richard A. Wasserstrom, 2nd ed. (New York: Macmillan, 1979), pp. 118–33.

[7] Greenwich, Conn.: Fawcett Publications, 1971. First published in 1869.

[8] Ibid., p. 70.

[9] See, for example, Judith Jarvis Thomson, "Preferential Hiring," *Philosophy & Public Affairs* 2 (1973): 384.

[10] See *Sail'er Inn, Inc.* v. *Kirby,* 5 Cal. 3d 1, 485 P.2d 529 (1971).

Bibliography on Equality of the Sexes

Bayles, Michael D. "Compensatory Reverse Discrimination in Hiring." *Social Theory and Practice* 2 (1973): 301–12.

Blackstone, William T., and Heslep, Robert D., eds. *Social Justice and Preferential Treatment.* Athens, Ga.: University of Georgia Press, 1977.

Bishop, Sharon, and Weinzweig, Marjorie, eds. *Philosophy and Women.* Encino, Calif.: Wadsworth, 1979.

English, Jane. "Sex Equality in Sports." *Philosophy & Public Affairs* 7 (1978): 269–77.

————, ed. *Sex Equality.* Englewood Cliffs, N.J.: Prentice-Hall, 1977.

Flew, Antony. "Who Are the Equals?" *Philosophia* 9 (1980): 131–54.

Fullinwider, Robert K. *The Reverse Discrimination Controversy: A Moral and Legal Analysis*. Totowa, N.J.: Rowman and Littlefield, 1980.

Goldman, Alan. *Justice and Reverse Discrimination*. Princeton, N.J.: Princeton University Press, 1979.

Gould, Carol C., and Wartofsky, Marx W., eds. *Women and Philosophy: Towards a Theory of Liberation*. New York: Putnam, Capricorn Books, 1976.

Gross, Barry R., ed. *Reverse Discrimination*. Buffalo, N.Y.: Prometheus Books, 1977.

Haack, Susan. "On the Moral Relevance of Sex." *Philosophy* 50 (1974): 90–98.

Hill, Thomas E., Jr. "Servility and Self-Respect." *The Monist* 57 (1973): 87–104.

Jagger, Alison M. "On Sexual Equality." *Ethics* 84 (1974): 278–97.

_____, and Struhl, Paula Rothenberg, eds. *Feminist Frameworks: Alternative Theoretical Accounts of the Relations Between Women and Men*. New York: McGraw-Hill, 1978.

Lucas, J. R. "Because You Are a Woman." *Philosophy* 48 (1973): 161–71.

_____. "Vive La Difference." *Philosophy* 53 (1978): 367–73.

Mill, John Stuart. *On the Subjection of Women*. Many editions.

Osborne, Martha Lee, ed. *Woman in Western Thought*. New York: Random House, 1979.

Sher, George. "Justifying Reverse Discrimination in Employment." *Philosophy & Public Affairs* 4 (1975): 159–70.

Thomas, Laurence, and Postow, B. C. "Symposium on Sexism and Racism." *Ethics* 90 (1980): 239–56.

Vetterling-Braggin, Mary; Elliston, Frederick A.; and English, Jane; eds. *Feminism and Philosophy*. Totowa, N.J.: Littlefield, Adams, 1977.

Wasserstrom, Richard A., ed. *Today's Moral Problems*. 2nd ed. New York: Macmillan, 1979. Chapters 2 and 3.

White, Stephen W. "Beautiful Losers: An Analysis of Radical Feminist Egalitarianism." *Journal of Value Inquiry* 11 (1977): 264–83.

Wolgast, Elizabeth H. *Equality and the Rights of Women*. Ithaca, N.Y.: Cornell University Press, 1980.

Problem Case
Goesaert v. Cleary, 335 U.S. 464 (1948)

Mr. Justice Frankfurter delivered the opinion of the Court.

As part of the Michigan system for controlling the sale of liquor, bartenders are required to be licensed in all cities having a population of 50,000 or more, but no female may be so licensed unless she be "the wife or daughter of the male owner" of a licensed liquor establishment. . . . The case is here on direct appeal from an order of the District Court of three judges, convened under § 266 of the old Judicial Code, now 28. U.S.C. § 2284, denying an injunction to restrain the enforcement of the Michigan law. The claim, denied below, one judge dissenting, 74 F. Supp. 735, and renewed here, is that Michigan cannot forbid females generally from being barmaids and at the same time make an exception in favor of the wives and daughters of the owners of liquor establishments. Beguiling as the subject is, it need not detain us long. To ask whether or not the Equal Protection of the Laws Clause of the Fourteenth Amendment barred Michigan from making the classification the State has made between wives and daughters of owners of liquor places and wives and daughters of non-owners, is one of those rare instances where to state the question is in effect to answer it.

STEVEN GOLDBERG
THE INEVITABILITY OF PATRIARCHY

THE FEMINIST ASSUMPTION

The view of man and woman in society that implicitly underlies all of the arguments of the feminists is this: there is nothing inherent in the nature of human beings or of society that necessitates that any role or task (save those requiring great strength or the ability to give birth) be associated with one sex or the other; there is no natural order of things decreeing that dyadic and social authority must be associated with men, nor is there any reason why it must be men who rule in every society. Patriarchy, matriarchy, and "equiarchy" are all equally possible and—while every society may invoke "the natural order of things" to justify its particular system—all the expectations we have of men and women are culturally determined and have nothing to do with any sort of basic male or female nature.

There is nothing internally contradictory in such a hypothesis; indeed, it is an ideal place from which to begin an empirical investigation into the nature of man, woman, and society. However, the feminist does not use this as a heuristic first step but unquestioningly accepts it as true. . . .

. . . *The only biological hypothesis included in this book states that those individuals whose male anatomy leads to a social identification as "male" have hormonal systems which generate a greater capacity for "aggression" (or a lower threshold for the release of "aggression"—for our purposes this is the same thing) than those individuals whose female anatomy leads to a social identification as "female" and that socialization and institutions conform to the reality of hormonal sexual differentiation and to the statistical reality of the "aggression advantage" which males derive from their hormonal systems. . . .*

AGGRESSION AND ATTAINMENT

In other words, I believe that in the past we have been looking in the wrong direction for the answer to the question of why every society rewards male roles with higher status than it does female roles (even when the male tasks in one society are the female tasks in another). While it is true that men are always in the positions of authority from which status tends to be defined, male roles are not given high status primarily *because* men fill these roles; men fill these roles because their biological aggression "advantage" can be manifested *in any non-child related area rewarded by high status in any society.* (Again: the line of reasoning used in this book demonstrates only that the biological factors we discuss would make the social institutions we discuss inevitable and does not preclude the existence of other forces also leading in the same direction; there may be a biologically based tendency for women to prefer male leadership, but there need not be for male attainment of leadership and high-status roles to be inevitable.) As we shall see, this aggression "advantage" can be most manifested and can most enable men to reap status rewards *not* in those relatively homogeneous, collectivist primitive societies in which both male and female must play similar economic roles if the society is to survive or in the monarchy (which guarantees an occasional female leader); this biological factor will be given freest play in the complex, relatively individualistic, bureaucratic, democratic society which, of necessity, must emphasize organizational authority and in which social mobility is relatively free of traditional barriers to advancement. There were more female heads of state in the first two-thirds of the sixteenth century than in the first two-thirds of the twentieth.

The mechanisms involved here are easily seen if we examine any roles that males have attained by channeling their aggression toward such attainment. We will assume for now that equivalent women could *perform* the tasks of roles as well as men if they could attain the roles. Here we can speak of the corporation president, the union leader, the governor, the chairman of an association, or any other role or position for which aggression is a precondition for attainment. Now the environmentalist and the feminist will say that the fact that all such roles are nearly always filled by men is attributable not to male aggression but to the fact that women have not been allowed to enter the competitive race to attain these positions, that they have been told that these positions are in male areas, and that girls are socialized away from competing with boys in general. Women *are* socialized in this way, but again we must ask why. If innate male aggression has nothing to do with male attainment of positions of authority and status in the political, academic, scientific, or financial spheres, if aggression has nothing to do with the reasons why *every* society socializes girls away from those areas which are given high status and away from competition in general, then why is it never the *girls* in any society who are socialized toward these areas, why is it never the nonbiological roles played by women that have high status, why is it always boys who are told to compete, and why do women never "force" men into the low-status, nonmaternal roles that women play in every society?

These questions pose no problem if we acknowledge a male aggression that enables men to attain any nonbiological role given high status by any society. For one need merely consider the result of a society's *not* socializing women away from competitions with men, from its *not* directing girls toward roles women are more capable of playing than are men or roles with status low enough that men will not strive for them. No doubt some women would be aggressive enough to succeed in competitions with men and there would be considerably more women in high-status positions than there are now. But most women would lose in such competitive struggles with men (because men have the aggression advantage) and so most women would be forced to live adult lives as failures in areas in which the society had *wanted them to succeed*. It is women, far more than men, who would never allow a situation in which girls were socialized in such a way that the vast majority of them were doomed to adult lifetimes of failure to live up to their own expectations. Now I have no doubt that there is a biological factor that gives women the desire to emphasize maternal and nurturance roles, but the point here is that we can accept the feminist assumption that there is no female propensity of this sort and still see that a society must socialize women away from roles that men will attain through their aggression. For if women did not develop an alternative set of criteria for success their sense of their own competence would suffer intolerably. It is undeniable that the resulting different values and expectations that are attached to men and women will tend to work against the aggressive woman while they work for the man who is no more aggressive. But this is the unavoidable result of the fact that most men are more aggressive than most women so that this woman, who is as aggressive as the average man, but more aggressive than most women, is an exception. Furthermore, even if the sense of competence of each sex did not necessitate society's attaching to each sex values and expectations based on those qualities possessed by each sex, observation of the majority of each sex by the population would "automatically" lead to these values and expectations being attached to men and women.

SOCIALIZATION'S CONFORMATION TO BIOLOGICAL REALITY

Socialization is the process by which society prepares children for adulthood. The way in which its goals conform to the reality of biology is seen quite clearly when we consider the method in which testosterone generates male aggression (testosterone's serially developing nature). Preadolescent boys and girls have roughly equal testosterone levels, yet young boys are far more aggressive than young girls. Eva Figes has used this observation to dismiss incorrectly the possibility of a hormone-aggression association.[1] Now it is quite probable that the boy is more aggressive than the girl for a purely biological reason. We have seen that it is simplistic to speak simply in terms of hormone levels and that there is evidence of male-female differences in the behavior of infants shortly after birth (when differential socialization is not a plausible explanation of such differences). The fetal alteration of the boy's brain by the testosterone that was generated by his testes has probably left him far more sensitive to the aggression-related properties of the testosterone that is present during boyhood than the girl, who did not receive such alteration. But let us for the moment assume that this is not the case. This does not at all reduce the importance of the hormonal factor. For even if the boy is more aggressive than the girl only because the society allows him to be, the boy's socialization still flows from society's acknowledging biological reality. Let us consider what would happen if girls have the same innate aggression as boys and if a society did not socialize girls away from aggressive competitions. Perhaps half of the third-grade baseball team would be female. As many girls as boys would frame their expectations in masculine values and girls would develop not their feminine abilities but their masculine ones. During adolescence, however, the same assertion of the male chromosomal program that causes the boys to grow beards raises their testosterone level, and their potential for aggression, to a level far above that of the adolescent woman. If society did not teach young girls that beating boys at competitions was unfeminine (behavior inappropriate for a woman), if it did not socialize them away from the political and economic areas in which aggression leads to attainment, these girls would grow into adulthood with self-images based not on succeeding in areas for which biology has left them better prepared than men, but on competitions that most women could not win. If women did not develop feminine qualities as girls (assuming that such qualities do not spring automatically from female biology) then they would be forced to deal with the world in the aggressive terms of men. They would lose every source of power their feminine abilities now give them and they would gain nothing. . . .

DISCRIMINATION OF A SORT

If one is convinced that sexual biology gives the male an advantage in aggression, competitiveness, and dominance, but he does not believe that it engenders in men and women different propensities, cognitive aptitudes, and modes of perception, and if he considers it discrimination when male aggression leads to attainment of position even when aggression is not relevant to the task to be performed, then the unavoidable conclusion is that discrimination so defined is unavoidable. Even if one is convinced from the discussion in the following sections that the differing biological substrates that underlie the mental apparatus of men and women *do* engender different propensities, cognitive aptitudes, and modes of perception, he will probably agree that the relevance of this to male attainment of male roles is small when compared to the importance of male biological aggression to attainment. Innate tendencies to specific aptitudes *would* indicate that at any given level of competence there will be more men than women or vice versa (depending on the qualities relevant to the task) and that the very best will, in all probability, come from the sex whose potentials are relevant to the task. Nonetheless, drastic sexual differences in occupational and authority roles reflect male aggression and society's acknowledgment of it far more than they do differences in aptitudes, yet they are still inevitable.

In addition, even if artificial means were used to place large numbers of women in authority positions, it is doubtful that stability could be maintained. Even in our present male bureaucracies problems arise whenever a subordinate is more aggressive than his superior and, if the more aggressive executive is not allowed to rise in the bureaucracy, delicate psy-

chological adjustments must be made. Such adjustments are also necessary
when a male bureaucrat has a female superior. When such situations are
rare exceptions adjustments can be made without any great instability oc-
curring, particularly if the woman in the superior position complements
her aggression with sensitivity and femininity. It would seem likely, however, that if women shared equally in power at each level of the bureaucracy,
chaos would result for two reasons. Even if we consider the bureaucracy as
a closed system, the excess of male aggression would soon manifest itself
either in men moving quickly up the hierarchy or in a male refusal to acknowledge female authority. But a bureaucracy is not a closed system, and
the discrepancy between male dominance in private life and bureaucratic
female dominance (from the point of view of the male whose superior is a
woman) would soon engender chaos. Consider that even the present minute
minority of women in high authority positions expend enormous amounts
of energy trying *not* to project the commanding authority that is seen as
the mark of a good male executive. It is true that the manner in which aggression is manifested will be affected by the values of the society in general and the nature of the field of competition in particular; aggression in
an academic environment is camouflaged far more than in the executive
arena. While a desire for control and power and a single-mindedness of
purpose are no doubt relevant, here aggression is not easily defined. One
might inject the theoretical argument that women could attain positions
of authority and leadership by countering the male's advantage in aggression with feminine abilities. Perhaps, but the equivalents of the executive
positions in every area of suprafamilial life in every society have been attained by men, and there seems no reason to believe that, suddenly, feminine means will be capable of neutralizing male aggression in these areas.
And, in any case, an emphasis on feminine abilities is hardly what the
feminists desire. All of this can be seen in a considerably more optimistic
light, from the point of view of most women, if one considers that the biological abilities possessed only by women are complemented by biologically generated propensities directing women to roles that can be filled only
by women. But it is still the same picture. . . .

"OPPRESSION"

All of this indicates that the theoretical model that conceives of male success in attaining positions of status, authority, and leadership as *oppression* of the female is incorrect if only because it sees male aggressive energies as *directed toward* females and sees the institutional mechanisms that
flow from the fact of male aggression as *directed toward* "oppressing"
women. In reality these male energies are directed toward attainment of
desired positions and toward succeeding in whatever areas a particular society considers important. The fact that women lose out in these competitions, so that the sex-role expectations of a society would have to become
different for men and women even if they were not different for other rea-

sons, is an inevitable byproduct of the reality of the male's aggression advantage and not the cause, purpose, or primary function of it. In other words, men who attain the more desired roles and positions do so because they channel their aggression advantage toward such attainment; whether the losers in such competitions are other men or women is important only in that—because so few women succeed in these competitions—the society will attach different expectations to men and women (making it more difficult for the exceptional, aggressive, woman to attain such positions even when her aggression is equal to that of the average man).

Notes

1 Eva Figes, *Patriarchal Attitudes* (Greenwich, Conn.: Fawcett World, 1971), p. 8.

BERNARD R. BOXILL
SEXUAL BLINDNESS AND SEXUAL EQUALITY

In a recent important essay, Richard Wasserstrom describes what he thinks the "good or just society" would make of racial and sexual differences.[1] The good or just society, he argues, would exemplify the "assimilationist ideal."[2] That is, it would make of racial and sexual differences what present society makes of differences in eye color. In present society, no "basic political rights and obligations are determined on the basis of eye-color"; no "institutional benefits and burdens are connected with eye color"; and "except for the mildest sort of aesthetic preferences, a person would be thought odd who even made private, social decisions by taking eye-color into account."[3] In the good or just society, Wasserstrom contends, race and sex would be of no greater significance.[4] And, he continues, just as the typical adult in present society is "virtually oblivious to the eye color of other persons for all major inter-personal relationships," so the typical adult in the assimilationist society would be "indifferent to the sexual, physiological differences of other persons for all inter-personal relationships."[5]

The assimilationist vision of the sexually and racially ideal society springs, no doubt, from the most humane sentiments. We are seemingly so drawn to invidious discrimination against those of a different race or sex that it must be few who have not yearned for a society where people are blind to both their racial and sexual differences. Yet I shall argue that the assimilationist ideal is defective. The problem it attempts but fails to solve is the old one that has long troubled egalitarians: How are we to deal with the fact that, though we are undeniably equal, we are also undeniably different? In this essay I focus on the defects in the assimilationist argument that are due to the fact that though we are equal because we are human,

From Bernard R. Boxill, "Sexual Blindness and Sexual Equality," published by *Social Theory and Practice* 6 (1980): 281–98, Tallahassee, Florida. Reprinted by permission.

we are also different because we are female and male. However, my arguments should apply as well to the assimilationist position on racial differences. My conclusion is that we cannot plan that the good and just society be either "sex-blind" or "color-blind."

1

As Wasserstrom allows, there can be no important sex-role differentiations in the assimilationist society. If women are better than men at certain significant activities, or if men are better than women at certain significant activities, people will not likely be oblivious to their sexual differences. The correlation of sexual differences with activities that are significant would tend to make sexual differences themselves appear significant. Accordingly he proposes to break down all sex-activity correlations by designing activities so that women and men can succeed and excel equally at every activity. To use his illustration, if lifeguarding at the ocean as now practiced puts a premium on the kind of strength that gives men an advantage over women, the sexually ideal society would change the way lifeguarding is now practiced so that this advantage is nullified.[6] . . .

Wasserstrom is aware that his reform may have costs. But he seems to think that the only such cost is a possible loss in efficiency. The question whether to institute his reforms, he says, is simply "whether the increased cost (or loss of efficiency) was worth the gain in terms of equality and the avoidance of sex-role differentiation."[7] But I argue that he is mistaken. There are two major possible costs he does not consider: the loss of a whole province of our most significant activities, and a loss of opportunities to acquire self-esteem.

Significant Activities. "It is likely," Wasserstrom writes, "that even in this ideal society, weightlifting contests and boxing matches would in fact be dominated, perhaps exclusively so, by men. But it is hard to find any *significant* activities or institutions that are analogous. And it is not clear that such insignificant activities would be worth continuing, especially since sports function in existing patriarchal societies to help maintain the dominance of males."[8] But surely this conclusion is hasty. Even if sports function in *existing* patriarchal societies to help maintain male dominance, it certainly does not follow that they will perform the same function in an *ideal* society. Consequently, the inference that they would not be "worth continuing" is invalid. But the deeper difficulties concern the claim that sports are *insignificant*.

What Wasserstrom may mean by this is suggested in the next paragraph where he allows that lifeguarding, which also requires considerable unaided strength, is "nontrivial."[9] Since lifeguarding is distinguished from say, weightlifting, because it performs a service, the implication is that sports are "trivial" and "insignificant" because they do not perform a service and (by extension) have no product. It is true that sports need not perform a service or have a product. Though "spectator sports" may be said to perform the service of entertaining the spectators, and sports in general may produce health, people can engage in sport without entertaining spectators or improving their health. But it is false that sports are for that reason "insignificant" and not worth continuing. There are many activities that, like sports, need have no product and need perform no service. But these activities are not "insignificant" or "not worth continuing." On the contrary some of them are among our more significant activities and are well worth continuing. They are significant and well worth continuing because of what they are in themselves. These activities are unalienated activities. First I shall describe their nature. Then I shall show that sports are among them.

Alienated activity is not itself "the satisfaction of a need, but only a means to satisfy needs outside itself."[10] These needs are "outside" the activity in the sense that they can, at least conceivably, be satisfied "outside," that is, without the activity that usually provides for their satisfaction. As I understand it, what is really essential about labor's being alienated is that it is not in this sense itself the satisfaction of a need. Consequently, though Marx may have believed otherwise, I describe alienated activity as not essentially, though perhaps usually, involving the other man or capitalist who owns the alienated activity.[11] Now the products and services that happen to be demanded by society, as, for example, shoes, ships, and safe swimming, are needs "outside" activities because they all can at least conceivably be satisfied without the usual human activities of shoemaking, shipbuilding and lifeguarding. Since alienated labor is "only a means" to satisfy such needs, the overwhelming consideration in its design is that it satisfy these needs efficiently. Hence, except inadvertently, that design will not allow the worker room to express himself or to "develop freely his mental and physical energies."[12] Further, if there is a need to engage in such activity, alienated labor cannot satisfy that need. Since such a need is for a particular kind of activity, and so can be satisfied only by engaging in that activity, it does not meet the condition of being "outside" the activity that satisfies it.

But if alienated labor is of this nature, unalienated activity must be activity that the worker has a need to engage in, and in particular, activity that is designed specifically to provide him with room to express and develop himself freely. This does not mean that it is unprincipled or undisciplined. As Marx wrote, "Really free labor, the composing of music, for example, is at the same time damned serious and requires the greatest effort."[13] That is to say, activity which is truly a form of self-expression and self-development is necessarily governed by the discipline of laws and principles. We can express ourselves in writing, music, painting and so on, and exercise our literary, musical, and in general our creative talents, only because there are laws governing literary, musical and artistic composition, and only if we submit ourselves to the discipline of these laws. As Marx put it most generally, in his free activity man "constructs in accordance with the laws of beauty."[14] . . .

In elaborating his Aristotelian Principle, Rawls comes to relevantly similar conclusions. The Aristotelian Principle is a "principle of motivation" that "accounts for many of our major desires."[15] According to it "human beings enjoy the exercise of their realized capacities . . . and this enjoyment increases the more the capacity is realized, or the greater its complexity." Thus, "of two activities they do equally well [people] prefer the one calling on a larger repertoire of intricate and subtle discriminations."[16] Presumably such activities are more enjoyable because they "satisfy the desire for variety and novelty of experience" and permit or even require "individual style and personal expression."[17] This desire is, moreover, "relatively strong" and it must be reckoned with in the design of social institutions; for "otherwise human beings will find their culture and form of life dull and empty. Their vitality and zest will fail as their life becomes a tiresome routine."[18] Thus human beings have a need to engage in activities that call on the exercise of their abilities "simply for their own sakes."[19]

In sum, then, activities can be significant in themselves both in the sense that they are forms of self-expression in which excellence can be achieved, and in the sense that human beings have a profound need to engage in them. I now show that the assimilationist proposes to eliminate a considerable class of these activities.

Consider first, sport: We have seen that Wasserstrom proposes to eliminate it for the sake of sexual blindness. Now in practically all cultures and societies people engage in sport for its own sake. Assuming that people tend to recognise their own needs, it would seem that engaging in sport is in itself the satisfaction of an important human need.[20] To forestall objections that this may be a "false need," I can show that sports can also be forms of self-expression in which excellence is achieved. Sports are not merely undisciplined, unprincipled explosions of physical energy. Though they are exercises of human energy that are freely engaged in because they are engaged in for themselves, they are governed by the most exacting rules. Moreover, since sport is not subservient to satisfying needs "outside" itself, in accordance with the Aristotelian Principle, its rules can be, and usually are, constructed to require the utmost in "intricate and subtle discriminations" that the players are capable of. Though Rawls allows that the Aristotelian Principle operates "even in games and pastimes,"[21] he unfortunately, but I think inadvertently, gives the notion of intricacy and subtlety involved an excessively intellectual interpretation. But anyone who has tried to describe a Dr. J stuff shot, or the fastidious shifts in balance and speed of the best high jumpers or shot-putters, and who also understands that what he or she would put into words is not the spontaneous perfection of the animal, but a deliberately acquired art, must acknowledge that sport, too, calls for "intricate and subtle discriminations." Further, as Rawls notes, since it is the very complexity of activities which makes them important avenues of self-expression—"for how could everyone do them in the same way?"[22]—being complex, sports too are important avenues of self-expression. And again, to prove this we need only take an educated look at the best practitioners of any sport. As infallibly as any maestro, they, too, put their personal stamp on their best performances. Finally, many sports are to a considerable extent art forms governed by the "laws of beauty." Few who have seen an accomplished performance of gymnastics or diving, or a perfect pole vault, or a well-run hurdles race, would care to deny this. In ancient Greece, Myron captured the beauty of the discus thrower in his famous discobolus. . . .

. . . [T]he assimilationist must eliminate sport. But it is not only sport he must eliminate. The sexes do not differ only in strength. They differ also in physical appearance, flexibility, grace, and texture of voice, for example. Further, the exercise of these differences is central to many of our most aesthetically appealing and culturally important activities. The exercise of man's greater natural strength and woman's greater natural flexibility and grace is of course obvious in many forms of dance. Similarly, the importance of woman's naturally higher, and man's naturally deeper, voice is obvious in practically all forms of singing. Anyone who thinks of questioning the importance of the aesthetic value of the mix of soprano and bass voices should recall the lengths to which—including in particular the castration of little boys—the medievals went to secure it.

Finally, these losses of the assimilationist society cannot be "made up." Sport and the other activities the assimilationist would suppress have their own peculiar standards of excellence and beauty, and exercise different and peculiar sets of our abilities. Hence given the human need to engage in, and express the self in, all-around activity, though we could, for example, engage in the unalienated activity of philosophizing in the assimilationist society, we could not *replace* sport with philosophizing.

Self-Esteem. Turning to the second cost of the assimilationist ideal, I now argue that in cutting off opportunities to engage in unalienated activity, the assimilationist society cuts off opportunities to acquire self-esteem.

Following Rawls, I take self-esteem as including "a person's sense of his own value, his secure conviction that his conception of his good, his plan of life, is worth carrying out."[23] As Rawls further notes, one of the two main sorts of circumstances that support a person's self-esteem is finding his "person and deeds appreciated and confirmed by others who are likewise esteemed and their association enjoyed" . . . "unless our endeavors are appreciated by our associates it is impossible for us to maintain the conviction that they are worthwhile."[24] This theory that a person's self-esteem depends on his associates' appreciation of his endeavors has long been recognized by social theorists. Without denying that appreciation of any of our endeavors is likely to support self-esteem, I argue that appreciation of our unalienated activity is especially important.

If alienated activity is activity one feels to be somehow not one's own activity, that is, not activity which expresses one's own ideas and aspirations, the fact that others appreciate it is unlikely to give much support to one's self-esteem. Support for one's self-esteem would seem to come more surely from others' appreciation of activity one feels to be an expression of one's own ideas and aspirations, that is, activity which is truly an expression of oneself. But such activity is unalienated activity. Further, since unalienated activity is done only for itself and for no ulterior motive, all other considerations can be set aside in order to achieve excellence and beauty. Consequently, there can be much for others to appreciate in one's unalienated activity. For these reasons, it would seem that an opportunity to engage in unalienated activity is also an important opportunity to acquire self-esteem. Hence in curtailing opportunities for unalienated activity, the assimilationists curtail opportunities to acquire self-esteem. And that is a serious cost.

However, it may seem that others' appreciation of one's endeavors, especially one's unalienated activity, is a chancy way to secure self-esteem. For what if one never achieves excellence or beauty? Must one lack self-esteem? This does not seem to be necessarily the case. If it is not, there must be another support for self-esteem that I have not mentioned. Further, if it flourishes in the assimilationist society, my present objection will seem less important.

What this other support for self-esteem could be may be suggested by Bernard Williams's distinction between regarding a person's life, and actions from a "technical point of view," and regarding them from "the human point of view."[25] It may be urged that what is important to persons' self-esteem is not so much that we appreciate their endeavors, which is only to see them from the technical point of view, but that we appreciate what it is for them to attempt what they attempted, which is to see them from the human point of view. I agree that because appreciation from the human point of view can be accorded irrespective of the success or importance of our endeavors—and is to that extent unconditional—it probably offers a far more secure support for self-esteem than the appreciation accorded from the technical point of view. The question is whether the human point of view is likely to flourish in the assimilationist society. Though it is possible, I think there is reason to doubt it. To regard persons from the "human point of view," we must consider their endeavors important just because they are important *to them*. Thus, as Williams notes, from the human point of view, we regard the failed inventor, "not merely as failed inventor, but as a man who wanted to be a successful inventor," that is, as one to whom inventing was important.[26] But, as we have seen, whatever its ultimate significance many people find sport important. Hence the assimilationist's proposal to eliminate it casts doubt on the assumption that he or she views the members of the ideal society from the human point of view.

Finally, the fact that the costs of the assimilationist society involve essentially unalienated activity shows how inadequate Wasserstrom's reassurance is that the "occupational cases" that would have to be phased out are "infrequent and peripheral."[27] It is inadequate because the important costs of his reforms are not the elimination of the few "occupational cases'' that the industrial revolution would have eliminated anyway. They are the elimination of the unalienated activity that the industrial revolution, by increasing our leisure time, has simultaneously made more possible and more important. Thus, perhaps what is most paradoxical is the assimilationist's belief that the industrial and technological revolution will reduce the significance of the differences between the sexes. For if I am right the very *opposite* is the truth.

2

At this point, critics may grant that I have pointed to some hitherto unnoticed costs of the sexually blind society, but maintain that I have not shown that society to be unjustified because I have not shown that it is not *worth* the costs. In particular, they may argue that the assimilationist society is worth the costs I mention because it gains so much for sexual equality. . . .

My first objection is that it is not necessary to incur the costs of the assimilationist society in order to have equality of opportunity between the sexes. These costs are the loss of opportunities to engage in unalienated activities and to achieve self-esteem, which are incurred by the elimination of all sex-activity correlations. But it is not necessary to eliminate correlations between sex and activity in order to have equality of opportunity between the sexes. Sex roles do subvert that equality, and perhaps human beings do tend to change sex-activity correlations into sex roles. Thus, the bare existence of correlations between sex and activities may engender a societal expectation that the sexes tend to excel at different activities, and this in turn can lead to societal factors that actively discourage women and men from pursuing certain activities.[28] When this occurs, sex roles exist and equality of opportunity ceases to exist. The point, however, is that sex-activity correlations need not thus develop into sex roles.[29] There is no reason that people cannot learn to successfully resist the tendency to move from a perception of sex-activity correlations to instituting sex roles. . . .

It could be said that though abolishing sex-activity correlations is not necessary for sexual equality, it makes that equality more secure: If we do not notice our sexual differences we can hardly discriminate against each other on their basis. Further, it could be argued that the alternative arrangement I propose would leave society with a built-in potential for conflict between the sexes, and that the more harmonious society that sexual blindness would secure would be infinitely superior. But even this considerably weakened case for sexual blindness collapses. Though sexual blindness may give us a safer enjoyment of sexual equality as equality of opportunity between the sexes, it does so at the expense of a more fundamental precept of egalitarianism, in terms of which equality of opportunity is itself justified.

That precept, which I refer to as equality of respect, is that each person has an equal right to the maximum opportunity, compatible with a like opportunity for others, to express himself or herself and to exercise and develop his or her talents as he or she sees fit.[30] It is clearly a stronger requirement than equality of opportunity. As I defined it, and as it is commonly understood, equality of opportunity is equality of opportunity to gain available positions or careers. Hence, since we can express ourselves and exercise and develop our talents *outside* our positions and careers, equality of respect makes broader and stronger demands than equality of opportunity. More importantly—for the egalitarian at least—it is the precept in terms of which equality of opportunity is justified. Thus one reason why equality of opportunity is so important is that although careers are not the only avenues of self-expression and self-realization, they are major avenues of self-expression and self-realization.

Now the assimilationists do propose to sacrifice equality of respect for equality of opportunity. As we have seen, they propose to eliminate a substantial portion of our unalienated activities for the sake of sexual blindness. These activities are an especially rich medium of self-expression and self-realization, and probably for some people more than others. Consequently, to eliminate such activities for the sake of sexual blindness is to sacrifice equality of respect for sexual blindness. But the purpose of sexual blindness is that it secures equality of opportunity between the sexes. Hence the assimilationists propose to sacrifice equality of respect for equality of opportunity. Finally, since it is equality of respect which justifies equality of opportunity, their position is incoherent.

Notes

[1] Richard A. Wasserstrom, "Racism, Sexism and Preferential Treatment: An Approach to the Topics," *U.C.L.A. Law Review 24* (February 1977): 603.

[2] Ibid., p. 604.

[3] Ibid.

[4] Ibid., p. 605.

[5] Ibid., p. 606.

[6] Ibid., p. 611 n 59.

[7] Ibid.

[8] Ibid., italics in the original.

[9] Ibid.

[10] Karl Marx, "Alienated Labour" in *Karl Marx Selected Writings*, edited by David McLellan (Oxford: Oxford University Press, 1977), p. 80.

[11] For further discussion of this see Richard Schact, *Alienation* (Garden City, NY: Anchor Books, 1971), pp. 100, 101.

[12] Karl Marx, "Alienated Labor" in *Karl Marx Selected Writings*, p. 80.

[13] Karl Marx, "Grundrisse" in *Karl Marx Selected Writings*, p. 368.

[14] Karl Marx, "Alienated Labor" in *Karl Marx Selected Writings*, p. 82.

[15] John Rawls, *A Theory of Justice* (Cambridge: Harvard University Press, 1971), p. 427.

[16] Ibid., p. 426.

[17] Ibid., p. 427.

[18] Ibid., p. 429.

[19] Ibid., p. 431.

[20] Jan Boxill develops this theme in "Sport as unalienated activity," unpublished manuscript.

[21] Rawls, *A Theory of Justice*, p. 429.

[22] Ibid., p. 427.

[23] Ibid., p. 440.

[24] Ibid., p. 441.

[25] Bernard Williams, "The Idea of Equality," in Joel Feinberg, editor, *Moral Concepts* (London: Oxford University Press, 1970), p. 159.

[26] Ibid.

[27] Wasserstrom, "Racism, Sexism and Preferential Treatment," p. 611, n 59.

[28] On this point see Joyce Trebilcot, "Sex Roles: The Argument From Nature," in *Sex Equality*, edited by Jane English (Englewood Cliffs, NJ: Prentice-Hall, 1977), p. 125. From *Ethics*, 85 (1975): 249–55.

[29] Ibid.

[30] This conception is close, though not identical with Dworkin's "equality of respect and concern." See Ronald Dworkin, *Taking Rights Seriously* (Cambridge: Harvard University Press, 1977), pp. 272, 273.

JOYCE TREBILCOT
TWO FORMS OF ANDROGYNISM

Traditional concepts of women and men, of what we are and should be as females and males, of the implications of sex for our relationships to one another and for our places in society, are not acceptable. But what models, if any, should we adopt to replace them? In this paper I consider just two of the alternatives discussed in recent literature—two versions of androgynism.

In discussing these two views I follow the convention of distinguishing between sex (female and male) and gender (feminine and masculine). Sex is biological, whereas gender is psychosocial. Thus, for example, a person who is biologically female may be—in terms of psychological characteristics or social roles—feminine or masculine, or both.

Although what counts as feminine and masculine varies among societies and over time, I use these terms here to refer to the gender concepts traditionally dominant in our own society. Femininity, on this traditional view, has nurturing as its core: it centers on the image of woman as mother, as provider of food, warmth, and emotional sustenance. Masculinity focuses on mastery: it comprises the notion of man struggling to overcome obstacles, to control nature, and also the notion of man as patriarch or leader in society and the family.

From Joyce Trebilcot, "Two Forms of Androgynism," *Journal of Social Philosophy* 8 (1977): 4–8. Reprinted with the permission of the editor and the author. An earlier version of this paper was read for the Society for Women in Philosophy at the American Philosophical Association meeting, Pacific Division, San Diego, California, March 1975. My thanks to Professors Jane English and Mary Anne Warren of SWIP and especially to Professor Kathryn Guberman of the Women's Studies Program at Washington University for discussions of this topic.

The first form of androgynism to be discussed here takes the word "androgyny" literally, so to speak. In this word the Greek roots for man (*andros*) and woman (*gynē*) exist side by side. According to the first form of androgynism, both feminine and masculine characteristics should exist "side by side" in every individual: each woman and man should develop personality traits and engage in activities traditionally assigned to only one sex. Because this view postulates a single ideal for everyone, I call it mono-androgynism, or, for brevity, M.

Monoandrogynism, insofar as it advocates shared roles, is now official policy in a number of countries. For example, the Swedish government presented a report to the United Nations in 1968 specifying that in Sweden, "every individual, regardless of sex, shall have the same practical opportunities not only for education and employment but also fundamentally the same responsibility for his or her own financial support as well as shared responsibility for child upbringing and housework."[1]

Closer to home, Jessie Bernard, in her discussion of women's roles, distinguishes the one-role view, according to which woman's place is in the home; the two-role pattern, which prescribes a combination of the traditional housewife-mother functions and work outside the home; and what she calls the "shared-role ideology" which holds "that children should have the care of both parents, that all who benefit from the services supplied in the household should contribute to them, and that both partners should share in supporting the household."[2]

Caroline Bird in her chapter "The Androgynous Life" writes with approval of role-sharing. She also suggests that the ideal person "combines characteristics usually attributed to men with characteristics usually attributed to women."[3]

The psychological dimension of M is stressed by Judith M. Bardwick. In her essay "Androgyny and Humanistic Goals, or Goodbye, Cardboard People," she discusses a view according to which the ideal or "healthy" person would have traits of both genders. "We would then expect," she says, "both nurturance and competence, openness and objectivity, compassion and competitiveness from both women and men, as individuals, according to what they were doing."[4]

The work of these and other writers provides the basis for a normative theory, M, which prescribes a single ideal for everyone: the person who is, in both psychological characteristics and social roles, both feminine and masculine.

The second form of androgynism shares with the first the principle that biological sex should not be a basis for judgments about the appropriateness of gender characteristics. It differs from the first, however, in that it advocates not a single ideal but rather a variety of options including "pure" femininity and masculinity as well as any combination of the two. According to this view, all alternatives with respect to gender should be equally available to and equally approved for everyone, regardless of sex. Thus, for example, a female might acceptably develop as a completely feminine sort of person, as both feminine and masculine in any proportion, or as wholly masculine. Because this view prescribes a variety of acceptable models, I call it polyandrogynism, or *P*.[5]

Constantina Safilios-Rothschild supports *P* in her recent book *Women and Social Policy*. In this work she makes a variety of policy recommendations aimed at bringing about the liberation of both sexes. Liberation requires, she says, that individuals live "according to their wishes, inclinations, potentials, abilities, and needs rather than according to the prevailing stereotypes about sex roles and sex-appropriate modes of thought and behavior." Some persons, she adds, "might *choose* to behave according to their sex's stereotypic . . . patterns. But some women and some men may *choose*, if they are so inclined, to take options in some or all of the life sectors now limited to the opposite sex."[6]

Carolyn Heilbrun's work also suggests *P*. In *Toward a Recognition of Androgyny* she writes, "The ideal toward which I believe we should move is best described by the term 'androgyny.' This ancient Greek word . . . defines a condition under which the characteristics of the sexes, and the human impulses expressed by men and women, are not rigidly assigned. Androgyny seeks to liberate the individual from the confines of the appropriate." Androgyny suggests, Heilbrun says, "a full range of experience open to individuals who may, as women, be aggressive, as men, tender; it suggests a spectrum upon which human beings choose their places without regard to propriety or custom."[7]

This second form of androgynism focuses on a variety of options rather than on the single model of the part-woman/part-man (that is, of the androgyne in the classic sense). It is appropriate, however, to extend the term "androgynism" to apply to it; for, like *M*, it seeks to break the connection between sex and gender.

For both forms of androgynism, the postulated ideals are best construed so as to exclude aspects of traditional gender concepts which are morally objectionable. Femininity should not be taken to include, for example, weakness, foolishness, or incompetence. Similarly, tendencies such as those to authoritarianism and violence should be eliminated from the concept of masculinity. Most importantly, aspects of the gender concepts which prescribe female submissiveness and male domination (over women and over other men) must, on moral grounds, be excluded from both the single ideal advocated by *M* and the range of options recommended by *P*.

Either form of androgyny may, in the long run, lead to major changes in human attributes. It is often suggested that the androgyne is a person who is feminine part of the time and masculine part of the time. But such compartmentalization might be expected to break down, so that the feminine and masculine qualities would influence one another and be modified. Imagine a person who is at the same time and in the same respect both nurturant and mastery-oriented, emotional and rational, cooperative and competitive, and so on. I shall not undertake here to speculate on whether this is possible, or, if it is, on how such qualities might combine.

The point is just that androgyny in the long run may lead to an integrating of femininity and masculinity that will yield new attributes, new kinds of personalities. The androgyne at this extreme would perhaps be not part feminine and part masculine, but neither feminine nor masculine, a person in whom the genders disappear.

I turn now to the question of which of these two forms of androgynism is more acceptable. I am not concerned here to evaluate these positions in relation to other alternatives (for example, to the traditional sexual consti- tution of society or to matriarchy).[8] For the sake of this discussion, I as- sume that either M or P is preferable to any alternative, and that the prob- lem is only to decide between them. Let us first consider this problem not as abstract speculation, and not as a problem for some distant society, but rather as an immediate issue for our own society. The question is then: Which form of androgynism is preferable as a guide to action for us here and now?

Suppose we adopt M. Our task then is to provide opportunities, en- couragement, and perhaps even incentives for those who are now feminine to be also masculine, and conversely. Suppose, on the other hand, that we adopt P. Our task is to create an environment in which, without reference to sex, people choose among all (moral) gender alternatives. How can this best be accomplished? What is required, clearly, is that the deeply- entrenched normative connection between sex and gender be severed. Vir- tually everyone now, in formulating preferences for the self and in judging the appropriateness of gender characteristics for others, at least on some occasions takes it, consciously or otherwise, that the sex of the individual in question is a relevant consideration: that one is female tends to count in favor of a feminine trait and against a masculine one, and conversely. In order to break this connection, it must be shown that masculinity is ac- ceptable for females and femininity for males. There must, then, be opportunities, encouragement, and perhaps even incentives for gender- crossing. But this is what is required by M. Hence, under present condi- tions, the two forms of androgynism prescribe the same course of action— that is, the promotion of gender-crossing.

The question "Which form of androgynism is preferable here and now?" then, is misconstrued. If one is an androgynist of either sort, what one must do now is seek to break the normative connection between sex and gender by bringing about gender-crossing. However, once the habit of taking sex as a reason for gender evaluation is overcome, or is at least much weaker and less widespread than it is today, then the two forms of androgynism do prescribe different courses of action. In particular, on M "pure" gender is condemned, but on P it is accepted. Let us consider, then, which version of androgynism is preferable for a hypothetical future society in which femininity and masculinity are no longer normatively associated with sex.

The major argument in favor of P is, of course, that because it stipu- lates a variety of acceptable gender alternatives it provides greater gender freedom than *M*. Now, freedom is a very high priority value, so arguments for *M* must be strong indeed. Let us consider, then, two arguments used to support *M* over *P*—one psychological, one ethical.

The psychological argument holds that in a society which is open with respect to gender, many people are likely to experience anxiety when faced with the need, or opportunity, to choose among different but equally acceptable gender models. Consider the words of Judith M. Bardwick:

> People need guidelines, directions that are agreed upon because they help each individual to know where one ought to go, how one can get there, and how far one is from one's goal. It is easier to sustain frustration that comes from knowing how far you are from your objective or what barriers are in your way than it is to sustain the anxiety that comes from not being sure about what you want to do or what others want you to do. It will be necessary, then, to develop new formulations by which people will guide their lives.[9]

Bardwick says that anxiety "comes from not being sure about what you want to do or what others want you to do." But in a society of the sort proposed by *P*, the notion that one should seek to please others in deciding among gender models would be rejected; ideally "what others want you to do" in such a society is to make your own decisions. Of course there is still the problem of not being sure about what *you* want to do. Presumably, under *P*, people would provide one another with help and support in finding suitable life styles. Nevertheless, it could be that for some, choosing among alternatives would be anxiety-producing. On the other hand, under *M*, the lack of approved alternatives could produce frustration. Hence, the argument from anxiety should be paired with an argument from frustration. In *M*, socialization is designed to make everyone androgynous (in ways similar, perhaps, to those which have traditionally produced exclusive femininity and masculinity in our own society), and frustration is part of the cost. In *P*, socialization is directed toward enabling people to perceive, evaluate, and choose among alternatives, and there is a risk of anxiety. We are not now in a position to decide whether the frustration or the anxiety is worse, for there are no data on the numbers of people likely to suffer these emotions nor on the extent of the harm that they are likely to do. Hence, neither the argument from anxiety nor the argument from frustration is of any help in deciding between the two forms of androgynism.

I turn now to a more persuasive argument for *M*, one which claims that androgyny has universal value. This argument supports *M* not, as the argument from anxiety does, because *M* prescribes some norm or other, but rather because of the content of the norm. The argument holds that both traditional genders include qualities that have value, qualities that it would be good for everyone to have. Among the elements of femininity, candidates for universal value are openness and responsiveness to needs and feelings, and being gentle, tender, intuitive, sensitive, expressive, considerate, cooperative, compassionate. Masculine qualities appealed to in this connection include being logical, rational, objective, efficient, responsible, independent, courageous. It is claimed, then, that there are some aspects of both genders (not necessarily all or only the ones I have mentioned) which are desirable for everyone, which we should value both in ourselves and in one another. But if there are aspects of femininity and masculinity which are valuable in this way—which are, as we might call them, virtues—they are *human* virtues, and are desirable for everyone. If Smith is a better person for being compassionate or courageous, then so is Jones, and never mind the sex of Smith or Jones. Hence, the argument concludes, the world envisioned by *M,* in which everyone or nearly everyone is both feminine and masculine, is one in which life for everyone is more rewarding than the world advocated by *P,* in which some people are of only one gender; therefore we should undertake to bring about *M.*

The argument claims, then, that both genders embody traits that it would be valuable for everyone to have. But how is this claim to be tested? Let us adopt the view that to say that something is valuable for everyone is, roughly, to say that if everyone were unbiased, well-informed, and thinking and feeling clearly, everyone would, in fact, value it. As things are now, it is difficult or impossible to predict what everyone would value under such conditions. But there is an alternative. We can seek to establish conditions in which people do make unbiased, informed, etc., choices, and see whether they then value both feminine and masculine traits.

But this reminds us, of course, of the program of *P. P* does not guarantee clear thought and emotional sensitivity, but it does propose an environment in which people are informed about all gender options and are unbiased with respect to them. If, in this context, all or most people, when they are thinking clearly, etc., tend to prefer, for themselves and others, both feminine and masculine virtues, we will have evidence to support the claim that androgyny has universal value. (In this case, *P* is likely to change into *M.*) On the other hand, if "pure" gender is preferred by many, we should be skeptical of the claim that androgyny has universal value. (In this case we should probably seek to preserve *P.*) It appears, then, that in order to discover whether *M* is preferable to *P,* we should seek to bring about *P.*

In summary, we have noted the argument from freedom, which supports *P;* arguments from anxiety and frustration, which are indecisive; and the argument from universal value, whose analysis suggests the provisional adoption of *P.* As far as I know, there are no additional major arguments which can plausibly be presented now for either side of the issue. Given, then, the problem of deciding between *M* and *P* without reference to other alternatives, my tentative conclusion is that because of the great value of freedom, and because in an atmosphere of gender-freedom we will be in a good position to evaluate the major argument for *M* (that is, the argument from the universal value of androgyny), *P* is preferable to *M.*

Of course all we have assumed about the specific nature of the hypothetical society for which we are making this judgment is that the connection between sex and gender would be absent, as would be the unacceptable components of traditional gender concepts, particularly dominance and submission. It might be, then, that particular social conditions would constitute grounds for supporting *M* rather than *P*. For example, if the society in question were hierarchical with leadership roles tightly held by the predominantly masculine individuals, and if leaders with feminine characteristics were more likely to bring about changes of significant value (for example, eliminating war or oppression), it could reasonably be argued that *M*, in which everyone, including leaders, has both feminine and masculine characteristics, would be preferable to *P*. But such considerations are only speculative now.

Notes

[1] Official Report to the United Nations on the Status of Women in Sweden, 1968. Quoted in Rita Liljeström, "The Swedish Model," in *Sex Roles in Changing Society*, ed. Georgene H. Seward and Robert C. Williamson (New York: Random House, 1970), p. 200.

[2] Jessie Bernard, *Women and the Public Interest* (Chicago: Aldine, 1971); and idem, *The Future of Marriage* (New York: Bantam Books, 1972). The quotation is from the latter book, p. 279.

[3] Caroline Bird, *Born Female* (New York: Pocket Books, 1968), p. xi.

[4] Judith M. Bardwick, "Androgyny and Humanistic Goals, or Goodbye, Cardboard People," in *The American Woman: Who Will She Be?* ed. Mary Louise McBee and Kathryn A. Blake (Beverly Hills, Calif.: Glencoe Press, 1974), p. 61.

[5] "Monoandrogynism" and "polyandrogynism" are perhaps not very happy terms, but I have been unable to find alternatives which are both descriptive and non-question-begging. In an earlier version of this paper I used "A_1" and "A_2" but these labels are not as perspicuous as "*M*" and "*P*." Mary Anne Warren, in "The Ideal of Androgyny" (unpublished) refers to "the strong thesis" and "the weak thesis," but this terminology tends to prejudice judgment as to which view is preferable. Hence, I use "*M*" and "*P*."

[6] Constantina Safilios-Rothschild, *Women and Social Policy* (Englewood Cliffs, N.J.: Prentice-Hall, 1974), p. 7; emphasis hers.

[7] Carolyn Heilbrun, *Toward a Recognition of Androgyny* (New York: Harper & Row, 1973), pp. 7–8.

[8] My current view is that we should work for the universal realization of women's values; but that is another paper. (For some arguments against the use of the term "androgyny" in feminist theory, see, for example, Mary Daly, "The Qualitative Leap beyond Patriarchal Religion," *Quest: A Feminist Quarterly*, vol. 1, no. 4 [Spring 1975], pp. 29ff.; and Janice Raymond, "The Illusion of Androgyny," *Quest*, vol. 2, no. 1 [Summer 1975].)

[9] Bardwick, op. cit., p. 50.

chapter 10

The Justice of Capitalism

INTRODUCTION

Do principles of right conduct have implications for the organization of the economy? More specifically, is capitalism a just system or is it inevitably unjust? These questions are complex, for not only is there disagreement about principles of right conduct, there is also disagreement about the nature of capitalism and its morally relevant characteristics.

Capitalism is the economic system within which private *capital* (wealth used to produce more wealth) controls the production of goods and services. It contrasts with earlier hierarchical and status systems (feudalism); with systems of centralized governmental control (state socialism); and with decentralized control by workers (syndicalism). The connection (or lack of connection) between these economic arrangements and such political arrangements as constitutional democracy is much debated.

The justice of capitalism cannot without extensive argument be based upon the justice of a democratic society with protection of individual political, legal, and religious liberty; there are socialists and syndicalists who argue against capitalism and yet consider such individual liberties all-important. There are, however, defenders of capitalism who claim that individual liberty in other spheres of life crucially depends upon the free enterprise system in the economic sphere. That dispute is not the topic of this chapter. Rather, the topic is the justice of capitalism understood as an *economic system,* and the primary question addressed is whether it is an injustice that capitalism leads to a very unequal distribution of wealth.

The Question of Distributive Justice   The question then of the justice of capitalism as an economic system is, first of all, the question of the *distributive justice* of this economic system. Are the workers treated unjustly when the company or the individual employer makes a profit by selling the product or service that the workers provide? Is it an injustice that middlemen such as real-estate brokers, bankers, and assorted speculators can become wealthy while some skilled and needed professionals (nurses, for instance) cannot become wealthy through their occupations? Is the

294

provision of equal opportunity to pursue success possible within a capitalist system?

Fulfillment in Work   But there are other questions of justice distinct from those of distribution. These concern the quality of life workers experience as they pursue their occupations. Critics of capitalism claim that workers are deprived not only of the full value of their work but are also deprived of meaningfulness and self-expression in their working lives. They are *alienated* from their work, seeing it as a mere instrumental, alien task that they must perform in order to "make a living." Workers in a capitalist system do not identify with their work, and so the time and energy spent in work is seen as a subtraction from their true lives. The critics of capitalism thus see even the well-paid industrial worker as a victim of injustice.

Defenders of capitalism emphasize the freedom from work created by advanced capitalism. Workers have an increasing amount of time to live their lives as they wish, finding significance and expressing themselves in leisure. For to be honest, even with worker participation in the control of a factory and such innovations as team responsibility forming an aspect of production, it is a romantic notion that workers feel fulfilled through working in a modern factory. It is in their personal lives, most importantly, that workers fulfill themselves, and capitalism offers the best chance for the most people to pursue such satisfactions successfully. But opponents of capitalism see the consumer society within which the worker must find fulfillment as itself distorted and degraded by manipulation for profit.

Natural Law   The natural-law theory can accept any of the major economic systems, though it will not accept all conduct within these economic systems. Natural resources, including the land itself, are for the common good. Even an individual's talents and energies are to be used, not only for his own welfare (though that use has a legitimate priority), but also for the welfare of others. Private property is a useful institution of the positive law of particular nations. Although not based on natural law, private property is a consistent addition to natural law, for it is more efficient to have particular persons responsible for administering particular property. However, in administering private property the owner ought to see himself as a steward attempting to contribute to the common good.[1] It is possible for a natural-law theorist to criticize a capitalist system to the extent that it abandons this stewardship of resources for the common good. The natural-law answer to the question of the distributive justice of capitalism is that whether a capitalist system is distributively just will depend upon the conduct of people within a system that is, in its general arrangements, *one* permissible way the positive law may strive to promote the common good. Whether to change such a system if it fails to promote the common good depends upon whether an achievable alternative will do better. In changing an economic system no violations of natural law can be morally justified no matter how good the goal (so, for instance, killing the innocent during a revolution would be prohibited).

The natural-law approach to the question of worker fulfillment depends upon the Aristotelian conception of happiness as activity in accordance with human excellence. A good human life requires the engagement of such distinctively human capacities as rationality. And so the reduction of work life to a set of mindless routines will be seen as unfortunate. Yet if capitalist production leaves workers increasingly at leisure to develop their humanity, all things considered, there *could* be a gain in human flourishing. Natural-law theorists, however, will find the hedonistic consumerism of capitalist culture a defective setting for human flourishing, and perhaps fault capitalism itself for this cultural degradation.

Natural Rights   Historically, the theory of natural rights developed at the same time as capitalism. Unlike the natural-law tradition out of which it grew, natural-rights theory is thoroughly individualist. Individual rights are central to this view, and private property is given a foundation in natural justice rather than merely being grounded in positive law. Natural-rights theory views private property as a right independent of and conceptually prior to the positive laws of the state. This right to hold property is filled out with theories of acquisition and the transfer of property. The just acquisition of property, in John Locke's view, occurs when someone mixes his labor with an object (for example, by picking an apple or by cultivating land). The object must be unowned, and there must be enough left for others. Also, one cannot rightfully appropriate more than one can use; however, this last qualification becomes inoperative once there is a monetary system, for possessions can then be converted to money, which does not spoil.[2] Transfer of property is at the discretion of the owner, as long as he does not violate the rights of other individuals.

Natural-rights theory in its traditional form gives capitalism a resounding endorsement. Governments are instituted to protect individual rights, including property rights. Freedom of contract is an important individual right in natural-rights theory and in capitalism. The company or individual employer offers an employment contract to a potential employee. Each contracting individual is free to enter into such a contract. Neither party has a legitimate claim of injustice as long as the terms of the contract are kept. It might be claimed that the employee who needs a job in order to make a living really has little freedom to turn down the offer. But on natural rights theory these differences in bargaining position are morally irrelevant, for the employer has no duty to use his property to promote the common good and the employee has no right to benefit from another individual's property.

The ethical minimalism of the theory of natural rights leads to a quick answer to the question of worker fulfillment. Although it might be desirable for workers to feel fulfilled in their work, there is no *right* of individuals to such fulfillment. Each person has the right to pursue his own conception of the good life, as long as the individual rights of others are respected.

But no one can demand of others that they aid in this pursuit of happiness. The worker and the employer are free contractors, owing each other no more than the contract specifies. No injustice would be done if the employer simply closed down his business, offering the workers no further opportunity for work, whether or not it were humanly fulfilling.

Kant A Kantian approach to the question of distributive justice depends upon the distinction between perfect and imperfect duties and the distinction between ethical and juridical duties. A *perfect duty* (for instance, the duty not to defraud) allows no discretion on the part of the agent. With *imperfect duties* (for instance, the duty to develop one's talents), there is discretion as to many details, for only the general goal is obligatory. A *juridical duty* is one that may be enforced by external coercion by the state; an *ethical duty* cannot be coerced. Justice is the name for perfect juridical rights. The employer has a property right in his capital and what it buys. Property is, for Kant, protected as a natural right. And so Kant's view coincides with the natural-rights approach. Employer and worker are related by contract, and it is no injustice to pay the worker only what was agreed.[3]

This is the view of Kant himself, and there is little doubt that he would have found no injustice in the system of capitalism. But there are two considerations that qualify a Kantian endorsement of capitalism. The first qualification is that Kant held that there is an imperfect, ethical duty to promote the happiness of others. This duty of beneficence allows great discretion on the part of the agent; each individual must decide *how* to help others. Although an employer will not be guilty of an injustice if he drives a hard bargain with a worker, he may still be acting immorally if this lack of beneficence is a general pattern in his life.

The second qualification concerns the question of worker fulfillment. The Kantian principle of respect for persons requires that humanity always be treated as an end in itself and never *merely* as a means. A slave is treated merely as a means, while a wage-laborer is not merely a tool. The free consent of the laborer to the contract allows the employer to make use of him without degrading him below the dignity of a rational, free agent. However, if the conditions of work deprive the worker of a sense of self-worth, it could be argued that there is a failure to respect the worker as an end in himself, regardless of the worker's consent to the contract. There could be a Kantian argument for worker participation based on the need to respect the rational humanity of all persons.

Marx Such an argument, in effect, is given in the early writings of Karl Marx.[4] In the "Economic and Philosophical Manuscripts of 1844," Marx attacked the way in which the worker is reduced to a mere thing in the process of capitalist production. Instead of expressing his free, conscious, *social* nature through his vital activity, the worker is reduced to an instrument. In alienated labor, "man makes his vital activity and essence a mere means to his existence."[5] In Marx's view, the freedom of individuals is itself social; it is through history that the *social* individual achieves freedom. Human freedom is not an existing metaphysical reality waiting for recognition (as Kant seems at times to think). Marx is not Kantian in this emphasis on the social and historical embeddedness of the rationality and consciousness that make humanity free. But the affirmation of the intrinsic value of free conscious activity is Kantian. Respect for the humanity of workers requires not only that they *see* themselves as autonomous and free in their private consciences (as in Kant) but also that they *make* themselves autonomous and free in their lives as economic producers.

Contractarianism   A contractarian view of the justice of capitalism depends upon two considerations. First, there must be fair equality of opportunity for everyone to pursue success within the system. Second, economic inequalities must be arranged so that they are to the greatest benefit of the least advantaged.[6] These conditions result from the self-interested calculation of the parties to the contract, who do not know what social and economic position they will occupy in the society.

Rawls's contractarian view has often been seen as a defense of welfare capitalism, if it is assumed that the least advantaged *do* indeed benefit economically from such a system. But Rawls himself has insisted that, regarding private property and socialist regimes, "which of these systems and the many intermediate forms most fully answers to the requirements of justice cannot . . . be determined in advance . . . since it depends in large part upon the traditions, institutions, and social forces of each country, and its particular historical circumstances."[7] It seems that Rawls, like Aquinas, has room for more than one permissible economic system.

However, there is more ground for an *attack* on capitalism within a contractarian approach than might at first appear. Mere economic benefit of the least advantaged will not suffice to show that in Rawls's sense they have benefited from the system. Benefit must include all of the primary goods, and self-respect is the most important of all. Although equality of basic liberties is crucial to fostering self-respect, there could be a contractarian argument that self-respect requires that workers have more dignity and self-determination in the workplace. Such an argument would lead the contractarian toward socialism on grounds that are Kantian in spirit, though not in letter.

Act Utilitarianism   Strictly speaking, there can be no such thing as an act-utilitarian approach to the question of whether the system of capitalism is just. An act utilitarian judges particular actions and so can approach the question of the justice of capitalism only by evaluating particular actions of (for instance) legislators, judges, corporate executives, and union officials. Voting for a statute or issuing a court order are particular actions, and an act utilitarian must evaluate each action by its consequences. In deliberating about what action to take, the agent will consider the foreseeable consequences of each alternative. Because of the complexity of particular cases, no general pattern of either supporting or modifying capitalism can be predicted for an act utilitarian. However, an act utilitarian will give little weight to arguments that a specific radical change in the economic system will promote the general welfare, for his *particular* action must be evaluated by foreseeable consequences, and any such radical change will require an improbable convergence of many particular actions of many individuals. If it is probable that the economic system will not change radically in the foreseeable future, then an act utilitarian will assume the continuation of the system in calculating the consequences of his particular actions, including actions which could have contributed to such an improbable change.

Rule Utilitarianism   Rule utilitarians can approach the justice of capitalism more directly, for they can evaluate alternative sets of rules. The acceptance-utility of a set of rules for economic arrangements is the net balance of happiness or satisfaction that would result from acceptance of the entire set of rules. The best economic system is the one that maximizes the amount of happiness. If the *distribution* of happiness is considered only as it effects the total amount of happiness (for instance, very unequal distribution may cause unhappiness), then rule utilitarianism will endorse capitalism to the extent that it does promote prosperity.

However, the distinction between *kinds* of pleasure or happiness found in John Stuart Mill might modify such an endorsement of capitalism.[8] If great importance is placed upon satisfactions deriving from the exercise of active rational faculties and the imagination, then a rule utilitarian might criticize capitalism on grounds of worker fulfillment. If the pleasures that are maximized for the workers (and perhaps even for the wealthy) are the passive pleasures which contribute little to human flourishing, then a truly human happiness might require modifications of capitalism to protect the interests of all. But if a utilitarian considers the distinction between *kinds* of satisfaction morally irrelevant (as did Jeremy Bentham), then such considerations of worker fulfillment will not be important as long as pleasures are maximized.

Readings   The problem case, *Lochner* v. *New York,* raises the issue of whether freedom of contract is the kind of right that proponents of human rights must view as fundamental. The issue is posed within American constitutional law, but it can be addressed as a moral question independent of that legal context.

The selection from F. A. Hayek argues within a natural-rights, individualistic framework. Hayek considers the very concept of social or distributive justice a confusion based upon a faulty comparison of "society" to an individual distributing rewards. For further discussion within this tradition, see the selection by Robert Nozick in Chapter 1.

The selection from Karl Marx attacks capitalist production as a form of alienation. To be alienated from something is to see it as foreign to the self, existing as a separate "other" rather than as an expression of oneself. Marx's critique of capitalism is Kantian in its emphasis upon free conscious activity as truly human, and in its attack on the degradation of the worker to the status of a mere tool.

The selection from John Stuart Mill is utilitarian, but with Mill's distinctive insistence that the satisfactions deriving from the higher faculties (intellect, imagination, and the sense of community) are all-important for human well-being. He argues for worker participation both on the grounds of efficiency and as a contribution to the cultivation of the higher faculties.

Notes

1 See St. Thomas Aquinas, *Summa Theologica*, II–II, Question 66.

2 John Locke, *Second Treatise of Civil Government*, chaps. 27–50.

3 See Immanuel Kant, *The Metaphysical Elements of Justice*, trans. John Ladd (Indianapolis, Ind.: Bobbs-Merrill, 1965), pp. 40, 98–99.

4 For a discussion of Marx as a humanist, see Erich Fromm, *Marx's Concept of Man* (New York: Frederick Unger, 1966); Kant's principle of respect for persons as ends in themselves is compared to Marx on pp. 53–54.

5 Karl Marx, "Economic and Philosophical Manuscripts of 1844," in *Karl Marx: Selected Writings*, ed. David McLellan (Oxford: Oxford University Press, 1977), p. 82.

6 John Rawls, *A Theory of Justice* (Cambridge, Mass.: Harvard University Press, 1971), p. 302.

7 Ibid., p. 274.

8 See John Stuart Mill, *Utilitarianism*, chap. 2, for an explanation of higher and lower pleasure.

Bibliography on the Justice of Capitalism

Cohen, G. A. "The Labor Theory of Value and the Concept of Exploitation." *Philosophy and Public Affairs* 8 (1979): 338–60.

De George, Richard, and Pichler, Joseph, eds. *Ethics, Free Enterprise, and Public Policy.* New York: Oxford University Press, 1978.

Feinberg, Joel. "Social Justice." *Social Philosophy.* Englewood Cliffs, N.J.: Prentice-Hall, 1973. Chapter 7.

Harrington, Michael. *Socialism.* New York: Bantam, 1973.

Hayek, F. A. *The Constitution of Liberty.* Chicago, Ill.: University of Chicago Press, 1960.

_____. *Law, Legislation and Liberty.* Vol. 1. *Rules and Order.* Chicago, Ill.: University of Chicago Press, 1973.

_____. *Law, Legislation and Liberty.* Vol. 2. *The Mirage of Social Justice.* Chicago, Ill.: University of Chicago Press, 1976.

Held, Virginia, ed. *Property, Profits, and Economic Justice.* Belmont, Calif.: Wadsworth, 1980.

Macpherson, C. B. *Democratic Theory: Essays in Retrieval.* Oxford: Oxford University Press, 1973.

_____. *The Political Theory of Possessive Individualism.* Oxford: Oxford University Press, 1962.

Marx, Karl. *Early Writings.* Translated and edited by T. B. Bottomore. New York: McGraw-Hill, 1964.

_____. *Selected Writings.* Edited by David McLellan. Oxford: Oxford University Press, 1977.

Nozick, Robert. *Anarchy, State, and Utopia.* New York: Basic Books, 1974.

Steiner, Hillel. "The Natural Right to the Means of Production." *Philosophical Quarterly*, 27 (1977): 41–49.

Wolff, Robert Paul. *The Poverty of Liberalism.* Boston: Beacon Press, 1968.

Problem Case

Lochner v. New York, 198 U.S. 45 (1905)

Joseph Lochner was convicted of violating the labor law of the state of New York. Lochner had permitted an employee to work for more than the sixty hours a week allowed for bakery workers by the statute. Lochner appealed to the federal courts, claiming that the statute deprived him of his rights under the U.S. Constitution and that it was not a valid exercise of the state's power to protect the public health and general welfare. The U.S. Supreme Court ruled that the relevant provision of the New York statute was unconstitutional as an arbitrary interference with the freedom of individuals to enter into contracts. The majority opinion stated that "the general right to make a contract in relation to his business is part of the liberty of the individual protected by the 14th Amendment to the Federal Constitution." In his dissenting opinion, Mr. Justice Holmes replied that "a Constitution is not intended to embody a particular economic theory, whether of paternalism and the organic relation of the citizen to the state or of *laissez faire*."

Does the state have the moral right to regulate the economy? What is the moral basis (if any) of freedom of contract?

F. A. HAYEK

THE ILLUSION OF "SOCIAL JUSTICE"

The most common attempts to give meaning to the concept of 'social justice' resort to egalitarian considerations and argue that every departure from equality of material benefits enjoyed has to be justified by some recognizable common interest which these differences serve. This is based on a specious analogy with the situation in which some human agency has to distribute rewards, in which case indeed justice would require that these rewards be determined in accordance with some recognizable rule of general applicability. But earnings in a market system, though people tend to regard them as rewards, do not serve such a function. Their rationale (if one may use this term for a role which was not designed but developed because it assisted human endeavour without people understanding how) is rather to indicate to people what they ought to do if the order is to be maintained on which they all rely. The prices which must be paid in a market economy for different kinds of labour and other factors of production if individual efforts are to match, although they will be affected by effort, diligence, skill, need, etc., cannot conform to any one of these magnitudes; and considerations of justice just do not make sense with respect to the determination of a magnitude which does not depend on anyone's will or desire, but on circumstances which nobody knows in their totality.

Reprinted from F. A. Hayek, *Law, Legislation and Liberty*, vol. 2, *The Mirage of Social Justice* (Chicago, Ill.: University of Chicago Press, 1976), by permission of the University of Chicago Press. © 1976 by F. A. Hayek.

The contention that all differences in earnings must be justified by some corresponding difference in deserts is one which would certainly not have been thought to be obvious in a community of farmers or merchants or artisans, that is, in a society in which success or failure were clearly seen to depend only in part on skill and industry, and in part on pure accident which might hit anyone—although even in such societies individuals were known to complain to God or fortune about the injustice of their fate. But, though people resent that their remuneration should in part depend on pure accident, that is in fact precisely what it must if the market order is to adjust itself promptly to the unavoidable and unforeseen changes in circumstances, and the individual is to be allowed to decide what to do. The now prevalent attitude could arise only in a society in which large numbers worked as members of organizations in which they were remunerated at stipulated rates for time worked. Such communities will not ascribe the different fortunes of its members to the operation of an impersonal mechanism which serves to guide the directions of efforts, but to some human power that ought to allocate shares according to merit.

The postulate of material equality would be a natural starting point only if it were a necessary circumstance that the shares of the different individuals or groups were in such a manner determined by deliberate human decision. In a society in which this were an unquestioned fact, justice would indeed demand that the allocation of the means for the satisfaction of human needs were effected according to some uniform principle such as merit or need (or some combination of these), and that, where the principle adopted did not justify a difference, the shares of the different individuals should be equal. The prevalent demand for material equality is probably often based on the belief that the existing inequalities are the effect of somebody's decision—a belief which would be wholly mistaken in a genuine market order and has still only very limited validity in the highly interventionist 'mixed' economy existing in most countries today. This now prevalent form of economic order has in fact attained its character largely as a result of governmental measures aiming at what was thought to be required by 'social justice.'

When the choice, however, is between a genuine market order, which does not and cannot achieve a distribution corresponding to any standard of material justice, and a system in which government uses its powers to put some such standard into effect, the question is not whether government ought to exercise, justly or unjustly, powers it must exercise in any case, but whether government should possess and exercise additional powers which can be used to determine the shares of the different members of society. The demand for 'social justice', in other words, does not merely require government to observe some principle of action according to uniform rules in those actions which it must perform in any case, but demands that it undertake additional activities, and thereby assume new responsibilities— tasks which are not necessary for maintaining law and order and providing for certain collective needs which the market could not satisfy.

The great problem is whether this new demand for equality does not conflict with the equality of the rules of conduct which government must enforce on all in a free society. There is, of course, a great difference between government treating all citizens according to the same rules in all the activities it undertakes for other purposes, and government doing what is required in order to place the different citizens in equal (or less unequal) material positions. Indeed, there may arise a sharp conflict between these two aims. Since people will differ in many attributes which government cannot alter, to secure for them the same material position would require that government treat them very differently. Indeed, to assure the same material position to people who differ greatly in strength, intelligence, skill, knowledge and perseverance as well as in their physical and social environment, government would clearly have to treat them very differently to compensate for those disadvantages and deficiencies it could not directly alter. Strict equality of those benefits which government could provide for all, on the other hand, would clearly lead to inequality of the material positions.

This, however, is not the only and not even the chief reason why a government aiming to secure for its citizens equal material positions (or any determined pattern of material welfare) would have to treat them very unequally. It would have to do so because under such a system it would have to undertake to tell people what to do. Once the rewards the individual can expect are no longer an appropriate indication of how to direct their efforts to where they are most needed, because these rewards correspond not to the value which their services have for their fellows, but to the moral merit or desert the persons are deemed to have earned, they lose the guiding function they have in the market order and would have to be replaced by the commands of the directing authority. A central planning office would, however, have to decide on the tasks to be allotted to the different groups or individuals wholly on grounds of expediency or efficiency and, in order to achieve its ends, would have to impose upon them very different duties and burdens. The individuals might be treated according to uniform rules so far as their rewards were concerned, but certainly not with respect to the different kinds of work they would have to be made to do. In assigning people to their different tasks, the central planning authority would have to be guided by considerations of efficiency and expediency and not by principles of justice or equality. No less than in the market order would the individuals in the common interest have to submit to great inequality—only these inequalities would be determined not by the interaction of individual skills in an impersonal process, but by the uncontradictable decision of authority.

As is becoming clear in ever increasing fields of welfare policy, an authority instructed to achieve particular results for the individuals must be given essentially arbitrary powers to make the individuals do what seems necessary to achieve the required result. Full equality for most cannot but mean the equal submission of the great masses under the command of some élite who manages their affairs. While an equality of rights under a limited government is possible and an essential condition of individual freedom, a claim for equality of material position can be met only by a government with totalitarian powers.

We are of course not wrong when we perceive that the effects on the different individuals and groups of the economic processes of a free society are not distributed according to some recognizable principle of justice. Where we go wrong is in concluding from this that they are unjust and that somebody is responsible and to be blamed for this. In a free society in which the position of the different individuals and groups is not the result of anybody's design—or could within such a society not be altered in accordance with a principle of general applicability—the differences in rewards cannot meaningfully be described as just or unjust. There are, no doubt, many kinds of individual actions which are aimed at affecting particular remunerations and which might be regarded as unjust. But there are no principles of individual conduct which would produce a pattern of distribution which as such could be called just, and therefore also no possibility for the individual to know what he would have to do to secure a just remuneration of his fellows.

Our whole system of morals is a system of rules of individual conduct, and in a Great Society no conduct guided by such rules, or by decisions of the individuals guided by such rules, could produce for the individuals results which would appear to us as just in the sense in which we regard designed rewards as just or unjust: simply because in such a society nobody has the power or the knowledge which would enable him to ensure that those affected by his actions will get what he thinks right for them to get. Nor could anyone who is assured remuneration according to some principle which is accepted as constituting 'social justice' be allowed to decide what he is to do: remuneration indicating how urgent it was that a certain work should be done could not be just in this sense, because the need for work of a particular kind would often depend on unforeseeable accidents and certainly not on the good intentions or efforts of those able to perform it. And an authority that fixed remunerations with the intention of thereby reducing the kind and number of people thought necessary in each occupation could not make these remunerations 'just', i.e. proportionate to desert, or need, or the merits of any other claim of the persons concerned, but would have to offer what was necessary to attract or retain the number of people wanted in each kind of activity.

. . . It is of course not to be denied that in the existing market order not only the results but also the initial chances of different individuals are often very different; they are affected by circumstances of their physical and social environment which are beyond their control but in many particular respects might be altered by some governmental action. The demand for equality of opportunity or equal starting conditions . . . appeals to, and has been supported by, many who in general favour the free market order. So far as this refers to such facilities and opportunities as are of necessity affected by governmental decisions (such as appointments to public office and the like), the demand was indeed one of the central points of classical liberalism, usually expressed by the French phrase 'la carrière ouverte aux talents'. There is also much to be said in favour of the government providing on an equal basis the means for the schooling of minors who are not yet fully responsible citizens, even though there are grave doubts whether we ought to allow government to administer them.

But all this would still be very far from creating real equality of opportunity, even for persons possessing the same abilities. To achieve this government would have to control the whole physical and human environment of all persons, and have to endeavour to provide at least equivalent chances for each; and the more government succeeded in these endeavours, the stronger would become the legitimate demand that, on the same principle, any still remaining handicaps must be removed—or compensated for by putting extra burden on the still relatively favoured. This would have to go on until government literally controlled every circumstance which could affect any person's well-being. Attractive as the phrase of equality of opportunity at first sounds, once the idea is extended beyond the facilities which for other reasons have to be provided by government, it becomes a wholly illusory ideal, and any attempt concretely to realize it apt to produce a nightmare.

. . . The idea that men ought to be rewarded in accordance with the assessed merits or deserts of their services 'to society' presupposes an authority which not only distributes these rewards but also assigns to the individuals the tasks for the performance of which they will be rewarded. In other words, if 'social justice' is to be brought about, the individuals must be required to obey not merely general rules but specific demands directed to them only. The type of social order in which the individuals are directed to serve a single system of ends is the organization and not the spontaneous order of the market, that is, not a system in which the individual is free because bound only by general rules of just conduct, but a system in which all are subject to specific directions by authority.

It appears sometimes to be imagined that a mere alteration of the rules of individual conduct could bring about the realization of 'social justice'. But there can be no set of such rules, no principles by which the individuals could so govern their conduct that in a Great Society the joint effect of their activities would be a distribution of benefits which could be described as materially just, or any other specific and intended allocation of advantages and disadvantages among particular people or groups. In order to achieve *any* particular pattern of distribution through the market process, each producer would have to know, not only whom his efforts will benefit (or harm), but also how well off all the other people (actually or potentially) affected by his activities will be as the result of the services they are receiving from other members of the society. As we have seen earlier, appropriate rules of conduct can determine only the formal character of the order of activities that will form itself, but not the specific advantages particular groups or individuals will derive from it. . . .

There is no reason why in a free society government should not assure to all protection against severe deprivation in the form of an assured minimum income, or a floor below which nobody need to descend. To enter into such an insurance against extreme misfortune may well be in the interest of all; or it may be felt to be a clear moral duty of all to assist, within the organized community, those who cannot help themselves. So long as such a uniform minimum income is provided outside the market to all those who, for any reason, are unable to earn in the market an adequate maintenance, this need not lead to a restriction of freedom, or conflict with the Rule of Law. The problems with which we are here concerned arise only when the remuneration for services rendered is determined by authority, and the impersonal mechanism of the market which guides the direction of individual efforts is thus suspended.

Perhaps the acutest sense of grievance about injustice inflicted on one, not by particular persons but by the 'system', is that about being deprived of opportunities for developing one's abilities which others enjoy. For this any difference of environment, social or physical, may be responsible, and at least some of them may be unavoidable. The most important of these is clearly inseparable from the institution of the family. This not only satisfies a strong psychological need but in general serves as an instrument for the transmission of important cultural values. There can be no doubt that those who are either wholly deprived of this benefit, or grew up in unfavourable conditions, are gravely handicapped; and few will question that it would be desirable that some public institution so far as possible should assist such unfortunate children when relatives and neighbours fail. Yet few will seriously believe (although Plato did) that we can fully make up for such a deficiency, and I trust even fewer that, because this benefit cannot be assured to all, it should, in the interest of equality, be taken from those who now enjoy it. Nor does it seem to me that even material equality could compensate for those differences in the capacity of enjoyment and of experiencing a lively interest in the cultural surroundings which a suitable upbringing confers.

There are of course many other irremediable inequalities which must seem as unreasonable as economic inequalities but which are less resented than the latter only because they do not appear to be man-made or the consequence of institutions which could be altered.

KARL MARX
ALIENATED LABOR

We shall begin from a *contemporary* economic fact. The worker becomes poorer the more wealth he produces and the more his production increases in power and extent. The worker becomes an ever cheaper commodity the more goods he creates. The *devaluation* of the human world increases in direct relation with the *increase in value* of the world of things. Labour does not only create goods; it also produces itself and the worker as a *commodity*, and indeed in the same proportion as it produces goods.

This fact simply implies that the object produced by labour, its product, now stands opposed to it as an *alien being*, as a *power independent* of the producer. The product of labour is labour which has been embodied in an object and turned into a physical thing; this product is an *objectification* of labour. The performance of work is at the same time its objectification. The performance of work appears in the sphere of political economy as a *vitiation* of the worker, objectification as a *loss* and as *servitude to the object*, and appropriation as *alienation*.

So much does the performance of work appear as vitiation that the worker is vitiated to the point of starvation. So much does objectification appear as loss of the object that the worker is deprived of the most essential things not only of life but also of work. Labour itself becomes an object which he can acquire only by the greatest effort and with unpredictable interruptions. So much does the appropriation of the object appear as alienation that the more objects the worker produces the fewer he can possess and the more he falls under the domination of his product, of capital.

All these consequences follow from the fact that the worker is related to the *product of his labour* as to an *alien* object. For it is clear on this presupposition that the more the worker expends himself in work the more powerful becomes the world of objects which he creates in face of himself, the poorer he becomes in his inner life, and the less he belongs to himself. It is just the same as in religion. The more of himself man attributes to God the less he has left in himself. The worker puts his life into the object, and his life then belongs no longer to himself but to the object. The greater his activity, therefore, the less he possesses. What is embodied in the product of his labour is no longer his own. The greater this product is, therefore, the more he is diminished. The *alienation* of the worker in his product means not only that his labour becomes an object, assumes an *external* existence, but that it exists independently, *outside himself,* and alien to him, and that it stands opposed to him as an autonomous power. The life which he has given to the object sets itself against him as an alien and hostile force.

. . . Let us now examine more closely the phenomenon of *objectifica-*

From Karl Marx, *Early Writings*, translated and edited by T. B. Bottomore (New York: McGraw-Hill, 1963), pp. 121–27, 129–31, by permission of the publisher.

tion; the worker's production and the *alienation* and *loss* of the object it produces, which is involved in it. The worker can create nothing without *nature*, without the *sensuous external world*. The latter is the material in which his labour is realized, in which it is active, out of which and through which it produces things.

But just as nature affords the *means of existence* of labour, in the sense that labour cannot *live* without objects upon which it can be exercised, so also it provides the *means of existence* in a narrower sense; namely the means of physical existence for the *worker* himself. Thus, the more the worker *appropriates* the external world of sensuous nature by his labour the more he deprives himself of *means of existence*, in two respects: first, that the sensuous external world becomes progressively less an object belonging to his labour or a means of existence of his labour, and secondly, that it becomes progressively less a means of existence in the direct sense, a means for the physical subsistence of the worker.

In both respects, therefore, the worker becomes a slave of the object; first, in that he receives an *object of work*, i.e. receives *work*, and secondly, in that he receives *means of subsistence*. Thus the object enables him to exist, first as a *worker* and secondly, as a *physical subject*. The culmination of this enslavement is that he can only maintain himself as a *physical subject* so far as he is a *worker*, and that it is only as a *physical subject* that he is a worker.

(The alienation of the worker in his object is expressed as follows in the laws of political economy: the more the worker produces the less he has to consume; the more value he creates the more worthless he becomes; the more refined his product the more crude and misshapen the worker; the more civilized the product the more barbarous the worker; the more powerful the work the more feeble the worker; the more the work manifests intelligence the more the worker declines in intelligence and becomes a slave of nature.) . . .

So far we have considered the alienation of the worker only from one aspect; namely, *his relationship with the products of his labour*. However, alienation appears not merely in the result but also in the *process of production*, within *productive activity* itself. How could the worker stand in an alien relationship to the product of his activity if he did not alienate himself in the act of production itself? The product is indeed only the *résumé* of activity, of production. Consequently, if the product of labour is alienation, production itself must be active alienation—the alienation of activity and the activity of alienation. The alienation of the object of labour merely summarizes the alienation in the work activity itself.

What constitutes the alienation of labour? First, that the work is *external* to the worker, that it is not part of his nature; and that, consequently, he does not fulfil himself in his work but denies himself, has a feeling of misery rather than well-being, does not develop freely his mental and physical energies but is physically exhausted and mentally debased. The worker, therefore, feels himself at home only during his leisure time, whereas at work he feels homeless. His work is not voluntary but imposed, *forced labour*. It is not the satisfaction of a need, but only a *means* for satisfying other needs. Its alien character is clearly shown by the fact that as soon as there is no physical or other compulsion it is avoided like the plague. External labour, labour in which man alienates himself, is a labour of self-sacrifice, of mortification. Finally, the external character of work for the worker is shown by the fact that it is not his own work but work for someone else, that in work he does not belong to himself but to another person.

Just as in religion the spontaneous activity of human fantasy, of the human brain and heart, reacts independently as an alien activity of gods or devils upon the individual, so the activity of the worker is not his own spontaneous activity. It is another's activity and a loss of his own spontaneity.

We arrive at the result that man (the worker) feels himself to be freely active only in his animal functions—eating, drinking and procreating, or at most also in his dwelling and in personal adornment—while in his human functions he is reduced to an animal. The animal becomes human and the human becomes animal.

Eating, drinking and procreating are of course also genuine human functions. But abstractly considered, apart from the environment of human activities, and turned into final and sole ends, they are animal functions.

We have now considered the act of alienation of practical human activity, labour, from two aspects: (1) the relationship of the worker to the *product of labour* as an alien object which dominates him. This relationship is at the same time the relationship to the sensuous external world, to natural objects, as an alien and hostile world; (2) the relationship of labour to the *act of production* within *labour*. This is the relationship of the worker to his own activity as something alien and not belonging to him, activity as suffering (passivity), strength as powerlessness, creation as emasculation, the *personal* physical and mental energy of the worker, his personal life (for what is life but activity?), as an activity which is directed against himself, independent of him and not belonging to him. This is *self-alienation* as against the above-mentioned alienation of the *thing*.

. . . We have now to infer a third characteristic of *alienated labour* from the two we have considered.

Man is a species-being not only in the sense that he makes the community (his own as well as those of other things) his object both practically and theoretically, but also (and this is simply another expression for the same thing) in the sense that he treats himself as the present, living species, as a *universal* and consequently free being.

Species-life, for man as for animals, has its physical basis in the fact that man (like animals) lives from inorganic nature, and since man is more universal than an animal so the range of inorganic nature from which he lives is more universal. Plants, animals, minerals, air, light, etc. constitute, from the theoretical aspect, a part of human consciousness as objects of natural science and art; they are man's spiritual inorganic nature, his intellectual means of life, which he must first prepare for enjoyment and perpetuation. So also, from the practical aspect, they form a part of human life and activity. In practice man lives only from these natural products, whether in the form of food, heating, clothing, housing, etc. The universality of man appears in practice in the universality which makes the whole of nature into his inorganic body: (1) as a direct means of life; and equally (2) as the material object and instrument of his life activity. Nature is the inorganic body of man; that is to say nature, excluding the human body itself. To say that man *lives* from nature means that nature is his *body* with which he must remain in a continuous interchange in order not to die. The statement that the physical and mental life of man, and nature, are interdependent means simply that nature is interdependent with itself, for man is a part of nature.

Since alienated labour: (1) alienates nature from man; and (2) alienates man from himself, from his own active function, his life activity; so it alienates him from the species. It makes *species-life* into a means of individual life. In the first place it alienates species-life and individual life, and secondly, it turns the latter, as an abstraction, into the purpose of the former, also in its abstract and alienated form.

For labour, *life activity, productive life*, now appear to man only as *means* for the satisfaction of a need, the need to maintain his physical existence. Productive life is, however, species-life. It is life creating life. In the type of life activity resides the whole character of a species, its species-character; and free, conscious activity is the species-character of human beings. Life itself appears only as a *means of life*.

The animal is one with its life activity. It does not distinguish the activity from itself. It is *its activity*. But man makes his life activity itself an object of his will and consciousness. He has a conscious life activity. It is not a determination with which he is completely identified. Conscious life activity distinguishes man from the life activity of animals. Only for this reason is he a species-being. Or rather, he is only a self-conscious being, i.e. his own life is an object for him, because he is a species-being. Only for this reason is his activity free activity. Alienated labour reverses the relationship, in that man because he is a self-conscious being makes his life activity, his *being*, only a means for his *existence*. . . .

Consciousness, which man has from his species, is transformed through alienation so that species-life becomes only a means for him. (3) Thus alienated labour turns the *species-life of man*, and also nature as his mental species-property, into an *alien* being and into a *means* for his *individual existence*. It alienates from man his own body, external nature, his mental life and his *human* life. (4) A direct consequence of the alienation of man from the product of his labour, from his life activity and from his species-life, is that *man is alienated* from other *men*. When man confronts himself he also confronts *other* men. What is true of man's relationship to his work, to the product of his work and to himself, is also true of his relationship to other men, to their labour and to the objects of their labour.

In general, the statement that man is alienated from his species-life means that each man is alienated from others, and that each of the others is likewise alienated from human life.

Human alienation, and above all the relation of man to himself, is first realized and expressed in the relationship between each man and other men. Thus in the relationship of alienated labour every man regards other men according to the standards and relationships in which he finds himself placed as a worker. . . .

Consider the earlier statement that the relation of man to himself is first *realized, objectified*, through his relation to other men. If he is related to the product of his labour, his objectified labour, as to an *alien,* hostile, powerful and independent object, he is related in such a way that another alien, hostile, powerful and independent man is the lord of this object. If he is related to his own activity as to unfree activity, then he is related to it as activity in the service, and under the domination, coercion and yoke, of another man.

Every self-alienation of man, from himself and from nature, appears in the relation which he postulates between other men and himself and nature. Thus religious self-alienation is necessarily exemplified in the relation between laity and priest, or, since it is here a question of the spiritual world, between the laity and a mediator. In the real world of practice this self-alienation can only be expressed in the real, practical relation of man to his fellow men. The medium through which alienation occurs is itself a *practical* one. Through alienated labour, therefore, man not only produces his relation to the object and to the process of production as to alien and hostile men; he also produces the relation of other men to his production and his product, and the relation between himself and other men. Just as he creates his own production as a vitiation, a punishment, and his own product as a loss, as a product which does not belong to him, so he creates the domination of the non-producer over production and its product. As he alienates his own activity, so he bestows upon the stranger an activity which is not his own. . . .

JOHN STUART MILL

WORKER PARTICIPATION

. . . The aim of improvement should be not solely to place human beings in a condition in which they will be able to do without one another, but to enable them to work with or for one another in relations not involving dependence. Hitherto there has been no alternative for those who lived by their labour, but that of labouring either each for himself alone, or for a master. But the civilizing and improving influences of association, and the efficiency and economy of production on a large scale, may be obtained

From John Stuart Mill, *Principles of Political Economy* (1848).

without dividing the producers into two parties with hostile interests and feelings, the many who do the work being mere servants under the command of the one who supplies the funds, and having no interest of their own in the enterprise except to earn their wages with as little labour as possible. The speculations and discussions of the last fifty years, and the events of the last thirty, are abundantly conclusive on this point. If the improvement which even triumphant military despotism has only retarded, not stopped, shall continue its course, there can be little doubt that the *status* of hired labourers will gradually tend to confine itself to the description of workpeople whose low moral qualities render them unfit for anything more independent: and that the relation of masters and workpeople will be gradually superseded by partnership, in one of two forms: in some cases, association of the labourers with the capitalist; in others, and perhaps finally in all, association of labourers among themselves.

. . . The first of these forms of association has long been practised, not indeed as a rule, but as an exception. In several departments of industry there are already cases in which every one who contributes to the work, either by labour or by pecuniary resources, has a partner's interest in it, proportional to the value of his contribution. It is already a common practice to remunerate those in whom peculiar trust is reposed, by means of a percentage on the profits: and cases exist in which the principle is, with excellent success, carried down to the class of mere manual labourers.

In the American ships trading to China, it has long been the custom for every sailor to have an interest in the profits of the voyage; and to this has been ascribed the general good conduct of those seamen, and the extreme rarity of any collision between them and the government or people of the country. An instance in England, not so well known as it deserves to be, is that of the Cornish miners. "In Cornwall the mines are worked strictly on the system of joint adventure; gangs of miners contracting with the agent, who represents the owner of the mine, to execute a certain portion of a vein and fit the ore for market, at the price of so much in the pound of the sum for which the ore is sold. These contracts are put up at certain regular periods, generally every two months, and taken by a voluntary partnership of men accustomed to the mine. This system has its disadvantages, in consequence of the uncertainty and irregularity of the earnings, and consequent necessity of living for long periods on credit; but it has advantages which more than counterbalance these drawbacks. It produces a degree of intelligence, independence, and moral elevation, which raise the condition and character of the Cornish miner far above that of the generality of the labouring class." . . .

Some attention has been excited by an experiment of this nature, commenced above thirty years ago by a Paris tradesman, a house-painter, M. Leclaire, and described by him in a pamphlet published in the year 1842. M. Leclaire, according to his statement, employs on an average two hundred workmen, whom he pays in the usual manner, by fixed wages or salaries. He assigns to himself, besides interest for his capital, a fixed allowance for his labour and responsibility as manager. At the end of the year, the surplus profits are divided among the body, himself included, in the proportion of their salaries. The reasons by which M. Leclaire was led to adopt this system are highly instructive. Finding the conduct of his workmen unsatisfactory, he first tried the effect of giving higher wages, and by this he managed to obtain a body of excellent workmen, who would not quit his service for any other. 'Having thus succeeded' (I quote from an abstract of the pamphlet in Chambers' Journal,) 'in producing some sort of stability in the arrangement of his establishment, M. Leclaire expected, he says, to enjoy greater peace of mind. In this, however, he was disappointed. So long as he was able to superintend everything himself, from the general concerns of his business down to its minutest details, he did enjoy a certain satisfaction; but from the moment that, owing to the increase of his business, he found that he could be nothing more than the centre from which orders were issued, and to which reports were brought in, his former anxiety and discomfort returned upon him.' He speaks lightly of the other sources of anxiety to which a tradesman is subject, but describes as an incessant cause of vexation the losses arising from the misconduct of workmen. An employer 'will find workmen whose indifference to his interests is such that they do not perform two-thirds of the amount of work which they are capable of; hence the continual fretting of masters, who, seeing their interests neglected, believe themselves entitled to suppose that workmen are constantly conspiring to ruin those from whom they derive their livelihood. If the journeyman were sure of constant employment, his position would in some respects be more enviable than that of the master, because he is assured of a certain amount of day's wages, which he will get whether he works much or little. He runs no risk, and has no other motive to stimulate him to do his best than his own sense of duty. The master, on the other hand, depends greatly on chance for his returns: his position is one of continual irritation and anxiety. This would no longer be the case to the same extent, if the interests of the master and those of the workmen were bound up with each other, connected by some bond of mutual security, such as that which would be obtained by the plan of a yearly division of profits.' . . .

. . . The form of association, however, which if mankind continue to improve, must be expected in the end to predominate, is not that which can exist between a capitalist as chief, and work-people without a voice in the management, but the association of the labourers themselves on terms of equality, collectively owning the capital with which they carry on their operations, and working under managers elected and removable by themselves. So long as this idea remained in a state of theory, in the writings of Owen or of Louis Blanc, it may have appeared, to the common modes of judgment, incapable of being realized, and not likely to be tried unless by seizing on the existing capital, and confiscating it for the benefit of the labourers; which is even now imagined by many persons, and pretended by more, both in England and on the Continent, to be the meaning and purpose of Socialism. But there is a capacity of exertion and self-denial in the masses of mankind, which is never known but on the rare occasions on which it is appealed to in the name of some great idea or elevated sentiment. Such an appeal was made by the French Revolution of 1848. For the first time it then seemed to the intelligent and generous of the working classes of a great nation, that they had obtained a government who sincerely desired the freedom and dignity of the many, and who did not look upon it as their natural and legitimate state to be instruments of production, worked for the benefit of the possessors of capital. Under this encouragement, the ideas sown by Socialist writers, of an emancipation of labour to be effected by means of association, throve and fructified; and many working people came to the resolution, not only that they would work for one another, instead of working for a master tradesman or manufacturer, but that they would also free themselves, at whatever cost of labour or privation, from the necessity of paying, out of the produce of their industry, a heavy tribute for the use of capital; that they would extinguish this tax, not by robbing the capitalists of what they or their predecessors had acquired by labour and preserved by economy, but by honestly acquiring capital for themselves. If only a few operatives had attempted this arduous task, or if, while many attempted it, a few only had succeeded, their success might have been deemed to furnish no argument for their system as a permanent mode of industrial organization. But, excluding all the instances of failure, there exist, or existed a short time ago, upwards of a hundred successful, and many eminently prosperous, associations of operatives in Paris alone, besides a considerable number in the departments.

The same admirable qualities by which the associations were carried through their early struggles, maintained them in their increasing prosperity. Their rules of discipline, instead of being more lax, are stricter than those of ordinary workshops; but being rules self-imposed, for the manifest good of the community, and not for the convenience of an employer regarded as having an opposite interest, they are far more scrupulously obeyed, and the voluntary obedience carries with it a sense of personal worth and dignity. With wonderful rapidity the associated workpeople have learnt to correct those of the ideas they set out with, which are in opposition to the teaching of reason and experience. Almost all the associations, at first, excluded piece-work, and gave equal wages whether the work done was more or less. Almost all have abandoned this system, and after allowing to every one a fixed minimum, sufficient for subsistence, they apportion all further remuneration according to the work done: most of them even dividing the profits at the end of the year, in the same proportion as the earnings.

It is the declared principle of most of these associations, that they do not exist for the mere private benefit of the individual members, but for the promotion of the co-operative cause. With every extension, therefore, of their business, they take in additional members, not (when they remain faithful to their original plan) to receive wages from them as hired labourers, but to enter at once into the full benefits of the association, without being required to bring anything in, except their labour: the only condition imposed is that of receiving during a few years a smaller share in the annual division of profits, as some equivalent for the sacrifices of the founders. When members quit the association, which they are always at liberty to do, they carry none of the capital with them: it remains an indivisible property, of which the members for the time being have the use, but not the arbitrary disposal: by the stipulations of most of the contracts, even if the association breaks up, the capital cannot be divided, but must be devoted entire to some work of beneficence or of public utility. A fixed, and generally a considerable, proportion of the annual profits is not shared among the members, but added to the capital of the association, or devoted to the repayment of advances previously made to it: another portion is set aside to provide for the sick and disabled, and another to form a fund for extending the practice of association, or aiding other associations in their need. The managers are paid, like other members, for the time which is occupied in management, usually at the rate of the highest paid labour: but the rule is adhered to, that the exercise of power shall never be an occasion of profit. . . .

From the progressive advance of the co-operative movement, a great increase may be looked for even in the aggregate productiveness of industry. The sources of the increase are twofold. In the first place, the class of mere distributors, who are not producers but auxiliaries of production, and whose inordinate numbers, far more than the gains of capitalists, are the cause why so great a portion of the wealth produced does not reach the producers—will be reduced to more modest dimensions. Distributors differ from producers in this, that when producers increase, even though in any given department of industry they may be too numerous, they actually produce more: but the multiplication of distributors does not make more distribution to be done, more wealth to be distributed; it does but divide the same work among a greater number of persons, seldom even cheapening the process. By limiting the distributors to the number really required for making the commodities accessible to the consumers—which is the direct effect of the co-operative system—a vast number of hands will be set free for production, and the capital which feeds and the gains which remunerate them will be applied to feed and remunerate producers. This great economy of the world's resources would be realized even if co-operation stopped at associations for purchase and consumption, without extending to production.

The other mode in which co-operation tends, still more efficaciously, to increase the productiveness of labour, consists in the vast stimulus given to productive energies, by placing the labourers, as a mass, in a relation to their work which would make it their principle and their interest—at present it is neither—to do the utmost, instead of the least possible, in exchange for their remuneration. It is scarcely possible to rate too highly this material benefit, which yet is as nothing compared with the moral revolution in society that would accompany it: the healing of the standing feud between capital and labour; the transformation of human life, from a conflict of classes struggling for opposite interests, to a friendly rivalry in the pursuit of a good common to all; the elevation of the dignity of labour; a new sense of security and independence in the labouring class; and the conversion of each human being's daily occupation into a school of the social sympathies and the practical intelligence.

Such is the noble idea which the promoters of Co-operation should have before them. But to attain, in any degree, these objects, it is indispensable that all, and not some only, of those who do the work should be identified in interest with the prosperity of the undertaking. Associations which, when they have been successful, renounce the essential principle of the system, and become joint-stock companies of a limited number of shareholders, who differ from those of other companies only in being working men; associations which employ hired labourers without any interest in the profits (and I grieve to say that the Manufacturing Society even of Rochdale has thus degenerated) are, no doubt, exercising a lawful right in honestly employing the existing system of society to improve their position as individuals, but it is not from them that anything need be expected towards replacing that system by a better. Neither will such societies, in the long run, succeed in keeping their ground against individual competition. Individual management, by the one person principally interested, has great advantages over every description of collective management. Co-operation has but one thing to oppose to those advantages—the common interest of all the workers in the work. When individual capitalists, as they will certainly do, add this to their other points of advantage; when, even if only to increase their gains, they take up the practice which these co-operative societies have dropped, and connect the pecuniary interest of every person in their employment with the most efficient and most economical management of the concern; they are likely to gain an easy victory over societies which retain the defects, while they cannot possess the full advantages, of the old system.

Under the most favourable supposition, it will be desirable, and perhaps for a considerable length of time, that individual capitalists, associating their work-people in the profits, should coexist with even those co-operative societies which are faithful to the co-operative principle. Unity of authority makes many things possible, which could not or would not be undertaken subject to the chance of divided councils or changes in the management. A private capitalist, exempt from the control of a body, if he is a person of capacity, is considerably more likely than almost any association to run judicious risks, and originate costly improvements. Co-operative societies may be depended on for adopting improvements after they have been tested by success, but individuals are more likely to commence things previously untried. Even in ordinary business, the competition of capable persons who in the event of failure are to have all the loss, and in the case of success the greater part of the gain, will be very useful in keeping the managers of co-operative societies up to the due pitch of activity and vigilance.

When, however, co-operative societies shall have sufficiently multiplied, it is not probable that any but the least valuable work-people will any longer consent to work all their lives for wages merely; both private capitalists and associations will gradually find it necessary to make the entire body of labourers participants in profits. Eventually, and in perhaps a less remote future than may be supposed, we may, through the co-operative principle, see our way to a change in society, which would combine the freedom and independence of the individual, with the moral, intellectual, and economical advantages of aggregate production; and which, without violence or spoliation, or even any sudden disturbance of existing habits and expectations, would realize, at least in the industrial department, the best aspirations of the democratic spirit, by putting an end to the division of society into the industrious and the idle, and effacing all social distinctions but those fairly earned by personal services and exertions. Associations like those which we have described, by the very process of their success, are a course of education in those moral and active qualities by which alone success can be either deserved or attained. As associations multiplied, they would tend more and more to absorb all work-people, except those who have too little understanding, or too little virtue, to be capable of learning to act on any other system than that of narrow selfishness. As this change proceeded, owners of capital would gradually find it to their advantage, instead of maintaining the struggle of the old system with work-people of only the worst description, to lend their capital to the associations; to do this at a diminishing rate of interest, and at last, perhaps, even to exchange their capital for terminable annuities. In this or some such mode, the existing accumulations of capital might honestly, and by a kind of spontaneous process, become in the end the joint property of all who participate in their productive employment: a transformation which, thus effected, (and assuming of course that both sexes participate equally in the rights and in the government of the association) would be the nearest approach to social justice, and the most beneficial ordering of industrial affairs for the universal good, which it is possible at present to foresee.

chapter *11*

*P*opulation, Hunger, and the Environment

INTRODUCTION

Approximately 75 million more people existed at the beginning of 1981 than did at the beginning of 1980. In mid-1981 about 4.5 billion people existed. By the end of the century, there will probably be over 6 billion people, and perhaps 90 million more will be added each year.[1] Predictions as to the ultimate size of the world population vary greatly—from 8 to 11 billion or more.[2] This growth will occur even though the rate of increase dropped from about 2 percent in the late 1960s to 1.7 percent in the late 1970s and will probably decline even more by the end of the century. Even if fertility rates dropped to a replacement level so that each person only replaced him- or herself, the world population would continue to grow for about sixty years simply because so many young people are entering their reproductive years.

This increase in world population will not be evenly distributed. To the end of this century, 90 percent of the increase will be in the developing countries, while only 10 percent will be in the developed ones. Indeed, although a few developed countries might decrease in population, some developing countries, such as Algeria, Iraq, Bangladesh, and Mexico, will almost double in size.

Rapid population growth affects the amount of food and resources available for each person. It is not the only factor that affects these matters —methods of production, for instance, are also relevant—but it is an important one. For example, using food production from 1961 to 1965 as a base, by 1976 the developing countries had increased their total food production slightly more than had the developed countries. However, while the per-capita food produced in the developed countries increased about 20 percent, in the developing countries it increased less than 10 percent.[3] The faster rate of population growth in the developing countries accounted for this difference. The same sort of relationship applies to the production of such other goods as housing. If a population grows by 2 percent a year, then 2 percent more houses must be built each year just to stay even. Also, more people produce more pollution even if each person

318

produces the same amount as before. However, much increased pollution is due to using more polluting methods of production and distribution—throw-away cans and bottles rather than returnable ones, individual automobiles rather than mass transit, and so on.

One of the major concerns about population is whether a vastly larger future population will confront a spoiled environment denuded of resources, such as energy, arable land, and water. All three resources present problems. So do each of the current forms of energy. World oil production has peaked, but its extraction often causes oil spills and other environmental damage. Although abundant coal exists, its extraction also causes environmental damage, and its consumption pollutes the air. Firewood is a primary source of energy in many less-developed countries, but the supply of trees is rapidly diminishing, leaving the earth subject to erosion and floods. Furthermore, the continued consumption of these fossil fuels might significantly increase the amount of carbon dioxide in the atmosphere, which could increase the earth's temperature and cause significant climatic changes. Alternative forms of energy, such as nuclear power, pose threats of radiation, primarily from stored radioactive wastes.

Arable land and water are necessary for the production of food for the growing world population. Almost all of the world's best farmland is now under cultivation, but hundreds of thousands of acres of prime farmland are lost each year to highways, industrial and residential developments, and erosion. Water for irrigation has become short in some developed countries. Unless significant changes occur in usage, parts of the United States could be seriously short of water by the end of the century. Many less developed countries even lack potable drinking water. Will future generations be bequeathed an environment without clean air or water, without sufficient land to grow food, and without natural beauty?

Two major ethical problems arise in trying to provide an ethical basis for dealing with population, hunger, and the environment. First, what precisely do people currently alive owe to future generations? How can one have an obligation to people who do not now exist? Even if some obligations to future generations exist, exactly what is owed: a minimum existence, a life of as good a quality as people now have, or an improved lot? Furthermore, how much one must provide future generations depends in part upon how many people there will be. The present generation can significantly influence how many people will exist in the future. It can allow population growth to continue until lack of food or other conditions bring it to a halt, or it can limit growth. Is there a reason to prefer a world of 6 billion people rather than one of 10 or even 14 billion? A second major ethical problem is that obligations to future generations could conflict with the wants and needs of, and obligations to, currently existing people. For example, in order to preserve resources and the environment for future generations, should poor people around the world be condemned to remain poor because making them better off would be too detrimental to the environment?

Obligations and Population Growth   The *natural-law* tradition generally recognizes a duty to procreate. The function of the natural human sexual inclination is reproduction because only sexual acts can lead to reproduction. The point of reproduction is the preservation of the species. The reproductive function of adding members to the species and community includes their upbringing and education.

Thomas Aquinas distinguished two types of duties, which can be called "individual" and "collective."[4] *Individual duties* must be fulfilled by each person, whereas *collective duties* fall upon a group and each person need not act so long as enough others do so to fulfill the duty. For example, an army needs sentries, but not every soldier need be a sentry so long as enough are. As the end of the duty to procreate is the preservation of the species, not everyone needs to have children and even those who do need not have as many as they can.

A natural-law theory of this sort thus does not require that the size of the population continuously increase. Although the population needs to be large enough to ensure the continuation of the species, as the end of procreation includes education and contribution to the social good, it should not increase to the point that it seriously damages the social good. Unfortunately, natural-law theory is not very explicit as to when continued growth is harmful to the social or common good. In short, there is a duty to provide for the existence and social good of future generations, and considerations of their social good can provide a good reason for not greatly increasing their number.

The *natural-rights* tradition seems to imply that one must not act so as to violate the rights of future generations. Of course, one must first admit that future generations can have rights. John Locke required that when one originally acquires property in the state of nature, one must leave "enough, and as good" for others.[5] If this is extended from property rights to future generations, then one would have to leave them "enough, and as good" natural resources. Other natural rights might also establish obligations of the present generation.

A general difficulty with a natural-rights approach to obligations to future generations is that the rights are usually negative ones, for instance, not to kill or torture others. They do not require that one provide things to people. However, if one adopted modern human-rights statements, such as the U.N. Declaration of Human Rights, as the basis for what is owed to future generations, then many positive rights would be included. Essentially, population growth should not be permitted to continue if it implies that the rights of people in the future cannot be fulfilled.

The only discussions of future generations and population in the *Kantian* and *contractarian* traditions are recent considerations of Rawlsian contractarianism. In the contractarian view, the principles for future generations depend significantly upon who the contractors are. They can be either (1) all presently existing people; (2) all who actually exist at some time or other; or (3) all possible people, that is, all those who might exist at some time or other. All possible people include all those who actually exist as well as all those who might have been conceived or born but were not.

If, like Rawls,[6] one assumes that only presently existing people are contractors, then the contractors will not agree to principles concerned with persons in the distant future. While they might have some concern for their children and grandchildren, they will not be concerned with people in the fifth or sixth generation.

If the contractors are all actual persons, including persons who will actually exist in the distant future, they will not agree to principles permitting population growth at the expense of future generations. Instead, they will accept principles that permit population growth and other conduct only as long as economic growth is not hindered and the point has not been reached where the principles of justice with the priority of liberty can be secured. They would have no reason to accept principles allowing detrimental population growth or environmental deterioration after justice is secured.

The actual-persons view faces a couple of major difficulties.[7] First, as all the contractors know they exist, they have no reason to permit population increase except to fulfill their own desires to have children. Second, it does not seem to make sense to have all actual persons choosing population principles that determine who will exist in the future. One cannot determine who will be a contractor until the contract is made, but the contract cannot be made until one knows who the contractors are. This is the chicken and the egg problem with a vengeance.

If all possible people were contractors, the principle agreed to would probably be to maximize one's chances for receiving some primary goods, which means bringing as many people as possible into existence.[8] The worst off possible people are those who do not exist, for they do not have any primary goods. Each contractor would wish to have as great a chance as possible to receive primary goods. This requires increasing the chance for existence by bringing as many people as possible into existence.

The *utilitarian* tradition is concerned to maximize net utility, and it makes no difference whether the utility is now or in the future. At first glance, this might seem to be a good basis for being concerned with the happiness of people existing in the future. (Indeed, utilitarians also emphasize a concern for the happiness that animals can have.) Great difficulties arise, however. Once population size is allowed to vary, two different interpretations are possible of the aim of a net utility as high as any other. (See Chapter 3 for the meaning of net utility.) The aim can be either as high a total net utility or as high an average net utility as possible. Total net utility is simply the sum of all the happiness minus the sum of all unhappiness. The average net utility is the total divided by the number of people. When the size of the population is constant, these two versions give the same results, because a change in total net utility produces a corresponding change in the average net utility. When the sizes of populations differ, this correspondence does not hold. For example, a small increase in the total net utility due to the addition of happy people might decrease the average net utility.

The total utilitarian view has a number of intuitively objectionable implications. First, the addition implication is that population size should be increased so long as the happiness from the addition is greater than the unhappiness. For example, a world population of 4 billion people ought to be increased to one of 8 billion people, if each of the 8 billion would have more than half the net utility of each of the 4 billion. Second, the sacrifice implication is that the happiness of people should be sacrificed if it will increase the total net utility. Two versions of the sacrifice implication exist. One states that the happiness of existing people should be sacrificed if the net utility of the additional people is greater than that lost by existing people. According to the other, the population should be increased even if the additional people have net disutility (are miserable), provided the gain in net utility to existing people is greater than the net disutility of the new people.

The average view avoids the addition implication of the total view, because, in the example above, the average happiness of a world of 8 billion people would be less than that of a world of 4 billion people. However, it has a converse addition implication. Suppose additional people would be quite happy but less happy than the average of those presently existing. Then by the average view, it would be wrong to allow the additional people, because the average would be lower. Also, while the average view moderates the sacrifice implications, it does not eliminate them. If the average net utility of additional people is great, then it might offset a decrease in the average utility of presently existing people. Similarly, the gain in the average net utility of presently existing people can be great enough to offset even an average net disutility of additional people.

Constraints   Once obligations to future generations have been established, fulfilling them can be subject to other obligations. In particular, obligations to help the poor, especially in less-developed countries, might conflict with conserving resources for the future. Other ethical obligations can also restrict the means of providing for the future.

In the *natural-law* tradition, perhaps the most significant constraints concern methods of limiting population growth. It basically opposes abortion and artificial contraception (the pill, IUDs, and so on). As the function of sexual activity is reproduction, interfering with the reproductive process to prevent generation is contrary to natural law and wrong.[9] Only the rhythm method, by which intercourse is avoided during the time a woman might conceive, accords with natural law.[10] Of course, abortion is also contrary to natural law (see Chapter 4). Finally, Pope Paul VI urged public authorities not to legally permit these practices as contrary to natural law.[11] Consequently, on this interpretation of natural law, the state should not foster the use of abortion or contraceptives in family-planning programs.

The constraint on providing for future generations on *natural-rights* views is that one cannot violate the natural rights of presently existing people. Thus, freedom and the right to life must be respected. Moreover, the United Nations has recognized a human right to determine the number of children one will have.

All couples and individuals have the basic right to decide freely and responsibly the number and spacing of their children and to have the information, education and means to do so; the responsibility of couples and individuals in the exercise of this right takes into account the needs of their living and future children, and their responsibilities towards the community.[12]

The right is a double-edged sword. As a positive right to assistance in family limitation, it supports efforts at population control. As a negative right to freedom from interference in making reproductive decisions, it prohibits coercive policies of population control.[13]

Little has been written in the *Kantian* tradition concerning methods of controlling population or protecting the environment, although the Kantian view probably has some interesting implications. Neither the formula of universal law nor that of treating humanity as an end is likely to show voluntary programs to be wrong, but they might forbid compulsory programs of population control.

A *contractarian* view is apt to provide more explicit guidance. First, the equal liberty and fair equality of opportunity principles imply that any permissible program should provide equal liberties—such as the freedom to have children. A policy of a flat tax per child would not be acceptable because wealthier couples would have a greater opportunity to have children than would poor ones. Second, the difference principle might imply that programs of social development to improve the lot of the least advantaged should have priority over programs of direct fertility control.[14] The underlying assumption is that as people's level of well-being increases, they will voluntarily decide to have fewer children. However, one cannot conclude that providing for the least advantaged in the present generation always takes precedence over providing for future generations, only that the burden should preferably fall upon the more rather than the less advantaged in the present generation.

Finally, *utilitarian* principles will, depending on the circumstances, justify any type of program as permissible. The difference between act and rule utilitarianism is not significant here, because programs or rules are being considered. One must always consider the net utility of one program versus other possible programs. Utilitarianism does not necessarily imply that one should choose the program most effective in reducing pollution or population growth. An outright ban on the use of coal, for example, might be the most effective program for reducing acid rain, but the unhappiness due to consequent unemployment and other economic dislocations would make it less useful than would limitations on pollution.

Readings The problem case briefly describes the situation in Brazil. It is the largest middle-income developing country in terms of population (122 million), land area, and total economic output (1980 per capita income $1,570 U.S.). Its present rate of natural increase is about 2.8 percent, and by the end of the century it will have a population of about 200 million. Also, while Brazil is rich in many resources, it has little coal or oil. On the basis of the description, one should consider whether Brazil's population size or growth is permissible or whether an obligation exists to further slow the rate of increase. One should also consider what form of energy development would be most appropriate. In August 1979 a new person became Secretary of Planning. Should he have recommended an official policy to decrease population growth? If so, what type of program would have been justified? What energy policy should he have recommended?

The selection by James Sterba presents a natural-rights perspective on population and hunger. He argues that the right to life, even as a negative right, justifies obligations to people in less-developed countries and future generations. He rebuts several reasons for believing that future people cannot have rights that obligate presently existing people. Finally, he briefly suggests what fulfilling these rights implies for the life of presently existing people in developed countries.

The selection by Ronald Green presents the core of his contractarian argument for obligations to future generations. Green uses the actual persons interpretation. He contends that a zero population growth policy is generally correct but that decreasing population size to provide a better life for people in the future is justifiable. Indeed, presently existing people have an obligation to provide future people a better life than at present. At the end of the selection, Green argues that due to the environmental hazards of the radioactive waste, plutonium breeder reactors for generating electricity violate obligations to future generations.

In the last selection, Garrett Hardin gives an essentially average utilitarian argument for not giving food aid to less developed countries and for restricting immigration. Although Hardin is not explicit about adopting the average-utility view, he does clearly count the well-being of future persons equally with that of presently existing persons. Moreover, he claims that giving aid now will cause greater unhappiness in the future. The reader should consider whether his argument is an example of the sacrifice implication.

Notes

[1] Jean van der Tak, Carl Haub, and Elaine Murphy, "Our Population Predicament: A New Look," *Population Bulletin* 34 (December 1979): 3–4.

[2] Ibid., p. 38.

[3] Ibid., p. 25, fig. 11.

[4] St. Thomas Aquinas, *Summa Theologica*, II–II, Question 152, Article 1, ad. 1.

[5] *Two Treatises of Government*, ed. Peter Laslett, rev. ed. (New York: New American Library, 1963), bk. 2, chap. 5, sec. 27, p. 329.

⁶ John Rawls, *A Theory of Justice* (Cambridge, Mass.: Harvard University Press, 1971), pp. 140, 292.

⁷ See Brian Barry, "Justice Between Generations," in *Law, Morality and Society: Essays in Honour of H. L. A. Hart,* ed. P. M. S. Hacker and J. Raz (Oxford: Clarendon Press, 1977), p. 281.

⁸ Brian Barry, "Rawls on Average and Total Utility: A Comment," *Philosophical Studies* 31 (1977): 322–24.

⁹ Aquinas, *Summa Theologica*, II–II, Question 154, Article 1.

¹⁰ See Pope Paul VI, "Humanae Vitae," in *Philosophy & Sex*, ed. Robert Baker and Frederick Elliston (Buffalo, N.Y.: Prometheus Books, 1975), pp. 139–40; and G. E. M. Anscombe, "Contraception and Chastity," in *Ethics and Population*, ed. Michael D. Bayles (Cambridge, Mass.: Schenkman, 1976), pp. 134–53.

¹¹ Ibid., p. 143.

¹² "World Population Plan of Action," in *The Population Debate: Dimensions and Perspectives*, vol. 1, U.N. Department of Economic and Social Affairs, Papers of the World Population Conference, Bucharest, 1974 (New York: United Nations, 1975), p. 157, par. 14 (f).

¹³ See Daniel Callahan, "Ethics and Population Limitation," in *Ethics and Population*, ed. Michael D. Bayles (Cambridge, Mass.: Schenkman, 1976), pp. 19–40, for a good discussion, largely based on a human-rights theory, of the ethical acceptability of population-control methods.

¹⁴ Ronald Michael Green, *Population Growth and Justice: An Examination of Moral Issues Raised by Rapid Population Growth*, Harvard Dissertations in Religion, no. 5 (Missoula, Mont.: Scholars Press, 1976), p. 237.

Bibliography on Population, Hunger, and the Environment

Aiken, William, and La Follette, Hugh, eds. *World Hunger and Moral Obligation*. Englewood Cliffs, N.J.: Prentice-Hall, 1977.

Bayles, Michael D. *Morality and Population Policy*. University, Ala.: University of Alabama Press, 1980.

_____, ed. *Ethics and Population*. Cambridge, Mass.: Schenkman, 1976.

Blackstone, William T., ed. *Philosophy and Environmental Crisis*. Athens, Ga.: University of Georgia Press, 1974.

_____. "The Search for an Environmental Ethic." In *Matters of Life and Death: New Introductory Essays in Moral Philosophy*, edited by Tom Regan. New York: Random House, 1980.

Brown, Peter G., and Shue, Henry, eds. *Food Policy: The Responsibility of the United States in the Life and Death Choices*. New York: Free Press, 1977.

Environmental Ethics. A journal devoted to these issues.

Green, Ronald Michael. *Population Growth and Justice: An Examination of Moral Issues Raised by Rapid Population Growth*. Harvard Dissertations in Religion, no. 5. Missoula, Mont.: Scholars Press, 1976.

Lucas, George R., Jr., and Ogletree, Thomas W., eds. *Lifeboat Ethics: The Moral Dilemmas of World Hunger*. New York: Harper & Row, 1976.

MacLean, Douglas, and Brown, Peter G., eds. *Energy Policy and Future Generations*. Totowa, N.J.: Rowman and Littlefield, forthcoming.

Miller, Frank, and Sartorius, Rolf. "Population Policy and Public Goods." *Philosophy and Public Affairs* 8 (1979): 148–74.

O'Neill, Onora. "The Moral Perplexities of Famine Relief." In *Matters of Life and Death:*

New Introductory Essays in Moral Philosophy, edited by Tom Regan. New York: Random House, 1980.

Partridge, Ernest, ed. Responsibilities to Future Generations: Environmental Ethics. Buffalo, N.Y.: Prometheus Books, 1981.

Passmore, John. Man's Responsibility for Nature. New York: Scribner's, 1974.

"Population Ethics" and "Population Policy Proposals." Encyclopedia of Bioethics, s.v.

Reich, Warren. "Responsible Parenthood and Overpopulation." Thomist 30 (1966): 362–433.

Schrader-Frechette, K. S. Nuclear Power and Public Policy: The Social and Ethical Problems of Fission Technology. Dordrecht: Reidel, 1980.

Sikora, R. I., and Barry, Brian, eds. Obligations to Future Generations. Philadelphia, Pa.: Temple University Press, 1978.

United Nations. Department of Economic and Social Affairs. The Population Debate: Dimensions and Perspectives. Papers of the World Population Conference, Bucharest, 1974. 2 vols. New York: United Nations, 1975.

United States, Commission on Population Growth and the American Future. Population and the American Future. New York: New American Library, Signet, 1972.

Veatch, Robert M., ed. Population Policy and Ethics: The American Tradition. New York: Irvington Publishers, 1977.

White, Stephen, ed. Population and the Environmental Crisis. Johnson City, Tenn.: Research Advisory Council, East Tennessee State University, 1975.

Problem Case
Population Growth in Brazil

Since the end of World War II, Brazil has experienced rapid population growth. Its present rate of growth of 2.8 percent will cause it to become the most populous country in the Western hemisphere during the twenty-first century. However, it is not one of the desperately poor developing countries. On the contrary, Brazil is quite rich in all natural resources except petroleum and coal. It has plentiful sugar cane and other biomass that might be used to produce alcohol. Although Brazil has had significant economic growth—about 10 percent per year between 1968 and 1973—the benefits have primarily gone to the rich. Capital-intensive growth has not reduced unemployment. As 40 percent of the population is under fifteen years of age, it will be very difficult in coming years to provide adequate employment for new workers. Also, population growth in the cities, from both natural increase and rural-urban migration, has created a serious challenge to the ability of the government to provide education, health, water, sanitation, and housing. Slower population growth would ease but not eliminate this challenge.

Prior to 1974 the government strongly opposed intervention in population matters. After the 1974 World Population Conference in Bucharest, it adopted a laissez-faire policy. Many couples, especially in the middle- and upper-income groups, practice modern contraception. Furthermore, private organizations, such as a branch of International

See Thomas W. Merrick, "Brazil's Population to Be Hemisphere's Largest in 21st Century," Intercom 7, nos. 11–12 (1979): 6–9.

Planned Parenthood Federation, have actively offered Brazilians family-planning information and devices, and some state governments have cooperated. In 1979 a new Secretary of Planning took office. One of his tasks was to prepare a statement on population for the next five-year development plan. He might also recommend an energy policy. What policies should he recommend?

JAMES P. STERBA
WELFARE RIGHTS OF FUTURE GENERATIONS

In order to formulate social policies to deal with issues like population control, world hunger and energy consumption, we clearly need solutions to many difficult and perplexing problems. Not the least of these problems is the determination of the moral side-constraints we should observe by virtue of our relationship to persons who are separated from us in space (distant peoples) and time (future generations). In this paper I wish, firstly, to show how these side-constraints, which I shall call "the welfare rights of distant peoples and future generations," can be grounded on fundamental moral requirements to which many of us are already committed and, secondly, to determine some of the practical requirements of these side-constraints for the issues of population control and world hunger.

THE WELFARE RIGHTS OF DISTANT PEOPLES

It used to be argued that the welfare rights of distant peoples would eventually be met as a byproduct of the continued economic growth of the technologically developed societies of the world. It was believed that the transfer of investment and technology to the less developed societies of the world would eventually, if not make everyone well off, at least satisfy everyone's basic needs. Now we are not so sure. Presently more and more evidence points to the conclusion that without some substantial sacrifice on the part of the technologically developed societies of the world, many of the less developed societies will never be able to provide their members with even the basic necessities for survival. For example, according to a study prepared by the World Bank in 1979, depending on the growth of world trade, between 470 and 710 million people will be living in conditions of absolute poverty as the 21st century dawns, unless, that is, the technologically developed societies of the world adopt some plausible policy of redistribution.[1] Even those, like Herman Kahn, who argue that an almost utopian world situation will obtain in the distant future, still would have to admit that unless some plausible policy of redistribution is adopted, malnutrition and starvation will continue in the less developed

From James P. Sterba, "The Welfare Rights of Distant Peoples and Future Generations," published by *Social Theory and Practice* 7 (1981): 99–119, Tallahassee, Florida. Reprinted by permission.

societies for many years to come.[2] Thus, a recognition of the welfare rights of distant peoples would appear to have significant consequences for developed and underdeveloped societies alike.

Of course, there are various senses in which distant peoples can be said to have welfare rights and various moral grounds on which those rights can be justified. First of all, the welfare rights of distant peoples can be understood to be either negative rights or positive rights.[3] A negative right is a right not to be interfered with in some specific manner. For example, a right to liberty is usually understood to be a negative right; it guarantees each person the right not to have his liberty interfered with provided that he does not unjustifiably interfere with the liberty of any other person. On the other hand, a positive right is a right to receive some specific goods or services. Typical positive rights are the right to have a loan repaid and the right to receive one's just earnings. Secondly, the welfare rights of distant peoples can be understood to be either *in personam* rights or *in rem* rights. *In personam* rights are rights that hold against some specific namable person or persons while *in rem* rights hold against everyone who is in a position to abide by the rights in question. A right to liberty is usually understood to be an *in rem* right while the right to have a loan repaid or the right to receive one's just earnings are typical *in personam* rights. . . .

Of the various moral grounds for justifying the welfare rights of distant peoples, quite possibly the most evident are those which appeal either to a right to life or a right to fair treatment. Indeed, whether a person's right to life is interpreted as a negative right (as political conservatives tend to do) or as a positive right (as political liberals tend to do), it is possible to show that the right justifies welfare rights that would amply provide for a person's basic needs. . . .

Thus suppose that a person's right to life is a positive right. So understood the person's right to life would most plausibly be interpreted as a right to receive those goods and resources that are necessary for satisfying his basic needs. For a person's basic needs are those which must be satisfied in order not to seriously endanger his health or sanity. Thus receiving the goods and resources that are necessary for satisfying his basic needs would preserve a person's life in the fullest sense. And if a person's positive right to life is to be universal in the sense that it is possessed by every person (as the right to life is generally understood to be) then it must be an *in rem* right. This is because an *in rem* right, unlike an *in personam* right, does not require for its possession the assumption by other persons of any special roles or contractual obligations. Interpreted as a positive *in rem* right, therefore, a person's right to life would clearly justify the welfare rights of distant peoples to have their basic needs satisfied.

Suppose, on the other hand, that a person's right to life is a negative right. Here again, if the right is to be universal in the sense that it is possessed by all persons then it must also be an *in rem* right. So understood the right would require that everyone who is in a position to do so not interfere in certain ways with a person's attempts to meet his basic needs.

But what sort of noninterference would this right to life justify? If one's basic needs have not been met, would a person's right to life require that others not interfere with his taking the goods he needs from the surplus possessions of those who already have satisfied their own basic needs? As it is standardly interpreted, a person's negative right to life would not require such noninterference. Instead, a person's negative right to life is usually understood to be limited in such circumstances by the property rights of those who have more than enough to satisfy their own basic needs.[4] Moreover, those who claim property rights to such surplus goods and resources are usually in a position to effectively prohibit those in need from taking what they require. For surely most underdeveloped nations of the world would be able to sponsor expeditions to the American Midwest or the Australian Plains for the purpose of collecting the grain necessary to satisfy the basic needs of their citizens if they were not effectively prohibited from doing so at almost every stage of the enterprise.

But are persons with such surplus goods and resources normally justified in so prohibiting others from satisfying their basic needs? Admittedly, such persons may have contributed greatly to the value of the surplus goods and resources they possess, but why should that give them power over the life and death of those less fortunate? While their contribution may well justify favoring their nonbasic needs over the nonbasic needs of others, how could it justify favoring their nonbasic needs over the basic needs of others? After all, a person's negative right to life, being an *in rem* right, does not depend on the assumption by other persons of any special roles or contractual obligations. By contrast, property rights that are *in personam* rights require the assumption by other persons of the relevant roles and contractual obligations which constitute a particular system of acquisition and exchange, such as the role of a neighbor and the obligations of a merchant. Consequently, with respect to such property rights, it would seem that a person could not justifiably be kept from acquiring the goods and resources necessary to satisfy his basic needs by the property rights of others to surplus possessions, unless the person himself had voluntarily agreed to be so constrained by those property rights. But obviously few people would voluntarily agree to have such constraints placed upon their ability to acquire the goods and resources necessary to satisfy their basic needs. For most people their right to acquire the goods and resources necessary to satisfy their basic needs would have priority over any other person's property rights to surplus possessions, or alternatively, they would conceive of property rights such that no one could have property rights to any surplus possessions which were required to satisfy their own basic needs.

Even if some property rights could arise, as *in rem* rights by a Lockean process of mixing one's labor with previously unowned goods and resources, there would still be a need for some sort of a restriction on such appropriations. For if these *in rem* property rights are to be *moral rights* then it must be reasonable for every affected party to accept such rights, since the requirements of morality cannot be contrary to reason. Accordingly, in order to give rise to *in rem* property rights, the appropriation of previously unowned goods and resources cannot justifiably limit anyone's ability to acquire the goods and resources necessary to satisfy his basic needs, unless it would be reasonable for the person to voluntarily agree to be so constrained. But obviously it would not be reasonable for many people, particularly those whose basic needs are not being met, to voluntarily agree to be so constrained by property rights. This means that whether property rights are *in personam* rights and arise by the assumption of the relevant roles and contractual obligations or are *in rem* rights and arise by a Lockean process of mixing one's labor with previously unowned goods and resources, such rights would rarely limit a negative right to life, interpreted as an *in rem* right to noninterference with one's attempts to acquire the goods and resources necessary to satisfy one's basic needs. So interpreted, a negative right to life would clearly justify the welfare rights of distant peoples. . . .

THE WELFARE RIGHTS OF FUTURE GENERATIONS

At first glance, the welfare rights of future generations appear to be just as firmly grounded as the welfare rights of distant peoples. For assuming that there will be future generations, then, they, like generations presently existing, will have their basic needs that must be satisfied. And just as we are now able to make provision for the basic needs of distant peoples, so likewise we are now able to make provision for the basic needs of future generations (for example, through capital investment and the conservation of resources). Consequently, it would seem that there are equally good grounds for taking into account the basic needs of future generations as there are for taking into account the basic needs of distant peoples.

But there is a problem. How can we claim that future generations *now* have rights that we make provision for their basic needs when they don't presently exist? How is it possible for persons who don't yet exist to have rights against those who do? For example, suppose we continue to use up the earth's resources at present or even greater rates, and, as a result, it turns out that the most pessimistic forecasts for the 22nd century are realized.[5] This means that future generations will face widespread famine, depleted resources, insufficient new technology to handle the crisis, and a drastic decline in the quality of life for nearly everyone. If this were to happen, could persons living in the 22nd century legitimately claim that we in the 20th century violated their rights by not restraining our consumption of the world's resources? Surely it would be odd to say that we violated their rights over one hundred years before they existed. But what exactly is the oddness?

Is it that future generations generally have no way of claiming their rights against existing generations? While this does make the recognition and enforcement of rights much more difficult (future generations would need strong advocates in the existing generations), it does not make it impossible for there to be such rights. After all, it is quite obvious that the recognition and enforcement of the rights of distant peoples is a difficult task as well.

Or is it that we don't believe that rights can legitimately exercise their influence over long durations of time? But if we can foresee and control at least some of the effects our actions will have on the ability of future generations to satisfy their basic needs then why should we not be responsible for those same effects? And if we are responsible for them then why should not future generations have a right that we take them into account?

Perhaps what troubles us is that future generations don't exist when their rights are said to demand action. But how else could persons have a right to benefit from the effects our actions will have in the distant future if they did not exist just when those effects would be felt? Those who exist contemporaneously with us could not legitimately make the same demand upon us, for they will not be around to experience those effects. Only future generations could have a right that the effects our actions will have in the distant future contribute to satisfying their basic needs. Nor need we assume that in order for persons to have rights, they must exist when their rights demand action. Thus, to say that future generations have rights against existing generations we can simply mean that there are enforceable requirements upon existing generations that would benefit or prevent harm to future generations.[6]

Yet most likely what really bothers us is that we cannot know for sure what effects our actions will have on future generations. For example, we may at some cost to ourselves conserve resources that will be of little value to future generations who have developed different technologies. Or, because we regard them as useless, we may destroy or deplete resources that future generations will find to be essential to their well-being. However, we should not allow such possibilities to blind us to the necessity for a social policy in this regard. After all, whatever we do will have its effect on future generations. The best approach, therefore, is to use the knowledge that we presently have and assume that future generations will also require those basic resources we now find to be valuable. If it turns out that future generations will require different resources to meet their basic needs from those we were led to expect, then at least we will not be blamable for acting on the basis of the knowledge we had.[7]

As in the case of the welfare rights of distant peoples, we can justify the welfare rights of future generations by appealing either to a right to life or to a right to fair treatment.

Justifying the welfare rights of future generations on the basis of a right to life presents no new problems. As we have seen, a right to life applied to distant peoples is a positive *in rem* right of existing persons to receive the goods and resources necessary to satisfy their basic needs or a negative *in rem* right of existing persons to noninterference with their attempts to acquire the goods and resources necessary to satisfy their basic needs. Accordingly, assuming that by "future generations" we mean "those whom we can definitely expect to come into existence," then a right to life applied to future generations would be a right of persons whom we can definitely expect to exist to receive the goods and resources necessary to satisfy their basic needs or to noninterference with their attempts to acquire the goods and resources necessary to satisfy their basic needs. Understood in this way, a right to life of future generations would justify the welfare rights of future generations for much the same reasons that a right to life of distant peoples justifies the welfare rights of distant peoples. For future generations clearly have not voluntarily agreed nor would it be reasonable for them to voluntarily agree to have their ability to receive or acquire the goods and resources necessary to satisfy their basic needs limited by the property rights of existing generations to surplus possessions. Thus a right to life of future generations, interpreted either as a positive *in rem* right or a negative *in rem* right, would clearly justify the welfare rights of future generations to have their basic needs satisfied. . . .

FUTURE GENERATIONS AND POPULATION CONTROL

The welfare rights of future generations are also closely connected with the population policy of existing generations. For example, under a population policy that places restrictions on the size of families and requires genetic screening, some persons will not be brought into existence who otherwise would have come into existence. Thus, the membership of future generations will surely be affected by whatever population policy existing generations adopt. Given that the size and genetic health of future generations will obviously affect their ability to provide for their basic needs, the welfare rights of future generations would require existing generations to adopt a population policy that takes these factors into account. . . .

Fortunately a policy with the desired restrictions can be grounded on the welfare rights of future generations. As we have seen, the welfare rights of future generations require existing generations to make provision for the basic needs of future generations. As a result, existing generations would have to evaluate their ability to provide both for their own basic needs and for the basic needs of future generations. Since existing generations by bringing persons into existence would be determining the membership of future generations, they would have to evaluate whether they are able to provide for that membership. Existing generations should not have to sacrifice the satisfaction of their basic needs for the sake of future generations, although they would be required to sacrifice some of their nonbasic needs on this account. Thus, if existing generations believe that were population to increase beyond a certain point, they would lack sufficient resources to make the necessary provision for each person's basic needs, then it would be incumbent upon them to restrict the membership of future generations so as not to exceed their ability to provide for each person's basic needs. For if the rights of future generations were respected, the membership of future generations would never increase beyond the ability of existing generations to make the necessary provision for the basic needs of future generations.

But this is to indicate only the "negative half" of the population policy that is grounded on the welfare rights of future generations, that is, the obligation to limit the size of future generations so as not to exceed the ability of existing generations to provide for the basic needs of future generations. The "positive half" of that population policy, which I have defended elsewhere,[8] is the obligation of existing generations, once their basic needs have been met, to bring into existence additional persons whose basic needs could also be met. . . .

WELFARE RIGHTS AND WORLD HUNGER

We have seen that the welfare rights of distant peoples and future generations guarantee each person a minimum of goods and resources necessary to meet the normal costs of satisfying his basic needs in the society in which he lives. Let us now determine some of the practical implications of these welfare rights for the issue of world hunger.

At present there is probably a sufficient world-wide supply of goods and resources to meet the normal costs of satisfying the basic nutritional needs of all existing persons in the societies in which they live. . . .

Needless to say, the adoption of a policy of meeting the basic nutritional needs of all existing persons would necessitate significant changes, especially in developed societies. For example, the large percentage of the U.S. population whose food consumption clearly exceeds even an adequately adjusted poverty index would have to substantially alter their eating habits. In particular, they would have to reduce their consumption of beef and pork so as to make more grain available for direct human consumption. (Presently the amount of grain fed American livestock is as much as all the people of China and India eat in a year.) Thus, at least the satisfaction of some of the nonbasic needs of the more advantaged in developed societies would have to be foregone so that the basic nutritional needs of all existing persons in developing and underdeveloped societies could be met. . . .

. . . Once the basic nutritional needs of future generations are also taken into account, then the satisfaction of the nonbasic needs of the more advantaged in developed societies would have to be further restricted in order to preserve the fertility of cropland and other food-related natural resources for the use of future generations.[9] And once basic needs other than nutritional needs are taken into account as well, still further restrictions would be required. For example, it has been estimated that presently a North American uses fifty times more resources than an Indian. This means that in terms of resource consumption the North American continent's population is the equivalent of 12.5 billion Indians.[10] Obviously, this would have to be radically altered if the basic needs of distant peoples and future generations are to be met. . . .

Notes

[1] *The Preliminary Report of the Presidential Commission on World Hunger,* December 1979. Section II, Chapter 3.

[2] Herman Kahn, William Brown and Leon Martel, *The Next 200 Years* (New York: William Morrow, 1976), Chapter 2.

[3] A distinction that is similar to the distinction between positive and negative rights is the distinction between recipient and action rights. Recipient rights, like positive rights, are rights to receive some specific goods or services. However, action rights are a bit more circumscribed than negative rights. Action rights are rights to act in some specific manner, whereas negative rights include both rights of noninterference with actions (and, hence, imply action rights) and rights of noninterference with things or states of affairs (such as a right to one's good name).

Having previously used the distinction between recipient and action rights (*The Demands of Justice* [Notre Dame: University of Notre Dame Press, 1980, Chapter 6]), in a defense of welfare rights, I now hope to show, in response to critics, particularly Jan Narveson, that the distinction between positive and negative rights can serve as well in the fuller defense of welfare rights which I am presenting in this paper.

[4] This is why a negative right to life is usually understood to impose lesser moral requirements than a positive right to life.

[5] Donella H. Meadows, Dennis L. Meadows, Jorgen Randers and William W. Behrens III, *The Limits to Growth*, second edition (New York: New American Library, 1974), Chapters 3 and 4.

[6] Indeed, right claims need not presuppose that there are any rightholders either in the present or in the future, as in the case of a right not to be born and a right to be born. On this point, see my paper "Abortion, Distant Peoples and Future Generations," *The Journal of Philosophy* 77 (1980): 422–40 and *The Demands of Justice*, Chapter 6.

[7] For a somewhat opposing view, see M. P. Golding, "Obligations to Future Generations," *The Monist*, 56 (1972): 85–99.

[8] See "Abortion, Distant Peoples and Future Generations," and *The Demands of Justice,* Chapter 6.

[9] Lester Brown, "Population, Cropland and Food Prices," *The National Forum* (1979), Vol. 69, No. 2, pp. 11–16.

[10] Janet Besecker and Phil Elder, "Lifeboat Ethics: A Reply to Hardin," in *Readings in Ecology, Energy and Human Society: Contemporary Perspectives*, edited by William R. Burch, Jr. (New York: Harper and Row, 1977), p. 229.

RONALD M. GREEN
INTERGENERATIONAL JUSTICE AND ENVIRONMENTAL RESPONSIBILITY

From the beginning of the nuclear age, through the Pugwash Conferences of the late 1950's, down to the environmental movement of our own decade, scientists have played a leading role in alerting us to the dangers posed by our present habits and technologies. Each problem in what Platt has

Reprinted from *BioScience*, Vol. 27, pp. 260–263, 265 (April 1977). Copyright © 1977 by the American Institute of Biological Sciences. Reprinted with permission of the copyright holder.

termed the "storm of crisis problems"[1] facing mankind today—population growth, resource depletion, environmental degradation, and the control of nuclear energy—has typically first been identified and publicized by members of the scientific community.

Since a distinguishing feature of all these problems is that they threaten massive evil for generations yet unborn, scientists have also performed the important task of reminding us of our moral responsibility to future generations. More than many of us, scientists have been alert to the fact that our moral obligations extend beyond our contemporaries to the generations that will follow us. But although scientists have tended to assume the existence of a responsibility to the future, they have not commonly discussed the more abstract question of the nature of that responsibility, its basis, extent, or limits.

As an ethicist, I want to take the modest step here of remedying this lack of discussion by proposing three very basic guides to our thinking about obligations to the future. I call these "axioms" of intergenerational responsibility. They are so "commonsensical" that I suspect that most scientists concerned with the future already share them. Nevertheless, each does involve some serious conceptual difficulties, and it may be useful to look at these moral axioms with some of the same care that scientists bring to questions of fact.

BONDS WITH THE FUTURE

The first axiom is: *We are bound by ties of justice to real future persons.*

Even though the belief that we have obligations to future generations is widely held, the very idea of obligations to persons in the future is quite odd. In a discussion of this issue, Stearns pointed this out when he asked: "Why should there be obligations to future generations? We have made no commitments to them. We have entered no social compacts with them. . . . Under any moral theory, why should there be obligations to nonexistent persons?"[2] . . .

. . . Morality does not really involve any kind of lofty commitment to maximizing human happiness, nor even, as some have believed . . . to minimizing suffering. Rather, morality has a far more mundane purpose: It is primarily an instrument for adjudicating possible conflicts between persons and for facilitating a noncoercive settlement of social disputes. It is an effort to replace the play of force and power in human affairs with principles to guide our conduct derived from reasoned, common agreement. . . .

Moral Reasoning

This understanding of morality is reflected in the recent return by some philosophers to a social contract method of moral reasoning. According to Rawls, for example, moral principles may be thought of as those basic rules agreed to by free, equal, self-interested and rational persons under conditions of strict impartiality.[3] Specifically, Rawls proposes that we view our moral principles as deriving from a hypothetical (not real) contract situation in which each of us seeks best to protect our possible interests. To prevent an unfair distortion of the outcome and to produce a result acceptable to all, however, he asks that we also think of ourselves as deprived of knowledge of our own particular strengths and weaknesses, advantages or disadvantages. The outcome of this hypothetical reasoning process would be a set of principles to which all could agree.

Rawls' view has many complexities, but the basic idea is as familiar as the everyday counsel to "put yourself in the other fellow's shoes." What Rawls is telling us is that if we are rationally to settle our social disputes and to construct a harmonious social order, we must adopt a moral point of view that involves choosing rationally but impartially before the array of competing interests and claims.

These considerations suggest just why we are obligated to future generations. It is not, as utilitarians mistakenly believe, because we have a duty to promote human happiness. Rather, it is because our wishes and behavior can conflict with those of future persons. We live, after all, in a finite world with limited space, resources, and opportunities, and not even the most optimistic prospects of technological change in the future are likely to remove all limits. By reducing these resources or opportunities, our conduct in the present can injure those who follow us, and they, in turn, in anger, resentment, or ignorance can inflict injury on their descendants.

For these reasons, moral obligations between generations are as important as any obligations we possess. In fact, they clearly form a part of the total requirements of distributive justice that bear upon us; as we must equitably distribute scarce goods and opportunities in the present, so must we do so over time. If we fail to do so, if we neglect our just responsibilities to the future, we risk reducing ongoing human relations to the Hobbesian "war of all with all" that morality aims to prevent.

Who Is the Future?

As elemental as this understanding is, it has some important implications. For one thing, it suggests that we need not morally concern ourselves with the welfare of merely "possible" future persons—with those human beings whose very coming into existence depends on our reproductive decisions. Persons who will never come into being cannot conceivably occasion social conflict, so merely "possible" persons need not enter into our moral thinking at all. Concretely, this means that there is no such thing as a "right to come into being" or a "right to be born."[4] It also means that in our collective population decisions we are primarily called upon to minimize injury to *real* future persons. Zero population growth, with its goal of improved life circumstances for smaller future numbers, is a valid conclusion from these basic premises.

Actually, the population issue is a bit more complex than this. Even with merely "possible" persons out of the picture, population policy can involve a conflict between generations. To some degree, it is in the interests of certain segments of present generations to have unrestrained procreative liberty, whereas it is generally in the interests of future generations to have earlier population growth limited. Apart from the emotional satisfactions produced by children, for example, there are often concrete reasons why parents in agrarian societies opt for numerous offspring. At the same time, larger family size can disadvantage the children themselves, a fact that has led some demographers to speak of the "parental exploitation of children" in the underdeveloped setting.[5]

This raises the question of how disputes of this sort are to be settled. The answer, I think, is furnished by the kind of contract method Rawls proposes. Specifically, each of us must ask: "If I were a member of a hypothetical contract situation seeking my possible advantage, but if I were denied knowledge of which generation I live in, what population policy would I propose?" Elsewhere I have tried to consider this question at length,[6] but a general answer seems clear: In view of the many future generations aided by stationary population levels, and the relatively slight sacrifices imposed on the present, a no-growth policy is a good choice under conditions of radical impartiality. Zero population growth is right. Indeed, negative growth rates to enhance the circumstances of future generations are also justifiable, and it goes without saying that rampant population growth under conditions of poverty is absolutely unacceptable. Quite apart from the question of whether such growth threatens physical survival, the miserable survival it produces is a severe injustice to those born into progressively more impoverished generations.

More important than this almost undisputed conclusion, however, is the method of arriving at it. What I am trying to suggest under the heading of this first axiom is a way of thinking about our obligations to the future and, at the same time, a rational way of determining the extent of those obligations. This method, moreover, is as applicable to other problems of intergenerational justice, including environmental responsibility and resource planning, as it is to population policy. In each of these cases, I suggest, we are called upon to ask a simple question: "Which policy would I find most advantageous if I were deprived of the knowledge of the generation to which I belonged?" Obviously, this question alone will not solve our problems. Complex factual matters must also be faced on each issue, and the expertise of many disciplines must be drawn upon. But it may be of some help at the outset to see that the right question is being asked.

FUTURE SHOULD BE BETTER

The second axiom is: *The lives of future persons ought ideally to be "better" than our own and certainly no worse.*

Ordinarily, when we act out of respect for other persons, we can at least entertain the possibility that when their turn comes, they will act out of respect for us as well. But virtually no possibility of such reciprocity exists between generations. Except, perhaps, by respecting our memory, future generations cannot really compensate us for the sacrifices we make on their behalf. This consideration has led some philosophers to suggest that human history displays a kind of chronological unfairness; the earliest generations are called upon to make sacrifices whose benefits they can never enjoy.[7] A similar oddity has been noted by economists and others who have discussed the matter of capital savings for the future. A policy of savings, they observe, benefits every generation but the first, which experiences only sacrifice.[8]

It is tempting to conclude that policies which disadvantage one individual or group for the sake of others must be unjust. This need not be true. Where circumstances allow no alternative, policies of this sort can be just, and this seems to be the case where obligations to the future are concerned. Not only is restraint on behalf of the future required, but deliberate sacrifices on our part aimed at making life better for all our descendants also are justified.

To see this, we need only regard the choices impartially. We can refuse to sacrifice or save, and we can insist on a strict equality of expectations across generations. This probably is to our advantage if we happen to be in any initial generation when savings are proposed. But it is clearly to our disadvantage if we belong to any subsequent generation. Each of these receives something from its predecessors and benefits generally from the process of savings as the circumstances of life continue to improve. Deprived of knowledge of the generation to which we belong, therefore, it seems reasonable to opt for some kind of saving policy. Morally this expresses itself as the duty to strive, even at some expense to ourselves, for the betterment of the conditions of life of those who follow us.

My use of the terms *savings* and *betterment* interchangeably may suggest that I construe this duty to improve the welfare of our descendants primarily in economic terms—as some kind of unending growth in material productivity. Certainly, money income and consumer goods of one sort or another are candidates for consideration among the values we ought to increase for our descendants. But they cannot be the sole goods because we know that increase in these goods has characteristically been accompanied by the degradation of other important and choice-worthy values, including human emotional health, cultural richness, and environmental quality.

The fact that many evils associated with an expanding economy are external to any one generation has led some economists to view commodity production and consumption as an undisputed good, something that persons with divergent ends can all support. But any perspective which takes future generations into account must question this emphasis. Even responsible economists today agree that adequate income measurements must encompass the cross-generational costs of environmental deterioration and resource depletion. . . .

The Quality of Life

These considerations raise the complex question of "quality of life." If we agree that we ought to improve the real quality of life of our descendants, which criteria should we select for doing so? What constitutes a good or "better" life? So many moralists have tried to answer this question, that it would be presumptuous of me to try to resolve it here. But a few modest suggestions may be in order. For one thing, the fact that it is far easier to identify what constitutes a deterioration in the quality of life than what constitutes an improvement makes it minimally incumbent upon us not to worsen the lot of our successors. This means that we must be careful not to squander or dissipate the legacy of natural and cultural values we have inherited from the past. In particular, we must respect the integrity of our physical environment, since all future progress presumes environmental stability.

In considering the direction actual progress in the future should take, we might keep in mind the fact that, here as elsewhere, moral choice requires a process of impartial but informed reasoning. This means that we must not allow our choices for the future to be guided by narrow preferences and special interest groups. Neither those who would make us into insatiable consumers nor those who would have us all become philosophers deserve our exclusive attention. A realistic assessment of the plurality of human ends must guide our thinking about the world we hand down to the future.

The fact that moral choice requires impartiality, however, does not mean that it presumes ignorance. On the contrary, full general information is essential to sound moral reasoning. Even the hypothetical contractors of Rawls' theory are assumed to know all the "general laws and theories" that bear on their choices.[9] . . .

It may well be that scientific inquiry will inform us that an overall improvement in our condition requires *less* of some of the goods or activities we presently cherish, or even, perhaps, a measure of deliberately programmed austerity and hardship in our lives. . . . Keeping this in mind, we should not forget that it is still our obligation to help improve the lives of those who follow us. Whatever the intent, appeals for an end to economic growth . . . may have recently had the effect of casting the very idea of progress into disrepute. Although this conclusion is understandable, it can encourage a defection from our obligation to the future. Our responsibility is not to abandon a striving for progress so much as to identify and develop those areas where significant human progress remains possible.

Whatever positive directions we select for the future, it remains true that we are minimally required not to worsen the future quality of life. Any historical process displaying a retrogression in human prospects would violate the deepest possibilities of the human enterprise. Unfortunately, an unprecedented capacity to inflict deliberate, mammoth, and irreversible injury on our descendants is a distinguishing feature of our era. Our exercise of this capacity is illustrated by our near exhaustion of petroleum resources and by the serious insults we inflict on delicate environmental systems. Among the most vivid illustrations of irresponsibility to the future, however, are the recent proposals for development of a plutonium recycle economy. Since these proposals furnish virtually a textbook case of how *not* to treat our descendants, I want briefly to dwell on them.

Possibility of a Plutonium Economy

The arguments in favor of a plutonium economy are fairly straightforward. Not only would such an economy enable us to use what is presently a troublesome waste-product of nuclear reactors, but with the development of the Liquid Metal Fast Breeder Reactor (LMFBR) we would be in a position to exploit abundantly available uranium 238 and thus vastly expand our energy resources. This would lower energy costs for decades to come and might also save lives by reducing the number of persons needed for uranium mining.[10]

The difficulties with this proposal are equally clear. Plutonium is one of the most toxic substances known. Lung burdens no larger than a millionth of a gram (the weight of a grain of pollen) produce cancer in animals with certainty. The problem is exacerbated by the fact that, with a half-life of 24,000 years, plutonium's radioactivity is undiminished within the span of human imagining.[11]

The fact that plutonium is virtually unknown in nature also means that we are uniquely responsible for every grain of this substance introduced into the environment. We have been creating plutonium, of course, from the beginning of the nuclear age, because it is a by-product of fission reactions. But the problem would assume new dimensions if we were to develop a plutonium recycle economy. Not only would this greatly increase the amount of plutonium produced—some projections foresee a cumulative flow of 100,000 tons of plutonium through the fuel cycle within roughly the next half-century—but because this plutonium would be in pure form it would be especially subject to theft and accidental dispersion.[12] The special safety problems of breeder reactors only further compound the risks.

By even the most conservative standards of intergenerational justice, these proposals seem grossly irresponsible. How can we justify introducing into the environment a substance that can seriously jeopardize the health and lives of countless future generations? The argument advanced at a recent government hearing—that because we will not be dependent on plutonium for more than a few hundred years it "will not be an important problem indefinitely"[13]—entirely misses the point. Though we may rely on plutonium for only a relatively brief period, the plutonium produced during that period may be with us indefinitely, and it may jeopardize the lives of many times the number of generations that profit from its use. Assuming there are alternatives to plutonium recyle, it is not the kind of policy that people deprived of knowledge of the generation to which they belong would favor. For a small probability of gain in the earlier generations, they would assume eons of risk to life and health.

It may be objected here that it is not possible to make such long-term calculations of risk. As some have observed, our future is "very open" with all sorts of scientific change possible.[14] We may someday be in a position to develop protective medical technologies against the somatic and genetic dangers plutonium represents.

The reply to this, of course, is that we may. But if we look at the matter impartially, it hardly seems acceptable to embark on programs that presently pose great foreseeable dangers merely in the hope that these dangers will vanish in the future. In matters of intergenerational responsibility, just as in more familiar moral choices, caution is in order where great evils are involved. This suggests that in considering policies that affect the future, we must evaluate our actions in terms of the best *available* estimate of their consequences.[15] By this standard, the proposals for a plutonium economy seem presently unacceptable.

It may finally be objected, however, that this kind of discussion proceeds in a vacuum. There is no such thing as an absolute evil. All the evils of any policy must be weighed against the evils of alternative policies. But any such weighing seems to favor a plutonium economy. All of our present energy alternatives, after all, involve serious risks. Do not the lives of hundreds of persons killed, maimed, or disabled in each generation by coal mining mean anything? And what about the many ordinary citizens whose health is jeopardized and whose lives are cut short by the air pollution caused by fossil fuels?

These are weighty arguments. Certainly it is true that policies involving generations, no less than individual moral choices, require a relative evaluation of goods and evils. Moral choices are always balancing judgments. It is also true that if we regard the matter impartially, it is very difficult to weigh a sure risk to the life and health of a series of present generations against the grave possible risks plutonium holds for future generations. If that were the choice before us, it would be a difficult one indeed. But is that the choice? Must we continue expending lives in order to protect distant future generations?

One answer to this, I suspect, is that the choice before us is not quite as dramatic as the defenders of a plutonium economy (or similar deleterious policies) would have us believe. Many of the present evils to which they allude can be eliminated or substantially reduced if we are prepared to spend money to do so. Thus, the dangers of coal mining and air pollution can both be substantially reduced for a price. Then, too, there is the prospect of developing relatively nonpolluting solar energy (or, less certainly, fusion energy) to replace much of our dependence on fossil fuel. The choice before us, in other words, is not the sacrifice of present life for future life. Rather, it is the choice of accepting material sacrifices in the present—in the form of higher energy and conservation costs—in order to protect the lives and health of our descendants.

By now it is clear that I believe we should choose against plutonium (and, perhaps by extension, any fission energy policy as well). Regarding the matter as though we did not know which generation were our own, it seems unreasonable to risk our lives and health in countless future generations (and the lives and health of those we love) simply to preserve high material living standards in the present.

Notes

1 J. Platt, "What We Must Do," *Science* 166 (1969): 1115–21.

2 J. B. Stearns, "Ecology and the Indefinite Unborn," *The Monist* 56 (1972): 612–25.

3 J. Rawls, *A Theory of Justice* (Cambridge, Mass.: Harvard University Press, 1971).

4 J. Feinberg, "The Rights of Animals and Unborn Generations," in *Philosophy & Environmental Crisis,* ed. W. T. Blackstone (Athens, Ga.: University of Georgia Press, 1974).

5 T. P. Schultz, "An Economic Perspective on Population Growth," in *Rapid Population Growth,* ed. National Academy of Sciences (Baltimore, Md.: Johns Hopkins Press, 1971).

6 R. Green, *Population Growth and Justice*, Harvard University Ph.D. Thesis (Missoula, Mont.: Scholars Press, 1976).

7 Immanuel Kant, "Idea for a Universal History with a Cosmopolitan Purpose," in *Kant's Political Writings*, ed. H. Reiss (Cambridge: Cambridge University Press, 1970).

8 D. C. Mueller, "Intergenerational Justice and the Social Discount Rate," *Theory and Decision* 5 (1974): 263–73; Rawls, *A Theory of Justice.*

9 Rawls, *A Theory of Justice.*

10 Environmental Protection Agency, *Proceedings of Public Hearings: Plutonium and Other Transuranium Elements* (Washington, D.C.: Environmental Protection Agency, 1974).

11 J. G. Speth, A. R. Tamplin, and T. B. Cochrane, "Plutonium Recycle: The Fateful Step," *Bulletin of Atomic Scientists* 30 (1974): 15–22.

12 B. T. Feld, "The Menace of a Fission Power Economy," *Bulletin of Atomic Scientists* 30 (1974): 32–34 and 34–36; L. Scheinman, "Safeguarding Nuclear Materials," *Bulletin of Atomic Scientists* 30 (1974): 34–36.

13 Environmental Protection Agency, *Proceedings of Public Hearings.*

14 M. Golding, "Obligations to Future Generations," *The Monist* 56 (1972): 85–99; K. Nielsen, "The Enforcement of Morality and Future Generations," *Philosophia* 3 (1973): 443–48.

15 D. Callahan, "What Obligations Do We Have to Future Generations?" *American Ecclesiastical Review* 144 (1971): 265–80.

GARRETT HARDIN
LIFEBOAT ETHICS

Environmentalists use the metaphor of the earth as a "spaceship" in trying to persuade countries, industries and people to stop wasting and polluting our natural resources. Since we all share life on this planet, they argue, no

From Garrett Hardin, "Lifeboat Ethics: The Case Against Helping the Poor," *Psychology Today* 8 (September 1974): 38, 40–43, 123–24, 126. Reprinted from *Psychology Today Magazine.* Copyright © 1974 Ziff-Davis Publishing Company.

single person or institution has the right to destroy, waste, or use more than a fair share of its resources.

But does everyone on earth have an equal right to an equal share of its resources? The spaceship metaphor can be dangerous when used by misguided idealists to justify suicidal policies for sharing our resources through uncontrolled immigration and foreign aid. In their enthusiastic but unrealistic generosity, they confuse the ethics of a spaceship with those of a lifeboat.

A true spaceship would have to be under the control of a captain, since no ship could possibly survive if its course were determined by committee. Spaceship Earth certainly has no captain; the United Nations is merely a toothless tiger, with little power to enforce any policy upon its bickering members.

If we divide the world crudely into rich nations and poor nations, two thirds of them are desperately poor, and only one third comparatively rich, with the United States the wealthiest of all. Metaphorically each rich nation can be seen as a lifeboat full of comparatively rich people. In the ocean outside each lifeboat swim the poor of the world, who would like to get in, or at least to share some of the wealth. What should the lifeboat passengers do?

First, we must recognize the limited capacity of any lifeboat. For example, a nation's land has a limited capacity to support a population and as the current energy crisis has shown us in some ways we have already exceeded the carrying capacity of our land.

Adrift in a Moral Sea

So here we sit, say 50 people in our lifeboat. To be generous, let us assume it has room for 10 more making a total capacity of 60. Suppose the 50 of us in the lifeboat see 100 others swimming in the water outside, begging for admission to our boat or for handouts. We have several options; we may be tempted to try to live by the Christian ideal of being "our brother's keeper," or by the Marxist ideal of "to each according to his needs." Since the needs of all in the water are the same, and since they can all be seen as "our brothers," we could take them all into our boat, making a total of 150 in a boat designed for 60. The boat swamps, everyone drowns. Complete justice, complete catastrophe.

Since the boat has an unused excess capacity of 10 more passengers, we could admit just 10 more to it. But which 10 do we let in? How do we choose? Do we pick the best 10, the neediest 10, "first come, first served"? And what do we say to the 90 we exclude? If we do let an extra 10 into our lifeboat, we will have lost our "safety factor," an engineering principle of critical importance. For example, if we don't leave room for excess capacity as a safety factor in our country's agriculture, a new plant disease or a bad change in the weather could have disastrous consequences.

Suppose we decide to preserve our small safety factor and admit no more to the lifeboat. Our survival is then possible, although we shall have to be constantly on guard against boarding parties.

While this last solution clearly offers the only means of our survival it is morally abhorrent to many people. Some say they feel guilty about their good luck. My reply is simple: "Get out and yield your place to others." This may solve the problem of the guilt-ridden person's conscience, but it does not change the ethics of the lifeboat. The needy person to whom the guilt-ridden person yields his place will not himself feel guilty about his good luck. If he did, he would not climb aboard. The net result of conscience-stricken people giving up their unjustly held seats is the elimination of that sort of conscience from the lifeboat.

This is the basic metaphor within which we must work out our solutions. Let us now enrich the image, step by step, with substantive additions from the real world, a world that must solve real and pressing problems of over-population and hunger.

The harsh ethics of the lifeboat become even harsher when we consider the reproductive differences between the rich nations and the poor nations. The people inside the lifeboats are doubling in numbers every 87 years; those swimming around outside are doubling, on the average, every 35 years, more than twice as fast as the rich. And since the world's resources are dwindling, the difference in prosperity between the rich and the poor can only increase.

As of 1973, the U.S. had a population of 210 million people, who were increasing by 0.8 percent per year. Outside our lifeboat, let us imagine another 210 million people, (say the combined populations of Colombia, Ecuador, Venezuela, Morocco, Pakistan, Thailand and the Philippines) who are increasing at a rate of 3.3 percent per year. Put differently, the doubling time for this aggregate population is 21 years, compared to 87 years for the U.S.

Multiplying the Rich and the Poor

Now suppose the U.S. agreed to pool its resources with those seven countries, with everyone receiving an equal share. Initially the ratio of Americans to non-Americans in this model would be one-to-one. But consider what the ratio would be after 87 years, by which time the Americans would have doubled to a population of 420 million. By then, doubling every 21 years, the other group would have swollen to 3.54 billion. Each American would have to share the available resources with more than eight people.

But, one could argue, this discussion assumes that current population trends will continue, and they may not. Quite so. Most likely the rate of population increase will decline much faster in the U.S. than it will in the other countries, and there does not seem to be much we can do about it. In sharing with "each according to his needs," we must recognize that needs are determined by population size, which is determined by the rate of reproduction, which at present is regarded as a sovereign right of every nation, poor or not. This being so, the philanthropic load created by the sharing ethic of the spaceship can only increase.

The Tragedy of the Commons

The fundamental error of spaceship ethics, and the sharing it requires, is that it leads to what I call "the tragedy of the commons." Under a system of private property, the men who own property recognize their responsibility to care for it, for if they don't they will eventually suffer. A farmer, for instance, will allow no more cattle in a pasture than its carrying capacity justifies. If he overloads it, erosion sets in, weeds take over, and he loses the use of the pasture.

If a pasture becomes a commons open to all, the right of each to use it may not be matched by a corresponding responsibility to protect it. Asking everyone to use it with discretion will hardly do, for the considerate herdsman who refrains from overloading the commons suffers more than a selfish one who says his needs are greater. If everyone would restrain himself, all would be well; but it takes only one less than everyone to ruin a system of voluntary restraint. In a crowded world of less than perfect human beings, mutual ruin is inevitable if there are no controls. This is the tragedy of the commons.

One of the major tasks of education today should be the creation of such an acute awareness of the dangers of the commons that people will recognize its many varieties. For example, the air and water have become polluted because they are treated as commons. Further growth in the population or per-capita conversion of natural resources into pollutants will only make the problem worse. The same holds true for the fish of the oceans. Fishing fleets have nearly disappeared in many parts of the world, technological improvements in the art of fishing are hastening the day of complete ruin. Only the replacement of the system of the commons with a responsible system of control will save the land, air, water and oceanic fisheries.

The World Food Bank

In recent years there has been a push to create a new commons called a World Food Bank, an international depository of food reserves to which nations would contribute according to their abilities and from which they would draw according to their needs. This humanitarian proposal has received support from many liberal international groups, and from such prominent citizens as Margaret Mead, U.N. Secretary General Kurt Waldheim, and Senators Edward Kennedy and George McGovern.

A world food bank appeals powerfully to our humanitarian impulses. . . .

. . . We must ask if such a program would actually do more good than harm, not only momentarily but also in the long run. Those who propose the food bank usually refer to a current "emergency" or "crisis" in terms of world food supply. But what is an emergency? Although they may be infrequent and sudden, everyone knows that emergencies will occur from time to time. A well-run family, company, organization or country prepares for the likelihood of accidents and emergencies. It expects them, it budgets for them, it saves for them.

Learning the Hard Way

What happens if some organizations or countries budget for accidents and others do not? If each country is solely responsible for its own well-being, poorly managed ones will suffer. But they can learn from experience. They may mend their ways, and learn to budget for infrequent but certain emergencies. For example, the weather varies from year to year, and periodic crop failures are certain. A wise and competent government saves out of the production of the good years in anticipation of bad years to come. Joseph taught this policy to Pharaoh in Egypt more than 2,000 years ago. Yet the great majority of the governments in the world today do not follow such a policy. They lack either the wisdom or the competence, or both. Should those nations that do manage to put something aside be forced to come to the rescue each time an emergency occurs among the poor nations?

"But it isn't their fault!" some kindhearted liberals argue. "How can we blame the poor people who are caught in an emergency? Why must they suffer for the sins of their governments?" The concept of blame is simply not relevant here. The real question is, what are the operational consequences of establishing a world food bank? If it is open to every country every time a need develops, slovenly rulers will not be motivated to take Joseph's advice. Someone will always come their aid. Some countries will deposit food in the world food bank, and others will withdraw it. There will be almost no overlap. As a result of such solutions to food shortage emergencies, the poor countries will not learn to mend their ways, and will suffer progressively greater emergencies as their populations grow.

Population Control the Crude Way

On the average, poor countries undergo a 2.5 percent increase in population each year; rich countries, about 0.8 percent. Only rich countries have anything in the way of food reserves set aside, and even they do not have as much as they should. Poor countries have none. If poor countries received no food from the outside, the rate of their population growth would be periodically checked by crop failures and famines. But if they can always draw on a world food bank in time of need, their population can continue to grow unchecked, and so will their "need" for aid. In the short run, a world food bank may diminish that need, but in the long run it actually increases the need without limit.

Without some system of worldwide food sharing, the proportion of people in the rich and poor nations might eventually stabilize. The overpopulated poor countries would decrease in numbers, while the rich countries that had room for more people would increase. But with a well-meaning system of sharing, such as a world food bank, the growth differential between the rich and the poor countries will not only persist, it will increase. Because of the higher rate of population growth in the poor countries of the world, 88 percent of today's children are born poor, and only 12 percent rich. Year by year the ratio becomes worse, as the fast-reproducing poor outnumber the slow-reproducing rich.

A world food bank is thus a commons in disguise. People will have more motivation to draw from it than to add to any common store. The less provident and less able will multiply at the expense of the abler and more provident, bringing eventual ruin upon all who share in the commons. Besides, any system of "sharing" that amounts to foreign aid from the rich nations to the poor nations will carry the taint of charity, which will contribute little to the world peace so devoutly desired by those who support the idea of a world food bank.

As past U.S. foreign-aid programs have amply and depressingly demonstrated, international charity frequently inspires mistrust and antagonism rather than gratitude on the part of the recipient nation. . . .

Chinese Fish and Miracle Rice

The modern approach to foreign aid stresses the export of technology and advice, rather than money and food. As an ancient Chinese proverb goes: "Give a man a fish and he will eat for a day, teach him how to fish and he will eat for the rest of his days." Acting on this advice, the Rockefeller and Ford Foundations have financed a number of programs for improving agriculture in the hungry nations. Known as the "Green Revolution," these programs have led to the development of "miracle rice" and "miracle wheat," new strains that offer bigger harvests and greater resistance to crop damage. Norman Borlaug, the Nobel Prize winning agronomist who, supported by the Rockefeller Foundation, developed "miracle wheat," is one of the most prominent advocates of a world food bank.

Whether or not the Green Revolution can increase food production as much as its champions claim is a debatable but possibly irrelevant point. Those who support this well-intended humanitarian effort should first consider some of the fundamentals of human ecology. Ironically, one man who did was the late Alan Gregg, a vice president of the Rockefeller Foundation. Two decades ago he expressed strong doubts about the wisdom of such attempts to increase food production. He likened the growth and spread of humanity over the surface of the earth to the spread of cancer in the human body, remarking that "cancerous growths demand food; but as far as I know, they have never been cured by getting it."

Overloading the Environment

Every human born constitutes a draft on all aspects of the environment: food, air, water, forests, beaches, wildlife, scenery and solitude. Food can, perhaps, be significantly increased to meet a growing demand. But what about clean beaches, unspoiled forests, and solitude? If we satisfy a growing

population's need for food, we necessarily decrease its per capita supply of
the other resources needed by men.

India, for example, now has a population of 600 million, which increases by 15 million each year. This population already puts a huge load
on a relatively impoverished environment. The country's forests are now
only a small fraction of what they were three centuries ago, and floods and
erosion continually destroy the insufficient farmland that remains. Every
one of the 15 million new lives added to India's population puts an additional burden on the environment and increases the economic and social
costs of crowding. However humanitarian our intent, every Indian life saved
through medical or nutritional assistance from abroad diminishes the
quality of life for those who remain, and for subsequent generations. If
rich countries make it possible, through foreign aid, for 600 million Indians to swell to 1.2 billion in a mere 28 years, as their current growth rate
threatens, will future generations of Indians thank us for hastening the destruction of their environment? Will our good intentions be sufficient excuse for the consequences of our actions?

My final example of a commons in action is one for which the public
has the least desire for rational discussion—immigration. Anyone who
publicly questions the wisdom of current U.S. immigration policy is
promptly charged with bigotry, prejudice, ethnocentrism, chauvinism,
isolationism, or selfishness. Rather than encounter such accusations one
would rather talk about other matters, leaving immigration policy to wal-
low in the crosscurrents of special interests that take no account of the
good of the whole, or the interests of posterity.

Perhaps we still feel guilty about things we said in the past. Two generations ago the popular press frequently referred to Dagos, Wops, Polacks,
Chinks and Krauts, in articles about how America was being "overrun"
by foreigners of supposedly inferior genetic stock. . . . But because the
implied inferiority of foreigners was used then as justification for keeping
them out, people now assume that restrictive policies could only be based
on such misguided notions. There are other grounds.

A Nation of Immigrants

Just consider the numbers involved. Our Government acknowledges a net
inflow of 400,000 immigrants a year. While we have no hard data on the
extent of illegal entries, educated guesses put the figure at about 600,000
a year. Since the natural increase (excess of births over deaths) of the resident population now runs about 1.7 million per year the yearly gain from
immigration amounts to at least 19 percent of the total annual increase,
and may be as much as 37 percent if we include the estimate for illegal
immigrants. Considering the growing use of birth control devices, the potential effect of educational campaigns by such organizations as Planned
Parenthood Federation of America and Zero Population Growth, and the
influence of inflation and the housing shortage, the fertility rate of American women may decline so much that immigration could account for all

the yearly increase in population. Should we not at least ask if that is what we want?

For the sake of those who worry about whether the "quality" of the average immigrant compares favorably with the quality of the average resident let us assume that immigrants and nativeborn citizens are of exactly equal quality, however one defines that term. We will focus here only on quantity, and since our conclusions will depend on nothing else, all charges of bigotry and chauvinism become irrelevant.

Immigration Vs. Food Supply

World food banks *move food to the people,* hastening the exhaustion of the environment of the poor countries. Unrestricted immigration, on the other hand, *moves people to the food,* thus speeding up the destruction of the environment of the rich countries. We can easily understand why poor people should want to make this latter transfer, but why should rich hosts encourage it?

As in the case of foreign-aid programs, immigration receives support from selfish interests and humanitarian impulses. The primary selfish interest in unimpeded immigration is the desire of employers for cheap labor, particularly in industries and trades that offer degrading work. In the past, one wave of foreigners after another was brought into the U.S. to work at wretched jobs for wretched wages. In recent years the Cubans, Puerto Ricans and Mexicans have had this dubious honor. The interests of the employers of cheap labor mesh well with the guilty silence of the country's liberal intelligentsia. White Anglo-Saxon Protestants are particularly reluctant to call for a closing of the doors to immigration for fear of being called bigots.

But not all countries have such reluctant leadership. Most educated Hawaiians, for example, are keenly aware of the limits of their environment, particularly in terms of population growth. There is only so much room on the islands, and the islanders know it. To Hawaiians, immigrants from the other 49 states present as great a threat as those from other nations. At a recent meeting of Hawaiian government officials in Honolulu, I had the ironic delight of hearing a speaker, who like most of his audience was of Japanese ancestry, ask how the country might practically and constitutionally close its doors to further immigration. One member of the audience countered: "How can we shut the doors now? We have many friends and relatives in Japan that we'd like to bring here some day so that they can enjoy Hawaii too." The Japanese-American speaker smiled sympathetically and answered: "Yes, but we have children now, and someday we'll have grandchildren too. We can bring more people here from Japan only by giving away some of the land that we hope to pass on to our grandchildren some day. What right to we have to do that?"

At this point, I can hear U.S. liberals asking: "How can you justify slamming the door once you're inside? You say that immigrants should be kept out. But aren't we all immigrants, or the descendants of immigrants?

If we insist on staying, must we not admit all others?'' Our craving for intellectual order leads us to seek and prefer symmetrical rules and morals: a single rule for me and everybody else; the same rule yesterday, today and tomorrow. Justice, we feel, should not change with time and place.

We Americans of non-Indian ancestry can look upon ourselves as the descendants of thieves who are guilty morally, if not legally, of stealing this land from its Indian owners. Should we then give back the land to the now living American descendants of those Indians? However morally or logically sound this proposal may be, I, for one, am unwilling to live by it and I know no one else who is. Besides, the logical consequence would be absurd. Suppose that, intoxicated with a sense of pure justice, we should decide to turn our land over to the Indians. Since all our other wealth has also been derived from the land, wouldn't we be morally obliged to give that back to the Indians too?

Pure Justice Vs. Reality

Clearly, the concept of pure justice produces an infinite regression to absurdity. Centuries ago, wise men invented statutes of limitations to justify the rejection of such pure justice, in the interest of preventing continual disorder. The law zealously defends property rights but only relatively recent property rights. Drawing a line after an arbitrary time has elapsed may be unjust, but the alternatives are worse.

We are all the descendants of thieves, and the world's resources are inequitably distributed. But we must begin the journey to tomorrow from the point where we are today. We cannot remake the past. We cannot safely divide the wealth equitably among all peoples so long as people reproduce at different rates. To do so would guarantee that our grandchildren, and everyone else's grandchildren, would have only a ruined world to inhabit.

To be generous with one's own possessions is quite different from being generous with those of posterity. We should call this point to the attention of those who, from a commendable love of justice and equality, would institute a system of the commons, either in the form of a world food bank, or of unrestricted immigration. We must convince them if we wish to save at least some parts of the world from environmental ruin.

Without a true world government to control reproduction and the use of available resources, the sharing ethic of the spaceship is impossible. For the foreseeable future, our survival demands that we govern our actions by the ethics of a lifeboat, harsh though they may be. Posterity will be satisfied with nothing less.

About the Editors

Michael D. Bayles is director of the Westminster Institute for Ethics and Human Values, Westminster College, and professor of philosophy, University of Western Ontario, in London, Canada. He has previously taught at the University of Kentucky, Brooklyn College, and the University of Idaho, and has been a fellow at Harvard Law School and the Hastings Center. He is the author of *Principles of Legislation* (1978), *Morality and Population Policy* (1980), and *Professional Ethics* (1981), as well as over fifty-five articles on ethics and political-legal philosophy. He has also edited *Contemporary Utilitarianism* (1968), *Ethics and Population* (1976), and, with Dallas High, *Medical Treatment of the Dying: Moral Issues* (1978).

Kenneth Henley is associate professor in the Department of Philosophy and Religion at Florida International University. He received his B.A. in English from the University of Virginia in 1967, and then turned to philosophy for his M.A. in 1969 and Ph.D. in 1972, both also from the University of Virginia. He has published articles on ethical theory and applied ethics in several philosophical journals and has contributed an article on "The Authority to Educate" to the anthology *Having Children: Philosophical and Legal Reflections on Parenthood*. His current work involves the role of rules and principles in moral and legal reasoning.